JEWS AND CHRISTIANS IN MEDIEVAL CASTILE

JEWS AND CHRISTIANS IN MEDIEVAL CASTILE

Tradition, Coexistence, and Change

MAYA SOIFER IRISH

The Catholic University of America Press
Washington, D.C.

Copyright © 2016
The Catholic University of America Press
All rights reserved

Library of Congress Cataloging-in-Publication Data
Names: Soifer Irish, Maya, author.
Title: Jews and Christians in medieval Castile : tradition, coexistence, and change / Maya Soifer Irish.
Description: Washington, D.C. : The Catholic University of America Press, [2016] | Includes bibliographical references and index.
Identifiers: LCCN 2016020880 | ISBN 9780813236339 (pbk : alk. paper) Subjects: LCSH: Jews—Spain—Castile—History—To 1500. | Christians—Spain—Castile—History—To 1500. | Castile (Spain)—Ethnic relations.
Classification: LCC DS135.S75 C3357 2016 | DDC 946/.300492400902—dc23
LC record available at https://lccn.loc.gov/2016020880

CONTENTS

Acknowledgments — vii

A Note on the Coinage Mentioned in the Book — xi

List of Abbreviations — xiii

Maps — xv

Introduction: Northern Castile—An Internal Frontier — 1

PART 1. THE JEWS OF NORTHERN CASTILE AND LEÓN (CA. 1050–CA. 1350)

1. The Castilian-Leonese Monarchy and the Jews: From Fernando I to Fernando III — 19

2. The Jews of the Camino de Santiago — 53

PART 2. *JUDEI NOSTRI:* THE CHURCH AND THE JEWS IN NORTHERN CASTILE

3. Enemy of the Faith, Asset to the Church — 77

4. *Insolentia judeorum:* The Jews and the Conciliar Legislation — 103

5. *Tamquam domino proprio:* The Bishop and His Jews in Medieval Palencia — 132

PART 3. JEWS AND CHRISTIANS IN NORTHERN CASTILE (CA. 1250–CA. 1370)

6. The Jews of Castile at the End of the *Reconquista* (Post–1250): Cultural and Communal Life — 151

7. Jews, Christians, and Royal Power in Northern Castile — 170

8. "Insolent, Wicked People": The Cortes and Anti-Jewish Discourse in Castile — 221

Bibliography — 263

Index — 291

ACKNOWLEDGMENTS

The journey to the completion of this book began in 2004, when I made the momentous decision to write about the Jews of medieval Northern Castile. I knew at the time that the road I was about to take would lead me through some barren landscapes that had persuaded many a researcher to seek greener pastures in the archives of the Crown of Aragon. But being young, curious, and stubborn, I persisted, and while much of what wiser and more experienced scholars had advised me about the paucity of the Castilian archives turned out to be true, today I do not regret having made this choice. My adviser and teacher at Princeton, Bill Jordan, was there for me at the inception of this project, guided it with a steady hand, and was still there for me at the end of the journey, helping this manuscript see the light of day. The impact of his intellectual mentorship is incalculable and can be felt on every page of this book. I was also very fortunate to benefit from the support and kindness of Teo Ruiz, who generously shared with me his knowledge of Castilian history and Castilian archives and saved me from many missteps and embarrassing mistakes. Without his pioneering work on medieval Northern Castile, I would have never even attempted this project. I owe a debt of gratitude to Mark Cohen, Peter Brown, and Anthony Grafton for making me into the historian that I am today. I am also thankful to my cohort of graduate students at Princeton, and especially to my fellow medievalists: Erica Gilles, Michelle Garceau (Hawkins), Holly Grieco, James Byrne, Hussein Fancy, Guy Geltner, Ariel Lopez, and Damian Fernandez.

As a young immigrant from Russia and an undergraduate student at the University of Colorado at Colorado Springs, I was extremely lucky to find support and encouragement from a group of talented scholars and teachers at the History Department. It was thanks to them that I decided to become a professional historian. Richard Wunderli nurtured my interest in medieval history and patiently corrected my early, shaky compositions, which read like literal translations from Russian. I will never forget the pivotal role he played in my life and career. From my other professors at UCCS, especially Jan Meyers, Robert Sackett, Judy Price, Harlow Sheidley, Gerald Broce, and Cecile Malek I learned countless lessons about writing, history, scholarship, and the life of the mind. Sue Marasco, a fellow graduate student in history, whom I first met during a seminar at Columbine Hall, has become a treasured lifelong friend.

Like any work of scholarship, this book is truly a collaborative project that would not have been written without the help of many colleagues and friends. I owe a special thank you to Thomas Barton for agreeing to join my session at the Sewanee Medieval Colloquium in 2009 and for becoming, since then, an incredible coauthor and friend. The final version of this book bears an unmistakable imprint of the virtual and in-person discussions we have had over the last six years and of the many things I have learned from Tom's own research on the Jews of Aragon. I would also like to thank Robin Vose for his very helpful commentary on an early version of part 2. Philippe Buc provided valuable feedback when the manuscript was in the early stages of revision. It was a privilege to serve as a teaching fellow in his class on mass violence at Stanford University for two years, and I am very grateful for his support. Michael Maas, my colleague in the History Department at Rice University, read the manuscript when it was close to completion, and his comments were instrumental in making it a more readable and approachable work. I would also like to thank the members of the Junior Faculty Writing Group at the History Department, and especially Aysha Pollnitz, Rebecca Goetz, Caleb McDaniel, Cyrus Mody, Emily Straus, Anne Chao, and Kathryn de Luna, for their friendship and support, and for giving feedback on Part 2. I am also thankful to Javier Castaño of the Consejo Superior de Investigaciones Científicas for the invitation to present a section from chapter 7 at a CSIC seminar in June 2014 and for helping me improve it for publication in *Sefarad*. This chapter also benefited from the critique given by the participants in the California Medieval Seminar at the Huntington Library in March 2008.

During my many trips to Spain, I received invaluable assistance from staff members at several archives in Castile. In particular, I would like to thank Don Matías Vicario of the Archivo de la Catedral de Burgos, Rafael del Valle of the Archivo Municipal de Palencia, and Carlos Díez of the Archivo Municipal de Miranda de Ebro. I am also thankful for the help I received from the hardworking staff at the Archivo Histórico Nacional, Biblioteca Nacional, and Biblioteca de la Real Academia de la Historia in Madrid, Archivo de la Catedral de León, Archivo Municipal de León, and Archivo Municipal de Burgos. In the United States, the Interlibrary Loan staff at the Firestone Library at Princeton, the Green Library at Stanford, and the Fondren Library at Rice have provided me with numerous articles and books that were absolutely essential for the completion of this work.

Over the years, the research for this book has received financial backing from many institutions and organizations. At Princeton, I would like to thank the History Department, the Graduate School, the Program in Judaic Studies, and the Princeton Institute for International and Regional Studies. A grant from the Mrs. Giles Whiting Foundation supported me through the last year of graduate school and provided funding for the archival research in the summer of 2009. At Rice, the Mosle Fund for junior faculty in the School of Humanities, the History Department, and the Jewish Studies program supported research and travel during the last stages of completing the manuscript. Teaching releases and a junior faculty leave provided by the History Department and the Dean of Humanities gave me the time necessary to finish the project. Jeffrey Piccirillo, working under the guidance of Jean Aroom at Rice's GIS/Data Center, spent many hours creating the maps of medieval Iberia included in this book. I am very grateful for their hard work and dedication.

I was very fortunate to be working on this book while enjoying the wonderfully collegial atmosphere at Stanford and Rice. At Stanford's Introduction to the Humanities Program, which had been my home for three years, I benefited greatly from the companionship of other postdoctoral teaching fellows, especially Jesse Kauffman, Phillip Horky, Gabriel Wolfenstein, Anise Strong, Gillian Goslinga, and Stephen Puryear. I also wish to thank the program's administrators—Russell Berman, Ellen Woods, and Parna Sengupta—for their unflagging support and for organizing the IHUM Research Colloquium. Galen Davis always had a solution for my computer-related issues, and I am grateful for his help and expertise. At Rice's History Department, Lora Wildenthal was absolutely the best chair a new faculty member could ever hope for: understanding, supportive, and caring. Her successor, Alida Metcalf, has been just as wonderful and kind. Paula Sanders has taught me a lot about pedagogy and academic life, and I am extremely grateful for her friendship. Diane Wolfthal has been a wonderful mentor and supporter of my work. I am grateful to Matthias Henze for shepherding our close-knit Jewish Studies community and supporting its endeavors. I also would like to recognize my other Rice colleagues for their mentorship and friendship: Jack Zammito, Lisa Balabanlilar, Moramay Lopez-Alonso, Jared Staller, Gisela Heffes, Rosemary Hennessy, and Melissa Weininger. Rachel Zepeda, Paula Platt, Lisa Tate, Beverly Konzem, and Chris Tennison in the History Department have provided indispensible administrative support.

I would like to extend my gratitude to the Catholic University of America Press, and especially to Trevor Lipscombe, for believing in my project and for guiding it so quickly and efficiently from submission to publication. I am also thankful to the anonymous reviewers of the manuscript for their helpful suggestions, which truly improved the quality of the book. Aldene Fredenburg and Theresa Walker expertly edited the manuscript. Any mistakes that still remain in the book are of course entirely my own.

The final revisions for this book were completed at my academic home, Rice University, and at my actual home in Katy, Texas, where Tim Sojka was instrumental in making it possible for my family to find happiness and prosperity. Above all, I would like to thank my friends and family in the United States, Russia, and Israel. It is to them that I owe the greatest debt of all. My in-laws—Patricia Irish Amez, Hal Irish and Henrietta Humphreys, Marilyn Taube, Nancy Irish and Doug Blumer, Michael and Pati Irish—welcomed me into their family and their hearts. I thank my parents, Konstantin and Larisa Kikoin, and my brother, Ilya Kikoin, for their unconditional love and support every step of the way. To my husband, Steve, I owe more than words can ever express. Setting aside his own goals and aspirations, he moved with me across the country and started a new career so that I could pursue my scholarly dreams. With profound love and gratitude, I dedicate this book to him and to our children—Isabelle, Leon, and little Keaton.

A NOTE ON THE COINAGE MENTIONED IN THE BOOK

Solidus, sueldo: an early unit of account (not an actual coin), with 1 sueldo, in theory, equivalent to 12 dineros.

Denarius, dinero: a silver coin, first issued in Castile-León around 1050, and minted throughout the period described in this book. As a unit of account, it was eventually replaced by the maravedí.

Maravedí: a unit of account used in Castile-León, it originally derived its value from the Almoravid morabitino (3.85 g of gold). From the late twelfth to the early thirteenth century, Almoravid-inspired gold morabitinos were minted in Toledo. King Alfonso X issued some silver maravedís and half-maravedís, but for the most part, maravedí was used as a value referent for Castilian coins (1 maravedí = 10 dineros). Its value fell progressively throughout the Middle Ages, until it represented the equivalent of about 0.05 g of gold.

Please note: the value of coins fluctuated considerably over time and from one region to another.

Miquel Crusafont, Anna M. Balaguer, and Philip Grierson, eds., *Medieval European Coinage*, vol. 6, *The Iberian Peninsula* (Cambridge: Cambridge University Press, 2013), 6–7, 11–12, 16–17, 202–3, 305–7, 561–62, 567, 573; Philip Grierson, *The Coins of Medieval Europe* (London: Seaby, 1991), 103, 137; and Teofilo Ruiz, *Crisis and Continuity: Land and Town in Late Medieval Castile* (Philadelphia: University of Pennsylvania Press, 1994), 327.

ABBREVIATIONS

ACB	Archivo de la catedral de Burgos
ACL	Archivo de la catedral de León
ACP	Archivo de la catedral de Palencia
AHDE	Anuario de historia del derecho español
AHN	Archivo histórico nacional
AMB	Archivo municipal de Burgos
AMME	Archivo municipal de Miranda de Ebro
AMP	Archivo municipal de Palencia
BN	Biblioteca nacional
CDACL	Colección documental del archivo de la catedral de León
CDADA	Colección documental del archivo diocesano de Astorga
CDAML	Colección documental del archivo municipal de León
CDCB	Colección diplomatica del concejo de Burgos
CDMR	Colección diplomatica medieval de la Rioja
CDMS	Colección diplomática del monasterio de Sahagún
Cortes 1 and 2	Cortes de los antiguos reinos de León y Castilla, vols. 1 and 2
DCB	Documentación de la catedral de Burgos
DCP	Documentación de la catedral de Palencia
DHR	Documentación del hospital del rey de Burgos
DMHB	Documentación del monasterio de Las Huelgas de Burgos
DMSSO	Documentación del monasterio de San Salvador de Oña
FR	Fuero Real
PL	Patrologia Latina
RAH	Real academia de la historia

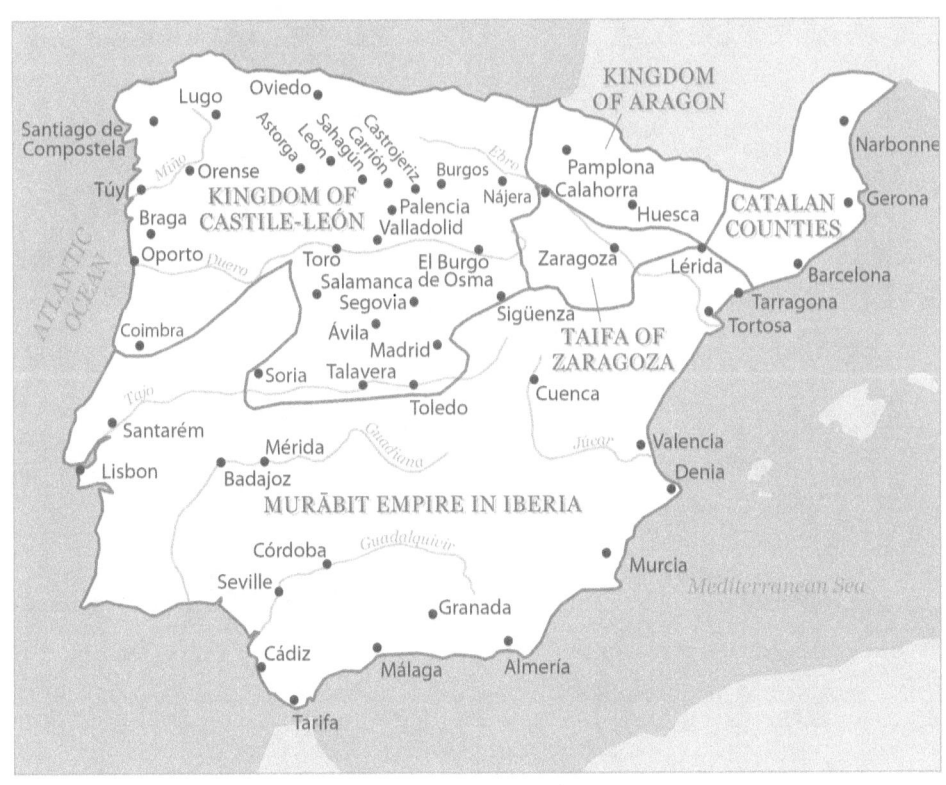

MAP 1. Iberia at the end of the eleventh century

MAP 2. Northern Castile and León (with the Camino de Santiago and other roads)

MAP 3. Iberia at the end of the thirteenth century

✝ Indicates the locations of the ecclesiastical institutions in Castile-León that are known to have had jurisdiction over Jewish communities and/or to have received taxes from them.

JEWS AND CHRISTIANS IN MEDIEVAL CASTILE

INTRODUCTION ~ Northern Castile—An Internal Frontier

Pilgrims on their way to Santiago de Compostela in the late thirteenth century entered the Northern Castilian city of Burgos through the gates of San Juan. Few things in the city would have struck these travelers from beyond the Pyrenees as particularly exotic. Built on the Camino de Santiago (the road to Santiago de Compostela), which evolved into an important commercial artery connecting Castile to the rest of Europe, Burgos was constantly subjected to an influx of people and ideas from the north.[1] Their impact could be seen in the Gothic forms of Burgos Cathedral, constructed with the participation of French masters. The somber walls of the Cluniac monastery of San Pedro de Cardeña and the Cistercian convent of Santa María la Real (Las Huelgas) in the Burgos environs testified to the presence in the city of the two great European monastic empires.[2] A pilgrim walking the road to Santiago through the city would inevitably pass by the houses of some Jews living along narrow Tenebregosa Street, where the local *judería* was located.[3] But not even the sight of Jewish moneychangers offering their services to the passing pilgrims would shock a visitor from the north. Until 1306, the kingdom of France had Jewish communities of its own, while the already large Jewish population in Provence received a further boost in the wake of Philip the Fair's Great Expulsion.[4] Rather

---

1. Teofilo Ruiz, "El siglo XIII y primera mitad del siglo XIV," in *Burgos en la edad media*, edited by Carlos Estepa Díez and Julio Valdeón Baruque, 106 (Valladolid: Junta de Castilla y León, 1984).

2. Estepa Díez, "De fines del siglo IX a principios del siglo XIII," in *Burgos en la edad media*, 74, 94.

3. Francisco Cantera Burgos, "La judería de Burgos," *Sefarad* 12 (1952): 60; Teófilo López Mata, "Morería y judería [de Burgos]," *Boletín de la Real Academia de la Historia* 129 (1951): 340–42.

4. William Chester Jordan, *The French Monarchy and the Jews: From Philip Augustus to the Last Capetians* (Philadelphia: University of Pennsylvania Press, 1989), 233.

more unusual would be the presence of some Castilian Muslims—*mudéjars*—busy about their *morería*, or working in the tanneries of the Hospital del Rey.[5] Such an encounter would be a distinctly Iberian phenomenon, unseen anywhere in northern Europe. Indeed, as visitors were bound to discover, Burgos was a city of three religions, a northern outpost of the fabled Iberian interfaith coexistence, often romanticized today as *convivencia*.

Yet, when historians discuss Jewish-Christian-Muslim coexistence in medieval Spain, this extreme north of Castile and León, which includes Burgos and other towns along the road to Santiago, rarely serves as the model.[6] Instead, they direct their attention to the Christian kingdoms' shifting military frontier with Islam—places like Toledo, Cuenca, and the Kingdom of Valencia.[7] It seems that the lure of the frontier is at least as strong for today's historians as it was for medieval settlers drawn by its many possibilities.[8] They see it as a place where the reconquest was still recent and raw, where the ever-present military threat forced both the rulers and the ruled to organize their society for war, and where Jews, Muslims, and Christians jostled for space and created a new cultural symbiosis.[9] It is these frontier contacts between Christians and Muslims,

---

5. Maria del Carmen Palacín Gálvez and Luis Martínez García, eds., *Documentación del hospital del rey de Burgos (1136–1277)* [DHR] (Burgos: Ediciones J. M. Garrido Garrido, 1990), 369–70.

6. Teofilo Ruiz's works are some of the very few exceptions: see Ruiz, "Judíos y cristianos en el ambito urbano bajomedieval: Ávila y Burgos, 1200–1350," in *Xudeus e conversos na historia*, edited by Carlos Barros, 2:69–93 (Santiago de Compostela: Editorial de la Historia, 1994), and Ruiz, "Trading with the 'Other': Economic Exchanges between Muslims, Jews, and Christians in Late Medieval Northern Castile," in *Medieval Spain: Culture, Conflict, and Coexistence; Studies in Honour of Angus MacKay*, edited by Roger Collins and Anthony Goodman, 63–78 (New York: Palgrave Macmillan, 2002).

7. Among others, see Robert I. Burns, *The Crusader Kingdom of Valencia: Reconstruction on a Thirteenth-Century Frontier* (Cambridge, Mass.: Harvard University Press, 1967); Jonathan Ray, *The Sephardic Frontier: "The Reconquista" and the Jewish Community in Medieval Iberia* (Ithaca: Cornell University Press, 2006); and James Powers, "Frontier Municipal Baths and Social Interaction in the Thirteenth-Century Spain," *American Historical Review* 84, no. 3 (June 1979): 649–67.

8. For a valuable discussion of the meaning of "frontier" in medieval historiography, see Nora Berend, *At the Gate of Christendom: Jews, Muslims and "Pagans" in Medieval Hungary, c.1000–c.1300* (Cambridge: Cambridge University Press, 2001), 6–17.

9. Elena Lourie, "A Society Organized for War: Medieval Spain," *Past and Present* 35 (1996): 54–76; Robert I. Burns, "The Significance of the Frontier in the Middle Ages," in *Medieval Frontier Societies*, edited by Robert Bartlett and Angus MacKay, 307–30 (Oxford: Clarendon Press, 1989).

scholars argue, that influenced the treatment of religious minorities in Christian Iberia and made Jewish-Christian interaction in Spain so markedly different from interfaith relations elsewhere in medieval Europe.[10]

In a departure from this historiographic tradition, this book emphasizes the central role of the northern regions in forging Jewish-Christian relations in the kingdom of Castile. According to the classic vocabulary of the reconquest, the land north of the Duero River had a short life as a real frontier. Muslims failed to establish permanent settlements here, crossing into this no man's land only occasionally during raiding expeditions against the Christians of Asturias-León.[11] Soon after Christian settlers had started colonizing this region in significant numbers, the 1085 capture of Toledo pushed the military frontier farther south.[12] Afterward, Muslims came here as slaves, merchants, or refugees from the south, never becoming particularly numerous. Portrayed by Christian chroniclers as the ancient seat of royal power inherited from the Visigoths, the northern lands were the symbolic antithesis of the frontier—the backwater of the reconquest.[13]

This said, the land crossed by pilgrims on their way to visit the relics of St. James was still a frontier, albeit of a different sort—an internal frontier.[14] From the eleventh to the early twelfth century, an influx of set-

10. Kenneth Stow, *Alienated Minority: The Jews of Medieval Latin Europe* (Cambridge, Mass.: Harvard University Press, 1992), 1; see Thomas F. Glick, *Islamic and Christian Spain in the Early Middle Ages*, rev. 2nd ed. (Leiden: Brill, 2005), 187–88: "when the Christians came to determine what their own comportment would be towards religious minorities ... they used the ready-made example afforded by Muslim treatment of dhimmis." For a critique of this position, see Mark Meyerson, *Jews in an Iberian Frontier Kingdom: Society, Economy, and Politics in Morvedre, 1248–1392* (Leiden: Brill, 2004), 6.

11. On the Muslim concept of the frontier and its distinction between thughūr (area of settlement) and 'awāsim (area of warfare, conquest), see Michael Bonner, "The Naming of the Frontier: 'Awāsim, Thughūr, and the Arab Geographies," *Bulletin of the School of Oriental and African Studies, University of London* 57, no. 1 (1994): 17–24.

12. Joseph O'Callaghan, *A History of Medieval Spain* (Ithaca: Cornell University Press, 1975), 100, 123, 206; Manuel González Jiménez, "Frontier and Settlement in the Kingdom of Castile (1085–1350)," in Bartlett and MacKay, *Medieval Frontier Societies*, 49–74.

13. Kenneth Baxter Wolf, *Conquerors and Chroniclers of Early Medieval Spain*, 2nd ed. (Liverpool: Liverpool University Press, 1999), 44–45.

14. In his highly influential 1958 article, Archibald Lewis talked of the "internal frontier" of Western Europe: the "new lands inside Europe's heartland" that underwent economic development between 1000 and 1250. It is in this sense that I use the term and apply it to the lands along the Camino de Santiago; Lewis, "The Closing of the Mediaeval

tlers to the region created an urban boom along the road from the Rioja to León: a new crop of towns, among them Logroño, Santo Domingo de la Calzada, Belorado, Castrojeriz, Carrión, and Sahagún, joined the older cities such as Burgos, Nájera, and León. Castilians, Gascons, Burgundians, Bretons, English, Germans, and Lombards, as well as Jews and Muslims, came as pilgrims or traders and established permanent settlements.[15] The mingling of ethnic and religious groups attracted by the region's resources created a frontier setting where the economic experiment was accompanied by social and institutional innovations. Old Castile and León became the birthplace of royal *fueros*—charters of privilege granted by kings to towns—that gave urban communities legal status, established basic political and judicial norms, and regulated relationships between ethnic and religious groups.[16] Until the appearance of centralized royal legislation in the mid-thirteenth century, the granting of *fueros* would continue to be the focus of the Castilian Crown's legislative activities.[17] These early *fueros* were the first laws in Castile to try to grapple with the reality of Jews living among Christians.[18]

This book contends that the basic elements of Jewish-Christian coexistence in Castile were first formed in this region. When Jews started coming to Old Castile and León, probably sometime in the tenth century, the region became the northern frontier of Jewish settlement in Castile.[19] The kings of Castile-León decided to accept their presence, despite the

---

Frontier, 1250–1350," *Speculum* 33, no. 4 (1958): 476–77; see also Burns, "Significance of the Frontier," 313.

15. Jean Gautier-Dalché, *Historia urbana de León y Castilla en la edad media (siglos IX–XIII)* (Madrid: Siglo XXI de España, 1979), 67–77.

16. Aquilino Iglesia Ferreirós, "Derecho municipal, derecho señorial, derecho regio," *Historia. Instituciones. Documentos* 4 (1977): 129–30.

17. Galo Sánchez, "Para la historia de la redacción del antiguo derecho territorial castellano," *Anuario de historia del derecho español* [AHDE] 6 (1929): 260–328.

18. As Hagith Sivan has argued, there appears to be a thorough break between the Jewish community of Visigothic Spain and their Jewish successors living in Spain beginning in the ninth century, who preserved no memory of the Visigothic persecutions; see Sivan, "The Invisible Jews of Visigothic Spain," *Revue des études juives* 159, nos. 3–4 (2000): 369–85.

19. Miguel Ángel Ladero Quesada accepts it as a given that the first Jews in Northern Spain "were of European origin"; Ladero Quesada, "Castile: An Overview (Thirteenth to Fifteenth Centuries)," in *The Jews of Europe in the Middle Ages (Tenth to Fifteenth Centuries): Proceedings of the International Symposium held at Speyer, 20–25 October 2002*, edited by Christoph Cluse, 51 (Turnhout: Brepols, 2004).

validity, in León, of the intemperately anti-Jewish old Visigothic Code, the *Liber iudicum*.[20] Contrary to what some historians have suggested, the legal and political arrangements for permitting Jewish life in Castile were not modeled on the Muslim *dhimma* system.[21] Rather, the practical exigencies of a continuous military campaign against Islam, as well as the need to attract settlers to the royal lands in the north, dictated the kings' policies toward these newcomers. Desirous of populating the region and fostering economic life, the kings extended to the Jews the same welcome they offered to other groups of settlers. They issued royal charters (*fueros*) that protected the Jews' judicial autonomy and guaranteed their legal equality with other groups in mixed litigation. Already in the eleventh century, the kings of Castile-León began to realize that the taxes of the Jews settled on the king's lands in Old Castile and León could be a lucrative source of income for the royal treasury. As the reconquest intensified, the collection of taxes from the Jews was transformed into a royal prerogative, until by the mid-twelfth century the Crown asserted the principle of royal ownership over the kingdom's Jewish communities. By the late twelfth century, some *fueros* explicitly referred to Jews as *servi regis*, binding them to the Crown by ties of fiscal obligation.[22] The grants of Jewish taxes given

20. *Fuero juzgo en Latín y Castellano*, edited by Joaquín Ibarra y Marín (Madrid: La Real Academia Española, 1815); S. P. Scott, ed., *The Visigothic Code (Forum Judicum)*, trans. S. P. Scott (Littleton, Colo.: Fred B. Rothman, 1982). According to Fernando Suárez Bilbao, Fernando I suspended the anti-Jewish provisions of the Visigothic Code sometime around 1066; see Suárez Bilbao, *El fuero judiego en la España cristiana: Las fuentes jurídicas, siglos V–XV* (Madrid: Dykinson, 2000), 17.

21. Larry Simon has argued that Alfonso X's legislation "may represent to some degree an adaptation of the Islamic dhimma system protecting and restricting alien religious groups," although he adds that "there may have been parallelism as well as adaptation"; Simon, "Jews in the Legal Corpus of Alfonso el Sabio," *Comitatus* 18 (1987): 89. Robert I. Burns offers a similarly vague assessment, arguing that the "insistent example" of Islamic society suggests "at least a strong supporting role for the dhimma in the evolution of the analogous Christian arrangements"; Burns, "Introduction to the Seventh Partida," in *Las siete partidas*, vol. 5, *Underworlds: The Dead, the Criminal, and the Marginalized*, edited by Robert I. Burns, xxviii (Philadelphia: University of Pennsylvania Press, 2001); see also Glick, *Islamic and Christian Spain*, 187–88, and Meyerson, *The Muslims of Valencia in the Age of Fernando and Isabel: Between Coexistence and Crusade* (Berkeley: University of California Press, 1991), 3. For a different assessment, see David Nirenberg, *Communities of Violence: Persecution of Minorities in the Middle Ages* (Princeton: Princeton University Press, 1996), 21: "What religious and legal arguments there were for permitting the existence of religious minorities were those current in the rest of Europe."

22. See Meyerson, *Jews in an Iberian Frontier Kingdom*, 98–175. No comparable arrangement

by kings to bishops and abbots starting in the eleventh century created extensive financial ties between Jewish communities and Northern Castile's ecclesiastical establishment, shaping the Castilian church's attitude toward the Jews.

These arrangements came together in the eleventh and twelfth centuries in the areas along the road to Santiago and influenced the Jews' subsequent history in the Kingdom of Castile. Therefore, the real frontier of Jewish-Christian relations during the early period of settlement ran along the road to Santiago. But even beyond this period, the northern towns—Burgos, Palencia, Sahagún, and other communities on or near the route to Santiago—remained important for the history of Jewish experiences in medieval Iberia.

There are further reasons that Jewish-Christian relations in the region north of Duero deserve greater attention. First, the pattern of Jewish settlement in this region does not fit the usual depiction of medieval Jews as inhabitants of major urban centers.[23] While the first mentions of Jewish presence in the Burgos environs date to as early as the tenth century, Burgos itself could hardly be called a real town until the mid-twelfth century.[24] As late as the thirteenth and fourteenth centuries,

---

is found in the *dhimma* law: "where the medieval Christian state ... progressively tightened its hold on the Jews until they constituted a special case of monarchical 'property' outside the umbrella of evolving public law, Islamic law never asserted the ruler's possessory rights over the non-Muslim"; Mark Cohen, *Under Crescent and Cross: The Jews in the Middle Ages* (Princeton: Princeton University Press, 1994), 52.

23. In explaining the Italian Jews' preference for settling in larger cities, Robert Bonfil mentions two main factors: economic considerations (business opportunities available in major urban centers) and religious-cultural needs (ten-male minyan; good religious education for the children and production of kosher foods; availability of a mikveh and a Jewish cemetery); see Bonfil, *Jewish Life in Renaissance Italy*, trans. Anthony Oldcorn (Berkeley: University of California Press, 1994), 55. Jews were predominantly urban in England (H. G. Richardson, *The English Jewry under Angevin Kings* [London: Methuen, 1960]); Gavin Langmuir concurs in "The Jews and the Archives of Angevin England: Reflections on Medieval Anti-Semitism," *Traditio* 19 (1963): 213. Jews might have lived in rural areas in Normandy, but were "almost exclusively" urban dwellers in the old French royal domain; Jordan, *French Monarchy and the Jews*, 53.

24. Jews are mentioned in the 974 *fuero* of Castrojeriz granted by Count Fernán González: Gonzalo Martínez Díez, ed., *Fueros locales en el territorio de la provincia de Burgos*, Biblioteca universitaria Burgalesa (Burgos: Caja de Ahorros Municipal de Burgos, 1982), 120; Pilar León Tello, "Disposiciones sobre judíos en los fueros de Castilla y León," *Sefarad* 46 (1986): 279; Estepa Díez, "De fines del siglo IX a principios del siglo XIII," 29.

Jews continued to reside in semi-urban settlements (Briviesca, Oña, Belorado, Medina de Pomar, Miranda de Ebro, Villadiego, Pancorbo) and to maintain strong ties to the countryside.[25] Second, in the late twelfth and early thirteenth centuries Burgos rose into prominence as an important center of Jewish life. After King Alfonso VIII had made it his kingdom's capital, the city known as *cabeza de Castilla* became a major commercial and political center of Northern Castile.[26] Perhaps as a consequence of this development, its Jewish population increased to the point that the city became home to the second largest *judería* in Castile, surpassed only by Toledo.[27] Finally, in the mid-thirteenth century the Jews of Burgos found themselves directly touched by Alfonso X's legislative program. Sahagún, Aguilar de Campóo, and Palencia, as well as Burgos, were some of the first Castilian municipalities to receive from the king, in 1255 and 1256, the *Fuero real* as their municipal law. With a special chapter dedicated to Jews (Título "de los iudíos"), the *Fuero real* represented a significant departure from earlier legislation and was an important watershed in Alfonso X *el Sabio*'s attempts to impose uniform law throughout his kingdom.[28] Even after the rebellion of the Castilian nobility in 1272 put a stop to the spread of Alfonsine legislation, Burgos preserved the *Fuero real* as its municipal code.[29]

In short, a detailed examination of the origins and characteristics of northern coexistence can help us understand the dynamics of Jewish-Christian relations in the Kingdom of Castile as a whole. My goal is not to undermine the significance of the southern frontier, but rather to make the story complete by bringing in the evidence from the north. Sometimes historians of medieval Spain assume that the story of Castilian Jewry begins in 1085, when the large and affluent *aljama* of Toledo was incor-

25. See Francisco Ruiz Gómez, "Juderías y aljamas en el mundo rural de la Castilla medieval," *Xudeus e conversos na historia*, 2:111–52. There are a number of useful local studies of Castilian juderías; see, for example, Luciano Huidobro y Serna, "La judería de Pancorbo (Burgos)," *Sefarad* 3 (1943): 155–66; Huidobro y Serna and Francisco Cantera Burgos, "Juderías burgalesas (Beleña, Belorado)," *Sefarad* 13 (1953): 35–59.

26. Martínez Díez, *Fueros locales*, 92.

27. According to the 1290 *Repartimiento de Huete*; Carlos Carrete Parrondo, "El repartimiento de Huete de 1290," *Sefarad* 36 (1976): 130, 126.

28. Azucena Palacios Alcaine, ed., *Alfonso X el Sabio: Fuero real* (Barcelona: PPU, 1991); Simon, "Jews in the Legal Corpus of Alfonso el Sabio," 81.

29. Ruiz, "El siglo XIII y primera mitad del siglo XIV," 113.

porated into the kingdom by the victorious King Alfonso VI.[30] Scholars of Castilian history tend to overlook the Jews' presence in the northern *meseta* before the late twelfth century.[31] Yet, the evidence from Old Castile and León belies the idea that toleration for the Jewish minority in Christian Castile was a cultural cross-pollination from the Islamic south. Américo Castro's dictum that "Spanish toleration was Islamic, and not Christian" is at odds with the Northern Castilian records, which consistently show an evolution of accommodations for the Jewish minority, independently from any models found in the Islamic world.[32]

At times, this study will seem painstakingly local, while at other times it will wander outside the regional confines to include other parts of Castile-León. Northern Castilian documentation, not particularly plentiful, needs to be supplemented and reinforced with evidence from other regions of the kingdom, both frontier and nonfrontier. Such an approach not only fills the gaps in the northern records, but also puts the data found in the archives along the road to Santiago into a broader context. In addition, the fortunes of the Castilian Jews were intimately tied to the exercise of royal power, whose arena of action expanded as the reconquest pushed farther and farther south. Going back and forth between a localized and a panoramic view, I weave the individual communities' experiences of interfaith relations into a larger story of Jewish-Christian coexistence in Northern Castile and the kingdom as a whole. In a broader sense, all of Castile was one big frontier, where the modus vivendi between the Jews and their Christian host society remained in a constant state of evolution.

As will become clear from the pages that follow, I do not employ the term *convivencia* that is often evoked to describe the state of interfaith relations in the medieval Iberian kingdoms.[33] I have come to the conclusion

---

30. See Thomas Glick's influential *Islamic and Christian Spain*, 185. The author implies that Castile became a "religiously heterogeneous" society only after 1085.

31. Bernard Reilly, for example, claims that a Jewish population was not in evidence in Palencia in mid-twelfth century, even though there is ample evidence of the Jews' presence in the region since at least the first decades of the twelfth century. By 1175, there were forty Jewish families in the town; see Reilly, *The Kingdom of León-Castilla Under King Alfonso VII, 1126–1157* (Philadelphia: University of Pennsylvania Press, 1998), 289.

32. Américo Castro, *España en su historia: Cristianos, moros y judíos* (Barcelona: Crítica, 2001), 202.

33. On the history of the concept, see Thomas Glick, "Convivencia: An Introductory Note," in *"Convivencia": Jews, Muslims, and Christians in Medieval Spain*, edited by Vivian Mann,

that the concept has been turned into a kind of brand name for the positive experiences of Jews and Muslims in Spain. Since much of the argument for Spanish *convivencia* hinges on its supposed origins in Islam's toleration for Jewish and Christian minorities, it is part of the nationalist myth, the reverse of the "Black Legend," that accords Spain a unique status in medieval Europe.[34] In Northern Castile, like in the rest of Christian Europe, religious coexistence rested on far less stable foundations than the precepts of the *shari'a* that governed the conduct and protection of the *dhimmī* in the Islamic world.[35] Because religious minorities were subject to secular jurisdictions, their position and security were especially sensitive to changes in the economic and social conditions and the vagaries of princely politics.[36]

A Diachronic Approach

My approach to the study of Jewish-Christian relations in Castile can best be described as diachronic. Some of the best recent contributions to the fields of medieval Jewish history and Jewish-Christian relations have taken a different path, emphasizing the persistence and stability of norms in interfaith relations. Ivan Marcus (*Rituals of Childhood*) and Israel Yuval (*Two Nations in Your Womb*) have focused on the sensitivity and adaptability of the Ashkenazi Jewry to the Christian cultural environment. Writing about Jews and Muslims in Aragon, David Nirenberg (*Communities of Violence*) has argued that ritualized outbursts of intercommunal violence

---

Glick, and Jerrilynn Dodds, 1–9 (New York: George Braziller, 1992); Glick, *Islamic and Christian Spain*, 338–66; Jonathan Ray, "Beyond Tolerance and Persecution: Reassessing Our Approach to Medieval *Convivencia*," *Jewish Social Studies* 11, no. 2 (2005): 1–18; Alex Novikoff, "Between Tolerance and Intolerance in Medieval Spain: An Historiographic Enigma," *Medieval Encounters* 11 (2005): 7–36; and Brian Catlos, "Contexto y conveniencia en la corona de Aragón: Propuesta de un modelo de interacción entre grupos etno-religiosos minoritarios y mayoritarios," *Rivista d'història medieval* 12 (2001–2): 259–68.

34. See Maya Soifer, "Beyond *Convivencia*: Critical Reflections on the Historiography of Interfaith Relations in Christian Spain," *Journal of Medieval Iberian Studies* 1, no. 1 (2009): 19–35.

35. Cohen, *Under Crescent and Cross*, 54.

36. When describing the negotiated contracts between subject Muslims (*mudéjars*) and Christian rulers, Brian Catlos notes that "they provided a medium-term stability: their durability often did not extend beyond the lifetimes of the authorities who signed them, their efficacy was only as clear as the power of the institutions that underwrote them, and they tended to be renegotiated either with each succeeding generation, or as the relative bargaining position of each of the parties changed"; see Catlos, *Muslims of Medieval Latin Christendom: c. 1050–1614* (Cambridge: Cambridge University Press, 2014), 525.

were a normal part of coexistence. In a study that is the closest to my own in geographic scope and subject matter, Jonathan Ray (*Sephardic Frontier*) has explored the ways in which individual Jews adapted to the fluid conditions of the southern frontier in Portugal, Castile, and Aragon.[37] These studies have greatly advanced our understanding of everyday Jewish-Christian coexistence by situating it within the context of the wider medieval European society and stressing the significance of long-term Jewish resilience and survival. The intellectual roots of this trend in historiography can be traced to the pioneering work of Salo Baron, who helped to shift "the focus of research from change to continuity, from the periodic explosion of Jew hatred to issues of status, structure, and context."[38] Historians today are understandably concerned that a renewed focus on the growth of anti-Judaism in the later Middle Ages will raise the specter of the "lachrymose conception of Jewish history," a famous term coined by Baron in the 1920s to counteract the assumption that hatred and persecutions had always shaped the Jewish experiences in the Diaspora.[39]

While I am cognizant of these concerns, I feel that this approach skirts the question that strikes me as crucial to understanding religious coexistence in medieval Spain: how did the changes in society affect Jewish-Christian relations over time? This book does not aspire to offer a sweeping, definitive answer to this question, but it does offer some suggestions that I hope will further our understanding of the major trends in interfaith coexistence in medieval Iberia. In exploring the ties between the Jews and the various sectors in the Christian Castilian society, especially the monarchy, the ecclesiastical institutions, and the municipal councils (*concejos*), I show that each group had its own relationship with

---

37. Ivan Marcus, *Rituals of Childhood: Jewish Acculturation in Medieval Europe* (New Haven: Yale University Press, 1987); Israel Yuval, *Two Nations in Your Womb: Perceptions of Jews and Christians in Late Antiquity and the Middle Ages*, trans. Barbara Harshav and Jonathan Chipman (Berkeley and Los Angeles: University of California Press, 2006); Nirenberg, *Communities of Violence*; Ray, *Sephardic Frontier*.

38. Ismar Schorsch, *From Text to Context: The Turn to History in Modern Judaism* (Hanover, N.H.: Brandeis University Press, 1994), 380.

39. Salo Baron, *History and Jewish Historians* (Philadelphia: Jewish Publication Society of America, 1964), 96. The most forceful recent articulation of the anti-lachrymose position can be found in Jonathan Elukin, *Living Together, Living Apart: Rethinking Jewish-Christian Relations in the Middle Ages* (Princeton: Princeton University Press, 2007).

the Jewish minority and its own reasons for accepting or rejecting the presence of the Jews. I also agree with the previous assessments that the conventional scheme of a "golden age" followed by a "decline" cannot adequately describe the Jews' history in the kingdom. The Jews' fortunes in Northern Castile waxed and waned during the period covered by this book—between the early 1000s and the third quarter of the fourteenth century. There was no "golden age" of Jewish life in Castile, but the community experienced its best years of growth and prosperity during the period of about one hundred years separating the reigns Alfonso VIII and Alfonso X (ca. 1160s to ca. 1260s).[40]

Throughout the book, my goal has been a careful and nuanced analysis of the sources, grounded in the local contexts and disengaged from any "master narratives." Nevertheless, one clear, overarching theme that did emerge from my reading of the evidence was the growing estrangement between Jews and Christians in Castile beginning in the late thirteenth century. The history of the Jews in Northern Castile that I trace in part 3 takes place against the background of dramatic changes and adjustments in the Castilian society that occurred between the last quarter of the thirteenth century and the end of the fourteenth century. I argue that these "long-term structural crises" were the underlying cause of the eventual deterioration of Jewish-Christian relations.[41] Adverse economic conditions, political realignments in towns, and the chronic fragility of royal power were what precipitated the tensions between Christians and Jews. Generally speaking, Castile's troubles were part of the crises plaguing all European kingdoms in the fourteenth century, but it had its distinctive features. The economic situation began to worsen in the late thirteenth century, when the shift of population from northern Spain to the southern regions after the conquest of Andalusia precipitated a decline in agricultural production. Rapid inflation and the kings' attempts to stabilize the currency by debasing the coinage only exacerbated the kingdom's economic woes.[42] The Crown's efforts to raise revenues by

---

40. See Meyerson, *Jews in an Iberian Frontier Kingdom*, 6. In Valencia, Meyerson argues, if the "golden age" existed at all, it was brief—thirty or forty years; see also his *A Jewish Renaissance in Fifteenth-Century Spain* (Princeton: Princeton University Press, 2004), 2–3.

41. T. Ruiz, *Spain's Centuries of Crisis: 1300–1474* (Malden: Wiley-Blackwell, 2011), 28.

42. Teofilo Ruiz, *Crisis and Continuity: Land and Town in Late Medieval Castile* (Philadelphia: University of Pennsylvania Press, 1994), 296–300.

imposing high taxes negatively affected all segments of Castilian society, but the Jews bore the brunt of the fiscal pressure. Burdened with the task of collecting outstanding loans from their impoverished Christian debtors, Jewish moneylenders were forced to operate in a climate increasingly hostile to them and to their business.

The decades of political instability also undermined the Jews' position in Northern Castile and the kingdom as a whole. Once the most active phase of the reconquest was over, the kings could no longer rely on their traditional role as military leaders in the war against the Muslims to protect their authority against the particularistic tendencies of the magnates. Starting late in the reign of Alfonso X and throughout the fourteenth century, the kingdom suffered from the devastating effects of political violence and multiple royal minorities. An alliance with the non-noble knights in towns (*caballeros villanos*), who had risen to prominence in the course of the thirteenth century, allowed the kings to recover some of the lost ground (often at the expense of the towns' autonomy), but also forced them to make concessions to urban procurators at the meetings of Castile's representative assembly—the cortes. The collective petitions submitted to the king by the urban representatives at the cortes became the outlet for an increasingly strident anti-Judaism percolating through the Castilian towns. Although the kings never officially rescinded their protected status, the legislation adopted at the cortes indicates a gradual erosion of the Jews' traditional privileges and shows the legislators' growing acceptance of "foreign" (i.e., northern European) ways of treating the Jewish minority.

The Sources

The reader will notice that Christian attitudes toward the Jews receive a much more thorough treatment in the book than the Jews' views of Christians. Much of this imbalance is due to the nature of the available documentation. Northern Castile was not a major center of Jewish learning during the High Middle Ages, and virtually no Jewish sources survive that could be helpful in my investigation. Christian documentation is by far the best source of information on Christian-Jewish relations in the region, but it affords only a limited view of the Jewish perspective on coexistence. Given the constraints imposed by the sources, whenever it seems fitting I make use of the Jewish writings that hail from other parts of Castile, from Aragon, and even from other European kingdoms. Most of the time, however, I choose to "squeeze the sources" of Northern Castilian provenance and hope that despite their limitations, they still have an important story to tell.[43]

A historian embarking on a study of Castilian coexistence also has to contend with the dearth of Christian sources.[44] The extant evidence from medieval Northern Castile is notoriously poor in both quantity and quality, and the shortage of documentation for the period before ca. 1250 is especially challenging to the work of historical reconstruction. The rest of Castile fares only slightly better, and the difficulty of making sense out of a very idiosyncratic and diverse set of records is the primary reason a definitive new history of the Castilian Jewry will probably remain a desideratum for some years to come.[45] I have tried to make the most of the surviving evidence by pulling together a wide variety of sources: royal charters and law codes, records of property transactions, lending contracts (of which very few survive), legal cases, papal letters, chronicles, and the legislation of the cortes. The bulk of the material that forms the archival basis for this book is found in the ecclesiastical holdings of the Archivo histórico nacional, sección de clero, in Madrid. I made an especially extensive use of the documentation that had come to the National Archive from Northern Castile and León's most prominent religious institutions, such as the monasteries of San Benito de Sahagún, Santa María la Real de Aguilar de Campóo, Santa María de Rioseco, and San Pedro de Arlanza. In addition, I consulted the local municipal and cathedral archives in Burgos, Miranda de Ebro, Palencia, and León. Quite indispensable to the project were the seventeenth-century copies of relevant medieval documents preserved in the Real Academia de la Historia and the Biblioteca Nacional in Madrid. My research greatly benefited from the publication,

43. Jordan, *French Monarchy*, ix.
44. Ray, *Sephardic Frontier*, 4.
45. More generally, on the difficulties of reconstructing Jewish life in medieval Spain, see José Hinojosa Montalvo, "La sociedad y la economía de los judíos en Castilla y la corona de Aragón durante la Baja Edad Media," in *II Semana de estudios medievales: Nájera, 5 al 9 de agosto de 1991* (Logroño: Instituto de Estudios Riojanos, 1992), 79.

over the last several decades, of the documents preserved in the archives of Castile's cathedral, monastic, and municipal institutions, such as the Las Huelgas monastery in Burgos, the Santa María cathedral in León, and the municipal archive in Palencia. Other published sources I analyze in this book are found in the still-indispensable *Die Juden im Christlichen Spanien* (edited by Yitzhak Baer), in the appendices of book-length studies, and in the journal *Sefarad*. Finally, I draw heavily on various published editions of the Castilian *fueros*, Alfonso X's legislative works (the *Fuero real*, *Las siete partidas*), the royal chronicles edited by Cayetano Rosell, and the cortes legislation published in the nineteenth century by the Real Academia de la Historia.

Part 1, "The Jews of Northern Castile and León (ca. 1050–ca. 1350)," opens with a discussion of the evolution of the relationship between the Castilian-Leonese monarchy and the Jews from the reign of Fernando I (1035–65) to the time of Fernando III (1217–52). It argues that the practical exigencies of a continuous military campaign against Islam, as well as the need to attract settlers to the royal lands in the north, dictated the kings' policies toward the Jews. As the reconquest intensified, the monarchy began to make claims of fiscal and jurisdictional monopoly on the Jews, and by the mid-twelfth century royal charters asserted that the Jews were a property of the royal fisc. Yet, from a very early date, the kings interpreted this monopoly as an unrestricted right to share the Jews and their taxes with the Crown's partners in the task of conquest and colonization—ecclesiastical institutions and lay retainers. Part 1 continues with an analysis of the Jews' civic status as reflected in the *fueros* of royal provenance, especially the *fuero* of Cuenca and the *fuero* of Haro, as well as the collection of customary laws from the Burgos region known as the *Libro de los fueros de Castilla*. The last chapter in part 1 details the Jews' arrival in the lands along the Camino de Santiago in Northern Castile-León and explores the role of the Camino and the subsidiary roads in Jewish urban life.

Part 2, "*Judei nostri*: The Church and the Jews in Northern Castile," examines the ties between Northern Castile's ecclesiastical establishment and the Jews. It subjects to critical scrutiny the prevailing theory that the presence in Spain of a large number of non-Christians led to an intensification of missionizing efforts directed at Jews and Muslims. The evidence from Northern Castile shows that ecclesiastical lords and institutions sought to turn the Jews' presence in Castile to their advantage, whether through routine economic transactions or by accepting donations of Jewish taxes and services, which were made by almost every Castilian king from Alfonso VI to Enrique II. When the popes pushed for an implementation of the edicts of the Fourth Lateran Council (1215) on the Jews, they were met with a stiff resistance from the Castilian Crown protective of its prerogatives, as well as an almost universal indifference of the local episcopate. Not even the clergy's widespread indebtedness to Jewish moneylenders and run-ins with Jewish tax farmers were enough to prompt Castilian ecclesiastics into uniting behind the papal initiatives. The clergy rarely took up anti-Jewish legislation during the meetings of the local church councils, and when they did complain to the king about the Jews, both before and after the Council of Zamora (1312), they emulated the strategies employed by the urban representatives at the meetings of the cortes. The arrival of mendicant orders in Northern Castile early in the thirteenth century did not alter the dynamics of the relationship between the church and the Jews.

Part 2 concludes with an analysis of the power relations in the episcopal city of Palencia, home to the Dominican convent of San Pablo established in 1219. At the end of the thirteenth century, the city's lord, the bishop, was engaged in a protracted struggle with the *concejo* (city council) over the extent of the bishop's seigniorial rights, including his jurisdiction in Palencia's Jewish and Muslim *aljamas*. This book suggests that an intense competition for sources of revenue between the city's lay and ecclesiastical powers, as well as between secular clergy and the mendicants, made it highly unlikely that a wealthy Jewish *aljama* like Palencia's would become a target of missionary proselytism.

Part 3, "Jews and Christians in Northern Castile (ca. 1250–ca. 1370)," traces the changes in the state of Jewish-Christian relations between the end of the active phase of the reconquest and the coming of the Trastámaras to the Castilian throne. It begins with an overview of the major trends in the cultural and religious life of the Castilian Jewry at the end of the active phase of the reconquest. During this period, a distinctive mystical tradition, the Kabbalah, emerged in Castile and Aragon in response to Maimonidean rationalism. There were also changes in the Jewish communal life as factionalism and social tensions intensified within the *aljamas* and the King of Castile endeavored to assert greater control over their affairs. Despite Alfonso X el Sabio's ("the Wise") reputation as a sponsor of cultural *convivencia* at his court, his policies had an overall negative effect on Jewish-Christian relations in Castile. His legislative works, most famously, the *Fuero real* and *Las siete partidas*, added restrictive provisions from Roman and canon law to the kingdom's legal discourse on religious minorities. Moreover, in an attempt to boost the Crown's flagging revenues, King Alfonso X initiated a tax hike on the Jewish *aljamas* and established a mechanism to maximize the monarchy's profits from moneylending, now officially closed to Christians. Even though the Jews continued to engage in artisanal pursuits and even own land, the fiscal pressure from the Crown drove the Jews in greater numbers than before to take up moneylending as their primary or secondary occupation.

At the heart of part 3 is a study of two small communities in Northern Castile—Belorado and Miranda de Ebro—where royal assistance with debt collections elicited strong protests from town officials, who accused Jewish moneylenders of violating local privileges and impoverishing Christian debtors. The Crown's relentless fiscal pressure left Jewish lenders with little choice but to enlist the help of royal officials, disrupting communal methods of conflict resolution and driving a permanent wedge between Christian and Jewish *vecinos*. The last chapter of the book argues that the drafting of collective petitions during the meetings of the cortes textualized the townsmen's grievances and transformed them into a potent anti-Jewish discourse. The cortes legislation, disseminated kingdom-wide through special booklets, *cuadernos*, that urban representatives took home with them, fostered hostile attitudes and stereotypes that did lasting damage to Jewish-Christian relations in the Kingdom of Castile. The book's conclusion leaves open the possibility that the intensification of anti-Jewish rhetoric under King Enrique II helped pave the way for the catastrophic violence of the late fourteenth century.

PART 1

The Jews of Northern Castile and León

(CA. 1050–CA. 1350)

ONE ⁜ The Castilian-Leonese Monarchy and the Jews

FROM FERNANDO I TO FERNANDO III

The Jews were destined to play a vital role in the formation of the Castilian state, first in a haphazard and limited fashion, but as time went on, more and more as the focus of the monarchy's deliberate policy of deriving substantial benefits from the "special property" of the royal treasury. From the first royal *fuero* acknowledging the Jews' presence on the Castilian soil and granting them privileges and incentives to stay, to the grim Edict of 1492 expelling them from the kingdom, the fortunes of Castilian Jewry changed with the ebb and flow of royal power. This was especially true early in its history, when the small geopolitical entity tucked into the northwestern corner of the Peninsula gradually transformed itself into a kingdom whose extraordinary imperial and military ambitions were matched only by its extraordinary expenses.[1]

Like the Castilian-Leonese monarchy itself, the Jews' legal and economic status was shaped by the two frontiers that cut through the body of the Peninsula roughly parallel to each other: in the north, the human and commercial traffic flowing along the road to Santiago, and in the south, the Spanish kingdoms' military frontier with Islam. It was the economic boom along the pilgrimage road that attracted the Jews to the areas around Burgos and León, which in the eleventh century were quickly becoming the centers of the emerging realm.[2] Most of them settled in

---

1. Joseph O'Callaghan, *Reconquest and Crusade in Medieval Spain* (Philadelphia: University of Pennsylvania Press, 2003), 175; Bernard Reilly, *The Kingdom of León-Castilla under King Alfonso VI, 1065–1109* (Princeton: Princeton University Press, 1988), 374–75; Maya Soifer Irish, "The Castilian Monarchy and the Jews (Eleventh to Thirteenth Centuries)," in *Center and Periphery: Studies on Power in the Medieval World in Honor of William Chester Jordan*, edited by Katherine L. Jansen, Guy Geltner, and Anne E. Lester, 39–49 (Leiden: Brill, 2013).
2. Reilly, *Kingdom of León-Castilla under King Alfonso VI*, xii.

big and small municipalities located on royal lands (*realengo*) and became the Crown's tenants, accepting the king's jurisdiction and paying tribute (*censum*) to the royal treasury.[3] To the king who needed money—and lots of it—to mobilize large armies on a regular basis for the ongoing war with Islam, the income from the relatively insignificant number of Jewish tenants probably seemed like a drop in the bucket. However, this revenue grew in significance and size, especially, one suspects, after the conquest of 1085 brought under the royal control the large and prosperous *aljama* of Toledo. Be that as it may, by the middle of the next century, one sees concerted efforts by the Crown to assert exclusive jurisdiction not only over Jews, but over Muslims as well, with the aim of advancing the monarchy's fiscal and administrative powers. But this claim of monopoly did not mean that the monarchy was the sole beneficiary of the Jews' fiscal services. From a very early date, the kings of Castile-León were committed to distributing fiscal and jurisdictional shares in the Jewish communities among royal retainers, both lay and ecclesiastical, whose loyalty and military support were indispensable to the monarchy engaged in the laborious process of war and colonization.

The development of the relationship between the Jews and the Crown, which spans the course of several centuries, left few traces in the records and is impossible to reconstruct in precise detail. The first explicit reference to the Jews' and Muslims' special status in the kingdom comes from the reign of Alfonso VII, whose 1141 extension of the *fuero* of Toledo to Calatalifa asserted that the property (*hereditatem*) of Jews and *mudéjars* settled in the town belonged to the king's palace (*sit de palatio*).[4] However, since *fueros* normally confirmed already existing practices, the claim of the Crown's proprietary rights over religious minorities must have predated the Calatalifa charter by several decades, if not longer. In fact, since at least the middle of the eleventh century the kings of Castile-León had been acting as if they had command over the revenues from

---

3. Gautier-Dalché, *Historia urbana*, 33; O'Callaghan, *History of Medieval Spain*, 174–75.

4. "Quicumque vero de populatoribus Calatalife, exceptis mauris et iudeis, tendam in sua hereditate fecerit, eam semper iure hereditario possideat. Maurus vero et iudeus si ibi hereditatem fecerit, sit de palatio"; Fritz (Yitzhak) Baer, ed., *Die Juden im Christlichen Spanien, Erster Teil, Urkunden und Regesten*, vol. 2, Kastilien, Inquisitionsakten (Berlin: Im Schocken Verlag, 1936), 13; D. Tomás Muños y Romero, ed., *Colección de fueros municipales y cartas pueblas* (Madrid: Imprenta de Don Jose Maria Alonso, 1847), 1:532–33.

the Jewish communities. There survives a letter written in 1074 by Bishop Pelayo of León that mentions an annual grant by Fernando I of Castile-León (1035–65) of five hundred *solidos* of pure silver to the church of Santa María de León. The grant is said to have been made during the episcopate of Pelayo's predecessor, Bishop Alvito, and to have come from the "Jewish rent" (*de censu judaeorum*).[5] By all appearances, the king's donation represented a part of his income from the Jewish community in the city of León. It is reasonable to suppose that other *aljamas* living on royal lands also owed the king a *census* (Castilian *censo*).

The term used to describe the Jewish community's payment suggests that the tribute originated as a rent submitted by Jewish settlers to the king for the right to settle on royal lands. The very ordinariness of the word *census*, which frequently appears in medieval charters to designate agrarian rents, indicates that no particular distinction was made between Christian and non-Christian settlers wishing to try their fortune on the northern *meseta*.[6] This evidence effectively undermines some scholars' claim that the taxes paid by Jewish communities secured their right to continue practicing their religion.[7] In fact, the Jews owed a tribute to the Crown simply by virtue of their being royal tenants and living and conducting business on the *realengo*. Already during this early period, the rulers of Castile-León seem to have viewed the Jews as a reliable financial reserve, the Crown's own cache of revenue, into which the king could tap at any time to support his various projects, including grants to favored religious institutions. Fernando I's gift of Jewish rents to Santa

5. "Olim quippe dederat domnus rex Fredenandus quingentos solidos argenti probatissimi de censu judaeorum ad ipsam sedem sanctae Mariae profuturos episcopo ipsius sedis vel cui ipse vellet. Tunc dominus Alvitus episcopus, meus antecessor, in quibus diebus hoc factum est, constituit, ut trecenti solidi ex ipsis deservirent in usus fratrum et clericorum ibidem deo servientium"; Baer, *Die Juden*, 2:4; José Amador de los Ríos, *Historia social, politica, y religiosa de los judíos de España y Portugal*, vol. 1 (Madrid: Ediciones Turner, 1984), 177.

6. Luis Garcia de Valdeavellano, *Curso de historia de las instituciones españolas: De los orígenes al final de la edad media* (Madrid: Ediciones de la Revista de Occidente, 1968), 251: "Los terrazgueros de los predios del señorío debían al señor el pago de una renta o censo por el disfrute de la tierra y en reconocimiento del dominio ajeno sobre el predio que poseían. Esta renta se había confundido con el antiguo tributo territorial romano y recibió nombres diversos según los territorios y las épocas: *censum, tributum, foro, infurción, pectum* (luego *pecha y pecho*)", see also Robert I. Burns, *Medieval Colonialism: Postcrusade Exploitation of Islamic Valencia* (Princeton: Princeton University Press, 1975), 107–8.

7. Reilly, *Kingdom of León-Castilla under King Alfonso VII*, 226–27.

María de León initiated what was to become the standard practice among Castilian-Leonese monarchs in later centuries. When Fernando's son and successor, Alfonso VI (1065–1109), founded a new hospital in Burgos for pilgrims traveling to Santiago, he endowed the new Hospital del Emperador with a daily tribute from the town's Jewish community in the amount of two *solidos* and one *denarius*, along with a *portazgo* (toll) on wood, coal, and salt.[8]

Although the evidence to support firm conclusions is lacking, one can speculate that it was during the reign of Alfonso VI, who styled himself the "Emperor of all Spain," that the royal income from the kingdom's Jewish communities acquired a new significance. Alfonso spent most of his reign in the saddle, leading his troops into battle against the Muslim armies of Andalusia and North Africa. A successful warrior-king, Alfonso needed a constant influx of revenue to mobilize large armies on a regular basis and to be able to replace the troops defeated one year with a new army the next year.[9] Fortunately for Alfonso, the king had several major sources of income at his disposal, including *parias* (tributes paid by the *taifa* kingdoms in exchange for nonaggression and protection), the income from the royal fisc, the revenues from traditional regalian rights, such as minting money, *fossataria* (payment in lieu of military service), and the levies on the church.[10] But the conquest of Toledo in 1085 created a new set of financial challenges for the king. Just when Alfonso was in dire need of resources to repopulate the newly conquered kingdom of Toledo and to defend it against the Islamic threat from the south, the Crown's main source of specie, the *parias*, became increasingly difficult to collect because of the Almoravid control of Andalusia.[11] In all likelihood, the king was eagerly looking for ways to compensate his treasury for this loss in revenue.

The kingdom's religious minorities could provide some of the shortfall faced by the Crown. Alfonso had just acquired a large and flourishing Jewish *aljama* of Toledo and could reasonably expect a drastic increase

8. "Etiam praedicto hospitali ut accipiat quotidie ab ipsis judaeis de Burgos duos solidos et unum denarium, et quinta feria accipiat portaticum de linea et de carbone et unam mensuram salis"; Archivo de la catedral de Burgos [ACB], no. 40.
9. Reilly, *Kingdom of León-Castilla under King Alfonso VI*, 211, 303.
10. Ibid., 204, 374–75.
11. Ibid., 257, 375.

in rents collected from his Jewish subjects. One suspects that the king immediately took the necessary steps to affirm his jurisdiction over the Jews of Toledo, extending to them the claim that had already become traditional in his domain to the north. In fact, the post-conquest situation in Toledo was ideal for asserting such a claim: most of the lands in and around the city were quickly secured for the *realengo*, and the royal power became the dominant force in the city, eclipsing all other jurisdictions, including that of the *concejo*.[12] The *fueros* the king granted to the city's religious minorities have not survived, but they probably affirmed the principle of royal authority over Jews and Muslims and stipulated their obligation to pay a tribute to the royal treasury, modeled after the *censum* paid by the Jews of the north.[13]

Alfonso VI's conquest of Toledo was thus an important watershed in the history of León-Castile's Jewish minority. The incorporation of the Toledan *aljama* significantly increased the number of the king's Jewish and Muslim subjects and made their presence and their financial value to the Crown much more palpable. While the evidence from the north indicates that the ties between the Crown and the Jews predated Alfonso VI's victories in the south, the taking of Toledo likely prompted Alfonso and his successors to further explore the ways in which the expanding Jewish community in Castile-León could benefit the Crown. In 1091, Alfonso issued a charter to the entire kingdom of León that regulated legal disputes between Jews and Christians. The charter stipulated that in cases involving serious injury or homicide, litigants could use judicial combat to resolve their disputes. If the combatant (*bastonario*) representing the Jewish party was defeated, the king and the Christian party each received fifty *sueldos*.[14] If, however, the Jew's *bastonario* prevailed, all the pecuniary

---

12. Gonzalo Martínez Díez, *Alfonso VIII, rey de Castilla y Toledo* (Burgos: Editorial La Olmeda, 1995), 279; Gautier-Dalché, *Historia urbana*, 117; Heather Ecker, "How to Administer a Conquered City in Al-Andalus: Mosques, Parish Churches and Parishes," in *Under the Influence: Questioning the Comparative in Medieval Castile*, edited by Cynthia Robinson and Leyla Rouhi, 63 (Leiden-Boston: Brill, 2005).

13. Many scholars think that these *fueros* existed, but have not survived; see Alfonso García-Gallo, "Los fueros de Toledo," AHDE 45 (1975): 345; Reilly, *Kingdom of León-Castilla under King Alfonso VI*, 171. However, see also Ricardo Izquierdo Benito, "Los judíos de Toledo en el contexto de la ciudad," *Espacio: Tiempo y Forma* 6, series 3 (1993): 82.

14. Bastonario was a nonprofessional fighter armed with a shield and a stick; Félix J. Martínez Llorente, "En torno al procedimiento judicial alto-medieval judeocristiano en el

damages went to the king.[15] The charter thus provides additional evidence that the claim of exclusive royal authority over the Jewish community was already in existence by the end of the eleventh century.[16] To the best of our knowledge, Alfonso VI was also the first Castilian ruler to systematically employ Jewish notables at his court. Jewish physicians, diplomats, and tribute collectors, such as Yishaq ibn Salib, Joseph ha-Nasi ben Ferruziel (known as Cidellus), and his nephew, Solomon ben Ferruziel, put their administrative and intellectual talents in the service of the Castilian-Leonese Crown.[17]

By the early twelfth century, Castile's rulers claimed an exclusive right to collect taxes from the kingdom's religious minorities. This development went hand-in-hand with the evolution of Castilian-Leonese kingship, whose strength and influence depended heavily on the ability of the monarch to exercise effective leadership in the war against Muslims. The exigencies of the reconquest during this period were the major reason the kings of Castile-León were able to command such extensive resources with few major challenges to their authority. Buoyed by their role as military leaders, they accumulated land holdings that "far exceeded the estates of any noble" and cleverly exploited financial benefits that flowed from their numerous regalian rights.[18] The king's claim of proprietary rights over Jews was made that much stronger by the implicit assumption that the revenues from Jewish communities were meant for the royal war chest.

To what extent such claims were enforced cannot be ascertained, but

---

reino de León: La 'Karta inter christianos et iudeos de foros illorum' (1091)," in *Proyección histórica de España en sus tres culturas: Castilla y León, América y el Mediterráneo* (Valladolid: Junta de Castilla y León, 1993), 1:205–10.

15. Muños y Romero, *Colección de fueros municipales y cartas pueblas*, 89–93; Baer, *Die Juden*, 2:6–8.

16. Yitzhak Baer, *A History of the Jews in Christian Spain*, trans. Louis Schoffman (Philadelphia: Jewish Publication Society of America, 1992), 1:45.

17. Baer, *History of the Jews*, 1:50–51; Enrique Cantera Montenegro, "Cristianos y judíos en la meseta norte castellana: La fractura del siglo XIII," in *Del pasado judío en los reinos medievales hispánicos: afinidad y distanciamiento*, edited by Yolanda Moreno Koch and Ricardo Izquierdo Benito (Cuenca: Ediciones de la Universidad de Castilla-La Mancha, 2005), 52; Haim Beinart, "The Jews in Castile," in *Moreshet Sepharad: The Sephardi Legacy*, edited by Haim Beinart, 1:21–22 (Jerusalem: Hebrew University Press, 1992).

18. Reilly, *Kingdom of León-Castilla under King Alfonso VI*, 204. On Castilian kingship, see also Ruiz, "Unsacred Monarchy: The Kings of Castile in the Late Middle Ages," in *Rites of Power: Symbolism, Ritual and Politics Since the Middle Ages*, edited by Sean Wilentz, 109–44 (Philadelphia: University of Pennsylvania Press, 1985).

some Jewish communities could and did escape royal control, especially during the times of political upheavals, when royal power was weakened. During Castile's "crisis of power," one of many that enveloped England and continental Europe in the twelfth century, the kingdom entered a period of political instability.[19] After the death of Alfonso VI in 1109, Queen Urraca (1109–26) struggled to maintain control over the unified kingdom of Castile-León her father had created. Dynastic struggles, factionalism, centrifugal tendencies of the kingdom's provinces, and, finally, the occupation of the Rioja and Old Castile by Urraca's estranged husband, Alfonso I of Aragon (1104–34), created a situation of continuous crisis that threatened the safety of Castilian and Leonese Jewish communities.[20] Only two years after Alfonso VI's death, in August 1110, a major massacre of Jews took place in Toledo.[21] Whoever attacked the judería of Toledo was clearly taking advantage of the weakening of the central authority in the kingdom, felt especially acutely in the frontier, peripheral regions of the realm. At the time, Alfonso I was in his native Aragon, taking care of the affairs of his own kingdom, while Queen Urraca, having just agreed to separate from her husband, was busy consolidating her power in the Rioja.[22] Later in Urraca's reign, the attacks spread to the Castilian heartland, where Jews were physically assaulted and their property looted in several small towns around Sahagún and Palencia. The pardon issued to the offending communities by the young Alfonso VII in 1127 shows that the Jews were targeted in a systematic assault on the royal holdings. The status of the Jews as the Crown's property was evident to the residents of Saldaña, Carrión, Cisneros, and a few other towns who assaulted them while

---

19. Thomas Bisson, *The Crisis of the Twelfth Century: Power, Lordship, and the Origins of European Government* (Princeton: Princeton University Press, 2009), esp. "Troubles on the Pilgrims' Road," 243–59.

20. Bernard Reilly, *The Kingdom of León-Castilla under Queen Urraca, 1109–1126* (Princeton: Princeton University Press, 1982).

21. The *Anales Toledanos* state, "Mataron a los judíos en Toledo dia de Domingo, Vispera de Santa María de Agosto, Era MCXLVI [year 1108]." However, as Reilly points out, it is unlikely that the Jews were attacked on the evening of August 14, 1108, because Alfonso VI was then visiting the city. Moreover, the Feast of the Assumption fell on a Saturday in 1108, but on a Monday in 1110. I agree with Reilly that 1110 is a more likely date for the massacre; see Reilly, *Kingdom of León-Castilla under King Alfonso VI*, 352; see also Nina Melechen, "The Jews of Medieval Toledo: Their Economic and Social Contact with Christians from 1150–1391" (Ph.D. dissertation, Fordham University, 1999), 300–303.

22. Reilly, *Kingdom of León-Castilla under Queen Urraca*, 67–68.

also robbing the royal palaces and burning the king's hunting grounds.[23]

Once Urraca's son, Alfonso, came to power, he moved to restore order, in part by reestablishing royal authority over the Jews. Alfonso VII (1126–57) was another great warrior-king, who was at war for twenty-four out of the thirty-one years he ruled Castile-León, and who adopted the imperial title at the start of his reign.[24] Besides fining the Jews' attackers near Sahagún and Palencia, in 1141 he apparently became the first Castilian-Leonese ruler to employ formulaic language in characterizing the possessions of Jews and Muslims as the property of the royal fisc (*sit de palacio*). Alfonso's attempt to formalize the Jews' status in relation to the Crown indicates that the king placed high value on the income he received from Jewish rents. In another first, Alfonso VII appears to have initiated the practice of tapping Jews to oversee royal finances.[25] He appointed Judah ibn Ezra (nephew of the celebrated poet Moses ibn Ezra) as his treasurer, or *almojarife*.[26] In later decades, the position of the royal *almojarife* would become an almost exclusive domain of Jewish financiers.[27] The Jewish community's status as the property of the royal treasury seems to have been one reason behind the custom of giving the stewardship of the royal coffers to one of their number, although the *almojarifes'* personal wealth was probably another important consideration. Alfonso VII also kept up the practice of dipping into his pockets to reward his surrogates—bishops and abbots—with revenues from Jewish communities. In 1144 the bishop of Ávila was granted one tenth of the levy the town's Jews paid annually to the Crown.[28] Eight years later, in 1152, Alfonso gave an even more valuable gift to the abbot of Sahagún,

---

23. Archivo historico nacional [AHN], sección de clero, Sahagún, carpeta 894, no. 3; published in León Tello, *Los judíos de Palencia* (Palencia: Publicaciones de la Institución Tello Téllez de Meneses, 1967), 37–38.

24. Reilly, *Kingdom of León-Castilla under King Alfonso VII*, 213, 36, 138.

25. Julio González, *El reino de Castilla en la epoca de Alfonso VIII*, vol. 1, Estudio (Madrid: Escuela de Estudios Medievales, 1969), 249.

26. Cantera Montenegro, "Cristianos y judíos en la meseta norte castellana," 61–62; Baer, *History of the Jews*, 1:60, 77; Abraham Ibn Daud, *The Book of Tradition (Sefer ha-Qabbalah)*, ed. and trans. Gerson D. Cohen (Philadelphia: Jewish Publication Society of America, 1967), 97–99.

27. Miguel Ángel Ladero Quesada, *Fiscalidad y poder real en Castilla (1252–1369)* (Madrid: Editorial Complutense, 1993), 234–35.

28. Reilly, *Kingdom of León-Castilla under King Alfonso VII*, 227.

declaring that all the Jews settled in that town would be considered vassals of the abbot and would pay him pecuniary damages as well as, presumably, the requisite tribute.[29]

As the unified kingdom of Castile-León did not survive the death of Alfonso VII in 1157, his heirs split the revenues from the Jewish communities along with the rest of the royal patrimony. The king of Castile, whose inheritance included the old kingdom of Toledo with its populous *aljamas*, received by far the largest piece of the pie. Yet, when in the early 1160s, during the minority of Alfonso VIII, Fernando II of León briefly occupied Castile, he likely helped himself to the revenues from the Jewish communities under his control.[30] After a period of war and confusion, Alfonso VIII (1158–1214) came of age and took the reins of power in Castile. The future conqueror of Cuenca (1177) and the victor at Las Navas de Tolosa (1212) understood the Jews' significance for the success of his military plans and the financial solvency of his kingdom. His 1196 assault, with Pedro II of Aragon, on the Castro de los Judíos near the city of León provides a glimpse into Alfonso's mindset. The king's decision to burn the Jewish settlement together with its synagogue was probably driven by a desire to undermine the fiscal strengths of his Leonese rival, Alfonso IX.[31] Like his grandfather, Alfonso employed Jewish *almojarifes* and may have been the first Castilian ruler to borrow large sums both from Jewish communities and individual Jews. By the end of his reign, Alfonso owed 18,000 *maravedís* to his *almojarife* Joseph ibn Shoshan and an unknown—but presumably significant—amount of money to the Jewish community of Zorita.[32] Also like his predecessors, the king generously shared his Jewish revenues with the members of the ecclesiastical hierar-

---

29. "Ut omnes iudei ville Sancti Facundi sint uassalli abbatis ... et omnes calumpnias quas ipsi fecerint et quas eis fecerint sint semper abbatis Sancti Facundi"; *Colección diplomática del monasterio de Sahagún (857–1300)* [CDMS] (1110–99), 4:230–33. The *fuero* granted to Sahagún in 1255 states that the town's Jews used to pay the abbot of Sahagún eighteen *dineros* as *cienso* (tribute) and that they should continue to do so, as well as to pay an annual tribute of 100 *maravedís* (which includes the *yantar* tax—to feed the bishop's household). ("Otrosi mandamos que los diezeocho dineros que suelen los judios al abad en razon del cienso, que ge los den, et mandamus que le den al abad por yantar et por todo servicio cient moravedis cada anno, et non mas"); Suárez Bilbao, *El fuero judiego en la España cristiana*, 209.
30. Martínez Díez, *Alfonso VIII*, 28–30.
31. González, *El reino de Castilla*, 719–20.
32. Ibid., 249–50; O'Callaghan, *Reconquest and Crusade in Medieval Spain*, 171.

chy, making several major donations in the course of his reign. Thus, he gave the church of Santa María in Aguilar de Campóo a tenth (*diezmo*) of all the taxes the Jews of Aguilar paid to the royal treasury.[33] In addition, Raimundo, the bishop of Palencia and Alfonso's uncle, enjoyed income from the Jewish and *mudéjar* communities after the 1177 royal grant (confirmed in 1185) had made him the lord of the city's *aljamas*.[34]

But Alfonso VIII left his most long-lasting mark on the history of Castilian Jewry in the 1190s, when he called the Jews *servi regis* ("slaves" or "serfs" of the king) in a *fuero* that he gave to the inhabitants of the newly conquered city of Cuenca. The *fuero* of Cuenca is a remarkable document in many ways, not the least because it contains detailed regulations of juridical, social, and economic relations between Jews and Christians in the city. The existence of such a clause in the Cuencan charter is not, in itself, surprising: as was previously shown, the principle that the king had proprietary rights over Jews had already appeared in Castilian customary law. However, the addition of the word *servi* to the traditional formula strikes one as an innovative move. The *fuero* states that all the pecuniary penalties of a Jew belonged not to other Jews, but to the Crown, because "the Jews are *servi* of the king and they are entrusted to his treasury (*fisco*)."[35] What, exactly, did Alfonso VIII mean when he referred to the Jews as his *servi*?

33. "Todo el diezmo de todos los derechos reales que el avia e haber devia en la villa de Aguilar ... et el diezmo de los pechos que dan los judios del aljama de Aguilar al Rey." The documentation for the original donation did not survive. It is described in the 1311 letter by the Infante don Pedro, which states that Fernando III, Alfonso X, and Fernando VI had confirmed the privilege. The letter preserved in the AHN (AHN, clero, Aguilar, carp. 1666, no. 18) is in very poor condition, but the description of it is found in Baer, *Die Juden*, 2:117, and in Huidobro y Serna and Cantera Burgos, "Los judíos en Aguilar de Campóo," *Sefarad* 14 (1954): 337.

34. "Dono, inquam, uobis et prefate ecclesie prenominatos, ut dictum est, sarracenos et iudeos iure hereditario in perpetuum cum omni eorum sobole habendos. Et mando et semper firmiter tenendum statuo quod nulli sarraceni neque iudei de Palencia fossaderam nec façenderam nec pectum aliquod cum concilio ciuitatis umquam persoluant sed absque omni alio domino episcopo tantum palentino semper seruiant, pectent et, tamquam domino proprio, in omnibus et per omnia hobediant"; Teresa Abajo Martín, ed., *Documentación de la catedral de Palencia* (1035–1247) [DCP] (Palencia: Ediciones J. M. Garrido Garrido, 1986), 158–60, 202–3.

35. "In calumpnia iudei, iudeus nullam habet partem, tota enim regis est. Nam iudei serui sunt regis et fisco deputati"; D. Rafael de Ureña y Smenjaud, ed., *El fuero de Cuenca: Formas primitiva y sistemática; Texto Latino, texto Castellano y adaptación del fuero de Iznatoraf* (1936;

The significance of this question is amplified by the fact that such language was not unique to Castile. The *servi regis* clause in the *fuero* of Cuenca was likely an importation from the near-contemporary *fuero* of Teruel, a town in Aragon recaptured from the Muslims in the early 1170s.[36] Within fifty years it would surface in legal texts throughout Christian Europe. In 1236, Emperor Frederick II introduced the notion of *servi regiae camerae* in Germany, at about the same time as the word *servi* was first employed to describe Jews in France and England.[37] The application to Jews of a term that carries a connotation of servile status has puzzled and frustrated historians seeking a plausible explanation for the concept. Those who translate the word *servi* as "serfs" think that the appearance of the concept of *servi regis* or *servi camerae* in Spain and Germany indicates degradation of the Jews' legal status.[38] In the opinion of Guido Kisch, it signaled the advent of *Kammerknechtschaft* ("chamber serfdom"), which meant a complete "appertainment" of the Jews, with their persons and possessions, to the imperial chamber.[39] Some of Kisch's successors have been less willing to

---

repr. Cuenca: Ediciones de la Universidad de Castilla-La Mancha, 2003), 633–34; trans. James Powers as *The Code of Cuenca: Municipal Law on the Twelfth-Century Castilian Frontier* (Philadelphia: University of Pennsylvania Press, 2000), 165.

36. There exists a disagreement on whether the *fuero* of Cuenca was modeled on that of Teruel. The towns' codes are indeed very similar, and both contain the *servi regis* clause. David Abulafia calls the claim that the Cuenca code served as the model for Teruel "a good example of modern Castilian triumphalism" ("'Nam iudei servi regis sunt, et semper fisco regio deputati': The Jews in the Municipal Fuero of Teruel (1176–77)," in *Jews, Muslims and Christians in and around the Crown of Aragon: Essays in Honour of Professor Elena Lourie*, edited by Harvey J. Hames, 99 (Leiden: Brill, 2004). Powers suggests that both codes reflect local customs, rather than borrow from one another; Powers, *Code of Cuenca*, 3.

37. For translations of Louis IX's Ordinance of Melun, 1230, which employs the clause "tamquam proprium servum," and Frederick II's 1236 charter of protection given to the Jews of Germany (his "servi"), see Robert Chazan, *Church, State, and Jew in the Middle Ages* (West Orange, N.J.: Behrman House, 1980), 123–26, 213–15. In 1275, the reference to Jews as "serfs" of the king (*ky serfs il sunt*) appears in England, in Edward I's Statute of the Jewry; see J. A. Watt, "The Jew, the Law, and the Church: The Concept of Jewish Serfdom in Thirteenth-Century England," in *The Church and Sovereignty c. 590–1918*, edited by Diana Wood, 160 (Oxford: Basil Blackwell, 1991). David Abulafia tries to trace the idea of the Jews as *servi* to Frederick Barbarossa's Germany; see his "Nam iudei servi regis sunt," 110.

38. Powers translates *servi* as "serfs"; *Code of Cuenca*, 165.

39. Guido Kisch, *The Jews in Medieval Germany: A Study of Their Legal and Social Status* (Chicago: The University of Chicago Press, 1949), 129. Alexander Patschovsky also speaks of "Jewish serfs"; Patschovsky, "The Relationship between the Jews of Germany and the King (11th–14th Centuries): A European Comparison," in *England and Germany in the Middle Ages*,

equate the Jews' position with that of serfs. For example, Gavin Langmuir has argued that the word *servi* was used metaphorically to indicate a unique, though not servile, Jewish status.⁴⁰ In a recent article, David Abulafia goes somewhat further than Langmuir, suggesting that *servi* had a plain, and not a metaphorical, meaning, but that it indicated a status close to that of German *ministeriales* (unfree knights), who were obligated to perform certain *services* for the king.⁴¹

The evidence from Castile validates Abulafia's and others' rendition of *servi camerae* and *servi regis* as, respectively, "servants of the royal chamber" and "servants of the king."⁴² Even though the word *servi* seems to evoke the status of an unfree northern European peasant, attached to the land and subjected to various juridical disabilities, Alfonso VIII's jurists could hardly have had such an analogy in mind. First, there were never any serfs in Castile, and there would be no serfs in Catalonia until the late thirteenth century.⁴³ Second, Castilian Jews enjoyed both the freedom

---

edited by Alfred Haverkamp and Hanna Vollrath, 193–218 (Oxford: Oxford University Press, 1996).

40. Gavin Langmuir, "Tanquam Servi": The Change in Jewish Status in French Law about 1200," in *Toward a Definition of Antisemitism* (Berkeley: University of California Press, 1990), 192. Maurice Kriegel understands it to be a subordinate, but not a servile, status; see Kriegel, *Les juifs à la fin du Moyen Âge dans l'Europe méditerranéenne* (Paris: Hachette, 1979), 16–17. William Chester Jordan has recently presented clear evidence that the French Jews were not serfs; Jordan, "Jew and Serf in Medieval France Revisited," in *Jews, Christians and Muslims in Medieval and Early Modern Times: A Festschrift in Honor of Mark R. Cohen*, edited by Arnold E. Franklin, Roxani Eleni Margariti, Marina Rustow, and Uriel Simonsohn, 248–56 (Leiden: Brill, 2014).

41. Abulafia, "Jews in the Municipal Fuero of Teruel (1176–77)," 104.

42. See also Norman Roth, "The Civic Status of the Jew in Medieval Spain," in *Iberia and the Mediterranean World of the Middle Ages*, edited by P. E. Chevedden, D. J. Kagay, and P. G. Padilla, 140–42 (Leiden: Brill, 1996); Anna Sapir Abulafia, *Christian-Jewish Relations, 1000–1300: Jews in the Service of Medieval Christendom* (Harlow: Pearson, 2011), 51–55; and Ilan Shoval, "'Servi regis' Re-Examined: On the Significance of the Earliest Appearance of the Term in Aragon, 1176," *Hispania Judaica Bulletin* 4 (2004): 22–69. J. A. Watt defends the use of the term "Jewish serfdom" ("the English Crown did regard its Jews as serfs"), but also stresses that the essence of the Jews' legal status consisted of the *service* they performed for the Crown ("The operative word was *servire*; Jews served. They served both Church and State"; see Watt, "The Jew, the Law, and the Church," 171, 172.)

43. Paul Freedman, *The Origins of Peasant Servitude in Medieval Catalonia* (Cambridge: Cambridge University Press, 1991), 119. Mark Meyerson is unapologetic in his use of the expression "serfs of the royal treasury" to define the status of Jews in the Crown of Aragon in the late thirteenth and early fourteenth centuries. The Aragonese monarchs' fiscal exploitation of the Jews and their attempt to limit the Jews' mobility seem to justify Meyerson's

of movement and the benefit of some judicial autonomy. Yet, it is clear that the word *servi* implied a relationship of dependency and obligation that bound the Jews to render a special service to their lord, the king of Castile.[44] "Service" was a well-known concept in medieval Castile, where all those who had obligations toward their lords—from knights to peasants—were referred to as *vasallos* (vassals). Peasant vassals owed their lords various manorial dues in exchange for protection and the right to use the land, but they were not bound to the land or subjected to the arbitrary will of their lords.[45] Jews, too, were occasionally designated as "vassals," as in an 1152 charter of Alfonso VII to the abbot of Sahagún.[46] The Jewish vassals' particular obligation consisted of making customary payments to the treasury and providing other fiscal services to the king.

The *fuero* Alfonso VIII gave to Cuenca thus contained the most forceful and straightforward articulation of the principle whose origins can be traced to the early settlement of the Jews in Northern Castile-León. What started as a simple tribute collected from Jewish tenants living on royal lands over time became an important royal prerogative, prompting the Crown to assert, most notably in the *fuero* of Calatalifa, that the Jews' property belonged to the royal fisc. The *fuero* of Cuenca went one step further. In addition to appropriating the Jews for the royal treasury (*fisco deputati*), it bound the Jews to the Crown by ties of fiscal obligation (*servi regis*) in an attempt to convert the Jewish communities of Castile into a permanent and unalienable conduit of revenue. At the same time, Castilian monarchs continued to interpret their monopoly on the Jews as an unrestricted right to give them away to royal supporters. The mid-thirteenth-century *Libro de los fueros de Castilla*, a private compilation of Castilian customary laws, allowed for the possibility of some Jews remaining under the control of pri-

---

use of the term "fiscal servitude," especially since by then peasant serfdom was already established in Aragon; see Meyerson's enlightening study *Jews in an Iberian Frontier Kingdom: Society, Economy, and Politics in Morvedre, 1248–1391* (Leiden: Brill, 2004), 98–175.

44. This is close to Norman Roth's translation of the word as "servants," but he understands it only in the sense of the Jews living "under royal protection" and ignores the *service*—i.e., the Jews' obligations—part of the clause; see Roth, "Civic Status of the Jew in Medieval Spain," 140. Meyerson, on the other hand, is right on the mark when he speaks of Jews' "fiscal service"; see Meyerson, *Jews in an Iberian Frontier Kingdom*, 98.

45. Ruiz, *Crisis and Continuity*, 47.

46. Baer, *Die Juden*, 2:15.

vate lords: "This is for a *fuero*: that the Jews are the king's; although they might be under the jurisdiction of magnates (*ricos omnes*) or their knights (*caualleros*) or other men, or under the jurisdiction of monasteries, all of the Jews ought to be the king's, under his protection (*goarda*) and for his service (*seruyçio*)."[47] Therefore, while the ultimate authority over the *servi regis* rested with the monarchy, the established custom was to share the Jews with other lords. Recent examinations of Iberian kingship, such as Janna Bianchini's study of Queen Berenguela of Castile, have shown that "peninsular monarchy was a collaborative endeavor, characterized by corule among members of the royal family." They have also emphasized the importance of patronage in cultivating the nobility's support for the Iberian monarchs' exercise of power.[48] The need to shore up the loyalty of the Castilian Crown's lay and ecclesiastical supporters helps explain its distributive approach to managing Jewish revenues.[49]

In the late twelfth century, political circumstances prompted the king to assert his dominion over the Jews in more forceful terms. The reign of Alfonso VIII encompassed an almost continuous warfare between the kingdoms of Castile, León, Navarre, and Portugal. This military effort, coupled with the struggle against the Almohad threat, which culminated in the brilliant Christian victory at Las Navas de Tolosa, required major expenditures from the Castilian Crown.[50] The cost of running the government also increased during this period, prompting the king to look for new sources of revenue. Both Alfonso VIII of Castile and Alfonso IX of León (1188–1230) placed their bets on the growing prosperity of towns. When calling together the first assemblies of representatives of their kingdoms, later known as the cortes, the monarchs included townsmen in the invitation. The kings' express purpose was to obtain financial help from towns.[51] Although the evidence is lacking, it is logical to assume

47. Galo Sánchez, ed., *Libro de los fueros de Castiella* (Barcelona: Ediciones El Albir, 1981), 54; Javier Alvarado Planas and Gonzalo Oliva Manso, eds., *Los fueros de Castilla* (Madrid: Boletín Oficial del Estado, 2004), 291.

48. Janna Bianchini, *The Queen's Hand: Power and Authority in the Reign of Berenguela of Castile* (Philadelphia: University of Pennsylvania Press, 2012), 7–10.

49. Soifer Irish, "Castilian Monarchy," 49.

50. Derek Lomax, *The Reconquest of Spain* (London: Longman, 1978), 112–26; O'Callaghan, *History of Medieval Spain*, 278.

51. O'Callaghan, *History of Medieval Spain*, 278; Joseph O'Callaghan, *The Cortes of Castile-León, 1188–1350* (Philadelphia: University of Pennsylvania Press, 1989), 16–19.

that, given the delicate state of royal finances, the importance of taxes levied on Jewish communities increased in significance during the reign of Alfonso VIII, enabling his grandson, Fernando III (1217–52), to view them as a major part of the royal revenue.

Unfortunately, no data exists from Fernando III's reign to gauge the size of the income the king of Castile received from Jewish *aljamas*. However, there is indirect evidence that it was rather substantial. After the Fourth Lateran Council (1215) had issued a series of canons, which included a requirement for Jews and Muslims to wear distinctive dress in Christian lands, Pope Honorius III wrote a letter to Castilian bishops, urging them to make the Jews of their dioceses comply with the decisions of the Council. Two years later, in 1219, prompted by the protests of King Fernando III, Honorius rescinded his order. The pope's letter, exempting the Jews of Castile from the requirement, quoted Fernando as saying that the Jews of his kingdom would rather flee to the Muslim lands than submit to wearing distinguishing signs (*signa*). If this were to happen, the kingdom would suffer a great loss (*dispendium*), because a large part of the king's income came from the Jews (*cuijus proventus in Judeis ipsis pro magna parte consistunt*).[52] There is no way to verify this startling claim or to ascertain in what form the king received this income, but Fernando's words can be taken to mean that the revenue was well-established and steady, probably paid as an annual tribute from every Jewish community living on royal lands. It need not have been exclusively a monetary tribute. The 1185 confirmation of privileges given to the bishop of Palencia by Alfonso VIII mentions a tribute of wax (*ceram*) and pepper (*piper*) customarily submitted by the Jews of the kingdom (*sicut mos est iudeorum in regno meo dare*) to the king and his men (*mihi uel hominibus meis*).[53]

The establishment of the customary tribute as early as the eleventh century sets the Castilian case apart from most other European examples. While there are unmistakable parallels between the Jews' status in Castile and that of their counterparts in the rest of Christian Europe, the

---

52. The letter is reproduced in Amador de los Ríos, *Historia social, política, y religiosa de los judíos*, 1 (Madrid: Ediciones Turner, 1984), 554–55.

53. León Tello, *Los judíos de Palencia*, 41–42. The copy at the Biblioteca nacional [BN], mss. 11170, f. 97 has a date "Era MCCXVIII, XVII Calenda de Novembris" [1180]. Also, it mentions a confirmation at the cortes of Burgos of 1367, February 20, by Enrique II, "al mismo tipo que otros Privilegios a aquella Iglesia."

Castilian Crown was more successful in converting the resources of Jewish communities into a steady flow of revenue by means of regular taxation, enshrined in the kingdom's customary law as a royal prerogative. The claim of royal proprietary rights over the Jews was not uncommon in Western European kingdoms and principalities. Yom Tov Assis has claimed that in the neighboring kingdom of Aragon the principle of royal ownership of the Jews already existed during the reign of Count Ramon Berenguer IV (1131–62).[54] However, Thomas Barton has recently provided a forceful counterargument to this assessment by showing that the royal authority over the Jews in Aragon advanced much more gradually and encountered strong opposition from seigniorial jurisdictions even as late as the second half of the thirteenth century.[55] In England, the assertion that the king could have the Jews "as his own" (tamquam proprium) surfaced for the first time around 1135 in the so-called "Laws of Edward the Confessor."[56] In France and Germany, the principle of the royal Jews' special dependence on their lord was not clearly stated until, respectively, 1230 and 1236, but one can argue that it was implicit in Philip Augustus's expulsion of the Jews from the royal domain in 1182.[57]

However, routine taxation never formed the basis for the English and French kings' dealings with the Jews. In 1159, Henry II of England imposed a tax on the Jews of London, Norwich, Lincoln, Winchester, Cambridge, and some other towns.[58] But for the most part, the English and French monarchs chose to rely on fines, confiscations of outstanding loans (captiones), and impositions of exorbitant and unexpected levies. This was the path taken by the kings of England after 1186, when Henry II confiscated

54. Yom Tov Assis, *The Golden Age of Aragonese Jewry: Community and Society in the Crown of Aragon, 1213–1327* (London: Littman Library of Jewish Civilization, 1997), 9; however, see Ray, *Sephardic Frontier*, 80–81.

55. Thomas W. Barton, *Contested Treasure: Jews and Authority in the Crown of Aragon* (University Park: Pennsylvania State University Press, 2015), 10–11, 14–15, 110–12, 171; see also Ray, *Sephardic Frontier*, 80–81.

56. Bruce O'Brien, *God's Peace and King's Peace: The Laws of Edward the Confessor* (Philadelphia: University of Pennsylvania Press, 1999), 184–85, 97, 248n203.

57. Langmuir, "Jews in the Archives of Angevin England," 199–200; Kisch, *Jews in Medieval Germany*, 331–33.

58. Robert Stacey, "Jewish Lending and the Medieval English economy," in *A Commercializing Economy: England 1086 to c. 1300*, edited by Richard Britnell and Bruce Campbell, 86 (Manchester and New York: Manchester University Press, 1995).

the valuable estate of Aaron of Lincoln.[59] Such was the policy adopted in 1181 by Philip Augustus, the king of France, who arrested the Jews in their synagogues, confiscated their precious objects, and canceled all outstanding debts owed to Jews, reserving the principal for the royal treasury.[60] In Castile-León, on the other hand, at least before the late thirteenth century, the Crown relied on custom rather than arbitrary power. It may be that the ability of Castilian-Leonese monarchs to secure important royal prerogatives and command large military and fiscal resources necessary for the war of the reconquest prevented them from having to embark on the same path of arbitrary exploitation of Jewish communities that became the norm in England and France.

For their part, the leadership of the Jewish communities in Castile-León readily accepted royal support and protection in exchange for the fiscal and administrative services they rendered the Crown. Many of the Jewish notables at the courts of Alfonso VI, Alfonso VII, and Alfonso VIII traced their origin to Islamic Spain, and by performing administrative tasks on behalf of the Christian kings they were following the tradition of providing similar services to the Muslim rulers of al-Andalus.[61] Abraham ibn Daud's spirited defense of the rabbinic tradition, the treatise *Sefer ha-Qabbalah* (1161), shows quite clearly why an alliance with the monarchy was a boon to the Jewish leadership in Christian Castile. According to Ibn Daud, in about the mid-eleventh century, there was a resurgence of Karaite Judaism in Castile after a scholar who had recently returned from the Holy Land "led many astray."[62] Joseph ben Ferruziel, the courtier of Alfonso VI, did much to suppress "the heretics," but during the reign of Alfonso VII they grew in strength once again. It appears that Carrión de los Condes, a town on the Camino de Santiago about halfway between Burgos and León,

59. Stacey, "Jews and Christians in Twelfth-Century England: Some Dynamics of a Changing Relationship," in *Jews and Christians in Twelfth-Century Europe*, edited by Michael Signer and John Van Engen, 347 (Notre Dame: University of Notre Dame Press, 2001).

60. Jordan, *French Monarchy and the Jews*, 31.

61. Bernard Septimus, *Hispano-Jewish Culture in Transition: The Career and Controversies of Ramah* (Cambridge, Mass.: Harvard University Press, 1982), 11.

62. Karaites rejected the binding authority of the rabbinic writings, the Mishnah and Talmud. On the history of Karaites and their conflict with Rabbanites, see Fred Astren, *Karaite Judaism and Historical Understanding* (Columbia: University of South Carolina Press, 2004), and Marina Rustow, *Heresy and the Politics of Community: The Jews of the Fatimid Caliphate* (Ithaca: Cornell University Press, 2008).

had a significant Karaite community.⁶³ The Jewish communal leaders then turned for help to Alfonso, whom Ibn Daud lauds as the *Emperador*, "king of kings, and a righteous king." Ibn Daud relates that the king showered his *almojarife*, Judah ibn Ezra, with favors, appointing him "ruler over all his possessions." When Ibn Ezra asked Alfonso to "forbid the heretics to open their mouths throughout the land of Castile," the king ordered that it be done. Not only did Alfonso assist the Jewish community in resolving its internal religious dispute, but he also put Ibn Ezra in charge of the frontier city of Calatrava, which then became a refuge for the Jews fleeing from the Almohad persecutions in the south. After taking care of the refugees' basic needs, Ibn Ezra helped resettle them elsewhere in Castile.⁶⁴

The positive attitude toward royal power expressed in Ibn Daud's treatise was typical of Jewish writers in Castile and Aragon from the twelfth century on. The prominent thirteenth-century Catalan rabbis Moses ben Nahman and his pupil Solomon ben Adret insisted that Christian kings ruled by divine right and should be obeyed as one would a Jewish king.⁶⁵ An echo of this attitude may have survived in the saying, popular among the Spanish Jews during this period, that favorably compared the Jews' treatment in Christian Iberia to the interfaith climate in Islamic lands: "Better under Edom [Christendom] than Ishmael [Islam]."⁶⁶ Jewish authorities continued to depend on the Crown's officials to settle internal disputes, confirm Jewish *aljamas*' privileges, and collect outstanding debts from Christians.⁶⁷ The taxes that the Jewish communities in Spain owed to the Christian rulers were seen as a guarantee of protection and safety. Meir ha-Levi Abulafia, the leader of the Jewish community in Toledo during the first half of the thirteenth century, argued that royal taxes should be classified as defense expenditures: "Paying taxes to the king is certainly no less [effective] than hiring horsemen and guards for defense. Quite

---

63. "He [Joseph ben Ferruziel] drove them out of all the strongholds of Castile except for one, which he granted them, since he did not want to put them to death"; Ibn Daud, *Book of Tradition*, 95. Scholars surmise that this town was Carrión; León Tello, *Los judíos de Palencia*, 8–9.

64. Ibn Daud, *Book of Tradition*, 98–99.

65. Assis, "Jewish Attitudes to Christian Power in Medieval Spain," *Sefarad* 52 (1992): 292.

66. Septimus, "Hispano-Jewish Views of Christendom and Islam," in *In Iberia and Beyond: Hispanic Jews between Cultures*, edited by Bernard Dov Cooperman, 46–47 (Newark: University of Delaware Press, 1998).

67. See part 3 of this volume and Ray, *Sephardic Frontier*, 130.

to the contrary, the protection provided by the king is certainly more effective."[68] Not even the fiscal pressure of the late thirteenth century and the removal of Jews from positions of power in Aragon changed many Jewish leaders' opinion that the monarchy was the Jews' most reliable ally in Christian Spain.[69]

It is often argued that the experience of Jews in Iberia was so distinctive that it "cannot be easily fit into the framework of medieval European Jewish history." The uniqueness of this experience is attributed to the proximity of the frontier with Islam, which created an environment in which Jews, Christians, and Muslims could mingle freely and influence each other's culture, thought, political institutions, and social norms.[70] A close scrutiny of the evolution of Jewish status under the Crown of Castile-León between the eleventh and early thirteenth centuries shows that this view needs some modifications. While the existence of the military frontier and the ongoing confrontation with the Muslims of Andalusia and North Africa left an indelible mark on the nature of Castilian-Leonese monarchy and on Castilian political institutions, the position of the Jews in the kingdom seems to have been shaped less by Christians' interaction with Islam along the southern frontier than by the developments in the Christian north before the major conquests of the late eleventh century. The appropriation of the Jews by the royal fisc and the Jews' traditional role as the king's fiscal servants (*servi regis*) had roots in the rudimentary taxation system of Fernando I and his immediate successors. Since no comparable arrangement existed for Jews living under Castile's Muslim neighbors, who collected a poll tax, or *jizya*, from Christians and Jews as a sign of their humiliation and second-class status, it is clear that the claim of royal proprietary rights over religious minorities in Castile was an outgrowth of the monarchy's political and military needs and ambitions, and not a borrowing from Islam.

68. Yad Ramah, Baba Batra (Warsaw: 1887), 1:87; cited in Septimus, *Hispano-Jewish Culture in Transition*, 13.
69. Assis, "Jewish Attitudes," 294. Other evidence from Spain indicates, however, that Jewish communities and individuals could be quite opportunistic in seeking non-royal patrons (both secular and ecclesiastical) if they thought that alternate arrangements would serve their interests; see Ray, *Sephardic Frontier*, 82–84, and Barton, *Contested Treasure*, 152, 186.
70. Stow, *Alienated Minority*, 1; Meyerson, *Jews in an Iberian Frontier Kingdom*, 2.

Castilian Jews' special status in relation to the monarchy places them firmly within the framework of medieval European Jewish history. In fact, the same pattern emerged in every Christian country with a significant Jewish population. In Aragon, Germany, England, France, and Castile, the kings sought to assert their regalian rights over the country's Jews, using a variation of the *servi regis* doctrine to bind them to the monarchy with ties of dependency and financial obligation.[71] The Castilian-Leonese monarchs received customary tributes from the Jewish communities and until the latter part of the thirteenth century eschewed the draconian, exploitative methods adopted by their counterparts in the north. However, the fact remains that the Jews of Castile were like their coreligionists everywhere in medieval Europe in having their fates tied to the needs of the royal treasury.[72]

What sets Castile apart from non-Iberian monarchies that tolerated a Jewish minority is the extent to which Jewish-Christian relations in the kingdom were shaped by conquest, expansionism, and colonization. This was a monarchy whose budget, in the words of Joseph O'Callaghan, "would likely show that the bulk of the revenue was expended on war."[73] The exigencies of continuous warfare left a profound mark on the Jews' status in the kingdom, bolstering the kings' claim that Jewish taxes were a permanent part of the royal treasury. It made the Jews' financial contributions indispensable to the Crown engaged in the war against the Almohads and about to score its greatest victories at Las Navas de Tolosa (1212), Córdoba (1236), and Seville (1248). Additionally, conquest and colonization prompted the monarchy to grant Jewish and Christian settlers special privileges, delineated in a number of municipal *fueros* issued by the Crown in the course of the eleventh and twelfth centuries.

---

71. Langmuir, "Tanquam Servi," 192–93. On France, see Jordan, "Jews, Regalian Rights, and the Constitution in Medieval France," *AJS Review* 23 (1998): 1–16. Hussein Fancy argues a similar point with regard to the king of Aragon's efforts to recruit Muslim soldiers (*jenets*) into his service: Fancy, "Theologies of Violence: The Recruitment of Muslim Soldiers by the Crown of Aragon," *Past and Present* 221 (November 2013): 39–73.

72. See Stow, *Alienated Minority*, 273–80.

73. O'Callaghan, *Reconquest and Crusade in Medieval Spain*, 175.

The Jews in the Castilian *Fueros*

The legal sources of royal provenance reveal the Castilian monarchy's efforts to make the Jews into a special category of royal servants, uniquely dependent on royal protection and responsive to the Crown's political and fiscal needs. But a wealth of information also found in these charters indicates that the Jews' actual status in Castilian communities was more fluid than the rigid language of royal pronouncements would suggest. What the *fueros* show is that while the Jews' status generally benefited from Castile's military expansion, a great deal of variation existed among different communities and regions of Castile in the degree of the Jews' participation in the civic life of Christian municipalities. Granted by kings, and in some cases by secular and ecclesiastical lords, to individual localities or to ethnic and religious groups, *fueros* also reflected community-specific customs that account for much of this variation.[74] As a type of source they are extremely heterogeneous, idiosyncratic, and notoriously difficult to date, reflecting the decentralized state of Castilian legal norms before the start of Alfonso X's ambitious legislative program. Taken together, this evidence does not present a very clear picture of Jewish-Christian relations during the early period of settlement in Castile-León, but it does suggest that local customs and circumstances had at least as big an impact on Jewish life in Castile as did the Crown's efforts at regulating the affairs of its special servants.[75]

Before the last quarter of the twelfth century, *fueros* tend to be brief (*fueros breves*), addressing such particular issues as exemptions from tribute, penalties for crimes and transgressions, and judicial procedures.[76] The first *fuero* to depart from this model is that of Cuenca in southern Castile (around 1190), which reads more like an extensive municipal code than a collection of privileges.[77] By their very nature, the *fueros* of the early type emphasize privileges and immunities of the recipients, rare-

---

74. O'Callaghan, *History of Medieval Spain*, 172.
75. On the value of the *fueros* for elucidating medieval Jewish history, see Ray, "The Jew in the Text: What Christian Charters Tell Us about Medieval Jewish Society," *Medieval Encounters* 16 (2010): 243–67.
76. Palacios Alcaine, ed., *Alfonso X el Sabio: Fuero real*, ii.
77. Powers, *Code of Cuenca*, 1.

ly going into the minutiae of local governance. There survives only one such *fuero* given specifically to a Jewish community—the *fuero* of Haro in northeastern Castile (around 1187).[78] An important source of information on the kind of privileges Jews could receive from the Crown, the *fuero* of Haro does not have much to say on the Jews' place within a Christian municipality. In contrast, the Code of Cuenca devotes much attention to the governance of this frontier town and to the Jews' civic status. Yet, it has its own shortcomings as a source, giving few details regarding the royal jurisdiction in the *aljama*. The latter subject is highlighted extensively in the so-called *Libro de los fueros de Castilla*—a collection of charters, local and territorial law, and judicial decisions from the Burgos region in Northern Castile.[79] However, being neither a monarchy-sanctioned *fuero* nor a municipal code, the *Libro de los fueros* does not deal with the Jews' privileges or their civic status.

In short, the three most informative sources on the Jews' status in Castile are seemingly incommensurable, coming as they do from different parts of the kingdom and serving dissimilar purposes. Other *fueros* either mention Jews only in passing or cannot be dated with any degree of certainty.[80] Nevertheless, sources as dissimilar as the *fuero* of Cuenca, the *fuero* of Madrid, and the *Libro de los fueros de Castilla* do agree on one critical point: that the Jews of Castile live under the king's special protection and jurisdiction.[81] Beyond this underlying principle, however, the

78. León Tello, "Nuevos documentos sobre la judería de Haro," *Sefarad* 15 (1955): 157–69.

79. Sánchez, ed., *Libro de los fueros de Castiella*. A more recent edition is found in Alvarado Planas and Oliva Manso, eds., *Los fueros de Castilla*, 253–354. Sánchez, ed., *Libro de los fueros de Castiella*.

80. In the first category I include all of the eleventh- and early-twelfth-century *fueros*, as well as the *fuero* of Madrid (around 1202). The *fuero* of Coria (between 1208 and 1210) is concerned mainly with business transactions between Jews and Christians. In the second category, there is the *fuero* of Usagre, given by the Master of the Order of Santiago between 1242 and 1275 (i.e., it is unclear whether it was granted before or after the promulgation of the *Fuero Real*), and the *fuero* of Soria, previously thought to have been granted by Alfonso VIII between 1190 and 1214, but now placed by some historians after the *Fuero Real*; see Agustín Millares Carlo, ed., *Fuero de Madrid* (Madrid: Publicaciones del Archivo de Villa, 1994); Suárez Bilbao, *El fuero judiego*; de Ureña y Smenjaud and Adolfo Bonilla y San Martín, eds., *Fuero de Usagre* (Madrid: Hijos de Reus, 1907); Sánchez, ed., *Fueros castellanos: De Soria y Alcalá de Henares* (Madrid: Centro de Estudios Históricos, 1919); Martínez Díez, "El fuero real y el fuero de Soria," *AHDE* 39 (1969).

81. The Code of Cuenca: "In calumpnia iudei, iudeus nullam habet partem, tota enim regis est. Nam iudei serui sunt regis et fisco deputati"; de Ureña y Smenjaud, ed., *El fuero de*

fueros vary widely on the specifics of the Jews' status in Castilian municipalities. Several examples suffice to illustrate this point. The royal fuero of Briviesca (1123) specifies the fine of one hundred solidos for murdering a Jew. The Code of Cuenca (late twelfth century) sets the fine for the same crime as high as five hundred solidi.[82] In Cuenca, cases between Jews and Christians require participation of two alcaldi (judges) from each religious community, whereas many other municipal fueros, such as that of Toledo, stipulate that such cases be taken to Christian judges only.[83] The fuero of Coria (between 1208 and 1210) forbids Jews to plead cases in the court of law, whereas the fuero of Salamanca, later in the century, allows them to serve as advocates for a client of their choice.[84] Such diversity of juridical norms is hardly surprising. Before the middle of the thirteenth century, Castilian law represented a bewildering patchwork of local customs.[85] While many fueros originated as royal privileges to towns, they relied on a body of local law, written down either by townsmen themselves or by royal lawyers.[86]

Cuenca, 632. The fuero of Madrid: "El iudize non tradat uocem nisi per homines de sua casa aut de homines de palazio uel de moros uel de iudeos qui pertinent ad regem"; Millares Carlo, ed., Fuero de Madrid, 51. The Libro de los fueros de Castiella: "Esto es por fuero: quelos judios son del rey; maguer que sean so poder de ricos omnes o con sus cauelleros o con otros omnes o sopoder de monesterios, todos deuen ser del rey en su goarda e para su seruyçio"; Sánchez, ed., Libro de los fueros de Castiella, 54.

82. Martínez Díez, Fueros locales, 136; Powers, Code of Cuenca, 164; León Tello, "Disposiciones sobre judíos en los fueros de Castilla y León," Sefarad 46 (1986), 284.

83. Ibid., 281; León Tello, Judíos de Toledo (Madrid: CSIC, 1979), 1:34–35; Suárez Bilbao, El fuero judiego, 72. On the 1118 fuero of Toledo, see García-Gallo, "Los fueros de Toledo," AHDE 45 (1975): 351–61.

84. The fuero of Coria: "Nengun judio non tenga su voz ni agena"; Suárez Bilbao, El fuero judiego, 189. The fuero of Salamanca: "Moros e iudíos den su voz a barayar a quien se quesieren"; Jose Luis Martin and Javier Coca, eds., Fuero de Salamanca (Salamanca: Ediciones de la Diputación de Salamanca, 1987), 106.

85. Alfonso García-Gallo, Manual de historia del derecho español, 2nd ed. (Madrid: Artes Gráficas y Ediciones, 1964), 1:88–89, 386.

86. In Powers, Code of Cuenca, 1; Ramon Fernández Espinar, Manual de historia del derecho español, vol. 1, Las fuentes (Madrid: Editorial Centro de Estudios, 1990), 298, 305. Paola Miceli rejects the idea that customary law reflected in the fueros arose spontaneously out of social practices. In her view, it was the product of legal decisions made by jurists working under the influence of surviving Roman law, such as the old Visigothic Liber iudicum, especially in León and Catalonia; see Miceli, "El derecho consuetudinario en Castilla: una crítica a la matriz romántica de las interpretaciones sobre la costumbre," Hispania: Revista Española de Historia 63/1, no. 213 (2003): 9–27. Earlier, Aquilino Iglesia Ferreirós has argued along the same lines; see Iglesia Ferreirós, "Derecho municipal," 134–35.

Given the multiplicity of customs, it is difficult to make a persuasive case that twelfth-century municipal *fueros* reflect "pro-Jewish" policies of the Castilian monarchs.[87] With the single exception of the *fuero* of Haro, there are no extant royal charters from the eleventh or twelfth century given specifically to Jews.[88] It may be that the Jews, along with other groups of settlers—among them, Castilian, French, and Catalan—benefited from the more general royal policies designed to attract new *pobladores* to the towns along the Camino de Santiago that sprang up as a consequence of the economic boom of the late eleventh and early twelfth centuries. The *fueros* granted by the kings of Castile and León freed these towns' inhabitants from traditional obligations, guaranteeing their personal freedom and the right to form a town council—*concejo*.[89] On most occasions, the kings specify that the *fuero* is being given to anyone who comes to settle in the town, whether Jew, Christian, or Muslim.[90] The recipients are not individual Jews, *francos*, Muslims, or Christians, but rather religious and ethnic *communities*, whose judicial autonomy is thereby recognized and whose members' legal equality in mixed litigation is guaranteed. For example, the 1116 *fuero* of Belorado, given by the king of Aragon, Alfonso I, who controlled the Burgos province at the time, states that Jews and Christians have to pay the same fine for inflicting injury on each other.[91] However, it is not clear whether the Jews' rights extended to participation in communal life on a par with the Christians.[92] The *fuero* of Belorado stipulates that *francos* and *castellanos* could elect their own judges and jointly select *alcaldes*, presumably to hear mixed cases. It is

---

87. Norman Roth, "Civic Status of the Jew," 149–50. Jonathan Ray argues that in the twelfth century there was a "royal campaign to establish legal equality among Jews, Muslims, and Christians"; Ray, *Sephardic Frontier*, 89.

88. León Tello, "Nuevos documentos sobre la judería de Haro." It is possible, however, that other such charters existed, but have not survived.

89. Gautier-Dalché, *Historia urbana*, 208–9; Garcia de Valdeavellano, *Curso de historia de las instituciones Españolas*, 531.

90. These privileges are granted to all settlers—Jews, Christians, and Muslims—in the *fueros* of Briviesca, Lerma, and Miranda. The *fuero* of Belorado does not include Jews in the list of *pobladores* to whom the charter is being given, even though it mentions them elsewhere in the text; see Martínez Díez, *Fueros locales*, 134, 136, 153, 164.

91. "Et iudaeo cum christiano, et christiano ad iudaeo qualem livorem fecit, talem pectet, sed duobus partibus fiant in terra pro anima mea, sicut supra scriptum est"; Martínez Díez, *Fueros locales*, 134.

92. Baer, *History of the Jews*, 1:87.

silent on the role of the Jews.⁹³ In fact, none of the early twelfth-century *fueros* mention the Jews' involvement in the selection of magistrates.⁹⁴ The picture that arises from the study of these *fueros* shows autonomous Jewish communities enjoying royal protection and privileges but remaining politically isolated from their Christian counterparts.

In contrast, the much-celebrated and studied *fuero* of Cuenca, granted by Alfonso VIII around 1190, seems to suggest a higher degree of integration between Christian and Jewish communities. Not only does it go into much greater detail regulating legal, social, and economic interaction between Jews and Christians, but it does so in a way that has led some scholars to believe that the Jews enjoyed the right of full citizenship in Cuenca.⁹⁵ For example, Jews could be selected by the town officials to be public sellers of commodities (*venditores*).⁹⁶ Mixed cases between Jews and Christians require a designation of two Jewish and two Christian judges (*alcaldi*), as well as a selection of two witnesses from each religious community.⁹⁷ Moreover, Jews are repeatedly referred to as *vicini*, a term that can be rendered in English as "citizens."⁹⁸ "*Iudeus uicinus*" (the Jewish citizen) is entitled to certain privileges, such as the right to take and give sureties, to be elected *venditor*, or to serve as an *alcaldus* or a witness in mixed litigations.⁹⁹ But other evidence indicates that the Jews possessed a distinct legal status within the Christian municipality.¹⁰⁰ By the end of

---

93. "Et vos francos mittatis iudice franco, atque tollite ad vestrum talentum; et castellanos similiter tollite, et mittite vestro iudice a vestro talento de mea gente; et omnes in unum mittatis alcaldes ad discurrendum iuditium"; Martínez Díez, *Fueros locales*, 134.

94. One has to note, however, that the early twelfth-century *fueros* were not comprehensive codes of law, and many customs remained unwritten; see, for example, Fernández Espinar, *Manual de historia del derecho español*, 393.

95. See Powers, *Code of Cuenca*, 12.

96. "Iudex et alcaldes statuant uenditorem publicum mercium uenalium, quem uulgo uocat corredorem, siue sit xristianus, siue iudeus, aut sarracenus"; de Ureña y Smenjaud, ed., *El fuero de Cuenca*, 442; Powers, *Code of Cuenca*, 113.

97. "Si Iudeus et xristianus super aliquot disceptauerint, faciant duos alcaldes uicinos, quorum unus sit xristianus, et aliter iudeus.... Firme sint inter xristianum et iudeum xristianus et iudeus vicini"; de Ureña y Smenjaud, ed., *El fuero de Cuenca*, 614, 616; Powers, *Code of Cuenca*, 160–61.

98. As Powers does in *Code of Cuenca*, 160–61.

99. See Powers, *Code of Cuenca*, 113, 160–64.

100. Baer argues that the Jewish communal organization (*kehillah*) originated during the period of the Second Temple, but received its fullest development in Western Europe starting in the late tenth to early eleventh century; see Baer, "The Origins of Jewish Communal

the twelfth century, Christian sources recognized the existence of self-governing Jewish communities and began to call them *aljamas*.[101] The *aljama* of Cuenca had its own administrative and judicial structure whose functions paralleled those of the *concejo*. The Cuenca code mentions one of the *aljama*'s officials—*albedí*, or "judge"—who is responsible for hearing legal cases and carrying out decisions of the court.[102] It is the *albedí* who imprisons Jewish debtors (even if the plaintiff is a Christian) and collects sureties from the Jews, while the Christian judge—*iudex*—performs the same functions for the Christians.[103]

This inconsistent articulation of the Jews' status within the Cuencan municipality makes it difficult to ascertain whether they could obtain the privilege of full citizenship.[104] The status of a *vecino* (citizen) in a twelfth-century Castilian town was predicated on several circumstances: one had to be a native or to have lived in the town for a certain period of time, to possess property there, to pay the requisite tribute to the king and to the *concejo*, and to be independent of any other lord except the king. A citizen enjoyed all the rights and privileges spelled out in the *fuero*, including the right to participate in the *concejo*, and he had an obligation to serve in the municipal militia.[105] The status of a Jewish *vecino* satisfied some of these conditions, but not all. The Jews settled in Cuenca could fulfill the residency and property ownership requirements, and it is in this sense that some late-thirteenth century *fueros* described the Jews as *vecinos*.[106] But

---

Organization in the Middle Ages," in *Binah: Studies in Jewish History, Thought and Culture*, edited by Joseph Dan, 1:59–82 (New York: Praeger, 1989).

101. See David Romano, "Aljama frente a judería, call y sus sinómimos," in *De historia judía hispánica* (Barcelona: Publicacions Universitat de Barcelona, 1991), 347–54.

102. In Powers, *Code of Cuenca*, 160–65; de Ureña y Smenjaud, ed., *El fuero de Cuenca*, 616–34.

103. Powers, *Code of Cuenca*, 160–61.

104. Norman Roth answers mostly in the affirmative, although he sees "an inconsistency" in the code; see Roth, "Civic Status of the Jew," 152. María Fuencisla G. Casar argues that Jews and Christians enjoyed the same rights and privileges in Cuenca, in "El tratamiento de los judíos en los fueros de la familia Cuenca-Teruel," *Revue des etudes juives* 144, nos. 1–3 (January–September 1985): 27–37; María Auxiliadora Caro Dugo emphasizes their equality in legal process in "Pleitos entre judíos y cristianos en el derecho municipal Castellano-Leonés," in *Proyección histórica de España en sus tres culturas: Castilla y León, América y el Mediterráneo* (Madrid: Junta de Castilla y León, 1993), 37–43.

105. As described in García de Valdeavellano, *Curso de historia de las instituciones españolas*, 543, and Gautier-Dalché, *Historia urbana*, 353–54.

106. Fuero of Salamanca, in its final version (second half of the thirteenth century) states,

the Cuencan charter also referred to the Jews as *servi regis* and indicated that they were to pay pecuniary damages directly to the king, whereas the Christian *iudex* had no share in them.[107] A real clue to the Jews' participation in municipal life would be some evidence that they contributed to the taxes that the Christian *vecinos* owed the *concejo* and the king. But like most *fueros*, the code of Cuenca is silent on this point.[108] The picture that emerges from other Castilian sources, mostly of administrative nature, is rather contradictory. In Burgos, Palencia, Briviesca, and Belorado the king ordered the Jews to contribute to the maintenance of city fortifications.[109] In some cities, Palencia being one example, the Jews paid certain taxes (such as *fonsadera*, *infurción*, and *martiniega*) jointly with the *concejo*.[110] As a general rule, however, the Jews' special status exempted them from paying a tribute to the *concejo* unless they were specifically ordered to do so by the king.[111] Late in the thirteenth century, the Jews' tax exemptions became a bone of contention during the meetings of Castile's representative assembly—the cortes.

On balance, it appears that the status of a Jewish *vecino* conferred certain tangible benefits on the members of Cuenca's *aljama*, but it re-

---

"Et los iudíos sean encotados ellos e sus heredades commo vezinos de Salamanca"; see Martin and Coca, eds., *Fuero de Salamanca*, 123. The *fuero* of Sahagún, granted by Alfonso X in 1255 as a supplement to the *Fuero Real*, mentions the abbot's right to appoint *judío, que sea vecino de S. Fagund*, as an *alvedi* over the Jewish community; Muños y Romero, *Colección de fueros municipales y cartas pueblas*, 1:519. But by the second half of the thirteenth century, the status of a *vecino* has lost some of its former luster. With social stratification growing within some Castilian municipalities, many *vecinos* were excluded from political power by the tax-exempt *Caballería villana*; see, for example, Ruiz, "The Transformation of the Castilian Municipalities: The Case of Burgos," *Past and Present* 77 (November 1977), esp. 20–22. I suspect that the term *vecino* came to signify "a resident of town in possession of some property." According to this definition, many Jews qualified as *vecinos*.

107. De Ureña y Smenjaud, ed., *El fuero de Cuenca*, 632, 634.

108. Suárez Bilbao, *El fuero judiego*, 57.

109. Burgos: Asunción López Dapena, ed., *Cuentas y gastos (1292–1294) del rey D. Sancho IV el Bravo (1284–1295)* (Maracena: Publicaciones del Monte de Piedad y Caja de Ahorros de Cordoba, 1984), 487; Briviesca: Carrete Parrondo, "El repartimiento de Huete," 130; Belorado: Biblioteca de la real academia de la historia, 66.981.O-16, ff.403v–4; Palencia: Archivo municipal de Palencia [AMP], Pergaminos no. 2; Baer, *Die Juden*, 2:22.

110. Archivo municipal de Palencia [AMP], *Pergaminos* no. 2; Baer, *Die Juden*, 2:22; Miguel Angel Ladero Quesada, *Fiscalidad y poder real en Castilla*, 75.

111. As eventually happened in Burgos, in 1301; Archivo municipal de Burgos [AMB], no. 93; Emiliano González Díez, ed. *Colección diplomatica del concejo de Burgos (884–1369)* [CDCB] (Burgos: Institutos de estudios castellanos, 1984), 264–68.

mained a distinct status, which only partly mirrored that of a Christian *vecino*. This said, compared to other areas of Castile, the Cuenca model of Jewish-Christian relations strikes one as rather indulgent and accommodating of non-Christian minorities. One should put an emphasis on the word "model," for law codes are not perfect reflections of real-life practices.[112] Nevertheless, the popularity of the Cuencan code among the towns of southern and western Castile, many of which adopted it for their own use, shows that the code's emphasis on municipal autonomy and freedom from royal interference suited the customs and aspirations of towns on the Castilian frontier.[113] Like their coreligionists in towns along the Camino de Santiago earlier in the century, the Jews of Cuenca might have benefited from conditions made favorable by the kings' desire to foster settlement in strategically important locations. However, the customs reflected in the *fuero* of Cuenca did not find universal application in Castile. Especially in the area north of the Duero River, Jews had to contend with circumstances that dictated different dynamics of interfaith relationships. Many Castilian municipalities had a harder time obtaining the kind of privileges readily available on the frontier. Some towns, controlled by powerful ecclesiastical institutions, faced an uphill battle for autonomy, as the revolt of the burgesses of Sahagún against the local abbot demonstrates. Even the towns of the *realengo* (royal lands) had to overcome the monarchs' reluctance to bestow urban liberties.[114]

The kings' active interference in urban affairs influenced the Jews' civic status in some communities. Many of the *fueros* granted by the kings of Castile and León in the late twelfth and early thirteenth centuries, with the direct adaptations of the Cuenca code being excluded, reflect the Jews' greater dependency on the king and an even lesser degree of involvement in the towns' communal life than is apparently the norm in Cuenca. All

---

112. See Powers, *Code of Cuenca*, 16–17. Juan Antonio Frago Gracia's linguistic study of the *fuero* of Cuenca emphasizes its "practical" nature and its connection with everyday life; see Gracia, "El fuero de Cuenca: Lengua, cultura y problemas del romanceamiento," *Boletín de la Real Academia Española* 79, no. 278 (1999): 319–54.

113. Powers, *Code of Cuenca*, 16; Gautier-Dalché, *Historia urbana*, 250. The Code of Cuenca was adopted by Iznatoraf, Baeza, Bejár, Alarcón, Alcaraz, Zorita de los Canes, and other towns; see, for example, Juan Gutierrez Cuadrado, ed., *Fuero de Bejár* (Salamanca: Universidad de Salamanca, 1974).

114. Gautier-Dalché, *Historia urbana*, 219, 231.

of these municipal codes share a telling detail: they never—not a single time—describe Jews as *vecinos* ("citizens"). The *fuero* of Haro (about 1187) is a case in point. As a charter of privileges awarded to a particular religious group, it harkens back to the royal *fueros* of the early twelfth century. The only known *fuero* granted by the king of Castile (Alfonso VIII) to a Jewish community, the Haro charter seems to provide Jews with conditions almost as favorable as those in Cuenca.[115] The Jews of Haro are housed in a "castle"—probably a fortified barrio—and a heavy fine is paid by those who try to attack it with "stones, arrows, or spears."[116] Unlike in Cuenca, where Jewish debtors are housed in the king's prison, in Haro they can only be taken to a Jewish jail.[117] Two witnesses, a Jew and a Christian, are required to convict a Jew of theft or of default on a debt. However, the Jews of Haro appear to have less judicial autonomy than their counterparts in Cuenca: there are no Jewish *alcaldi* (judges); instead, the *dominus villae* (royal representative in the town), Haro's Christian *alcaldi*, and royal judges have the authority to hear cases involving Jews.[118] In business matters, on the other hand, the Jews have considerable leeway. The local *alcaldus* is told not to interfere in money-lending agreements between Jews and Christians.[119] The Jews of Haro can freely fish, construct mills and channels, and wash their garments in "all the waters of the kingdom."[120] Overall, the *fuero* of Haro is concerned more with protecting business interests and the wellbeing of the Jews than with defining their rights within a Christian municipality. They are treated as the valuable "property" of the Crown, but are never called "citizens" or "Jewish citizens."

115. This is due, perhaps, to Haro's position on the frontier with Navarre; León Tello, "Nuevos documentos sobre la judería de Haro," 157.

116. "Quicumque petra aut sagitta aut lancea aut aliquibus armis castellum impugnauerit, pectet mille aureos regi"; ibid., 162.

117. See Powers, *Code of Cuenca*, 160; "Judeo qui aliquo tenebitur debito domino ville aut cuilibus alii in carcerem aut in compedes non mitatur, sed in quandam domo ad hunc usum a judeis destinata"; León Tello, "Nuevos documentos sobre la judería de Haro," 162.

118. "Nullus judeus a domino ville aut ab aliquo alio de furto aut debito conuincatur nisi cum duobus testibus christiano et judeo.... Omnis judeus posit se alçare de judicio alcaldum de Faro et ad las justicias regis"; ibid., 162, 163.

119. "Judeus aut Judea qui sub certa pactione usure, aut pro ceuera ad nouum aut pro vuis ad nouum pecuniam cristiano mutuauerit, capitale et lucrum secundum factam pactionem recipiat nec alcaldus contra hoc posit judicare"; ibid., 162.

120. "In omnibus aquis regiis judei de Faro possint libere piscari et molinos facere et canales et pannos suos lauare"; ibid.

In the area of Old Castile—Burgos and its surroundings—royal control appears to have been the single greatest factor shaping the Jews' status. Until the promulgation of the *Fuero real* in the middle of the thirteenth century, Burgos and the surrounding towns lacked extensive municipal codes (*fueros extensos*) that can shed light on the nature of Jewish-Christian interaction within these communities.[121] However, the *Libro de los fueros de Castilla*—a collection of customs, royal privileges, and juridical decisions (*fazañas*) from the Burgos area—portrays Jewish communities physically and socially isolated from their Christian neighbors. According to Galo Sánchez, the *Libro de los fueros* was compiled by an anonymous author or authors shortly after the conquest of Seville by Fernando III in 1248. Much of its material comes from the reigns of Alfonso VIII and Fernando III.[122] The authors of a recent edition of the *Libro de los fueros* emphasize the collection's royal provenance, arguing that it originated in royal privileges and in legal decisions handed down by the king and his officials.[123] Not being a cohesive body of law, the *Libro de los fueros* is hardly a northern counterpart to the Code of Cuenca.[124] Nevertheless, taken together, its often-disjointed stipulations create a surprisingly wide-ranging portrayal of Jewish life in and around Burgos.

To a greater extent than any royal Castilian *fuero*, the *Libro de los fueros* aims to delineate the scope and the substance of the Jewish *aljamas'* jurisdiction vis-à-vis the royal authority. Several of the chapters (216, 217, and 220) describe the *judería* as a fortified settlement (*castiello*), whose walls mark the boundaries of the *aljama*'s special authority. In this sense, it is not unlike the Christian burg: just like the walls of a Castilian town symbolize the juridical personality of the *concejo*, so do the fortifications of a *judería* designate it as a self-governing community.[125] By all indications, this situation was a common one for Castilian towns. For example, the Code of Cuenca states that cases between Jews and Christians should be settled before the gate of the *alcacería* (a fortified barrio)—that is, right on

---

121. Martínez Díez, *Fueros locales*, 113.
122. Sánchez, "Para la historia de la redacción," AHDE 6:273; Sánchez, *Libro de los fueros de Castiella*, x.
123. Alvarado Planas and Oliva Manso, *Los fueros de Castilla*, 57.
124. Sánchez, "Para la historia de la redacción," 275; Fernández Espinar, *Manual de historia del derecho español*, 1:393.
125. Garcia de Valdeavellano, *Curso de historia de las instituciones españolas*, 531.

the boundary between Christian and Jewish areas of jurisdiction.[126] The *Libro de los fueros* is concerned not so much with mixed cases as with the degree of the royal officials' involvement in the inner affairs of the *aljama*. For instance, it stipulates that the amount of the Jews' pecuniary damages depends on whether the transgression occurred inside or outside the "castle": those committed outside the walls—in the area of royal jurisdiction—elicit greater penalties.[127] If the royal official (*merino*) demands pecuniary damages from the *aljama*, the accused has to find a guarantor in his own community. The *merino* waits outside the gates while the Jews decide the amount of damages.[128] However, if the king's interests so require, this rule can be overridden.[129] In some cases, to collect pecuniary damages or to apprehend criminals (*mal fechores*), the *merino* can demand from the Jews the keys to their "castle." The Jews should hand over the keys and help the *merino* look for the offenders. If a Jew dares to open the gates and let the criminals flee, he has to pay a fine.[130]

One striking feature of the *Libro de los fueros* is the direct involvement of royal officials—*merinos, alcaldes*, and the *señor*—in the administration of the *aljama*. Working in close cooperation with the Jewish judge—*vedin* (*albedí, albedín*)—royal representatives hear cases and assess pecuniary damages. If a Christian and a Jew wound or kill each other, it is the Christian judge (*alcalde*) who is authorized to set the fine, which is collected by the *merino*. The procedure is the same if a Jew kills or wounds another Jew.[131] Besides the *alcalde* and the *merino*, there is a higher official who

---

126. In Powers, *Code of Cuenca*, 162.

127. "Et non tan grand calonnia por muchas cosas dentro en castiello commo fuera"; Sánchez, *Libro de los fueros*, chap. 220, 117.

128. "Et sy demandare el merino al judio calonnias o otra demanda, deue dar el judio fiadores al meryno en su aliama e non en otro logar; e non entrara el meryno dentro, mas estara al puerta de fuera; e jusgar los judios e non el meryno"; ibid., chap. 216, 112.

129. One has to note that the *Libro de los fueros* is not a systematic law code: its stipulations can come from different locales and in some cases might contradict one another.

130. "Et sy demanda el meryno al judio calonnyas o otra cosa o mal fechores que an en su castiello, et nombrar quien son, e quel den las llaues del castiello que non se vayan, deuen le dar las llaues e catar los luego. Et sy sobre esto abriesse el castiello algun judio e se fuessen los ladronnes, el lo deue pechar el que abrio la puerta"; Sánchez, *Libro de los fueros*, chap. 217, 113.

131. "[S]y cristiano fiere a judio o judio a cristiano e fueren apreçiados del alcalle, qual fuere la calonnia tal la pechara. Et sy matare a cristiano el judio o la judia, el que matare seyendo apreçiado del alcalle, peche quinyentos sueldos al meryno. Et judio sy matare a judio,

acts as the surrogate for the royal authority in the *aljama*. *Señor* or "lord [of the city]" (*senior civitatis*) is the title of the royal representative in many Castilian towns who was responsible mainly for military defense, collection of tribute for the king, and protection of the royal prerogatives.[132] By the thirteenth century, the power of the *señor* to interfere in municipal affairs had declined throughout Castile, but more so south than north of the Duero. In Cuenca, the *señor* had very limited participation in the government and, apparently, played no role in administering the *aljama*.[133]

The *Libro de los fueros*, on the other hand, accords important functions to the *señor*, who represented royal jurisdiction in the *aljama*.[134] He was served by a subordinate official from within the Jewish community: the judge, or *vedín*. The *vedin* had the authority to gather the Jews in the synagogue and threaten them with excommunication (*aladma*) in order to produce witnesses to an alleged transgression. The *señor* was entitled to whatever pecuniary damages might be awarded by the Jewish court.[135] He also collected fines for various violations of Jewish law. For example, if a member of the *aljama* led his animal on a chain to drink outside the house on a Sabbath day and the *vedin* saw it, the animal was to be confiscated and given to the *señor* (*dar gela al sennor dela villa e seer suya*).[136] A Jew who rode an animal on a Sabbath or a Holy Day (*di santo*) had the animal confiscated in the *señor*'s favor, and was required to pay 30 sueldos.[137] If the *vedin* saw a Jewess leave her clothes hanging outside the house on a Sabbath, he was to take them to the *señor*.[138] Although the *Libro de los fueros* does not specify how pecuniary damages were distributed, the *señor* most likely kept part of the fines collected from the *aljama*, while the rest went to other royal officials and to the king.[139]

---

peche tresientos sueldos.... Et sy firiere vn judio a otro e se apreciare al alcalle, pechara la calonnya commo por cristiano"; ibid., chap. 217, 113.

132. Garcia de Valdeavellano, *Curso de historia de las instituciones españolas*, 547.
133. Gautier-Dalché, *Historia urbana*, 249, 347.
134. Baer, *History of the Jews*, 1:234.
135. "Et sy vedin demandar al aliama aque den aladma aque salgan sus testigos que el fiso testigos e que aya el sennor sus calonnyas, deuen dar aladma en la synoga.... Et sy judio feriere a otro de a tuerto de ferida ode denuesto e fisiere testigos e se querellare al vedin, deuen dar aladma que salga su testimonio por que aya el sennor su derecho"; Sánchez, *Libro de los fueros*, chap. 217, 113–14.
136. Ibid., chap. 219, 115.
137. Ibid., chap. 220, 116.
138. Ibid.
139. Gautier-Dalché, *Historia urbana*, 194.

While nominally all Castilian Jews were considered to be *servi regis* under the Crown's direct jurisdiction, in practice the degree of the king's involvement in the affairs of royal *aljamas* must have fluctuated a great deal depending on local customs and circumstances. In Haro, the *dominus villae* (*señor*) could try Jews in court for theft or nonpayment of a debt.[140] In the Cuenca code neither the *merino* nor the *señor* are pictured as having any functions in the *aljama*, and it is not clear how the king exercised his jurisdiction and collected pecuniary damages from Jews.[141] The *Libro de los fueros de Castilla*, on the other hand, betrays minute interest in the inner workings of the *aljama*, with the *señor*, and through him the king, standing to profit from fines imposed for violations as minor as verbal insult and as major as murder. Jews had to pay for extramarital pregnancies and for carrying iron weapons on the Sabbath, for calling people lepers, and for committing perjury.[142] The *vedin* and the other Jewish officials in the *aljama* also benefited from the involvement of the royal administrators who enforced observance of Jewish law and possibly shared some of the income with the Jewish authorities. The *Libro de los fueros* points to a far closer relationship of interdependence between the Crown and the Jews than ever indicated by any royal *fuero*, including the famous extensive *fuero* of Cuenca. It is reasonable to expect that in the towns of the northern *realengo*, along the Camino de Santiago, where the Crown exercised tighter control over municipal affairs, the Jewish communities also felt its effects in profound ways.

As the evidence from the surviving *fueros* indicates, there is little consistency on the Jews' status in Castilian municipalities. The Code of Cuenca accords a special privileged status to the Jews—that of a "Jewish citizen"—that allows them to participate, albeit to a limited extent, in the communal life of this frontier town. The *fuero* of Haro, and especially

140. León Tello, "Nuevos documentos sobre la judería de Haro," 162.
141. The Code of Cuenca states only that the king is entitled to collect pecuniary damages from the Jews and that the Christian judge (*iudex*) has no share in them; Powers, *Code of Cuenca*, 165.
142. "Esto es por fuero de judia que es por casar e fuere prennada e pariere: a de pechar el judio quela enprenno e la judia al merino trenta sueldos"; Sánchez, *Libro de los fueros*, 34 (chap. 62); "Et sy traxiere el dia de sabado arma que aya fierro, deue pechar veynte dos sueldos.... Et quien dise a otro judio 'malato prouado,' peche veynte çinco sueldos.... Et sy judio periurare de su jura, peche dose sueldos e medio"; Sánchez, *Libro de los fueros*, 116–17 (chap. 220).

the customary laws found in the *Libro de los fueros de Castilla*, treat the Jews strictly as the king's special subjects and the source of revenue for the Crown and its representatives. What unites these *fueros*, however, is the tacit acknowledgment that Castile is a kingdom of multiple religious and ethnic communities, each with its own controls and regulations. With regard to the Jews, the Crown's task consists of protecting their microsociety for the benefit of the royal treasury and using *fueros* to regulate its contacts with the larger Christian polity.

TWO ⁕ The Jews of the Camino de Santiago

The Origins of the Jews' Settlement in Northern Castile-León

Surveying the state of Jewish-Christian relations along the Camino de Santiago at the end of the Middle Ages, Francisco Cantera Burgos, renowned scholar of Castilian Jews, tries to imagine what it was like for the pilgrims from northern Europe to encounter Castilian interfaith coexistence firsthand. He envisions the pilgrims experiencing a strong culture shock: "How greatly would such state of toleration between Christians, Jews, and *conversos* surprise the foreign pilgrims in whose own countries it had become highly unusual!"[1] Cantera's enthusiasm is contagious, but his conjecture about the pilgrims' reaction is probably wrong. Rather than contemplate the wonders of the Jews' presence in Castile at the time they had been expelled from much of northern Europe, a pilgrim from abroad would be too focused on the rigors of the journey to pay such matters much attention. The section of the Camino running through the Northern Castilian plateau could put a traveler's mental and physical health to a severe test. As one modern study of the medieval pilgrimage to Compostela puts it, "those long, arid stretches and rocky defiles" seemed "not only metaphorically a 'return to the desert' but literally such."[2] Seemingly endless harsh winters and short, hot summers provided an appropriate stage for the journey "to the end of the world" (*finis terrae*). The Northern Castilian *meseta* was a barren and forbidding land.[3] If the pilgrims were

---

1. Francisco Cantera Burgos, "Las juderías españolas y el camino de Santiago," in *XII semana de estudios medievales, 1974* (Pamplona: Diputacion Foral de Navarra, 1976), 103.
2. Horton Davies and Marie-Hélène Davies, *Holy Days and Holidays: The Medieval Pilgrimage to Compostela* (London: Associated University Presses, 1982), 51.
3. See Ruiz's masterful description of Castile's climate in *Crisis and Continuity*, 18–23.

indeed surprised by the Jews' presence, it was probably because they were wondering why the Jews came here at all.

And yet the Jews came, in fairly large numbers, to settle in this region and form numerous *aljamas* along this stretch of the Camino, from Logroño (the Rioja) to Astorga (León). Many of them came from al-Andalus, where the intolerant policies of the Almoravids in the late eleventh century and the Almohads in the second half of the twelfth century made the distant Northern Castilian lands seem like a safe haven for refugees.[4] An economic and urban boom along the Camino in the early twelfth century provided another strong incentive. The Camino beckoned to the Jews, even if they were not destined to achieve much success in the region's long-distance trade. It is telling that most of the largest Castilian-Leonese *juderías* north of Duero—in Burgos, Carrión, León, Sahagún, Nájera, and Logroño, with the notable exceptions of Palencia and (farther south) Valladolid—were located directly on the Camino. Two other large and prosperous *juderías*—in Briviesca and Pancorbo—lay on a subsidiary route that ran from Vitoria to Burgos. It would not be an exaggeration to say that without the Camino and a variety of other roads, major and secondary, Jewish life in the region would be unimaginable.

The origins of Jewish settlement near the Camino in Northern Castile and León are obscure. The earliest evidence indicates that Jews were already present in the Burgos area during the reign of Fernán González, the count of Castile (923–70) and possessed stable settlements during the dominion over Castile of Sancho III Garcés, king of Navarre (1000–1035).[5] Documentation from León indicates the Jews' presence there in the tenth century.[6] The 1017 *fuero* granted by Alfonso V to the city of León mentions Jews in a way that suggests the existence of a Jewish commu-

---

4. Ray, *Sephardic Frontier*, 11. On the Jewish refugees from the Almohad persecutions, see chapter 1 of this volume.

5. Fuero of Castrojeriz (974): "Et si homines de castro matarent Judeo tantum pectet pro illo quo modo pro christiano et libores similiter hominem villarum"; Martínez Díez, *Fueros locales*, 120.

6. M. Fátima Carrera de la Red, "Árabes y judíos en la documentación del monasterio de Sahagún," in *Proyección histórica de España en sus tres culturas: Castilla y León, América y el Mediterráneo* (Madrid: Junta de Castilla y León, 1993), 1:46. On the presence of Jewish merchants in tenth-century León, see Claudio Sánchez-Albornoz, *Una ciudad de la España cristiana hace mil años: Estampas de la vida en León*, 5th ed. (Madrid: Ediciones Rialp, 1966), 32.

nity in the city.⁷ Significantly, some of the earliest evidence comes from sources that describe violent attacks on Jews. According to the *fuero* of Castrojeriz, upon the death of Sancho III in 1035, some "men" (*homines*) from the castle rose up in rebellion and killed four royal officials and sixty Jews at the nearby royal palace in Mercatello. The others were promptly removed to the castle.⁸ In the first two decades of the twelfth century, assaults on Jews occurred in several Castilian towns. In 1110 the walled *judería* in Toledo suffered an attack, with a number of Jews killed and some houses looted.⁹ Riots that simultaneously targeted royal property and the Jews occurred shortly thereafter in the diocese of Palencia. In 1127 King Alfonso VII issued a pardon to the inhabitants of Saldaña, Cea, Carrión, Cisneros, and several other towns, forgiving the perpetrators for killing Jews and taking their property, as well as for robbing the royal palaces and burning the king's hunting grounds. He accepted a fine of two silver coins from each perpetrator's household.¹⁰ The underlying causes of these events are difficult to ascertain. Religious hostility as well as dynastic struggles, temporary setbacks to the reconquest, and general political instability of these years might have contributed to outbursts of violence against Jews.¹¹

The frequency and seriousness of such attacks will remain unknown, but it is clear that the Jews felt sufficiently threatened to seek protection behind the walls of fortified settlements. Sources from the eleventh through the thirteenth centuries frequently refer to the so-called "castles" of the Jews. One such *castrum iudaeorum* was located at the Pu-

---

7. "Pero si quisiese [el dueño del suelo] por su voluntad vender su casa, que dos cristianos y dos judíos aprecien su labor"; Suárez Bilbao, *El fuero judiego*, 197.

8. "Migravit a seculo Sanctius rex, et surrexerunt homines de Castro et occiderunt IIII saiones [royal officials] in palacio de Rex in Mercatello et LX judeos; et illos alios prendamus totos et traximus illos de suas casas et de suas hereditates et fecerunt populare ad Castrello, regnante rex Ferrandus filius eius pro eo"; Martínez Díez, *Fueros locales*, 120.

9. Baer, *History of the Jews*, 2.51; Melechen, "Jews of Medieval Toledo," 300–301.

10. "Ad istos homines supra dictos facio hanc cartam perdonationis, de morte Ildefonsi Regis mei auui usque hodie, de malis que fecistis in iudeos quos occidistis et accepistis suum auere, et in meos palazios quos dextruxistis et panen et uinum que inde accepistis et aurum et argentum et alia omnia multa, et meos montes quos comburastis et abscidistis et extinguistis uenatu.... Et insuper accepi pecunias II solidos de argento de unaqueque casa istorum hominum quos supra diximus"; *Archivo historico nacional, sección de clero, Sahagún*, carpeta 894, no. 3; published in Leon Tello, *Los judíos de Palencia*, 37–38.

11. O'Callaghan, *History of Medieval Spain*, 211–14.

ente Castro near the city of León.[12] In 1112, the Jews "of the Castle" were paying the bishop of León an annual tribute of five hundred *solidos*, "by old custom."[13] In 1196 it was attacked and burned by the joint forces of Alfonso VIII of Castile and Pedro II of Aragon.[14] Another *Castro de los judíos* existed in the Leonese town of Astorga.[15] Around 1187, in the diocese of Calahorra, adjacent to Burgos province, Alfonso VIII gave the "castle" of Haro to the Jewish community. The king added that whoever attacked the castle with "stone, arrow, lance, or any weapons" would pay a thousand gold coins to him.[16] Thirteenth-century Burgalese sources often mention *Castiello de los iudios*, or *Castil de judíos*, which can probably be identified with the Jewish settlement in Castrojeriz.[17] While it is not clear how many Castilian *juderías* were located in "castles," the practice was sufficiently common to be mentioned in the mid-thirteenth century collection of Castilian laws *Libro de los fueros de Castilla*, which delineated the limits of Jews' autonomy within these fortified settlements.[18]

12. José Luis Lacave, *Juderías y sinagogas españolas* (Madrid: Editorial MAPFRE, 1992), 244–45; see also Jorge Sánchez-Lafuente Pérez and José Luis Avello Álvarez, "La judería de Puente Castro y la población altomedieval de la Ciudad de León (siglos X–XIII)," in *El mundo judío en la Península Ibérica: sociedad y economía*, edited by Sánchez-Lafuente Pérez and Avello Álvarez, 142–51 (Cuenca: Alderabán Ediciones, 2012).

13. "Dono, et concede predictis altaribus, et archidiaconatum de Tria Castella, et quinquaginta solidos de quingentis quos reddunt nobis iudei de Castro in festiuitate beati Martini, more antiquo"; Archivo de la catedral de León [ACL], no. 1383; published in José María Fernández Catón, ed., *Colección documental del archivo de la catedral de León (775–1230)* [CDACL], vol. 5, (1109–1187) (León: CSIC-CECEL, 1990), 92.

14. León Tello, "La estancia de judíos in castillos," *Anuario de Estudios Medievales* 19 (1989), 454; José Vicente Niclós, "San Martin de León y la controversia con los judíos en el siglo XII," *La controversia judeocristiana en España (desde los orígenes hasta el siglo XIII)* (Madrid: CSIC, 1998), 248.

15. Justiniano Rodríguez Fernández, *Las juderías de la provincia de León* (León: Centro de Estudios e Investigación "San Isidoro," 1976), 78–81.

16. "Petra aut sagitta aut lancea aut aliquibus armis"; León Tello, "Nuevos documentos sobre la judería de Haro," 161–62.

17. For example, Sancho IV's 1285 prohibition of gambling houses in Burgos and *Castil de judíos* (Archivo municipal de Burgos, #2939). The *Repartimiento de Huete* of 1290 states that the Jewish *aljama* in *Castriello* in the diocese of Burgos ought to pay 4,200 *maravedís*; Carrete Parrondo, "El repartimiento de Huete de 1290," 130. This is the same fortified Jewish barrio known as *Castrillo de Matajudíos* in Castrojeriz.

18. Sánchez, ed., *Libro de los fueros de Castiella*, 115–17. It states that the fine payable by Jews was higher outside their castles than inside: *Et non tan grand calonnia por muchas cosas dentro en castiello como fuera.*

Faced with such evidence, Baer and others have concluded that Spanish kings used the Jews to garrison forts in expectation that they would defend their castles against foreign and domestic enemies.[19] Castilian and Leonese evidence, at least, does not support this assumption. With the exception of the *fuero* of Haro, there is no evidence to suggest that the kings of Castile-León had a policy of settling Jews in "castles." Moreover, it is doubtful that they counted on the Jews to provide military assistance in times of war or rebellion. Neither the *fuero* of Haro nor the *Libro de los fueros* mentions such an arrangement. The closest the Jewish communities ever came to helping the king with the defense of castles was contributing financially to the upkeep of royal fortifications.[20] Late thirteenth-century evidence shows that the Jews of Burgos paid the king a large sum "for the work done on the Castle of Burgos," while the *juderías* of Briviesca and Belorado in the vicinity of Burgos contributed to the maintenance of royal fortifications in their towns.[21] The word *castrum* (*castillo*, castle) could have several different meanings. In non-Castilian medieval sources, the word was used to signify a number of things, including fortified buildings, the territory under the power of the castellan, or a fortified village.[22] Since there is no indication that the "castles of the Jews" were centers of power with military functions, it is more reasonable to conclude that they were no more than Jewish quarters surrounded by walls, perhaps built by the Jews themselves in order to protect their settlements from assaults by local or foreign Christians. Certainly not all Castilian and Leonese *juderías* were fortified. From at least the eleventh century, a "village of Jews" existed near the town of Pancorbo. It was variously known as "Villanueva de Pancorbo" and "Villanueva

---

19. Baer, *History of the Jews*, 2:80–81; León Tello, "La estancia de judíos en castillos," 451.

20. This does not preclude the possibility that occasionally Castilian Jews did take up arms. There is evidence that during the civil war of the 1360s the Jews of Toledo helped defend the city against the army of Enrique Trastámara; see Julio Valdeón Baruque, *Los judíos de Castilla y la revolución Trastámara* (Valladolid: Universidad de Valladolid, 1968), 45.

21. Burgos: Asunción López Dapena, ed., *Cuentas y gastos (1292–1294) del rey D. Sancho IV el Bravo (1284–1295)* (Maracena: Publicaciones del Monte de Piedad y Caja de Ahorros de Cordoba, 1984), 487; Briviesca: Carrete Parrondo, "El repartimiento de Huete," 130; Belorado: Biblioteca de la real academia de la historia, 66.981.O-16, ff.403v–4; Palencia: Archivo municipal de Palencia [AMP], Pergaminos no. 2; Fritz (Yitzhak) Baer, *Die Juden*, 2:22.

22. Pierre Bonnassie, *From Slavery to Feudalism in South-Western Europe*, trans. Jean Birrell (Cambridge: Cambridge University Press, 1991), 136.

de los judíos." Presumably most, if not all, of its inhabitants were Jews, who at the end of the thirteenth century paid the third-largest tribute to the Crown in the diocese of Burgos.[23] There is no evidence that it was a fortified settlement.[24] However, due to the scarcity of documentation, it is impossible to make broad generalizations on the extent of Jewish settlements in "castles."

The existence of Jewish "castles" is not the only sign that the Jewish *pobladores* (settlers) in Northern Castile were in need of protection. The early *fueros* (*fueros breves*) recognized the possibility of violence between Jews and Christians and sought to delimit it by specifying the amount of fines to be paid by Jews and Christians in cases of murder or injury. Some early twelfth-century *fueros* set the same amount of pecuniary damages for all settlers, regardless of their ethnicity or religion, thus casting doubt on the argument that the kings of Castile-León set higher than customary fines for injury done to Jews because they treated Jews as their "property."[25] The 1116 *fuero* of Belorado, granted by Alfonso I of Aragon, who controlled the Burgos region at the time, specified that in case of injury the fine should be the same for Jews and Christians.[26] The *fuero* given by Alfonso VII of Castile to Briviesca in 1123 set the fine for murdering a Jew at one hundred *solidos*, the same amount as for any homicide.[27] The *fuero* of Nájera (1076), on the other hand, mandated a much higher fine for a Jew's murder—two hundred fifty *solidos*, the same as for a knight (*infanzon*)—than for the murder of a common villager (*homine villano*), whose

---

23. Carrete Parrondo, "El repartimiento de Huete," 130.

24. Huidobro y Serna, "La judería de Pancorbo (Burgos)," 155–56. The Jews of Villanova de Pontecurbo were mentioned for the first time in 1097, when Domingo Laínez and his wife donated some land purchased from the Jews of Villanova to the monastery of San Millán de la Cogolla; Serrano, ed., *Cartulario de San Millán de la Cogolla* (Madrid: Centro de Estudios Históricos, 1930), 290. Among several other references to Villanueva and its Jews is the 1286 exchange of land between the monasteries of San Millán and San Salvador de Oña, when the former received some land in "Villanueua de los Iudios"; Isabel Oceja Gonzalo, ed., *Documentación del monasterio de San Salvador de Oña [DMSSO] (1285–1310)* (Burgos: Ediciones J. M. Garrido Garrido, 1983), 45.

25. Haim Beinart, *Los judíos en España* (Madrid: Editorial MAPFRE, 1992), 79.

26. "Et iudaeo cum christiano, et christiano ad iudaeo qualem livorem fecit, talem pectet, sed duobus partibus fiant in terra pro anima mea, sicut supra scriptum est"; Martínez Díez, *Fueros locales*, 134.

27. "Homicidium etenim quod omnibus manifestum fuerit pro eo C solidos persoluere confirmo.... Si quis iudeus ad hanc ciuitatem habitare uenerit uestrum habeat forum; et si aliquis eum necauerit centum solidos pectet"; ibid., 135–36.

slayer was required to pay a fine of one hundred *solidos*.[28] The diversity of juridical norms found in Castilian *fueros* makes it difficult to generalize on the direction of royal policies, but it appears that in many instances the kings' desire to attract new settlers by granting them the same legal protections outweighed other considerations.

The granting of privileges to towns was part of the Castilian Crown's efforts to facilitate economic development in the region. Protection from violence and freedom from seigniorial impositions mattered to traders and pilgrims at least as much as the new bridges and roads constructed on the orders of Alfonso VI.[29] With the growth of commercial activities along the road to Santiago in the twelfth century, Burgos's location at the intersection of routes propelled the city into the position of a major center of long-distance trade. It became a magnet for foreign merchants—French, Italian, German, Navarese, Aragonese, Catalan—many of whom became the city's permanent residents and citizens (*vecinos*).[30] In fact, many of the *caballeros villanos*—Burgos's ruling oligarchs in the thirteenth century—were descendants of foreign merchants.[31] *Francos*, as foreigners were generally called in Castile, also settled in smaller towns in the Burgos region. Some of the royal *fueros* explicitly addressed the rights of these new settlers. For instance, Alfonso I, the king of Aragon, gave his 1116 charter to the residents of Belorado, addressing them as "my settlers, *francos* and Castilians of Belorado."[32] *Francos* also lived in Medina de Pomar and Miranda de Ebro.[33] There is every reason to believe that Jews were part of this wave of foreign settlers, drawn in part by the promise of royal protection and in part by the commercial opportunities offered by the intersection of many trade routes in and around Burgos.[34]

28. "Per homicidium de inffancione, vel de scapulato, aut de judeo, non debent aliud dare plebs de Naiera, nisi CCL solidos sine saionia. Per homicidium de homine villano non debent dare nisi C. solidos sine saionia"; Muños y Romero, *Colección de fueros municipales y cartas pueblas*, 1:288.
29. O'Callaghan, *History of Medieval Spain*, 294.
30. Carlos Estepa Díez, "De fines del siglo IX a principios del siglo XIII," in *Burgos en la edad media*, 52–53.
31. Ruiz, "El siglo XIII y primera mitad del siglo XIV," in *Burgos en la edad media*, 140.
32. "Meos pobladores, francos et castellanos de Bilforad"; Martínez Díez, *Fueros locales*, 134.
33. Ibid., 59–62.
34. Huidobro y Serna, "La judería de Pancorbo (Burgos)," 155–56; Huidobro y Serna and Cantera Burgos, "Juderías burgalesas (Beleña, Belorado)," 38.

The evidence to document Jews' commercial and other activities during the first two centuries of their settlement in the Burgos area is woefully limited. Still, one can attempt a few tentative generalizations. Michael Toch has suggested that the Jews cannot be regarded as the only traders in early medieval Europe and that their role in long-distance trade diminished by the end of the eleventh century. The evidence from Northern Castile supports his argument.[35] By the thirteenth century, Christian merchants controlled the economic life of Burgos and of other towns along the road to Santiago.[36] However, the Jews did find their niche as local traders, moneylenders, owners of small agricultural properties, and, occasionally, artisans. In this respect, their situation was not much different from that of their counterparts in northern France.[37] As early as 1099, three Jews were present as witnesses when the prior of the monastery of San Miguel de Pedroso, in Belorado, claimed his monastery's ownership of the estate of Redecilla. In all likelihood, the Jews acted as the monastery's financial agents.[38] The documents are not explicit on the subject of Jewish moneylending until 1231, when King Fernando III gave the Jews of Villadiego dependent on the Hospital del Rey (Burgos) a royal official, *portero*, in order to enforce demands for payment from their debtors.[39] However, the *Libro de los fueros de Castilla*, compiled shortly after 1248, devotes much space to regulating Jewish moneylending. One judicial decision (*fazaña*) describes a lawsuit between Ferrant Yuannes and Mose Amordosiel, a Jew of Burgos, over a debt owed by Ferrant's father, now deceased.[40] Other evidence, somewhat more abundant after 1250, shows that by the mid-thirteenth century moneylending had become a major source of income for Jews in Burgos and its environs.[41]

The Jews living in Burgos, Villanueva de Pancorbo, Aguilar de Campóo,

---

35. Michael Toch, "Between Impotence and Power: The Jews in the Economy and Polity of Medieval Europe," in Toch, *Peasants and Jews in Medieval Germany: Studies in Cultural, Social, and Economic History* (Aldershot: Ashgate, 2003).

36. Ruiz, *Crisis and Continuity*, 275; Ruiz, "Judíos y cristianos en el ambito urbano bajomedieval," 73.

37. Jordan, *French Monarchy and the Jews*, 60.

38. "Et ex iudeis fuerunt ibi testes: Naamias maior testis, Naamias minor testis, Cide testis"; Serrano, *Cartulario de San Millán de la Cogolla*, 292–93.

39. DHR, 137.

40. Sánchez, ed., *Libro de los fueros de Castiella*, 134–35.

41. Ruiz, *Crisis and Continuity*, 276.

and other towns and villages possessed rural properties and showed a remarkable predilection for buying vineyards. Just like the Christian inhabitants of urban and semi-urban settlements, they sought to supplement their income with rural rents.[42] A small number of Jews of Villanueva de Pancorbo owned eight *solares* (allodial lands) near their town, which they sold, in 1097, to Domingo Laínez and his wife, who, in turn, donated them to the monastery of San Millán de la Cogolla.[43] The property included a common pasture, with the right of free access from Pancorbo and Villanueva.[44] Mill rights also appear to have been popular among some Jews as a financial investment. In 1187, Mael (or Mair), a Jew from Aguilar de Campóo, and his wife, Merian, bought some rights in the mills of la Vega from a number of Christians, including Juan, son of Petro Penilla, and Martino, Juan's brother. According to the long list of Jewish witnesses, many of whom have *ferrero* appended to their names (Jusep *ferrero*, Hazecrin *ferrero*), the occupation of blacksmith appears to have been open to the Jews of Aguilar.[45] More than thirty years later, the widow and son of one of the witnesses in the 1187 sale, a certain Iuseph de Levanza, decided to sell their rights in the mill of la Ravia, in the town's market, to Don Miguel, abbot of the monastery of Santa María la Real in Aguilar de Campóo. In 1219, Oro Sol and her son sold to the monastery three-fourths of the mill, including the mill's water ducts and its stream of water, for 210 *maravedís*.[46] Six months later, they sold to the monastery the remaining part of the mills belonging to them in the market for 100 *maravedís*.[47]

Viticulture appears to have been a particularly popular pursuit among the Jews of Northern Castile and León. Grapes were valued as a commercial commodity, but were also needed to make kosher wine. The Jews of

---

42. Ibid., 150, 152; see also Ray, *Sephardic Frontier*, 37.

43. In the general usage, *allodial property* means nonfeudal property; i.e., it is owned outright, without any obligation to a lord.

44. "Hec predicta solares, sicut mos fuit iudeis ibi commorantibus, habeant communem pastum et exitum atque regressum cum Ponticurbo et cum aliis vicinis de Villanova"; Serrano, *Cartulario de San Millán de la Cogolla*, 290–91.

45. AHN, sección clero, Palencia, Aguilar, carp. 1649, no. 2; AHN, codices, Cartulario de Aguilar de Campóo, fol. 15r; published by Huidobro y Serna and Cantera Burgos, "Los judíos en Aguilar de Campóo, 347–48.

46. AHN, codices, Cartulario de Aguilar de Campóo, fol. 62r; published by Huidobro y Serna and Cantera Burgos, "Los judíos en Aguilar de Campoó," 348–49.

47. Ibid., fol. 64r.; 349–50. Both documents appear to have been composed or dictated by

castrum iudeorum near the city of León possessed vineyards (*uineas*) and agricultural land—both cultivated and uncultivated (*terras tam cultas quam incultas*) inside or near their "castle."[48] A document from 1145 mentions the sale of a Jewish vineyard near León to an archdeacon.[49] The archive of the cathedral of León contains seven documents, written in Hebrew by Jewish scribes, recording sales of vineyards by the Jews of the "castle" to Christians—both laymen and members of the clergy—between 1053 and 1175.[50]

The Jews of Burgos also grew grapes for wine. In 1162 Alfonso VIII granted a privilege to the inhabitants of Burgos, abolishing the custom of waiting to collect the grape harvest until after the feast of St. Michael (September 29). Christians as well as Jews were mentioned as the recipients of the king's charter.[51] The royal convent of Las Huelgas near Burgos, apparently wishing to consolidate its estates in the first decade of the thirteenth century, bought a number of rural properties from the Burgalese Jews. First came the purchase, in 1204, of an estate in Vegamediana, which belonged to the Jew Rabi and his brother, Cemal. This land was situated between a river, a stream, and two properties belonging to the monastery.[52] In 1207, Salomón Atrugel sold to the abbess of Las Huelgas three vineyards in Arcos. The first, in the place called Molares, went for 13 *maravedís* and 15 *dineros*; the second, called Naiarilla (Najarilla), was sold for 71 *maravedís*; and the third for 60 *maravedís*. All three documents for the transactions include Christian and Jewish witnesses.[53] As the re-

---

Jews, since they are dated according to the Jewish calendar. The first one is dated "the fourth day of Marfesvan [Cheshvan], year 4980," the second, "the 27th day of Adar, year 4980."

48. In 1197, a year after the devastating attack on the castle by the kings of Castile and Aragon, the castle and the lands that had belonged to the Jews were given by Alfonso IX to the cathedral of León; ACL no. 1073, published in CDACL, 6:1188–1230, edited by J. M. Fernández Catón, 6:83–85 (León: Centro de Estudios e investigación "San Isidoro," 1991).

49. Ibid., 233–34.

50. Javier Castaño, "Los documentos hebreos de León en su contexto prenotarial," in *Judaísmo hispano: Estudios en memoria de José Luis Lacave Riaño*, edited by Elena Romero, 2:459–81 (Madrid: Junta de Castilla y León, 2002).

51. Archivo de la catedral de Burgos [ACB], no. 12, fol. 63; Estepa Díez, "De fines del siglo IX a principios del siglo XIII," 57.

52. José Manuel Lizoain Garrido, ed., *Documentación del monasterio de Las Huelgas de Burgos* [DMHB], vol. 1, 1116–1230 (Burgos: J. M. Garrido Garrido, 1985), 132–33; also cited in Baer, *Die Juden*, 2:28.

53. The witnesses are: "De iudei: Abraham Euellatef, Abraham Çaçon, Abraham el leui, Salamon Enpollegar," in DMHB, 1:140–43; also cited in Baer, *Die Juden*, 2:28.

cord of a 1209 purchase by Jews Avolafia Çaçon and Çach Cota indicates, Burgalese Jews likely produced their own wine, either for sale or for their own consumption. The two Jews bought houses with a wine press (lagar) and an adjacent orchard (orto) in the Burgalese neighborhood of Vega from Don Martín Illán and his wife for a very large sum of 200 gold maravedís.[54] Jews continued to own vineyards in the Burgos area well into the thirteenth century. The 1232 survey of property belonging to the convent of Las Huelgas mentions the Jew Çabarchylon as the owner of some land in the vicinity of the convent's estates. That the property in question is a vineyard is clear from it being included in the list of vineyards belonging to Las Huelgas.[55] In 1286, Juçef Haraçon, a Burgalese Jew, sold two parts of a vineyard in Villalgamar to Pero Sarracín, dean of the cathedral chapter, for 2,000 maravedís.[56]

The evidence may be sketchy, but it does illuminate several features of Jewish life along the road to Santiago between the late eleventh century and the first half of the thirteenth century. Like other newcomers to Northern Castile, Jews enjoyed the protection of royal *fueros*, settling in fortified villages or semi-urban communities, making a living as small-scale traders, artisans, moneychangers, and moneylenders, and supplementing their income with rents from mills and rural properties. At least as far as their occupations were concerned, the Jews were not dramatically different from their Christian neighbors. Even though anti-Jewish violence always remained a possibility and some *aljamas* sought protection against it behind the walls of fortified *juderías*, there is little doubt that Jewish settlers continued to be drawn by the favorable economic conditions in the lands along the Camino, over time transforming the region into one of the most prominent centers of Jewish life in medieval Iberia.

---

54. José Manuel Garrido Garrido, ed., *Documentacion de la catedral de Burgos* [DCB], vol. 2, 1184–1222 (Burgos: Ediciones J. M. Garrido Garrido, 1983), 221. The purchase is discussed in Ruiz, "Trading with the 'Other,'" 73.

55. "Estas son vinias del pie del monesterio.... Otra vinna de La Condessa, que es entre amas las carreras, de XXX obreros; aledanos, don Gregorio e el iudio Çabarchylon. Otra vinna en Arenas, de XVI obreros"; DMHB, vol. 2, 1231–62, 23.

56. F. Javier Pereda Llarena, ed., DCB, vol. 4, 1254–93, 276; Ruiz, *Crisis and Continuity*, 275–76.

The Role of the Camino de Santiago in Jewish Urban Life

There were many reasons why the network of roads linked to the pilgrimage route loomed large in the experiences of Northern Castilian Jews. The roads made it possible for some Jews to move out of major towns and settle in nearby smaller communities, in time forming sizable *juderías* of their own.[57] Even after they had become independent, these *aljamas* turned to their mother communities for religious and legal guidance. The *aljama* of Burgos was the nerve center of the Jewish life in the region. The rabbis of Burgos appointed Jewish judges in towns as far away as Sahagún.[58] Messengers from distant *juderías* must have arrived in Burgos on a regular basis. The Jews of Belorado, a community located on a long and sparsely populated stretch of the Camino about thirty miles east of Burgos, probably found it easier to communicate with the *aljama* of Burgos than with that of Briviesca—only fifteen miles north, but not connected to Belorado by a major road.[59]

While the east-west axis provided by the Camino was vital for communication between various *aljamas*, the routes running north-south were indispensable as well.[60] Roads radiated from Burgos in many directions: south, to the small *judería* in Lerma; north, to the Jewish community in Medina de Pomar; northeast, to the flourishing *aljama* in Briviesca. As much as these roads held together the delicate fabric of Jewish life in the region, they also helped alleviate occasional pains of coexistence by facilitating a more effective response to interreligious tensions. Negotiations always being an integral part of Jewish-Christian coexistence in Castile, smaller and less influential *aljamas* sometimes had to come together to face a challenge from the Christian *vecinos*. Thus in 1294, the Jews of Miranda de Ebro summoned two Jews from the neighboring *juderías*—David

---

57. For a similar situation in Normandy, see Jordan, *French Monarchy and the Jews*, 52–54.

58. AHN, clero, Sahagún, carp. 917, no. 13; José Antonio Fernández Flórez, ed., CDMS, 5:325–26.

59. Even today, the unpaved road from Belorado to Briviesca runs through sparsely populated agricultural lands, with not a single person to be seen for miles around.

60. On the role of the Camino in the spatial organization of medieval Castile, see José Ángel García de Cortázar, "El Camino de Santiago y la articulación del espacio en Castilla," in *XX semana de estudios medievales, 1993* (Pamplona: Gobierno de Navarra, 1994), 157–83.

of Haro and Moshe of Pancorbo—to serve as their witnesses in an agreement with the *concejo* of Miranda. The two representatives traveled to Miranda and duly affixed their signatures to the end of the contract regulating collection of debts.[61] When no mutually acceptable agreement could be reached, the *aljamas* often had to send a messenger to present the matter at the peripatetic royal court. In 1278, the Jews of Burgos, feeling that they had been wronged by the actions of the Burgos *concejo*, dispatched representatives to Segovia, where the king heard their complaint and sent back a charter supporting the *aljama*'s side.[62]

The exigencies of making a living also provided a powerful incentive for setting out on the road. Jewish traders, tax collectors, and even moneylenders traversing the northern plains must have been a common sight. The 1371 petition of town representatives even requested that Jews not be allowed to ride mules—to make it easy to distinguish them from Christian travelers.[63] Like their Christian neighbors, the Jews visited nearby towns on market days to sell their wares and to buy goods not available in their hometowns. A Jewish trader could start his week in Sahagún, where the market day was Monday, and then travel to León by Wednesday to attend the market there, perhaps with an intermediate stop on Tuesday in Mansilla de las Mulas.[64] Until 1301, when a royal charter barred the Jews from entering Belorado on market days, the Jews from the surrounding area regularly attended the town's market on Mondays.[65] The frequent mention of the Jews in royal charters exempting the inhabitants of a particular locale from *portazgo* (toll) is another sign of the ubiquitous presence of Jewish traders on Castilian roads. Among others, the Jews of Palencia and Belorado enjoyed this privilege.[66] In Sahagún, the Jews were expected to pay *portazgo* on merchandise they transported

---

61. Archivo municipal de Miranda de Ebro [AMME], no. L-H0213-053; Cantera Burgos, "La judería de Miranda de Ebro (1099–1350)," *Sefarad* 1 (1941): 112–13.

62. ACB, no. 4125; Emiliano Gonzales Díez, ed., *CDCB*, 150–51.

63. *Cortes* 2, 203–4.

64. Pascual Martínez Sopena, "El Camino de Santiago y la articulación del espacio en Tierra de Campos y León," in *XX semana de estudios medievales*, 202.

65. *Real academia de la historia* [RAH], ms. 66.981.O-16, ff. 403v–404; Huidobro y Serna and Cantera Burgos, "Juderías burgalesas," 52–53.

66. AMP, Pergaminos, no. 10; León Tello, *Los judíos de Palencia*, 106; RAH, ms. 66.981.O-16, ff. 402r–v; Huidobro y Serna and Cantera Burgos, "Juderías burgalesas," 56.

in the town; if they brought along cattle or purchased some in the town's market, a toll was imposed on each head of livestock.[67]

Another group of frequent travelers were Jewish moneylenders, who ventured out of their hometowns to take advantage of the ever-present need for credit in the nearby towns and villages. Once the deadline for payment had elapsed, the creditors went back to collect their debts or sent representatives to plead cases on their behalf. For instance, the Jewish moneylenders in Pancorbo and Haro lent money to Christians in the small town of Miranda de Ebro. In 1296, some of them sent an agent, a Jew by the name of Varon, to Miranda; he carried letters of obligation and attempted to collect the debts owed by some of the town's Christians.[68] Abraham, a resident of Briviesca, provided credit for a Christian family that lived about fifteen miles north of his town in a small village near Oña.[69] Abraham Ruvielo, a Jew living in León, had debtors in Mansilla de las Mulas, about ten miles away.[70] While there are other examples, they all reveal the existence of semi-urban credit networks that heavily depended on a good system of local roads.[71]

Even longer distances were covered by the Jewish tax farmers, who traveled the country collecting a variety of taxes for the king. As a rule, the collectors' hometowns were located in the general area where they conducted their business, but they still must have spent a great deal of their time on the road. In 1359 Yusef Cordiella and Abraham Enpollegar, residents of Palenzuela, a small town between Burgos and Palencia, traveled to Seville, where they signed a contract with Salomon Bien Veniste and Çag el Levi, who lived in the *juderías* of Burgos. The agreement stated that the *tercias* of the *alcabala* (sales tax) in Valladolid, formerly collected by Salomon and Çag, would now be farmed by Yusef and Abraham. It is tempting to speculate that the long commute of nearly eighty miles from

67. CDMS, 5:592.
68. AMME, no. L-H0039-031; Cantera Burgos, "La judería de Miranda de Ebro (1099–1350)," *Sefarad* 1 (1941): 119.
69. Isabel Oceja Gonzalo, ed., DMSSO, 3:220–21.
70. AHN, clero, León, Escalada, carp. 833, no. 10; Rodríguez Fernández, *Las juderías de la provincia de León*, 360–61.
71. See Robin R. Mundill, *England's Jewish Solution: Experiment and Expulsion, 1262–1290* (Cambridge: Cambridge University Press, 1998), 236–42, on the significance of local roads for the Jews' credit operations.

Burgos to Valladolid had something to do with the Burgalese Jews' decision to rent the tax out to the Jews of Palenzuela, a town "only" fifty miles away from Valladolid.[72] In another example, Sento Cidicaro, a Jew from Villadiego, a small town northwest of Burgos, was responsible for the collection of the tithe on livestock (*diezmos de los ganados*) in the bishoprics of Burgos, Palencia, Calahorra, and the Castilian part of the bishopric of León. The area was too large for one man to manage, so in 1365, he entrusted Mose Abaltax with collecting the tax in the region of León. Mose, in his turn, tapped Çag Merdohay and his sons. Unlike Sento, both tax farmers lived near León: Mose in Saldaña and Çag in Sahagún.[73] What would have been a major undertaking for Sento was a short one- or two-day trip for Mose and Çag.

In short, the Jews of the Camino were in reality the Jews of many *caminos* (roads). Like threads in a web spread over the Northern Castilian *meseta*, these roads connected small towns and villages to larger urban centers. The Jews depended on them all the more because, unlike their counterparts in some parts of Europe, they were not confined to a few major cities but resided in a variety of towns and semi-urban settlements.[74] In fact, only one *judería* in the region was located in what could be unequivocally called a large city—Burgos. Most Jews found their home in communities that were considerably smaller and ranged between good-sized towns and large villages. Although any estimates of the size of the Jewish population in these towns are bound to remain guesswork, some guidance is provided by the two surviving *particiones* (partitions) of Jewish taxes drafted by the royal chancery in 1287 and 1290 for the *aljamas* of the kingdoms of León and Castile, respectively.[75] Judging by the data contained in the Partition of Huete (1290), the *aljama* of Burgos was by far the largest and the most prosperous Jewish community in Northern Castile and León, with a tax payment of 87,769 *maravedís*. No other communi-

---

72. RAH, v. O-11, ff. 65–66; D. Luciano Serrano, ed., *Colección diplomatica de San Salvador de el Moral* (Valladolid: 1906), 155–57.

73. AHN, clero, León, carp. 936, no. 8; Baer, *Die Juden*, 2:202–3.

74. England's Jews exemplified the opposite extreme: they were "overwhelmingly urban"; see Stacey, "Jews and Christians in Twelfth-Century England," 342.

75. Both were published by Francisco J. Hernández, in *Las rentas del rey: Sociedad y fisco en el reino castellano del siglo XIII*, vol. 1, Estudio y documentos (Madrid: Fundación Ramón Areces, 1993), 138–41 (Castile), 337–88 (León).

ty came within a 10,000-*maravedís* range of the Burgos *aljama*'s payment.[76]

With a caveat that the partitions of Huete and Burgos (1287) measure not only the relative size of the *aljamas*, but also their relative prosperity, the rest of the *aljamas* can be roughly divided into three categories.[77] The first category comprised small Jewish communities (1,000–6,000-*maravedís* range), such as Miranda de Ebro, Dueñas, Castil de Judíos (Castriello), Lerma, Palenzuela, Oña, Medina de Pomar, Cea, and Peñafiel in Castile and Bembibre, Mayorga, and Oviedo in León. Numerically, this was the largest category, with eighteen *aljamas* listed. The next group was composed of "medium-sized" *aljamas* (circa 8,000–15,000 *maravedís*), and included Aguilar, Belorado, Villadiego, and Paredes de Nava (with Cisneros) in Castile; Calahorra and Logroño in the Rioja; and Astorga, Valencia de Don Juan, and Mansilla in León. Finally, the largest *aljamas* in Northern Castile, León, and the Rioja (20,000-plus *maravedís* range) were in Palencia, Sahagún, Nájera, León, Pancorbo, Briviesca, Haro, Carrión, Valladolid, and Burgos, with the last three (40,000-plus *maravedís*) forming a subcategory of their own. One suspects that at least some of the *aljamas* in this last group were not necessarily numerically superior to the medium-sized communities, but that their prosperity was the cause of higher taxation rates. The Jewish moneylenders of Haro and Pancorbo, in particular, must have shouldered much of their *aljamas*' fiscal burden.

As for the absolute size of the *aljamas*, as opposed to their relative size, any calculations must be considered very tenuous. By a lucky chance, a 1294 document survives from Miranda de Ebro listing thirteen adult Jews (twelve men and one woman, a widow) settled in the town. The Jews present at a meeting with Christian officials claimed that no Jews beyond these thirteen lived in Miranda, meaning, no doubt, the number of the heads of households.[78] Assuming that some *aljamas* (Dueñas, Tariego)

---

76. The *aljama* of Carrión paid 73,480 *maravedís*, but that sum included taxes from several other communities ("con los lugares que pechan con ellos"), one of them likely being Frómista, as it is not mentioned otherwise.

77. The need for this caveat becomes clear if one compares data for Burgos with that of Miranda de Ebro, one of the smallest *aljamas* in the region. It is known from other sources that Miranda had about thirteen Jewish families who paid 3,312 *maravedís* in taxes. If this coefficient (254.8) is applied to Burgos, then it turns out that Burgos had about four hundred Jewish families—a clear impossibility. A more likely explanation is that the *aljama* of Burgos was much more prosperous than that of Miranda, and therefore paid more per capita.

78. AMME, no. L-H0213-053; Cantera, "La judería de Miranda de Ebro (1099–1350)," 112.

were even smaller than the one in Miranda, 10 to 15 families (35 to 70 people) were probably the minimum sustainable level of population for Jewish communities in semi-urban settings. At the other end of the spectrum, the Burgos *aljama* probably had about 150 families, or between 540 and 675 people.[79] The rest of the *aljamas* in Northern Castile and León fell somewhere in between. For instance, at the end of the twelfth century, Palencia had 40 Jewish families.[80] Considering the purported prosperity of the *aljama* of Palencia, that number must have at least doubled by the end of the thirteenth century. At 80 to 100 families, the *aljama* of Palencia would be one of the largest Jewish communities in Northern Castile.

The high number of small and medium-sized *aljamas* is perhaps the most striking aspect of Jewish life along the Camino. There are some obvious reasons that life in smaller *aljamas* could be precarious for the Jews settled in the midst of the Castilian *meseta*. A community whose numbers dipped too low could face difficulties maintaining the essential synagogue personnel and a kosher slaughterer (*shochet*), as well as providing the ten adult males necessary for the *minyan*. In addition, small-town Jews had to deal with the issue of making a living in what essentially was a semi-rural setting. The difficulty is amply illustrated by the Jews of Miranda de Ebro, some of whom worked as manual laborers in the countryside. At least four Mirandese Jews were said to be working (*laurar*) in the *aldeas* (small villages) outside of the town at the time of the 1294 meeting with the *concejo* of Miranda.[81] In 1312, six poor Jewish laborers (*judíos poures menestrales*) in Miranda were allowed by the king to pay the same amount in purveyance (*yantar*) as poor Christians.[82]

The economic fortunes of some Mirandese Jews were evidently on

---

The following heads of Jewish households are mentioned in the document: Rabbi Çagui (son of Ordoña?), Çagui Pardo, Sento (Shem Tov) the physician, his sons Çagui and Hamuy, his nephews Semuel and Yuçe, Alazar the tailor (*alfayat*), his brothers Çagui and Mosse, brothers Yuçe and Hazen, and Hazibuena (widow of Barzilay). The number is fourteen, if Rabbi Çagui and Çagui, son of Ordoña, are two different persons.

79. Teofilo Ruiz's calculations seem reasonable; see his *Crisis and Continuity*, 273, and his "El siglo XIII y primera mitad del siglo XIV," 118; see also Baer, *History of the Jews*, 1:191–92.

80. Abajo Martín, ed., DCP, 153–54.

81. AMME, no. L-H0213-053; Cantera Burgos, "La judería de Miranda de Ebro (1099–1350)," 112. The verb *labrar* connotes physical labor.

82. AMME, no. L-H0112-022; Cantera Burgos, "La judería de Miranda de Ebro (1099–1350)," 130.

the decline, likely because they failed to establish themselves in the occupation that appears to have been the key to the Jews' survival in small-town Castile—moneylending. Some Jews from Miranda did lend money at interest to their Christian neighbors, but they faced competition from the moneylenders in the neighboring *aljamas* of Haro and Pancorbo, who expanded their commercial operations beyond their immediate communities. The Jews in many *aljamas* of small and medium size, such as Briviesca, Oña, Belorado, Medina de Pomar, Aguilar de Campóo, Villadiego, Astorga, and Valderas, lent money at interest to Christians. It is clear that the need for consumer credit among small farmers and artisans allowed these *aljamas* to survive and even prosper. Tax farming by some of their members was also a boon to many small *aljamas*. Samuel of Belorado, Sento Cidicaro of Villadiego, Mose Abaltax of Saldaña, and Yusef Cordiella and Abraham Enpollegar of Palenzuela were all collectors of royal taxes who lived in *aljamas* of small and medium size. Most small-town Jews were engaged in other pursuits—physicians, carpenters, and tailors are specifically mentioned—and some (probably a minority) even continued to possess land in the countryside.[83] However, the popularity of moneylending and tax farming in smaller *aljamas* suggests that only these activities could bring in the revenues necessary both to sustain the exigencies of Jewish life in semi-rural Castile and fulfill the *aljamas*' fiscal obligations to the Crown.

Yet, no matter how well the Jews mastered the task of making a living in semi-rural Castile, life in larger, urban *aljamas* had some clear advantages. The *aljama* of Burgos is the case in point. In a city the size of Burgos, there were many more economic opportunities available to the residents of the city's large *aljama*. The rate of taxation imposed on the Jews of Burgos by the Partition of Huete, unprecedented for Northern Castile, is a testimony to the prosperity of the Burgalese community. Some of

83. There were Jewish physicians in Briviesca, a Jewish carpenter in Astorga, and a Jewish tailor in Miranda; DMHB, 3:51–54; Gregorio C. Domínguez, César A. Álvarez, and José A. Martín Fuertes, eds., *Coleccion documental del archivo diocesano de Astorga* (León: Centro de Estudios e investigación "San Isidoro," 2001), 305; Cantera Burgos, "La judería de Miranda de Ebro (1099–1350)," 111. There are scattered references to Jews holding rural estates even in the fourteenth century. For example, in 1315, a Jew Mose bought some land in la Nava near Aguilar de Campóo; AHN, clero, Palencia, Aguilar, carp. 1667, no. 14; Salvador de Moxó, "Los judios castellanos en el reinado de Alfonso XI," *Sefarad* 36 (1976): 88–89.

Castile's richest Jewish tax farmers and financiers resided in Burgos, as did moneylenders, artisans, and traders.[84] That the *aljama*'s economic success raised the fortunes of many individual Jews is evident from the repeated complaints by the Christian *vecinos* of Burgos in the last decades of the thirteenth century that the Jews were buying taxable properties in the city.[85]

This prosperity had another significant consequence: it strengthened the *aljamas*' bargaining position in their disputes with the *concejos*. Given the importance of the Burgalese *aljama* to the fiscal needs of the Crown, the king could ill afford to shrug off their complaints the way he did in his communications with other, less prominent communities. Alfonso X and Sancho IV especially were inclined to grant favorable judgments to the Jews of Burgos. For instance, for the duration of Alfonso's and Sancho's reigns, the Burgalese *aljama* was able to protect its right to have separate judges—appointed directly by the king—in mixed litigation, despite the *concejo*'s best efforts to obtain a cancellation of the *aljama*'s privilege.[86] The large *aljama* in the city of León was still enjoying the right to retain separate judges as late as 1305, even as the Jews in the smaller *aljamas* of Belorado and Miranda de Ebro had no choice but to make use of the judges provided by the *concejo*.[87]

The size of a Jewish community was not a factor, however, in determining its place in the physical landscape of Northern Castilian towns. Whether big or small, most *juderías* provided unencumbered access to non-Jews and served as living quarters to Jews, Christians, and Muslims alike. By the same token, although Jews tended to congregate in one specific area of a city, giving it the name of the *judería*, Jewish houses and workshops were scattered throughout the urban space. The *judería* in the city of León appears to have had a particularly lively real estate market, with Jews, Christians, and Muslims residing side-by-side and engaging in numerous property transactions. For example, in 1274, the provost of the fraternity *Los Bachilleres de los Ciento* purchased a number of houses in

---

84. Ruiz, Crisis and Continuity, 274–76.
85. The first complaint came in 1268; AMB, no. 99.
86. AMB, nos. 4125, 125; CDCB, 150–51, 247–49.
87. Rodríguez Fernández, *La judería de la ciudad de León* (León: Centro de Estudios e investigación "San Isidoro," 1969), 204–7.

the city's *judería*. The first transaction involved several houses that belonged to don Llorente, a butcher. The properties abutted the neighborhood's synagogue and the houses of a Muslim woman, doña Miora, and her son Abrahan. Only a month later, the fraternity bought more houses in the *judería*, once again in the vicinity of Don Llorente's properties. This time, the sellers were doña Miora's sons, Yucep and Abrahan. Jews sometimes acquired properties from Christians living in the *judería*. In 1290, Salamon, a Jewish tanner, bought a house in Cal Silvana, located in the *judería*, from don Lorente (probably the same man who had appeared in the 1274 transaction). Salamon's new neighbors included Domingo Andrés, a Christian carpenter.[88]

The religious diversity found in León was fairly typical for Northern Castilian *juderías*. As the extant documentation indicates, in Valladolid and Ávila, Christians also shared neighborhoods and streets with Jews and Muslims.[89] The evidence for Burgos is more ambiguous, as the records of property transactions in the Burgalese *judería* have not survived. However, one suspects that the pattern of Jewish settlement in Burgos was not substantially different from that of other towns. The highest concentration of Jews in Burgos was found in the *judería*, located in the western part of the city, on the slopes of the hill that housed the royal castle.[90] Like the Jewish quarter of León, the Burgalese *judería* was probably the area of the city where many non-Jewish artisans and other commoners also found their home. That some Christian *pecheros* (taxpayers, or commoners) lived in this neighborhood is clear from the frequent complaints by the *concejo* about acquisition of taxable properties by the Jews.[91] The mingling of Jews and Christians in the *judería* was made all the more likely by the presence of pilgrims, who had to cross the Jew-

---

88. Rodríguez Fernández, *La judería de la ciudad de León*, 200–202.

89. According to a 1303 survey of property belonging to the cathedral chapter of Ávila, more than fifty Jews rented urban property from the chapter, living next door to Christians and Muslims; see Angel Barrios García, ed., *Documentación medieval de la catedral de Ávila* (Salamanca: Ediciones Universidad de Salamanca, 1981); León Tello, *Judíos de Ávila* (Ávila: Diputación Provincial de Ávila, 1963), 9. On the Jews of Valladolid, see Adeline Rucquoi, *Valladolid en la edad media*, vol. 1, *Genesis de un poder* (Valladolid: Junta de Castilla y León, 1987), 228–30.

90. López Mata, "Moreria y judería," 335.

91. Estepa Díez et al, eds., *Burgos en la edad media*, 147.

ish quarter on their way to the gate of San Martín (where the city's synagogue was apparently located) and the Hospital del Emperador.[92]

On the other hand, the long-term trend was toward greater segregation of the city's Jewish and Muslim minorities. With Burgos's new outer wall completed in the fourteenth century, the expanding *judería* and *morería* acquired a gate that allowed the Jews to come and go without having to be in prolonged contact with the Christian *vecinos*.[93] The trend apparently affected the entire kingdom and reflected the desire of Christian townsmen for a greater degree of separation from their Jewish neighbors.[94] One of the petitions presented at the cortes of Valladolid in 1351 asserted that some *concejos* had already reached an understanding with Jewish *aljamas*, reserving certain streets and neighborhoods for the Jews' exclusive use. King Pedro I, to whom the petition was addressed, did not go so far as to make spatial segregation a universal requirement, but he did approve the existing agreements.[95]

The walls of the *castillos de los judíos* afforded the Jews a greater degree of protection, but in times of peace they were quite permeable to non-Jews. For instance, a small Jewish *aljama* inhabited a fortified town known as *Castil de judíos*, located near Burgos.[96] The castle also housed a gambling establishment (*tafurería*), where members of all three religious communities likely came together to play games of chance, the way they were known to have done in many other Iberian towns.[97] In 1285, a royal decree ordered the gambling house to be shut down, for the ostensible reason of causing many disturbances and quarrels in the castle.[98] For lack of other docu-

92. López Mata, "Moreria y judería," 343.
93. Ruiz, *Crisis and Continuity*, 277.
94. As we will see in chapter 6, some leaders of the Jewish community also advocated separation from the gentiles.
95. "Alo que me pedieron por merçed porque algunas aljamas delos judios delos mios rregnos han conpusiçion e abenençias con algunas çibdades e villas e llugares del mio sennorio, con algunos prellados, en que tengan barrios e calles çiertas e apartadas en que moren; e que tenga por bien e mande que en los llugares e con las personas quelas dichas aljamas han auenençia o conpusiçion enesta rrazon, queles ssea guardada"; *Cortes* 2, 19.
96. According to the 1290 Partition of Huete, the Jews of "Castriello" paid 4,200 maravedís to the king; Francisco Hernández, *Las rentas del rey*, 140.
97. Nirenberg, *Communities of Violence*, 30–31, 158–59. On Jewish gambling in Aragon, see Assis, *Golden Age of Aragonese Jewry*, 285–86.
98. AMB, no. 2939; CDCB, 236–37. Gambling was briefly banned in Castile in the late

mentation, the exact nature of these interfaith disputes is best left to one's imagination. The "castles of the Jews" were still a prominent fixture of the Castilian countryside in the late 1360s, when some townsmen at the cortes of Burgos (1367) argued in favor of taking the castles away from Jews and Muslims and transferring them to Christians.[99]

The Jewish communities of the Camino did remarkably well in adapting to the idiosyncrasies of life on the northern *meseta*. Undeterred by long distances and inhospitable surroundings, the Jews relied on the system of local roads to take advantage of the economic opportunities available in the Northern Castilian hinterland. With Jewish *aljamas* established in a variety of urban and semi-urban settings, virtually every town that was large enough to have a marketplace and a *concejo* housed a Jewish community. Within towns, *juderías* were home to most local Jews, but there was as yet no significant amount of voluntary or forced segregation to dampen social and economic transactions across religious lines. Yet, living on the Northern Castilian *meseta* entailed much more than traveling long distances across barren landscape or finding prosperity in a land of limited natural resources. The Jews of the Camino also had to create a *modus vivendi* with Christians, who faced many of the same challenges peculiar to life in Northern Castile. Among the Jews' most prominent neighbors were the region's numerous ecclesiastical institutions, which developed strong ties to the Jewish communities. It is to the analysis of these ties that we now turn.

1260s, but was soon made legal again. The right to establish gambling houses in public places was granted to individuals by royal concessions. A code of law, *Libro de las Tahurerías*, completed in 1276 on the orders of Alfonso X, regulated gambling in Castile. Among other things, it meted out punishment to Jewish and Muslim gamblers for blaspheming God, St. Mary, and other saints. It also contained the texts of Christian, Jewish, and Muslim oaths taken by witnesses in gambling cases; see Robert MacDonald, ed., *Libro de las Tahurerías: A Special Code of Law, Concerning Gambling, Drawn Up by Maestro Roldán at the Command of Alfonso X of Castile* (Madison, Wisc.: Hispanic Seminary of Medieval Studies, 1995), 287, 296–97.

99. *Cortes* 2, 147. As the reason for their demand, townsmen cited the great "disservice" the existence of such castles did to royal power. One suspects that the real reason was the resistance shown by some "Jewish castles" to the military advances of Enrique Trastámara during the civil war of the 1360s.

PART 2

Judei nostri

THE CHURCH AND THE JEWS
IN NORTHERN CASTILE

THREE ⁓ Enemy of the Faith, Asset to the Church

Sometime in the late twelfth century, from his cell at the monastery of San Isidoro, the man who would be known as St. Martin of León made an urgent plea: "O, Jews, it is for the sake of your own salvation that I admonish you time and again, for I wish you to become part of the body of Jesus Christ."[1] Time was running out for the stubborn adherents of the carnal law: the arrival of the anti-Christ was imminent and the Apocalypse near.[2] Yet, the Jews he exhorted in this manner were not his neighbors from the old *aljama* of the city of León. They were a theological abstraction, the polemical adversaries of Augustine, Tertullian, Isidore of Seville, and a good many theologians of Martin's own time.[3] Even as San Isidoro's most famous canon was sketching the unflattering portrait of the "Eschatological Jew," only about fifty miles east from León, in Sahagún, another clergyman and Martin's contemporary had very different concerns involving the Jews.[4] Don Gutierre, the abbot of the monastery

---

1. PL 208, 1170C.
2. On St. Martin's eschatological ideas, see Klaus Reinhardt, "La exegesis escrituristica de Santo Martino," in *Santo Martino de León: Ponencias del I congreso internacional sobre Santo Martino en el VIII centenario de su obra literaria (1185–1985)* (León: Isidoriana Editorial, 1987), 583–94. Other works on St. Martin of León and the Jews include Manuel Mandianes Castro, "La personalidad del judío en la obra de Martino de León," in *Santo Martino de León*, 89–95; Antonio Viñayo González, *San Martín de León y su apologética antijudía* (Madrid and Barcelona, 1948); and José Vicente Niclós, "San Martin de León y la controversia con los judíos en el siglo XII," 243–52.
3. The number of works on the subject of Christian anti-Jewish polemics in the Middle Ages is too great for them all to be listed here. Two of the recent surveys are Heinz Schreckenberg, *Die christlichen Adversus-Judaeos-Texte (11.–13. Jh.), mit einer Ikonographie des Judenthemas bis zum 4. Laterankonzil* (Frankfurt am Main: Peter Lang, 1991), and Gilbert Dahan, *La polémique chrétienne contre le judaïsme au Moyen Âge* (Paris: Albin Michel, 1991); see also Maya Soifer [Irish], "'You Say That the Messiah Has Come ... ,'" 287–307.
4. Jeremy Cohen, "*Synagoga conversa*: Honorius Augustodunensis, the Song of Songs, and Christianity's 'Eschatological Jew,'" *Speculum* 79, no. 2 (2004): 309–40.

of San Benito de Sahagún, was the lord of a sizable Jewish *aljama*. By 1171 the growing Jewish community in Sahagún needed more space for the cemetery. The abbot felt compelled to step in and help out "his men":

> We believe that it pertains to the works of charity to show indulgence to our men, even though they are hostile to our religion and faith. All men are our neighbors, whether Jews or pagans; for one should not act wrongfully with anyone, but on the contrary one should be vigilant and toil for the salvation of all souls. Consequently in order to carry out the commandment of the Christian religion, we Christians are ordered to extend the fullness of charity even to our enemies. Therefore, I, abbot Gutierre, together with the convent, grant a charter to our Jews over a certain land of the apothecary's shop, in order for them and their progeny to have and to possess it for the purpose of burying their dead.[5]

By all appearances, Abbot Gutierre had as little sympathy for the Jews as did Martin of León. In his eyes, the Jews were "enemies," full of hostility toward the Christian faith. However, this particular Jewish community had a claim to the abbot's protection and support. By the terms of the 1152 donation made to the abbot of San Benito by Alfonso VII, the king of Castile-León, the Jews of Sahagún were "vassals of the abbot" (*uassalli abbatis*), who paid him pecuniary damages.[6] The supposed act of "charity" was in effect the granting of land in tenancy, conditional upon the Jews' remaining under the abbot's protection. Whatever the abbot's personal feelings toward the Jews may have been, they were of little importance in the face of the formal agreement binding the lord of Sahagún to his Jewish vassals. Such was the reality of twelfth-century León: members of Martin's "synagogue of the Satan" were a protected part of San Benito's patrimony.

---

5. "Censsemus enim, pertinere ad opera misericordie hominibus uestris, licet a nostra religione et fide sint alieni, indulgentiam exibere. Omnes, enim, siue iudei siue pagani, proximi nostri sunt; quia cum nullis male agendum est, immo, saluti animarum omnium inuigilandum et insudandum est. Quippe cum christiane religionis mandatum sit latum nimis, iubemur, enim, nos christiani caritatis amplitudinem etiam usque ad inimicos extendere. Idcirco, ego Guterius abbas, una cum omni conuentu, facimus cartulam iudeis nostris de quadam terra de apotecca, ut habeant et possideant ipsi et omnis posteritas sua ad sepeliendos mortuos suos"; AHN, clero, Sahagún, carp. 901, no. 8; published in Fernández Flórez, ed., *Colección diplomática del monasterio de Sahagún*, (857–1300) [CDMS] (León: Centro de Estudios e investigación "San Isidoro," 1991), (1110–1199), 4:334–35.

6. AHN, clero, Sahagún, carp. 898, no. 9, carp. 917, no. 13; CDMS, 4:231–32.

This apparent absence of convergence between the theoretical discourse and the lived experience was perhaps the most salient characteristic of the relations between *synagoga* and *ecclesia* in Spain not only during the twelfth century, but also in the 1200s, and even beyond.[7] One of this study's more surprising findings is the apparent absence in Northern Castile of a transition toward a practical application of argumentative strategies developed by Christian polemicists to counter the unbelief of Jews and Muslims.[8] It has been argued that by the middle of the thirteenth century ecclesiastical leadership decided to dedicate significant material and intellectual resources to the goal of proselytizing among nonbelievers in Spain and converting them to the "true faith." The newly created Mendicant Orders were entrusted by the papacy with the task of pursuing converts among Jews and Muslims, and Spain became the natural setting for the new missionizing campaign because it was home to a large number of non-Christians.[9] Several scholars have recently found problems with this theory. Robin Vose has argued that it is drawn from a limited documentary base—mainly scholarly treatises written by a few prominent Spanish polemicists such as Raymond Penyafort, Raymond Martini, and Raymond Lull. Analyzing the activities of the Dominican Order as a whole, both in Iberia and in the broader Mediterranean, he has found that the friars were far more focused on "internal missionary work" than on proselytizing among non-Christians.[10] Concurring with Vose, Harvey Hames has suggested that the Dominicans' efforts to convert the infidels to Christianity in the thirteenth century were desultory at best. He thinks that the Barcelona Disputation (1263) and the works of Raymond Martini were intended primarily for internal consumption

---

7. See Sara Lipton's review of John Van Engen, ed., *Jews and Christians in Twelfth-Century Europe*, *Speculum* (October 2003): 996.

8. David Berger, "Mission to the Jews and Jewish-Christian Contacts in the Polemical Literature of the High Middle Ages," *American Historical Review* 91, no. 3 (1986): 576 91.

9. Robert Chazan, *Daggers of Faith: Thirteenth-Century Christian Missionizing and Jewish Response* (Berkeley: University of California Press, 1989); Chazan, *Barcelona and Beyond: The Disputation of 1263 and Its Aftermath* (Berkeley: University of California Press, 1992); and more recently, Chazan, *The Jews of Western Christendom, 1000–1500* (Cambridge: Cambridge University Press, 2006), 100–101; see also Jeremy Cohen, *The Friars and the Jews* (Ithaca: Cornell University Press, 1982).

10. Robin Vose, *Dominicans, Muslims and Jews in the Medieval Crown of Aragon* (Cambridge: Cambridge University Press, 2009), 21.

and aimed at strengthening Christian belief. Only Lull, a Franciscan tertiary, and Alfonso of Valladolid, a convert from Judaism, developed missionizing argumentation that presented a serious intellectual challenge to Jews.[11] Adding to the growing consensus, Alex Novikoff also accepts Vose's conclusions and argues that the Barcelona Disputation "was organized and geared toward a predominantly Christian public as an educative performance of theological truth."[12]

One of the goals of the present book is to examine this theory in the light of the Castilian evidence. It seems premature at best to conclude, based solely on the records from Aragon, that the Spanish church found itself in the "forefront of thirteenth-century efforts to win over ... the nonbelievers" and yet ignore the broad central swath of the Iberian Peninsula occupied by the kingdom of Castile-León.[13] One well-researched recent study of the Dominican Order's expansion in Castile fails to turn up any solid evidence of the friars' involvement with the Jews and Muslims during the first hundred and thirty years of the Order's existence.[14] The relative scarcity of records does not mean that the history of ecclesiastical attitudes toward religious minorities in thirteenth-century Castile must remain an impenetrable enigma. Lucy Pick proves as much in her insightful study of Archbishop Rodrigo Jiménez de Rada's (cc. 1170–1247) polemics against the Jews. Rodrigo's public roles as a head of the Christian community of Toledo, a titular head of the Spanish church, and a leader in the *reconquista*, did not prevent him from having a generally positive interaction with the local Jewish community. He successfully protected his city's Jews against the distinctive dress regulations mandated

---

11. Vose, Dominicans, Muslims and Jews, 152; Harvey J. Hames, "Truly Seeking Conversion? The Mendicants, Ramon Llull and Alfonso de Valladolid," *Morgen-Glantz* 20 (2010): 43–44, 51–52; Hames, "Through Ramon Llull's Looking Glass: What Was the Thirteenth-Century Dominican Mission Really About?" in Ramon Llull i el "lul·lisme": Pensament i llenguatge; Actes de les jornades en homenatge a J. N. Hillgarth i A. Bonner, edited by Maria Isabel Ripoll and Margalida Tortella, 52, 61, 64, 71 (Palma: Edicions UIB, 2012).

12. Novikoff, *The Medieval Culture of Disputation: Pedagogy, Practice, and Performance* (Pennsylvania: University of Pennsylvania Press, 2013), 211. For an analysis of Nahmanides's Hebrew account of the Disputation, see Nina Caputo, *Nahmanides in Medieval Catalonia: History, Community, and Messianism* (Notre Dame: University of Notre Dame Press, 2007), 91–127.

13. Chazan, *Daggers of Faith*, 5.

14. Francisco García Serrano, *Preachers of the City: The Expansion of the Dominican Order in Castile (1217–1348)* (New Orleans: University Press of the South, 1996).

by the Fourth Lateran Council (1215) and might have personally debated the merits of Jewish exegesis with Rabbi Meir ben Todros Abulafia, the head of the Jewish community of Toledo.[15] Even Rodrigo's polemical treatises were intended not to promote a mission to the Jews or to encourage their conversion but to educate fellow Christians in the articles of the faith. It appears that Rodrigo differentiated between the Exegetical Jew, whose interpretation of scripture he could debunk in order to make manifest the truth of Christianity, and the Jewish members of Rodrigo's own community, who paid a head tax to his treasury and provided a number of administrative and financial services in the archdiocese.[16]

In the same vein, I propose that we distinguish between the church as the source and guardian of anti-Jewish policies and attitudes propagated through canon law and the edicts of the church councils and the church as it existed in the real world—an amalgam of discrete institutions and individuals, whose distinct interests only rarely produced coordinated strategy to put these policies into practice.[17] When it came to dealing with Jews, these individual churchmen were guided by many different considerations, among which the church's official doctrine was only one element, and often not the most important one. To the churchmen of Castile, the Jews appeared under a variety of guises—as neighbors and sellers of property, traders and purveyors of credit, tax collectors and vassals. Some clergymen suffered under the burden of unpaid debt to Jewish moneylenders, while others enjoyed valuable and steady income from the subordinate *juderías*. My goal is not to deny the role of theological discourses or to downplay the importance of the church's anti-Jewish policies, but to draw attention to the often-overlooked practical side of the relations between the church and the Jews.[18] In truth,

---

15. On R. Abulafia, also known as the Ramah, see Septimus, *Hispano-Jewish Culture in Transition*.

16. Lucy Pick, *Conflict and Coexistence: Archbishop Rodrigo and the Muslims and Jews of Medieval Spain* (Ann Arbor: The University of Michigan Press, 2004), 165, 172, 141, 179; see also Pick, "Rodrigo Jiménez de Rada and the Jews: Pragmatism and Patronage in Thirteenth-Century Toledo," *Viator* 28 (1997): 203–22.

17. As Thomas Bisson has put it, "the church was an aggregate of landlords"; Bisson, *Crisis of the Twelfth Century*, 5.

18. This is also the premise of Jonathan Ray's "The Jews between Church and State in Reconquest Iberia: The Evidence of the Ecclesiastical Tithe," *Viator* 38, no. 1 (2007): 155–65; see also Larry Simon, "Intimate Enemies: Mendicant-Jewish Interaction in Thirteenth-Century

Rodrigo's pragmatic attitude toward his Jewish contemporaries was rather common among the Castilian clergymen. To reach this conclusion, I delve into the substrata of the ordinary and the uneventful, in which the majority of the church's encounters with the Jews seem to have occurred.

The Castilian records have not preserved any examples of proselytizing activities among the Jews, but they do bear evidence to frequent contacts between the Jews and the members of the Castilian clergy and allow us to take a fairly accurate measure of the clergy's attitude toward the kingdom's Jews. Overall, the evidence indicates that the clergy accepted the Jews' place in Castilian society and even sought to turn their presence to the church's advantage. Much of this advantage had to do with the regular payments the Jews submitted to Rodrigo and other Castilian prelates. The monarchy's proprietary claim on Jewish taxes, described in part 1, meant that the royal largesse channeled some of this money into the coffers of ecclesiastical institutions. Like the royal policies, the Castilian church's institutional attitudes toward the Jews were shaped by the early centuries of settlement in Northern Castile. When the kings of Castile-León claimed the Jews for their fisc and began using them as a convenient source of revenue, the lords of the *abadengo* (ecclesiastical lands) quickly became co-opted into the emerging arrangement. Beginning with Sancho III el mayor (1000–1035), the kings of Castile-León showed themselves to be generous patrons of the religious institutions along the road to Santiago de Compostela, initiating the building of hospitals and inns for pilgrims and granting privileges and land to the favored Benedictine and, later, Cistercian monasteries.[19] The fledgling Northern Castilian and Leonese bishoprics also received a boost from royal subsidies.[20] The Castilian church's dependence on the monarchy, much abused by the latter in the thirteenth century, can be traced to the early centuries of the *reconquista*, when the role of the king

---

Mediterranean Spain," in *Friars and Jews in the Middle Ages and Renaissance*, edited by Steven McMichael and Susan Myers, 53–80 (Leiden and Boston: Brill, 2004).

19. María Asunción Esteban Recio and Julio Valdeón Baruque, "La provincia de Palencia en la época medieval," in Germán Delibes de Castro, *Historia de Palencia*, vol. 1, *De la prehistoria a la época medieval*, (Palencia: Ediciones Cálamo, 2002), 130.

20. On this process in the diocese of Palencia, see Emiliano González Diez, "Formación y desarrollo del dominio señorial de la iglesia Palentina (1035–1351)," in *Actas del I congreso de historia de Palencia*, vol. 2, *Fuentes documentales y edad media* (Palencia: Excma. Diputación Provincial de Palencia, 1985), 275–308.

as the dispenser of conquered lands to his loyal followers first emerged as the governing principle of Castilian politics.[21]

One of these early warrior-kings, most likely Fernando I, king of León (1035–65), decided that the gift of revenues from a Jewish community would greatly benefit a church.[22] His successors had similar notions, and soon a number of religious establishments along the road to Santiago became grateful recipients of Jewish taxes or acquired jurisdiction over entire Jewish communities. In the provinces of León, Palencia, and Burgos no fewer than twelve ecclesiastical institutions had or claimed to have had some rights over Jewish communities in the period between the eleventh and fourteenth centuries.[23] Some of them, like the Cistercian convent of Santa María la Real de las Huelgas in Burgos, were among the elite monasteries and bishoprics that enjoyed special royal patronage. The granting of Jewish taxes to the church was so common that nearly every Castilian king from Alfonso VI (1065–1109) to Enrique II (1369–79) used it as a routine form of donation.

The giving of Jewish taxes to ecclesiastical institutions, an established practice among the lay rulers of Western and Eastern Christendom, may help explain the Castilian churchmen's reluctance to engage in matters of religious controversy with the Jews.[24] It cannot, however, fully account

21. O'Callaghan, *A History of Medieval Spain*, 167. On church-state relations in medieval Castile, see Peter Linehan, *The Spanish Church and the Papacy in the Thirteenth Century* (Cambridge: Cambridge University Press, 1971), and José Manuel Nieto Soria, *Iglesia y poder real en Castilla: El episcopado (1250–1350)* (Madrid: Universidad Complutense, 1988).

22. Rodríguez Fernández, *La judería de la ciudad de León*, 181.

23. No one has endeavored to calculate the total number of religious communities in Castile receiving Jewish revenues; see José Monsalvo Antón, *Teoría y evolución de un conflicto social: El antisemitismo en la corona de Castilla en la baja edad media* (Madrid: Siglo XXI de España Editores, 1985), 72–73.

24. No specialized study of this phenomenon exists; however, see Shlomo Simonsohn, *The Apostolic See and the Jews*, vol. 7, *History* (Toronto: Pontifical Institute of Mediaeval Studies, 1991), 102–10; Nicolas Oikonomides, "The Jews of Chios (1049): A Group of Excusati," in *Intercultural Contacts in the Medieval Mediterranean* (London and Portland, Ore.: Frank Cass, 1996), 218–25; Robert Chazan, "Anti-Usury Efforts in Thirteenth Century Narbonne and the Jewish Response," *American Academy for Jewish Research* 41–42 (1973–74): 45–67; A. Graboïs, "L'Abbaye de Saint-Denis et les Juifs sous l'abbatiat de Suger," *Annales: Économies, sociétés, civilisations* 24 (1969): 1187–95. Yom Tov Assis states that in the Crown of Aragon, "[m]embers of monastic orders and churchmen benefited from income that Jewish communities had to provide from their taxes," but does not elaborate; see Assis, *Jewish Economy in the Medieval Crown of Aragon, 1213–1327: Money and Power* (Leiden: Brill, 1997), 155.

for their tepid interest in adopting anti-Jewish measures in Castile. After all, many ecclesiastical and secular authorities in Western European kingdoms benefited from Jewish taxes and services, but self-interest did not prevent them from promoting policies that were hostile to Jews.[25] Like any medieval monarch, King Louis IX of France stood to profit from Jewish moneylending, but the king's personal piety and sense of justice required that usury be banned in the royal domain.[26] Guillaume de Broue, the archbishop of Narbonne, who presided over a large Jewry and undoubtedly benefited from usury, nevertheless supported the royal initiative, arguing that lending at interest "is a sin whose punishment is weighty."[27] The thirteenth-century popes intensified their efforts at restricting Jewish life in Europe while at the same time exercising a profitable temporal lordship over Jews in the Papal States.[28]

A far more significant obstacle to enacting anti-Jewish measures in Castile was the Crown's vigilant control over its Jewish revenues. Any campaign to convert the Jews or at the very least to enforce the decisions of church councils regarding the Jews, if it were to have any chance of success, had to enlist the help of the Castilian Jews' main overlord—the king. Yet, as the successive thirteenth-century popes found out the hard way, the Castilian monarchy looked upon such efforts with suspicion bordering on animosity. The fate of the papal program directed at Castilian Jews, discussed in chapter 4, illustrates the monarchy's all-too-evident reluctance to risk losing an important source of revenue by letting churchmen meddle in the affairs of the Jews.

Until the fourteenth century, the Castilian churchmen showed little interest in addressing the issue of the Jews' place in Christian society, and when they finally acted, it was in reaction to the papal initiatives and the rise of anti-Judaism in the lay society. In Castile and elsewhere, one must

25. In this sense, I do not entirely agree with Brian Catlos's contention that self-interest was what sustained interfaith coexistence in Iberia, although I share his view that it played a very important role; see Catlos, "Contexto y conveniencia en la corona de Aragón," 268; *The Victors and the Vanquished: Christians and Muslims of Catalonia and Aragon, 1050–1300* (Cambridge: Cambridge University Press, 2004), 407; *Muslims of Medieval Latin Christendom*, 524.
26. Jordan, *French Monarchy and the Jews*.
27. Chazan, "Anti-Usury Efforts in Thirteenth-Century Narbonne and the Jewish Response," 50.
28. Simonsohn, *Apostolic See and the Jews*, 7:402–61.

not assume that the medieval church invariably took the lead in fanning the flames of anti-Judaism and pursuing anti-Jewish measures. Notwithstanding the strident rhetoric of a few prominent churchmen like Abbot Peter the Venerable of Cluny, ecclesiastical leadership generally followed an ambivalent and cautious policy toward the Jews, vacillating between the impulse to strike out more forcefully against the Jewish "errors" and the need to remain faithful to the Augustinian doctrine of protecting Jewish life and worship.[29] In the thirteenth century, for instance, the popes merely prohibited "immoderate usury," while the lay rulers like Louis IX of France and Edward I of England went much further, banning Jewish usury defined as any interest beyond the principal.[30]

None of the above is meant to imply that Castilian churchmen had no shared assumptions and negative stereotypes about the Jews. Individual churchmen contributed to the formation of an anti-Jewish discourse that began to coalesce in Castile during the latter part of the thirteenth century and fully developed in the following century. Clerics trained in canon law who helped draft Alfonso X's municipal code, the *Fuero real*, were likely responsible for placing the chapters on the Jews in the Fourth Book of the Code—the book dedicated to criminal acts and their punishment. It enumerates the many ways that the Jews can harm Christians and Christianity.[31] They probably also helped disseminate in Castile the little previously known accusation of ritual murder, which appears in Alfonso's other legislative creation, *Las siete partidas*.[32] In his *Los milagros de nuestra*

---

29. Jeremy Cohen, "Christian Theology and Anti-Jewish Violence in the Middle Ages: Connections and Disjunctions," in *Religious Violence between Christians and Jews: Medieval Roots, Modern Perspectives*, edited by Anna Sapir Abulafia, 44–60 (New York: Palgrave, 2002).

30. Kenneth Stow, "The Good of the Church, the Good of the State: The Popes and Jewish Money," in *Christianity and Judaism: Papers Read at the 1991 Summer Meeting and the 1992 Winter Meeting of the Ecclesiastical History Society*, edited by Diana Wood (Oxford: Blackwell, 1992), 237–52. According to Simonsohn, papal policies on usury lacked consistency: "From the end of the twelfth century, papal policy toward Jewish money-lending at interest was to prohibit it in theory, but permit it in practice, with one exception: in the fourteenth century, following the Council of Vienne, Jewish money-lending was completely outlawed. In the thirteenth century, there appears to have been a line drawn between exorbitant usury, which was strictly forbidden, and moderate usury, which was allowed. Toward the end of the fourteenth century and throughout the fifteenth and sixteenth centuries Jewish banking was generally tolerated inside and outside the papal dominions"; Simonsohn, *Apostolic See and the Jews*, 7:226.

31. See chapter 5.

32. Burns, ed., *Las siete partidas*, 5:1433.

señora, Gonzalo de Berceo (ca. 1196–ca. 1264), a Riojan poet and cleric connected to the monastery of San Millán de la Cogolla, included a version of the sixth-century Marian story of the Jewish Boy, "El Judiezno," who is thrown into a burning oven by his own father after confessing that he had fallen in love with an image of the Virgin but is rescued from the flames by Mary herself.[33] Such stories of "witness and conversion" were an important source for the rapidly spreading narrative of the Jews' desecration of the Eucharistic host.[34] Other tales in Berceo's poetic work portray the Jews in the most unflattering light, calling them "greedy and usurious," "false," and "disloyal," and associating them with the devil and black magic.[35] Occasionally, Castilian bishops took up anti-Jewish measures in their dioceses. For example, in 1297, Almoravid, the bishop of Calahorra, issued constitutions that included a prohibition for Christians to eat Jewish meat or drink Jewish wine; violators were to be excommunicated.[36] Almost a hundred years later, in 1379, the bishop of Oviedo, Gutierre de Toledo, took possession of the synagogue in Valencia de Don Juan (a town in León) and turned it into a church because the local Jews allegedly had enlarged and decorated it without royal permission.[37] The anti-Jewish campaign led by Ferrán Martínez, canon at the Cathedral of Seville and archdeacon of Écija, which triggered the catastrophic violence of 1391, will be discussed later.[38]

Yet the records of the local church councils summoned between the early thirteenth century and the end of the fourteenth century tell a very different story. Collectively, the Castilian churchmen never developed a coordinated strategy on the Jews or even showed much interest in the issue. Antonio García y García has analyzed the edicts of the

33. Gonzalo de Berceo, *Miracles of Our Lady*, trans. Richard Terry Mount and Annette Grant Cash (Lexington: University Press of Kentucky, 1997), 77–80.

34. Miri Rubin, *Gentile Tales: The Narrative Assault on Late Medieval Jews* (New Haven: Yale University Press, 1999), 7–39; see also Mary Jane Kelley, "Ascendant Eloquence: Language and Sanctity in the Works of Gonzalo de Berceo," Speculum 79 (2004): 80–81.

35. De Berceo, *Miracles of Our Lady*, 120, 131, 136, 143.

36. Ildefonso Rodriguez de Lama, ed., *Colección diplomatica medieval de la Rioja (923–siglo XIII)* [CDMR] (Logroño: Servicio de Cultura de la Excma. Diputación Provincial, 1976–89), 4:455.

37. Juan Ignacio Ruiz de la Peña, "La politica antijudaica del Obispo don Gutierre de Toledo (1377–1389)," Archivos Leoneses (1974): 282–84.

38. See conclusions to part 2 of this volume.

church councils that took place in Spain during this period and found a striking difference between the councils summoned and presided over by papal legates and those led by the local episcopate. The legatine councils of Valladolid (1228), Lérida (1229), Tarragona (1239), Valladolid (1322), and Palencia (1388) all legislated on Jewish and Muslim affairs, aiming to bring the local regulations into line with the general policy of the church on religious minorities. By contrast, the non-legatine councils were much less likely to take up these issues, and when they did so, the legislation gave Jews and Muslims a rather cursory treatment.[39] The only exceptions in Castile were the Council of Zamora (1312–13) and the Council of Salamanca (1335), with the latter enacting considerably less anti-Jewish legislation than the former. As García y García notes, the ostensible goal of the Council of Zamora was to implement the decisions of the ecumenical Council of Vienne (1311–12), but it went much further, reiterating virtually all the medieval canon legislation on the Jews.[40] Among other measures, it forbade Jews to hold public offices and engage in usury and ordered them to wear distinguishing signs and return renovated synagogues to their previous condition.[41]

By the time the Castilian prelates met in Zamora, a potent anti-Jewish discourse had been building in the kingdom for two decades. It was constructed and disseminated by the town representatives, who submitted their grievances against the Jews to the king at virtually every gathering of the Castilian representative assembly—the cortes.[42] It was they, and not the leaders of the Castilian church, who had been putting pressure on the king to curb Jewish moneylending and remove Jews from positions of power. It is easy to detect the influence of traditional theological attitudes on the procurators' discourse, but the absence of explicitly religious

39. Antonio García y García, "Judíos y moros en el ordenamiento canonico medieval," in Actas del II congreso internacional Encuentro de las Tres Culturas (Toledo: Ayuntamiento de Toledo, 1985), 176–77. The Council of Valladolid (1228), presided over by the papal legate, John of Abbeville, ordered the Jews to pay tithes and forbade them to wear clerical closed cloaks (cappae clausae), thus omitting virtually all of the Fourth Lateran Council's edicts on Jews; Linehan, Spanish Church and the Papacy, 29. See also Juan Tejada y Ramiro, ed., Colección de canones y de todos los concilios de la iglesia de España y de America (Madrid: 1861), 3:327, 335, 368, 404, 441, 499–501, 538, 545, 617–18.
40. García y García, "Judíos y moros," 177–78.
41. Tejada y Ramiro, Colección de canones, 3:575; ibid. (1863), 5: 676–77.
42. See chapter 8.

language in most of the petitions suggests that churchmen did not play a very active role in the drafting of these documents.[43] In fact, there is much more evidence that shows the clergy taking cues from the lay society, rather than vice versa. In their dealings with the Jews, members of the clergy—from prelates such as the abbot of Sahagún to ordinary priests—acted in ways that were remarkably similar to those of lay Christians. As chapter 4 shows, even when tensions arose and opportunities were created for the clergy to deploy their rich arsenal of theological argumentation against Jewish moneylenders and tax collectors, they tended to couch their complaints in terms that were virtually indistinguishable from the grievances of their lay counterparts. The failure to take the lead in propagating a cogent anti-Jewish discourse was symptomatic of the Castilian clergy's lack of interest in confronting their theological adversaries.

The arrival on the scene of the mendicant friars in the first quarter of the thirteenth century made no visible alteration, either in the pattern of royal patronage of the Jews or in the older ecclesiastical establishment's assiduous avoidance of interreligious controversies. While the Dominicans in particular have been characterized by scholars as having a predilection for preaching to non-Christians, Castilian evidence does not bear out this claim. A case study of the intricate power relations in the episcopal city of Palencia, which concludes part 2 of this volume, suggests that the friars of one of the first Dominican convents founded in Castile (1219) would face tremendous difficulties had they tried to convert the Jews. Throughout the second half of the thirteenth century, the Jews' overlord, the bishop, waged a protracted struggle with the city council over the scope of his authority, including the right to collect revenues from the city's religious minorities—Jews and Muslims. In this epic battle of jurisdictions, involving the bishop, the king, and the city council, the Jews mattered only insofar as they could supply the winning party with much-coveted revenues. Given the situation, the Dominicans, who faced a delicate task of finding a niche for themselves in a city already permeated with ecclesiastical presence, were in no position to bypass this daunting web of conflicting jurisdictions and take their message to the Jews and Muslims of the city's *aljamas*.

43. However, Rodrigo de Padrón, archbishop of Santiago de Compostela and one of the chief participants in the Council of Zamora, did assist in preparing the legislation issued by the cortes of Palencia; Antonio García y García, "Judíos y moros," 178.

The situation in Palencia exemplified the hands-off approach generally taken by Castilian churchmen with regard to the Jews. One of the most consistently conservative institutions in Castile, the church was deeply committed to the preservation of the status quo as it was understood by the early thirteenth century: the Jews "belonged" to the king, who generously shared with the church some of the financial benefits that flowed from this arrangement.[44] Any suggestion that the church in Spain could embark on a campaign to convert the unbelievers ignores the multitude of factors that could render such a campaign dead upon inception. When it came to the Jews, the Castilian church was not a monolithic institution with a unified strategy and purpose. For every Martin of León there were prelates like the abbot of Sahagún, the archbishop of Toledo, and the bishop of Palencia, ready to pour the cold water of common sense and proprietary interest on the fire of the former's eschatological yearnings.

"*Proximi nostri*": The Clergy and the Jews in Economic Contacts

The Jews may have been the "enemy of the faith," but they were no strangers to Castile's ecclesiastical establishment. Living, working, and trading right around the corner from many a church or a monastery, the Jews were drawn into property transactions and other business dealings with the clergy. While it is far from obvious that such contacts made the Jews' presence more palatable to the clergy, neither is there any indication that members of the church resisted doing business with the Jews. On the contrary, whenever possible, they sought to derive advantage from the Jews' presence in their neighborhoods. Whether they were buying the Jews' rural or urban property, acting as their landlords, employing Jewish artisans, or collecting tariffs from Jewish merchants, the clergy found a way to make the Jews useful to the church.[45]

---

44. On the Castilian church's commitment to preservation of its customs and privileges ("peculiar institutions"), see Linehan, *Spanish Church and the Papacy*, 2; see Ruiz, "Judíos y cristianos en el ámbito urbano bajomedieval: Ávila y Burgos, 1200–1350," 2:79–80: "El rey, la mayoría de los ricos hombres y de las más altas dignidades eclesiásticas mantenían un marcado interés en proteger a los judíos."

45. On the everyday relations between the Dominican friars and non-Christians in Aragon, see Vose, *Dominicans, Muslims and Jews*, 250–56.

Numerous religious institutions shared urban and rural space with the Jews. The abbot of Sahagún probably was not exaggerating when he called the Jews his *proximi* (neighbors). At the end of the thirteenth century, San Benito owned houses in the Jewish quarter of Sahagún. In 1297, the monastery received some houses in the *judería* as part of a pious donation from Domingo Cabrero de Villada, resident of Sahagún, who had earlier purchased them from Xabiça, a Jew.[46] The 1340 survey of the monastery's possessions in the city of Sahagún mentions some properties in the *judería*.[47]

In the twelfth and early thirteenth centuries, bishops, monasteries, and cathedral chapters embarked on a policy of aggressive land acquisitions.[48] Many of the small property owners who sold their lands to ecclesiastical institutions were the clergy's Jewish neighbors. In the surviving records of property transactions, the Jews almost invariably appear as the sellers of property, while the religious institutions and individual clerics are overwhelmingly the buyers.[49] Thus, in the 1110s, Pelayo, bishop of Astorga (west of León), went on a "shopping spree," acquiring several properties from the family of the Jew Buen, his wife Matrona, and their sons, Xap, Zamal, Jozef, and Pedro.[50] Bishop Pelayo's evident goal was to consolidate his episcopal estates right outside the city of Astorga. The same objective prompted the abbess of the Las Huelgas convent near Burgos to acquire several estates from the local Jews in the early 1200s. In 1204, the Jew Rabí and his brother Cemal sold to the monastery an estate in Vegamediana. In 1207, the abbess of Las Huelgas bought two vineyards in Arcos from Solomon Atrugel.[51] Such examples of religious institutions buying more than one property from the same Jewish individual or family suggest a fairly aggressive quest for adjoining estates that might have involved an element of coercion. The abbot of Sahagún acknowledged as much in 1229, when he took advantage of his Jewish

---

46. AHN, Clero, Sahagún, carp. 922, no. 5; CDMS, 5:566–67.

47. AHN, Codices, 225B, vol. 95v; CDMS, 6:66.

48. Ruiz, *Crisis and Continuity*, 156–57; Ruiz, "Transformation of the Castilian Municipalities," 15; see also Luis Fernández, "La abadia de Sahagún e el obispado de Palencia durante los siglos XIII y XIV," *Archivos Leoneses* 50 (1971): 209–29.

49. This relationship is highlighted in Ruiz, "Trading with the 'Other,'" 63–78. On the other hand, in some areas of Iberia, there existed restrictions on the sale of Jewish property out of royal control; see Ray, *Sephardic Frontier*, 42–45.

50. Rodríguez Fernández, *Las juderías de la provincia de León*, 346–47; 248–49; 86–87.

51. DMHB (1116–1230), 132–33, 140–43; see also chapter 1 of this volume.

vassals' need for yet another expansion of their cemetery. Unlike his predecessor, don Guillermo felt no need to present the exchange as an act of "charity," stating flatly that the vineyard the abbacy acquired in the trade was "much better" (*multo meliore*) than the land the Jews had received for their burial grounds.[52] The Jews had little choice in the matter, since the abbot was their overlord, and they were in a dire need of a piece of land adjacent to the old cemetery.[53]

As a result of the active pursuit of real estate by bishops, monasteries, abbeys, and cathedral chapters, many Jewish holdings passed into ecclesiastical hands. By the middle of the thirteenth century, the process stalled—in part because there were fewer Jewish rural properties available for purchase, but mostly because religious institutions now faced growing competition in the land market from the urban oligarchs.[54] One still sees occasional property transactions between Jews and individual clergymen. Thus, in 1286, Pedro Sarracín, dean of the cathedral chapter of Burgos, bought two parts of a vineyard in Villalgamar from Juçef Harçon and his wife.[55] In the town of Mancilla near the city of León, Johan and Johanna, the children of Juan Alfonso, a cleric (*sic, clerigo*), acquired a few houses from Çag Tintor and his wife, Hana, in 1347.[56] However, such purchases were done for the benefit of individual churchmen's families and not for the purpose of institutional aggrandizement.

It seems plausible that the quest for rural estates by Northern Castile's religious institutions contributed to the declining role of the Jews in agriculture—a trend noticeable throughout Europe.[57] Still, there are indications that the clergy continued to have business dealings with the Jews in the real estate market. No longer acting as sellers of rural properties, the Jews reappear in a limited number of sources as tenants of monasteries and

52. AHN, Clero, Sahagún, carp. 313, no. 3; CDMS, 5:167.
53. On the territorial expansion of the monastery of San Benito de Sahagún, see Evelio Martínez Liébana, *El dominio señorial del monasterio de San Benito de Sahagún en la baja edad media (siglos XIII–XV)* (Ph.D. diss., Universidad Complutense de Madrid, 1990), esp. 333–39.
54. Ruiz, *Crisis and Continuity*, 157.
55. José Manuel Garrido Garrido and F. Javier Pereda Llarena, eds., *Documentacion de la catedral de Burgos (1254–1293)* [DCB] (Burgos: Ediciones J. M. Garrido Garrido, 1983), 276. This sale is discussed in Ruiz, "Judíos y cristianos en el ámbito urbano bajomedieval," 73–74.
56. AHN, clero, León, S. Pedro de Eolonza, carp. 970, no. 12; described in Rodriguez Fernández, *Las juderías de la provincia de León*, 362.
57. Jordan, *French Monarchy and the Jews*, 26.

cathedral chapters. For example, in 1283, Salamon del Portiello rented an orchard from the cathedral chapter of Calahorra, while a year later Mosse Gamiz rented a *mayuelo* (new vine) from the same proprietor.⁵⁸ As late as the second half of the fourteenth century, the convent of Santa María de Otero de las Dueñas had Jewish tenants in Mansilla and León. In 1365, the Jew Baru and his wife rented some houses in Mansilla from the monastery for an annual payment of eight *maravedís*, due on Christmas Day.⁵⁹ In 1370 Semuel Franco held under a lifelong lease a plot of land (*solar*) belonging to the monastery in the city of León, for ten *maravedís* payable on the feast of St. John.⁶⁰

Business dealings between the clergy and the Jews were not limited to sales and leases of real estate. The extant documentation offers rare but fascinating glimpses into such encounters. For instance, Jews were sometimes called upon to witness property transactions between members of the clergy and lay Christians. In one such case, in 1262, "Yucefe, judío" of Villibañe witnessed a sale of a vineyard to a canon of Santa María de Regla in León.⁶¹ In 1303, "Salamon, son of Leui" was one of the witnesses who certified the sale of rural estates to the monastery of Las Huelgas in Burgos.⁶² Since in both contracts the Jews' names appear in a long list of witnesses, it seems likely that they were merely performing their duties as neighbors and not acting in any official capacity. Another possibility is to interpret their participation in these otherwise all-Christian transactions as evidence of their work as financial agents for the religious institutions involved in the exchange. There is at least one known example, from the Rioja, of a Jew working as a "manager" for a cathedral chapter. In 1297, Iuçe Finistriella, *judío*, acted as a representative of the cathedral chapter of Calahorra, receiving the guarantors (*fiadores*) of Doña Dominga and her daughters, who were renting the chapter's estates in Cervera.⁶³

---

58. CDMR, 4:349, 355; see also Francisco Cantera Burgos, "La judería de Calahorra," *Sefarad* 15 (1955): 356; and *Sefarad* 16 (1956), 77. For more on the Jews of Calahorra, see Enrique Cantera Montenegro, *Las juderías de la diocesis de Calahorra en la baja edad media* (Logroño: Instituto de Estudios Riojanos, 1987).

59. Rodríguez Fernández, *Las juderías de la provincia de León*, 364–65.

60. Rodríguez Fernández, *La judería de la ciudad de León*, 221.

61. Archivo de la catedral de León [ACL], no. 630; CDACL (1230–1269) (León: CECEL, 1993), 8:390–91.

62. DMHB, 4:260–62.   63. CDMR, 4:457–58.

Even more common, albeit transient, contacts were of the kind that have rarely left a trace in the documentary record. One should not ignore Jewish merchants and artisans, who were a fixture in Northern Castilian towns and interacted with the clergy in a variety of settings. Jewish traders bringing goods into cities paid tariffs to religious institutions that had the right to collect them. At the end of the thirteenth century, San Benito of Sahagún expected to collect one *dinero* in *portazgo* (toll) from every Jew transporting merchandise in the city of Sahagún—the same as from a traveling salesman (*buffon*).[64] In Burgos, the Las Huelgas monastery charged Jews and Moors a tariff (*cuezas*) on grain and flour they sold in the city.[65] It was not unusual for Jewish and Moorish artisans to labor in workshops that belonged to religious institutions. The case in point is the tanneries of the Hospital del Rey of Burgos, which since the early thirteenth century had been under the jurisdiction of the Las Huelgas monastery.[66] Jewish, Moorish, and Christian tanners worked there, and all were granted an exemption from *portazgo* by Alfonso X in 1277.[67] Several enigmatic entries in the accounts book (*Cuadernos de contabilidad*) kept by the canons of the cathedral chapter of Burgos suggest that a Jew employed by one of the Burgalese tanneries submitted rent payments to the chapter in four consecutive years from 1284 to 1287.[68]

By all appearances, the clergy were accustomed to sharing streets, neighborhoods, and markets with the Jews and engaging them in routine economic transactions. However, the Jews were more essential to the economic well-being of the Castilian church than these simple business exchanges would suggest. The true extent of the Jews' ties to Castile's religious establishment was hidden from view in the dusty folios of accounts books and in the old royal charters zealously watched over by the guardians of ancient ecclesiastical privileges.

64. CDMS, 5:592.
65. Archivo municipal de Burgos [AMB], no. 1784; CDCB, 336.
66. Luis Martínez García, *El Hospital del Rey de Burgos: El señorío medieval en la expansion y en la crisis (siglos XIII y XIV)* (Burgos: Ediciones J. M. Garrido Garrido, 1986), 49–81.
67. DHR, 369–70.
68. A typical entry reads, "La taneria del prior [?] Yuayuanez—el judio, VI mrs"; Archivo catedral de Burgos [ACB], Cuadernos de Contabilidad, years 1267 to 1320 (?), ff. 72, 84, 94, 104.

De Censu Judeorum: Grants of Jewish Rents to the Church in Northern Castile

As elsewhere in Iberia and beyond, the Jews of Castile were considered to be "the king's" and could not be owned or held in vassalage by private individuals without the king's explicit permission. The great majority of Jews in Northern Castile lived on royal lands under the Crown's direct jurisdiction and paid all taxes to the royal treasury. However, this seemingly straightforward arrangement had a caveat. As part of the royal patrimony, Jewish communities or their taxes could be awarded by the beneficent sovereign to a recipient of his choice. In Northern Castile, most of the royal grants of this nature went to religious institutions—monasteries, bishoprics, cathedral chapters, and hospitals. So it happened that many Jews in the region paid their "head tax" (*cabeza del pecho*) not to the king, but to the church, and some even had a bishop or an abbot for a lord. In theory, the principle declared in some royal *fueros* was not violated: the king could always rescind the privilege and take "his" Jews back. With time, however, and especially in the latter part of the thirteenth century, the situation began to appear anomalous to many who felt cheated by the arrangement: to townsmen, the Jews, and even the king himself.

Royal donations of Jewish taxes to the church in Castile had a long and at times turbulent history that largely depended on political and social developments in Castilian society. One discerns three broadly defined periods. The first period, which lasted from about the middle of the eleventh century until late into the reign of Alfonso X (1270s), was the "golden age" of such donations, both in quantity and in quality. The second period encompassed the reigns of Sancho IV, Fernando IV, Alfonso XI, and Pedro I. This was the time when royal grants of Jewish taxes to the church hit a clearly discernible snag. Sancho IV and Fernando IV not only put a stop to such grants, but also attempted to scale back some of the already existing privileges. Alfonso XI and Pedro I, on the other hand, chose to merely preserve the status quo. Finally, with the ascent to power of a Trastámara king, Enrique II, in the late 1360s, donations started flowing freely once again, many of them made to the mendicant orders.

As far as one can tell from the surviving evidence, the earliest grant of Jewish taxes to a religious institution in Castile-León was made by Fernando I of León (1035–65), celebrated for his patronage of the Cluniac order and the translation of the relics of St. Isidore from Seville to the city of León.[69] The king ordered that the bishop and the church of León receive 500 *sueldos* of pure silver from the "Jewish rent" (*de censu judeorum*). Bishop Alvito, during whose episcopate the grant was made, reserved 300 *sueldos* for the use of the episcopal see, while giving the rest to the clerics of the church of Santa María de León. During the next fifty years, it became a custom for the bishops of León to assign small sums from their share of the Jewish tax for nighttime illumination of several altars in Santa María.[70] The Jewish community whose payments kept the candles burning brightly at the altars of Christian saints was not named until 1120, when the bishop, don Diego, mentioned the customary tribute paid by "the Jews of the Castle" annually on the feast of St. Martin. The Jews in question lived in a fortified settlement outside the city of León known as *Castro de los judíos* or *Puente del castro*. With the castle being royal property, the Jews who first settled on its premises paid a rent to the king, who in turn donated part of it to the church of León. At the end of the twelfth century, the bishop of León was receiving not only the 500 *sueldos*, but also a tribute of a "good hide" and two *godomecios* (embossed leather)—apparently the finest products of the Jewish artisans living in the castle.[71] The church of León lost this reliable source of income in 1196, when a joint Castilian-Aragonese force attacked and burned the castle, together with its *judería* and the synagogue.[72]

69. O'Callaghan, *History of Medieval Spain*, 196, 310.

70. In 1074, Bishop Pelagius was the first to assign thirty *sueldos* for the illumination of the altars of St. Salvador, St. Mary, and St. Cyprian; this is also the first mention of the grant made years earlier by Fernando I; Rodríguez Fernández, *La judería de la ciudad de León*, 181–82. In 1092, Bishop Pedro added another twenty *sueldos* to be used for the same purpose; ibid., 186–88. In 1120, Bishop Diego allocated fifty *sueldos* from the five hundred paid to the church by the Jews of Puente del Castro, for the altars of St. Mary, St. Salvador, and St. John the Baptist: "et quinquaginta solidos de quingentis quos reddunt nobis iudei de Castro in festiuitate beati Martini, more antiquo"; ACL, no. 1383; CDACL, 5:90–93. Interestingly, in the mid-twelfth century, the Jews of Genoa were also paying an annual tribute for the illumination of the high altar in the church of St. Lorenzo. Was it a coincidence, or an unknown Mediterranean custom with some symbolic significance? See Cecil Roth, *The History of the Jews of Italy* (Philadelphia: Jewish Publication Society of America, 1946), 74–75.

71. ACL, no. 1073; CDACL, 6:83–85.

72. On the history of Puente del Castro and the remains of a Jewish cemetery with Hebrew inscriptions on the gravestones, see Rodríguez Fernández, *La judería de la ciudad de*

The kings of Castile were not far behind in initiating the same policy of donations in their kingdom. In the late eleventh century, the Jews of Burgos were helping support Christian pilgrims who fell ill en route to or from Santiago de Compostela, thanks to a 1085 grant by Alfonso VI to the Hospital del Emperador of a daily tribute of two *solidos* and one *denarius* and a *portazgo* (toll) on wood, coal, and salt.[73] In the second half of the twelfth century, Alfonso VII and Alfonso VIII made two of the most momentous grants ever recorded in Northern Castile. Not only their taxes, but also Jewish communities in their entirety were given in tenancy to ecclesiastical lords. The precedent was set in 1152, when Alfonso VII awarded the abbot of Sahagún jurisdiction over the Jews residing in his city. The royal charter proclaimed all the Jews residing in Sahagún to be "the abbot's vassals" and ordered them to pay their pecuniary damages directly to their new lord.[74] One can speculate that the present was occasioned by the granting of a new royal *fuero* to Sahagún, which attempted to reduce the longstanding tensions between the town's *concejo* and its ecclesiastical lord by limiting some of the abbot's monopolies and immunities. Perhaps the gift of jurisdiction over the town's Jews was meant to sweeten the bitter pill.[75] Then, in 1175, another ecclesiastical dignitary benefited from the royal largesse by becoming the lord of a sizable Jewish *aljama*. Don Raimundo, the bishop of Palencia and a close relative of King Alfonso VIII, spent most of his life at the royal court, accompanying the king on his military and diplomatic missions.[76] The gift of forty Jewish families—likely the entire Jewish population of Palencia—as *vasallos*

León, 25–61; Cantera Burgos, "Nuevas inscripciones hebraicas leonesas," *Sefarad* 3 (1943): 329–58; Cantera Burgos, "Nuevo hallazgo epigráfico en León," *Sefarad* 14 (1954), 119–21; Javier Castaño and José Luis Avello, "Dos nuevos epitafios hebreos de la necrópolis del Castro de los Judíos (Puente del Castro, León)," *Sefarad* 61 (2001): 299–318.

73. ACB, no. 40.

74. AHN, clero, Sahagún, San Benito, carp. 898, no. 9; another draft states that "thirty Jewish families" were passing under the abbot's jurisdiction—probably the total number of Jewish families living in Sahagún at the time; see CDMS, 4:230–33; see also Fátima Carrera de la Red, "Huellas de las culturas árabe y hebrea en torno al monasterio de Sahagún," *Archivos Leoneses*" 46 (1992): 375–90, and Carrera de la Red, "Árabes y judíos en la documentación del monasterio de Sahagún," 1:45–51.

75. Gautier-Dalché, *Historia urbana*, 242.

76. D. Antonio Alvarez Reyero, *Crónicas episcopales Palentinas* (Palencia: 1898), 79–86; León Tello, *Los judíos de Palencia*, 9.

of the bishop was one of the rewards for his faithful services.[77] In 1177 the gift was amplified by a concession of jurisdiction over the entire Muslim population (*sarracenos*) of Palencia. The charter declared that both Muslims and Jews and all their descendants would serve the bishop, pay him taxes, and obey him "as their own lord."[78]

Such outright concessions of jurisdictional rights over Jewish *aljamas* were relatively rare not only in Northern Castile, but also in the kingdom as a whole.[79] Even so, the *aljamas* of Palencia and Sahagún were not the only Jewish communities in Northern Castile to pass from royal to ecclesiastical jurisdiction during the first wave of royal donations. The royal convent of Santa María la Real de Las Huelgas in Burgos received its first Jewish vassals in 1221, when Fernando III's charter transferred all the Jews settled on the monastery's estate in the village of Dueñas to the lordship of the abbess of Las Huelgas.[80] A document from circa 1230 reveals how much some of these Jews were expected to pay the monastery in rent: Abraam "the Fat" (*el gordo*) owed two *maravedís*, Abraam of Burgos paid the same as "the rabbi"—one *maravedí*. A short list of Christian names immediately follows, enumerating the convent's servitors who

---

77. DCP, 153–54.

78. "*Tamquam domino proprio*," DCP, 158–60.

79. I was unable to find any example of such donations outside of Northern Castile in the period from the eleventh to the late fourteenth century. However, further research is needed to ascertain this preliminary observation; see Monsalvo Antón, *Teoria y evolucion de un conflicto social*, 72–73. Temporal lordship over Jews by ecclesiastical lords was quite common elsewhere in medieval Europe, although no general study of this phenomenon exists yet. On the ecclesiastical lordship over Jews in the cathedral cities of the Rhineland, see Werner Transier, "Speyer: The Jewish Community in the Middle Ages," in *The Jews of Europe in the Middle Ages (Tenth to Fifteenth Centuries): Proceedings of the International Symposium Held at Speyer, 20–25 October 2002*, edited by Christoph Cluse, 435–47 (Turnhout: Brepols, 2004); Gerold Bönnen, "Worms: The Jews between the City, the Bishops, and the Crown," in ibid., 449–58; and Matthias Schmandt, "Cologne, Jewish Centre on the Lower Rhine," in ibid, 367–78. On the efforts by the clerical elites to symbolically "constrain" the Jews through the sculptural representations of Synagoga and Ecclesia in the cathedrals of the episcopal cities of Reims, Bamberg, and Strasbourg, see Nina Rowe, *The Jew, the Cathedral, and the Medieval City* (Cambridge: Cambridge University Press, 2011). For a brief overview of ecclesiastical lordship over Jews, see Maya Soifer Irish, "*Tamquam domino proprio*: Contesting Ecclesiastical Lordship over Jews in Thirteenth-Century Castile," *Medieval Encounters* 19 (2013): 536–41.

80. "Concedo quod omnes illi iudei qui uoluerint uenire populare ad uestram sernam quam habetis in Duennas iuxta domos uestras sint uestri et uestro tantum dominio sint su biecti uobisque faciant forum et seruicium et nulli alii teneantur"; DMHB, 1:242–44; Baer, *Die Juden*, 2:26.

would receive the Jews' money: Pedro [of] Briviesca, for instance, was to receive one and a half *maravedí*. The document concludes with twenty-five Jewish names—presumably all heads of households who had to obey the *fuero* of Las Huelgas and pay *pechos* to the convent.[81]

More common were grants of a portion—traditionally, one-tenth—of Jewish taxes collected by the king in a community where the benefiting institution was located. According to Leon Tello, the cathedral of Ávila received such a grant from Alfonso VII in 1144.[82] El Emperador's grandson, Alfonso VIII, gave the monastery of Santa María de Aguilar de Campóo one tenth of the *pechos* received by the king from the Jews in the town of Aguilar.[83] The tradition was apparently still alive in the mid-thirteenth century, for in 1254, Alfonso X gave one-tenth of Jewish and Muslim *pechos* in the bishopric of Jaén to the bishop of Jaén.[84]

However, not long after the bishop received his gift, King Alfonso seemingly began to question the wisdom of making liberal donations of Jewish taxes and services to the church. In 1270, Las Huelgas became one of the last (and perhaps the last) religious institutions in Northern Castile to receive a grant of Jewish vassals. In his charter, Alfonso listed the names of seven Jews from the barrio of Santa Cecilia in Briviesca who henceforward would pay *pechos* to the convent. All seven were apparently skilled physicians, since they were also expected to take care of sick nuns. However, gone were the days when the king did not hesitate to

---

81. Among them are "Beniamin Zac, alfayath; el rabi Coxo; suo filio Abraam; Zac Marroqui; Daui Zapatero; Ridales; Aozac," and others. DMHB, 1:357–58; José Manuel Lizoain and Juan José García, El monasterio de Las Huelgas de Burgos: historia de un señorío cisterciense burgales (siglos XII y XIII) (Burgos: Ediciones J. M. Garrido Garrido, 1988), 291.

82. Leon Tello, *Judíos de Ávila*, 6.

83. At least such was the claim put forward by the monastery in 1311 and validated by Fernando IV a year later. In 1311 the monastery petitioned Infante Pedro, the king's brother, complaining that it was being denied some of its privileges, including one-tenth of the Jews' *pechos*. Infante sided with the monastery, as did Fernando IV; AHN, clero, Palencia, Aguilar de Campóo, carp. 1666, no. 18 (deteriorated) and no. 19: "Por que uos mando acada unos de uos que ffagades al aljama delos judios de y de Aguilar que dan cada anno al abbat e al conuento ssobredicho de y de Aguilar todo el diezmo delos dineros del pecho [torn] an a dar bien e cumplidamientre en guisa queles non mengue ende ninguna cosa segunt sse contienen en las dichas [torn] assi commo el infante don Pedro mio hermano manda quelos dades por sus cartas." See also Huidobro y Serna and Cantera Burgos, "Los judíos en Aguilar de Campóo," 337; Baer, *Die Juden*, 2:117; León Tello, *Los judíos de Palencia*, 107–108.

84. Nieto Soria, *Iglesia y poder real en Castilla*, 100.

give an entire Jewish *aljama* to a favored monastery. As a sign of changing times, Alfonso was careful to note that only the direct descendants of the seven would remain assigned to the nuns' service. Any other Jews who settled in Santa Cecilia would still be attached to the king and pay him *pechos* "like all the other Jews of our kingdoms."[85]

In fact, Alfonso's charter had implications that went far beyond the fate of the Jews in the village of Briviesca. It appeared as if the era of generous royal donations of taxes and services from Jewish communities had come to an end. This change was part and parcel of a growing estrangement between the monarchy and Castile's ecclesiastical elite. Although during the first half of his reign Alfonso could still afford to dispense favors with relative ease, after 1257, his quixotic quest for the imperial throne demanded greater and greater expenditures that strained the resources of the entire kingdom.[86] The church, in particular, was suffering under the burden of royal taxation.[87] Given this state of affairs, the Crown could ill afford to give the church a share in one of its most important sources of revenue. Now more than ever before, the king had to rely on "his" Jews to fill the royal coffers.[88] Furthermore, the ascent to the Castilian throne of Alfonso's rebellious son, Sancho IV, in 1284, did not mean a return to the earlier policies. On the contrary, while Sancho confirmed some old privileges, he made no new donations of Jewish taxes.[89]

---

85. "E si algunos otros iudios ha agora en aquel logar o uinieren morar daqui adelante en aquel barrio sobredicho, que finquen pora nos e que ayamos dellos nuestros pechos e nuestros derechos, assi como de todos los otros iudios de nuestros regnos"; DMHB, 3:51–54; see also Baer, *Die Juden*, 2:61–62; José María Escrivá, *La abadesa de Las Huelgas* (Madrid: Editorial Luz, 1944), 29.

86. Joseph O'Callaghan, *The Learned King: The Reign of Alfonso X of Castile* (Philadelphia: University of Pennsylvania Press, 1993), 205.

87. Linehan, *Spanish Church and the Papacy*, 154–61.

88. Nieto Soria also notes the drop in royal subsidies to the church in the latter part of Alfonso X's reign, the leveling off of donations during the reigns of Sancho IV and Fernando IV, and their virtual absence under Alfonso XI; see Nieto Soria, *Iglesia y poder real in Castilla*, 100–101.

89. In making a donation to the bishop of Cartagena and Murcia of *el diezmo* (one-tenth) of the royal income from the bishopric, Sancho excluded the tributes of Jews and Muslims, as well as the *tercias*—third of the ecclesiastical tithe: "saluo el diezmo del pecho delos Judios et delos Moros de los nuestros Logares e las tercias"; see Mercedes Gaibrois de Ballesteros, *Historia del reinado de Sancho IV de Castilla* (Madrid: Tip. de la Revista de archivos, bibliotecas y museos, 1928), 3:170, doc. no. 279. In 1285, Sancho confirmed the Las Huelgas

In 1285, he reversed his father's decision to claim all the *pechos* from the Jews of San Martín de Albelda that had previously belonged to the bishop of Calahorra and the church of San Martín de Albelda.[90] But Sancho also failed to give the bishop of Palencia the unambiguous support he needed in his dispute with the *concejo* of Palencia over the fate of the Jewish and Muslim *pechos* and services in that city. In fact, Sancho took advantage of the bishop's weakness by taking half of these *pechos* for his own use.[91]

The years following the minority of Fernando IV (1296–1312) were the time of constant turmoil, at home and abroad. Violence and economic ills precipitated a demographic decline, which, in turn, led to a major decrease in royal income.[92] It is in this context that one should understand Fernando IV's two charters exchanging the revenues received by the Las Huelgas monastery from the *aljamas* of Dueñas and Briviesca for other donations. In 1306 Fernando swapped the convent's 9,000 *maravedís* of annual tribute from the Jews of Dueñas and 12,200 *maravedís* in other income, for a lump sum of 21,200 *maravedís* from the *diezmos de la mar* tax in the port of Castro Urdiales.[93] Five years later, the *pechos* paid by the convent's Jewish vassals in Briviesca—another 9,000 *maravedís*—were also claimed by the king, once again exchanged for a comparable income from the *diezmos* in Castro Urdiales.[94] Even though neither charter addressed matters of jurisdiction, it is to be assumed that the Jews were reclaimed by the royal do-

---

monastery's jurisdiction over the Jews settled in Dueñas (DMHB, 4:67–70); as well as Alfonso X's 1270 donation to Las Huelgas of the seven Jews of Briviesca (DMHB, 4:70–72). In 1286, Sancho forbade royal tax collectors to demand payments from the descendants of the seven Jews, since they owed their *pechos* only to the abbess of Las Huelgas: "Onde uos mando que aquellos siete iudios e los que uinieren dellos por linea derecha que sean escusados de los mios pechos e que pechen e den sus derechos a la abbadesa e al conuiento sobredicho e non a otro ninguno"; DMHB, 4:99–100; Baer, *Die Juden*, 2:62.

90. Baer, *Die Juden*, 2:74–76; Nieto Soria, "Los judíos como conflicto jurisdiccional entre monarquia e iglesia en la Castilla de fines del siglo XIII: su casuistica," in *Encuentro de las tres culturas: Actas del II Congreso internacional, 3–6 Octubre 1983* (Toledo: Ayuntamiento de Toledo, 1985), 247.

91. See chapter 5 of this volume. On the parallel efforts by the king of Aragon to extract tributes from private Jewish *aljamas* and to assert royal jurisdictional control over them, see Barton, *Contested Treasure*, 128–29, 144–45.

92. Ruiz, *Crisis and Continuity*, 307–310.

93. DCB, 5:197–201.

94. DMHB, 5:68–69. Another charter with the same date (October 17, 1311), compensates Las Huelgas for the loss of Jewish *pechos* from Briviesca with 9,000 *maravedís* from the salt mines of Atienza; DMHB, 5:70. I cannot explain the discrepancy.

main. One can think of two plausible explanations for the king's actions. It is possible that economic and demographic malaise did not spare the *juderías* of Dueñas and Briviesca, and the king stepped in to supplant the convent's diminishing rents there with a more steady and reliable source of income. On the other hand, it is doubtful that the Crown would engage in acts of charity at a time when the royal treasury was in a pitiful state. Perhaps the king, convinced of the great value of this income, was seeking to consolidate the revenues from the *juderías* of Northern Castile into royal hands. After all, it was the same king who on his visit to Palencia circa 1305 attempted to claim some local Jews as his own—despite their having been vassals of the bishops of Palencia—because he was persuaded to believe that they were "his," just like "the Jews and Moors who live in other towns and villages of our [royal] domain."[95]

Fernando's son and heir saw little reason to alter this policy. Apart from an occasional confirmation of earlier royal privileges, no grants of Jewish taxes to the church in Northern Castile were issued by Alfonso XI's chancery.[96] In fact, not until Enrique II of Trastámara invaded Castile in 1366 did such donations return as a matter of royal policy. When they did reappear, in the midst of a bloody civil war that witnessed the destruction and despoliation of many *juderías* in Northern Castile, many of them went not to the older religious houses (Benedictines and Cistercians) that traditionally had been recipients of Jewish taxes, but to a new crop of religious orders. The precedent had been set in 1308, when Fernando IV allocated

---

95. "Et agora quando nos fuemos en Palencia porque algunos omes callando esto nos dixieron quelos iudios et los moros deste logar heran nuestros assi commo lo heran los iudios et los moros que moran en las otras villas et logares de nuestro sennorio, et nos por esta razon mandamos prender algunos delos judios desto logar cuydando que eran nuestros assi commo nos lo facian entender"; Archivo de la catedral de Palencia (ACP), no. 348; Baer, *Die Juden*, 2:109–10; León Tello, *Los judíos de Palencia*, 107.

96. Ruiz notes a general drop in the number of documents issued by the royal chancery after 1312; *Crisis and Continuity*, 316. Nieto Soria mentions the virtual absence of royal donations to the church during Alfonso XI's reign; *Iglesia y poder real en Castilla*, 101. Alfonso XI did confirm Fernando IV's 1306 privilege to Las Huelgas; DMHB, 5:215–20. One should note, also, the successful bid by the bishop of Astorga to reclaim the rights over the *judería* of Astorga in 1313; Rodríguez Fernández, *Las juderías de la provincia de León*, 359–60. In 1323 the cathedral chapter of Burgos was trying to enforce its right to collect *pechos* from the *judería* of Valencia (Valencia de Don Juan, in the province of León), given to the chapter by Infante Juan, the son of Alfonso X and regent to Alfonso XI, who died in 1319. It is unclear if the chapter's bid was successful; ACB, nos. 1193 and 1197.

800 maravedís to the Dominicans of Toro from the revenues of the judería of that town.⁹⁷ Out of Enrique II's four known grants of Jewish taxes in Northern Castile, two went to female convents of the order of St. Clare (in Burgos and in Astudillo) and one to a male Dominican monastery (San Pablo in Palencia).⁹⁸

Enrique's return to the policy of his thirteenth-century predecessors is a testament to the strength of the reciprocal triangle that traditionally connected the church, the Crown, and the Jews in the kingdom of Castile. The practice of rewarding the monarchy's ecclesiastical supporters with the Jews' taxes and services survived the times of upheaval, even if the ability of the *aljamas* to pay the requisite tribute was greatly reduced.⁹⁹ After decades of uncertainty surrounding the fate of such donations, old privileges were confirmed and new ones were secured by religious institutions still counting on the Jews' tribute as one of their greatest financial assets. In an ironic twist, the mendicants—purported authors of innovative argumentation against the Jews—now joined the elite group of religious establishments benefiting from Jewish taxes.

97. Baer, *Die Juden*, 2:114.
98. López Mata, "Morería y judería [de Burgos]," 370; AHN, clero, Palencia, San Pablo, carp. 1725, nos. 13 and 15. Enrique II's 1371 confirmation is published in León Tello, *Los judíos de Palencia*, 49–51. The Jews of Palencia were also expected to pay an annual tribute to the convent of Santa Clara de Astudillo, according to Enrique's 1367 charter (111).
99. In 1370, the Jews of Aguilar de Campóo complained that they could not pay the 3,000 *maravedís* in annual tribute to Santa María de Aguilar because of depopulation and impoverishment brought about by the attacks of "the English"; see Huidobro y Serna and Cantera Burgos, "Los judíos en Aguilar de Campóo," 339–40.

FOUR ~ Insolentia judeorum

THE JEWS AND THE CONCILIAR LEGISLATION

By all indications, the Castilian churchmen had no compunction about receiving royal grants of Jewish taxes: on the contrary, bishops and abbots were grateful for the privilege of being given a share in this valuable revenue. By accepting these gifts, prelates gave their implicit imprimatur to the king's jurisdiction over the Jewish communities and affirmed his right to decide all matters involving the kingdom's Jews. Yet there was another occupant of a throne—the throne of St. Peter—who eyed the Jews of Castile with disapproval and wished to have a greater say in their affairs. The ambitious legislative program of the Fourth Lateran Council summoned by Pope Innocent III in 1215 addressed issues of such momentous importance to the church as education and pastoral responsibilities of the clergy, episcopal elections, eradication of heresy, and spiritual discipline of lay Christians. Its overall goal was to create a more orderly Christian society by enforcing clear division lines according to "social and religious identity, class, economic status, and sexuality."[1] Only a handful of the canons in the Council's voluminous output dealt specifically with the Jews, condemning "heavy and immoderate usury," prohibiting the Jews to hold public office over Christians, and ordering them to wear distinctive clothing and pay tithes on properties that formerly belonged to Christians. However, the fact that a number of Innocent's successors on the throne of St. Peter penned letters to Europe's secular rulers, urging them to ensure that the Jews obey the decisions of the Council, shows

---

1. Olivia Remie Constable, "Clothing, Iron, and Timber: The Growth of Christian Anxiety about Islam in the Long Twelfth Century," in *European Transformations: The Long Twelfth Century*, edited by Thomas F. X. Noble and John Van Engen, 290 (Notre Dame: University of Notre Dame Press, 2012).

that the question of the Jews' proper place within the Christian community was one of the papal government's top concerns. More often than not, papal appeals fell on deaf ears as rulers resisted the pope's meddling in the affairs of the "special property" of the royal treasury.² The Jews living in the kingdom of Castile proved to be a particularly hard nut to crack. Throughout the thirteenth century, the pontiffs fought to overcome the stiff resistance from the Crown and the intractable passivity of the Castilian ecclesiastical establishment in order to breathe some life into the reform program directed at the Jews by Lateran IV.

If the campaign to enforce the decisions of church councils on the Jews in Castile were to have any chance of success, it had to enlist the help of the Jews' main overlord—the king. That the papacy understood this basic fact of Castilian life even before the decisions of Lateran IV gave the task new urgency is clear from its pre-thirteenth-century efforts to implement the edicts of church councils. In a 1205 letter to King Alfonso VIII of Castile, Pope Innocent III mentioned apostolic letters he had sent to the monarch previously, urging him to compel Jews and Muslims to pay tithes on properties purchased from Christians.³ These letters, the pontiff charged, went unheeded, and the synagogue grew in power as the church became weaker.⁴

At the time Lateran IV issued its edicts on the Jews, very little headway had been made in enforcing the payment of tithes.⁵ However, two years after the Council had met, in January of 1217, Pope Honorius III initiated a

---

2. Solomon Grayzel, *The Church and the Jews in the XIIIth Century* (New York: Hermon Press, 1966), 47–48.

3. On the history of the struggle over the Jews' payment of the ecclesiastical tithe, see Ray, "Jews between Church and State in Reconquest Iberia," 155–65, and Simonsohn, *Apostolic See and the Jews*, 7:180–85. The payment of tithes by Muslims was also a subject of controversy; see Thomas W. Barton, "Constructing a Diocese in a Post-Conquest Landscape: A Comparative Approach to the Lay Possession of Tithes," *Journal of Medieval History* 35, no. 1 (2009): 17.

4. "[L]icet, super eo quod Judeos et Sarracenos tui regni compelli ad solvendas decimas de possessionibus non permittis, litteras tibi apostolicas duxerimus transmittendas, tu tamen, nedum eos noluisti ad decimarum solutionem inducere, verum etiam liberiorem eis decimas non solvendi et emendi ampliores possessiones licentiam tribuistsi, ut, Synagoga crescente, decrescat ecclesia, et libere preponatur ancilla"; Grayzel, *Church and the Jews*, 112–13.

5. As late as 1222, the bishop of Calahorra complained to the king about the nonpayment of tithes by the Jews of his diocese; CDMR, 3:268–69.

sustained push for the implementation of the Council's decisions on the Jews in Castile. The pontiff's interest in the kingdom was not accidental, but was prompted by a letter written by Mauricio, the bishop of Burgos, who had complained—and this was the first of his two appeals to the pope—that the Jews of his diocese were not wearing distinctive dress or paying tithes to the church. Honorius responded by sending a dispatch addressed to the bishop of Palencia (don Tello), the abbot of Husillos, and the dean of Toledo, in which he urged the prelates to uphold the decisions of the Council with regard to the Jews.[6] A year later, apparently feeling that the issue needed to be brought to the attention of the man whose primacy in the Spanish church was still being questioned, but whose power and influence were already beyond doubt, Honorius wrote another letter—to Rodrigo Jiménez de Rada, archbishop of Toledo.

Lucy Pick, who has traced the events that led to the exemption of the Jews of Castile from the dress regulations of the Council, correctly emphasized the pragmatic nature of considerations that guided Rodrigo's negotiations with the papacy over the fate of anti-Jewish measures in Toledo.[7] Together with King Fernando III, at whose court he played a prominent diplomatic and military role, the archbishop successfully lobbied the pope to rescind the distinctive dress requirement, arguing that that the Jews of Castile would rather flee to the Muslim lands than submit to wearing distinguishing signs (*signa*). If this were to happen, the kingdom would suffer a great loss (*dispendium*) because a large part of the king's income came from the Jews.[8] However disingenuous the argument appears to modern scholars (the Almohad regime in southern Spain was anything but friendly to Jews), Honorius accepted it, and the exemption desired by the archbishop and the king was granted in a papal letter writ-

---

6. "Iudei commorantes in dioecesi et civitate Burgen, nec se a Christianis per habitus qualitatem distinguere, nec pro decimis et oblationibus supradictis satisfactionem curant ecclesiis exhibere, sicut venerabilis fratris nostri Burgensis episcopi oblata nobis petitio patefecit"; Simonsohn, ed., *The Apostolic See and the Jews: Documents, 492–1404* (Toronto: Pontifical Institute of Mediaeval Studies, 1988), 1:101; Grayzel, *The Church and the Jews*, 142–43.

7. Pick, "Rodrigo Jiménez de Rada and the Jews," 203–22; see also Rica Amran, "El arzobispo Rodrigo Jiménez de Rada y los judíos de Toledo: La Concordia del 16 junio de 1219," *Cahiers de linguistique et de civilisation hispaniques médiévales* 26 (2003): 73–85.

8. Simonsohn, ed., *Apostolic See and the Jews*, 1:105–6; Amador de los Ríos, *Historia social, política, y religiosa de los judíos*, 893–94.

ten in March 1219. As it turned out, the pope's decision spelled the end of this particular part of the papal reform in Castile: for the time being, the distinctive dress requirement for the Jews was dead. Even though Honorius reversed his decision in 1221 after a falling-out with Rodrigo, when John of Abbeville convened a provincial council in Valladolid in 1228, the Jews were merely forbidden to wear a certain cape worn by clerics.[9]

Yet, even as Honorius's letter exempted the Jews of Castile from wearing distinctive dress, the pope remained steadfast on the other issue brought to his attention by the bishop of Burgos: the Jews still had to pay tithes to bishops on properties they acquired from Christians.[10] Like the distinctive dress requirement, this papal initiative seemingly had very little chance of succeeding. By Castilian custom, an imposition of *any* payment on a Jewish community in the kingdom had to be initiated, or at least approved, by the royal court. Fernando III was no more inclined to acquiesce to this demand than Alfonso VIII, who had assiduously ignored the appeals of Innocent III. Once again, the ever-resourceful archbishop Rodrigo jumped into action. Somehow, likely after negotiating with both the king and the pope, Rodrigo managed to conclude a pact with the *aljama* of Toledo and have it confirmed by King Fernando. By the terms of the pact, the Jews were freed from paying the tithe on most properties, but every adult Jewish male now owed Rodrigo an annual head tax.[11] Other bishops, less enterprising than Rodrigo and with less clout at the royal court, were left empty-handed. In a testimony to the firmness of the king's control over the Castilian *aljamas*, Honorius's call for the payment of tithes by the Jews continued to be ignored in the rest of the kingdom.[12]

One of those undoubtedly disappointed by the outcome of this tug-of-war over Jewish tithes was Mauricio, the bishop of Burgos. Unlike Rodrigo, who now had a steady income from the *aljama* of Toledo, and Tello, the bishop of Palencia, who was the lord of his city's *aljamas* and collected taxes from both Jews and Muslims, Mauricio had no share in the reve-

---

9. Simonsohn, ed., *Apostolic See and the Jews*, 1:118; Pick, "Rodrigo Jiménez de Rada and the Jews," 208; Linehan, *Spanish Church and the Papacy*, 29.

10. Pick, "Rodrigo Jiménez de Rada and the Jews," 207–8.

11. Jews still had to pay tithes for the land acquired from Christians after the date of the pact, unless a property of equal value passed into Christian hands at the same time; ibid., 208; Baer, *Die Juden*, 2:24–25.

12. Pick, "Rodrigo Jiménez de Rada and the Jews," 210.

nues from the large and prosperous Jewish *aljama* of Burgos. After the papal legate in Spain, John of Abbeville, reiterated the demand for Jewish tithes at the provincial council at Valladolid in 1228, Mauricio penned another letter to Pope Gregory IX, complaining about the insolence of the Jews in the neighboring diocese of Palencia. Acting on the bishop's tip, in the spring of 1229, Gregory wrote to John of Abbeville about what he characterized as arrogant and provocative behavior displayed by the Jews in the diocese of Palencia:

> [they] refuse to pay [ecclesiastical] tithes, extort immoderate usury from Christians, raise violent hands against men of the church, and do not fear violating churches and cemeteries [with their presence], nor do they wish to answer for this in the ecclesiastical court. And whenever they answer, they say that only the testimony of one Jew and one Christian can be permitted against them, according to that region's evil custom established in the Jews' contracts. Also, with the demise of their old synagogues, they build other [synagogues], much better and more expensive ones, and they dare to construct them anew in places where they had never existed before, against the statutes of general councils; and they make their cemeteries in the vicinity of Christian ones, and whenever a Christian and a Jew are buried at the same time, the Christian rites are hindered by the clamor of the Jews, and it inevitably happens that the holy water customarily sprinkled by Christians lands on Jews.[13]

Several months later, in the fall of 1229, Gregory initiated a new round of attempts to bring Castile's Jews into compliance with the edicts of Lateran IV by dictating two almost identical letters to the bishops of Burgos and Palencia. Rather than reiterate the long list of offences supposedly committed by the Jews of Palencia, Gregory focused on the two issues that would remain at the heart of the papacy's policies toward the Castilian Jewry for the rest of the century. The Jews of Palencia and Burgos, Gregory asserted, were extorting "immoderate usury" from Christians and refusing to pay tithes to the church on properties that used to be in the hands of Christians.[14] Whether Mauricio or Tello took any ac-

---

13. RAH, ms. 9-24-5/4558, f. 194v. The document is cited, in part, in Linehan, *Spanish Church and the Papacy*, 147. Linehan thinks that it was John himself who informed the pope after passing through Palencia in the fall of 1228. On the efforts of the papacy to implement the decisions of the IV Lateran Council in Castile and on the role of Mauricio and Tello, bishops of Burgos and Palencia, see Linehan, *Spanish Church and the Papacy*, esp. 1–34.

14. Gregory IX's letters to the bishops of Burgos and Palencia are virtually identical, with

tion in response to the pope's letters is unclear, but the matter eventually came to the attention of King Fernando III, who once again waved the distinctive dress and tithing requirements for his kingdom's Jews. At least such was the intelligence received at the papal court, and in 1231 Gregory reacted by commanding the bishop of Burgos and the deans of Burgos and Calahorra to investigate.[15]

With the monarchy consistently resisting papal initiatives, in the quarter century after Lateran IV virtually no progress had been made on bringing the Jews of Castile into compliance with the decisions of the Council. Yet, the situation was not entirely hopeless for the papacy. Of all the causes championed by Gregory and his successors, the tithing requirement had the best prospects, since it could build upon the tradition of customary payments the Jews of Castile had been making to the church.[16] This is clear from the early success of another ecclesiastical tax initiative, which, unlike the tithing, Fernando III chose to support. Sometime in the 1230s the demand for tithes was quietly transformed into a requirement for all of the kingdom's adult male Jews to pay the so-called thirty *dineros* tax. Its first appearance early in the thirteenth century might have been related to the formulation by Innocent III in his 1205 bull *Etsi iudaeos* of the doctrine of the Jews' "perpetual servitude" (*perpetua servitudo*) as a punishment for their role in the Crucifixion. It symbolized the thirty pieces of silver Judas purportedly had received for betraying Christ.[17] In Castile, this tax debuted in 1238, when the ecclesiastical head tax the Jews of Toledo had been paying since 1219 was identified with the "thirty *dineros*" tribute.[18] Only two years

---

the exception of an additional sentence in the letter to the bishop of Burgos, from which it follows that the bishop complained to the pope about the Jews: "Quare nobis humiliter supplicasti ut ad eorum [i.e., Jews'] insolentiam cohibendam super nos circumspectione dignitate apostolica providere." The two letters were written several weeks apart from each other, in September and October 1229. For the letter to the bishop of Palencia, see Simonsohn, ed., *Apostolic See and the Jews*, 1:129–30; to the bishop of Burgos—ACB, v. 48, f. 46.

15. "In contemptum insuper statuti editi de Iudeis in concilio generali, pro sue prohibuit arbitrio voluntatis, ne signa ipsi Iudei deferant quibus a fidelibus discernantur, aut de hereditatibus que ad ipsos a Christianis pervenisse noscuntur, decimas debeant exhibere"; Simonsohn, ed., *Apostolic See and the Jews*, 1:133.

16. On the payment of the ecclesiastical tithe by the Jews, see Ray, "Jews between Church and State in Reconquest Iberia," 155–65.

17. Javier Castaño, "Una fiscalidad sagrada: Los 'treinta dineros' y los judíos de Castilla," *Studi medievali* 42, fasc. 1 (2001): 165–204.

18. Ibid., 180.

later, in 1240, Fernando III ordered the Jews of the diocese of Burgos to pay an annual tribute of thirty *dineros* to the metropolitan church.¹⁹

Why did the monarch who resisted subjecting his kingdom's Jews to ecclesiastical tithes embrace the thirty *dineros* tax without any apparent hesitation? Fernando might have believed that the enforcement of the thirty-*dineros* tribute was part of the monarch's sacred function as a protector of the kingdom's Christian community.²⁰ At the same time, however, it is easy to see that Fernando III was acting entirely within the tradition established by his predecessors. Never extending this grant to the Castilian church *as a whole*, he proceeded by granting the privilege to individual bishops and cathedral chapters. From his point of view, the grant of the thirty *dineros* tax was little different from the donations of Jewish taxes and services to ecclesiastical lords, which the kings of Castile had been practicing since the eleventh century. By contrast, giving permission to the church to collect tithes on Jewish properties must have appeared to Fernando III like a radical innovation that could jeopardize the Crown's control over Jewish *aljamas*.

The precedent set by Fernando with the thirty-*dineros* tax might have opened the door for a greater acceptance by the Crown of ecclesiastical tithing of Jewish properties, but the change in royal policies did not happen overnight. The popes made several other unsuccessful attempts to collect tithes from the Jews. In 1239, Gregory wrote to the canons of the cathedral chapter of Calahorra, giving them the power to compel Bano Papieto and other Jews to pay tithes on properties bought from Christians.²¹ The pope's missives were evidently not producing the desired effect. In 1252, Innocent IV was still complaining about the nonpayment of tithes by the Jews of Calahorra, and in 1254 he leveled the same charge against the Jews of Toledo.²² In 1264, Pope Urban IV asked the bishop of Burgos

---

19. Baer, *Die Juden*, 2:28.

20. Castaño, "Una fiscalidad sagrada," 198. However, some studies suggest that the Castilian monarchy never developed a strong sense of sacrality and retained a very pragmatic attitude in its dealings with the church; see Ruiz, "Une royauté sans sacré: La monarchie castillane du Bas Moyen Age," *Annales* (May–June 1984): 429–53, and Linehan, *Spanish Church and the Papacy*. For the opposing view see the works of José Manuel Nieto Soria—for example, his "Religión y política en la Castilla bajomedieval: Algunas perspectives de análisis en torno al poder real," *Cuadernos de Historia de España* 76 (2000): 99–120.

21. CDMR, 4:120.

22. CDMR, 4:187; Nieto Soria, "Los judíos de Toledo en sus relaciones financieras con

to resolve the impasse that the bishop of Calahorra had reached with the Jews and Muslims of his diocese over their nonpayment of tithes.[23] Such efforts were bound to remain fruitless, however, since the Jews of Castile were fully aware of the fact that only the king had the authority to compel them to make payments to the church.

Fortunately for the papacy and the church of Castile, Fernando's son, Alfonso X el Sabio, proved to be much more receptive to their demand, especially after embarking, in the 1260s, on a long and ultimately unsuccessful quest to become Holy Roman Emperor. The image of a benefactor and protector of the church was something the would-be emperor was eager to cultivate, even if his actions all too often contradicted it. Enforcing the church's request for tithes from Jews was a low-cost way to appease the episcopate at a time when relentless royal taxation was driving them into bankruptcy.[24] Moreover, under Alfonso, the pace of royal donations of Jewish taxes to the prelates slackened and then stopped altogether, since the king could no longer afford to give the church a share in one of his most important sources of revenue. One can speculate that the enforcement of the tithe was intended as a substitute for such donations.

Be it as it may, beginning in 1255, when Alfonso sent letters to Seville and Cordoba meant to ensure the payment of tithes by the Andalusian Jews, royal intervention in the matter became regular occurrence. Other surviving examples of such letters come from Salamanca and Segovia.[25] In 1282, it was the turn of the Jews of Burgos to be pressed for tithes, when Infante Sancho, Alfonso's son, acting on the request of Fray Fernando, bishop of Burgos, ordered the royal officials in the diocese to compel the Jews to pay tithes to local churches.[26] That the king lent his own alcaldes and merinos to enforce the order was a good indication that he meant business. Apparently the officials performed their duties well, for the early fourteenth-century evidence shows the bishop of Burgos in possession of large revenue from the local Jewish community. In 1316, Bishop Gonzalo even shared it with the cathedral chapter by giving the

---

la monarquia y la iglesia (1252–1312)," part 2, Sefarad 42 (1982): 79 (Nieto Soria is not sure about the date of Innocent's letter).

23. CDMR, 4:256.
24. Linehan, Spanish Church and the Papacy, chaps. 8–10.
25. Nieto Soria, Iglesia y poder real en Castilla, 111–13.
26. ACB, no. 45.

canons an annual income of 450 maravedís from the judería of Burgos.[27] Since the bishop of Burgos never received a grant of Jewish taxes from the king, one can cautiously assume that the money came from the tithe. Bishop Mauricio, dead since 1238, would have been pleased to see his church finally join the elite ranks of ecclesiastical institutions—recipients of taxes from Jewish communities.

Other papal initiatives faced considerably greater obstacles in Castile. The case in point is the accusation of "immoderate usury" allegedly practiced by the Jews of Castile. The legal interest rate in Castile, stipulated by the royal code *Fuero real* and repeatedly confirmed by the Castilian cortes legislation was 33.3 percent—well above the "moderate" rate of 20 percent allowed in Aragon and approved by Pope Gregory IX.[28] From the church's point of view, even this legal rate could well be considered "usurious." In reality, it probably often exceeded that amount. It is no wonder, then, that the papacy was greatly concerned about the practice of Jewish moneylending in the kingdom and used every available opportunity to try and invalidate "usurious" loans. Much to the popes' disappointment, however, the kings of Castile proved to be noticeably less cooperative on this issue than on the problem of Jewish tithing. The difficulty was compounded by the fact that there was no papal inquisition in medieval Castile, unlike in Aragon, where Dominican and Franciscan inquisitors sometimes conducted investigations to "protect" Christians from the "sin" of usury.[29]

Nevertheless, there were sporadic attempts to bring Castilian Jews to ecclesiastical courts on the charges of usury. One such attempt occurred during the pontificate of Gregory IX, in 1239, when the rector and the religious brothers of the Hospital del Emperador in Burgos asked the pope to interfere in their quarrel with Abohab and other Jews of Burgos. The Jews, so the brothers charged, were causing the hospital to lose "houses, property, and other things" "over a certain sum of money."[30] Gregory

27. DCB, 3:381–83.
28. Kenneth Stow, "Papal and Royal Attitudes toward Jewish Lending in the Thirteenth Century," AJS Review 6 (1981): 165.
29. Jill R. Webster, "Conversion and Co-existence: The Franciscan Mission in the Crown of Aragon," in *Iberia and the Mediterranean World of the Middle Ages*, edited by P. E. Chevedden, D. J. Kagay, and P. G. Padilla, 168 (Leiden: E.J. Brill, 1996).
30. "Dilecti filii rector et fratres Hospitalis Imperatoris Burgensis nobis conquerendo

undoubtedly knew that the Jews, as *servi regis*, were answerable only to the king. The unusual order for the Jews of Burgos to appear in the ecclesiastical court and respond to the charges indicates that the pope believed usury to be involved in the case. From the papacy's point of view, the presence of usurious loans made by the Jews of Burgos put the case within the purview of ecclesiastical jurisdiction.[31] It is highly improbable that the Jews, confident of the king's protection, paid any heed to the papal summons.

A major blow to the papal initiatives against Jewish usury in Castile was dealt in 1268, when Alfonso X forbade Christians to lend money at interest.[32] With Christian usury banned, and Muslims as far as we can tell not actively participating in moneylending, the Jews were in effect functioning as the royal usurers. They were encouraged to lend money to Christians at the official rate of 33.3 percent, even as a steep increase in taxes the Jews had to pay the Crown all but ensured that more and more Jews were forced into moneylending. Under these circumstances, the papacy seems to have shifted tactics and began issuing excommunication letters against Christians who took out loans from Jews at usurious rates. In 1325, the cortes legislation forbade Christians the use of such letters for the purpose of evading debt.[33] The royal opposition to the papacy's attempts to invalidate usurious loan contracts was equally strong. In the early fourteenth century, in the diocese of Toledo, several clerics and lay people asked Pope Clement V to cancel their debts to Jews because they believed the loans to be usurious. The pope's order for the interest to be returned is unlikely to have had any effect, since the king intervened, prohibiting the cathedral chapter to use the papal letters.[34]

It is within this context that we must understand Gregory IX's accu-

---

monstrarunt quod Abohab et alii judei Burgenses super quadam summa pecunie, domibus, possessionibus et rebus aliis ad idem hospitale de jure spectantibus injuriantur eisdem"; ACB, f. 5, p.I, f.58; published in P. Alfonso Andrés, "El Hospital del Emperador en Burgos," *Boletín de la comisión provincial de monumentos históricos y artísticos de Burgos* 23, nos. 88–89 (1944): 389–90.

31. On the claims of jurisdiction over Jews made by thirteenth-century popes, see Simonsohn, ed., *Apostolic See and the Jews*, 7:103.

32. "[C]a tengo quelos cristianos non deuen dar a vsuras por ley nin por derecho"; *Cortes* 1, 80.

33. *Cortes* 1, 379.

34. Melechen, "Jews of Toledo," 214; Nieto Soria, "Los judíos de Toledo," part 2, *Sefarad* 42 (1982): 83–84.

sation, cited above, that the Jews "[rose] violent hands against men of the church." By the late 1220s the news of the Castilian clergy's indebtedness to Jewish moneylenders had reached the papal court. The pope must have heard, with alarm, about members of the clergy who had defaulted on their loans being taken to court by Jewish moneylenders seeking to recoup some of their money. From the pope's perspective, this was a detestable violation of the natural order: condemned to "perpetual servitude," the Jews were not supposed to take legal action against members of the holy church. Their acquisition of power over Christians was yet another unwelcome consequence of a practice that was already inherently problematic from the theological and moral point of view.

Immoderata usura: The Clergy and Jewish Credit

The permissibility of lending money at interest confounded both Christian and Jewish jurists, and the problem became even more pressing with the development of the money economy in the twelfth and thirteenth centuries and the growing need for readily available credit. Jewish and Christian attitudes toward usury were built on a shared theological ground: the passage in the Bible (Dt 23:19–20) that disallowed usurious transactions between coreligionists but permitted lending money at interest to "foreigners."[35] This seemingly straightforward rule proved to be rather impractical when tested against the realities of medieval economic life. The Talmud and the medieval Jewish commentators interpreted the passage to mean that Jews could not legally lend money at interest to other Jews. The prohibition put the Jews seeking credit at an obvious disadvantage, since they could only borrow money at interest from gentiles. Some tried to evade the rule and obtain loans from other Jews by using non-Jewish intermediaries.[36] From the Jewish legal point of view, problems also arose when Jews acted as guarantors in usurious transactions between Jewish borrowers and Christian creditors. Some halakhists argued that this situation created a usurious loan between two Jews—the borrower and the guarantor—and therefore such transactions were for-

---

35. Other passages in the Jewish Bible specifically prohibit taking interest from the poor (Ex 22:25; Lv 25:35–37).

36. Haym Soloveitchik, "Pawnbroking: A Study in Ribbit and of the Halakah in Exile," *Proceedings of the American Academy for Jewish Research* 38 and 39 (1970–71): 203–68.

bidden.[37] No serious objections were raised against lending at interest to Christians. Not only was moneylending considered a matter of economic necessity for the Jewish minority, but also some Jewish commentators argued that moneylenders were performing a valuable service for their Christian hosts. Meir bar Simon of Narbonne, the author of *Milhemet Mizvah*, a mid-thirteenth-century compilation of discussions between a Jewish spokesman and the bishop of Narbonne, pointed out that usury played a vital role in the French society: "Who could imagine that society might exist without usury? Even officers and kings must borrow—indeed even the great king, the king of France.... Why then don't the great leaders of the land consider that, if they need to borrow at interest, what of the vast majority."[38]

Christian theologians and churchmen were even more conflicted on the subject of usury and ambivalent about viewing the Jews as "foreigners" to whom the prohibition to lend at interest did not extend.[39] In addition to citing the Deuteronomic passage, Christian theorists devised elaborate arguments against usury, suggesting that money was "sterile" and could not "fructify" and therefore usury was unnatural; or that the charging of interest was equivalent to selling time and thus was a theft from God.[40] The church categorically prohibited Christians to engage in usury, and several church councils starting in the late twelfth century legislated against it, a campaign that culminated in the Council of Vienne in 1311–12.[41] The church's approach to Jewish moneylending was much more cautious and contradictory. Some theologians held that usury was wrong, no matter whether it was done by Christians or Jews, and called for its prohibition, while others accepted Jewish moneylending as a necessary evil. A number of provincial church councils in the thirteenth century issued edicts that forbade Jews to take any interest from Chris-

---

37. Haym Soloveitchik, "Jewish and Provençal Law: A Study in Interaction," *Mélanges Roger Aubenas* (Montpellier: Faculté de Droit et des Sciences Économiques de Montpellier, 1974), 711–23.

38. Chazan, "Anti-Usury Efforts in Thirteenth Century Narbonne," 61.

39. Macarena Crespo Álvarez, "Judíos, préstamos y usuras en la Castilla medieval: De Alfonso X a Enrique III," *Edad Media: Revista de Historia* 5 (2002): 182–83.

40. N. J. G. Pounds, *An Economic History of Medieval Europe* (London: Longman, 1974), 405; Martha C. Howell, *Commerce before Capitalism in Europe, 1300–1600* (Cambridge: Cambridge University Press, 2010), 265–68.

41. Mundill, *England's Jewish Solution*, 109–10.

tians.⁴² Nevertheless, even though popes felt uneasy about Jewish moneylending and frequently released potential crusaders from the payment of interest, they did not issue a general ban on Jewish usury. The decrees of Lateran IV in 1215 stated that the Jews could not "extort heavy and immoderate usury" from Christians, and the subsequent papal initiatives focused on enforcing this rule.⁴³ As in the Castilian cases described above, the papal government periodically investigated complaints submitted by Christian debtors and ordered Jewish moneylenders to return the interest they had collected, but this was done on a case-by-case basis and never amounted to a universal policy.⁴⁴

Even though usury remained illegal and Jewish usury specifically was described as oppressive and injurious to Christians, the papacy in effect allowed it to continue.⁴⁵ It appears that medieval popes subscribed to the same wisdom as the author of *Milhemet Mizvah* and many other Jews and Christians: lending money at interest was an economic necessity, and the Jews (who from the Christian perspective were damned anyway) were best positioned to fulfill the need. Members of the church frequently availed themselves of the services of Jewish moneylenders, and Castilian clergymen were no exception. The records surviving from the north of the kingdom shed some light on the extent of the Jews' credit operations among the Castilian clergy. They indicate that it was quite common for the clerics of Northern Castile to turn to Jews for credit. Unfortunately, virtually no lending contracts between Jews and Christians survive from the region.⁴⁶ Most of the evidence comes from rental or sales agreements on property that is changing hands because of their former owners' debts to Jews. Given the fact that most small consumption loans were never recorded and that only a small percentage of credit agreements led to property transactions, it is clear that the loans discussed here are but

42. Simonsohn, *Apostolic See and the Jews*, 7:188–202.
43. Grayzel, *Church and the Jews*, 307.
44. Simonsohn, ed., *Apostolic See and the Jews*, 7:204–10.
45. Stow, "Good of the Church, the Good of the State," 242–45.
46. See Ruiz, "Trading with the 'Other,'" 70; but see chapter 7 of this volume. This scarcity of documentation is regrettable, especially in comparison to the richness of the sources in the Crown of Aragon, where the royal, municipal, notarial, and ecclesiastical archives preserve plentiful data on the economic life of the Jewish communities; see Assis, *Jewish Economy*, 10–13.

a small sample of a much greater number of such transactions that took place in Northern Castile.[47] Even so, while the cases under consideration might not be representative of the entire group, they do show that indebtedness to Jews touched the religious hierarchy at every level—from priests to powerful prelates. Significantly, the Castilian sample mirrors the situation in the Crown of Aragon, where high-ranking churchmen, friars, and priests also borrowed money from Jews.[48]

It would be tempting to assume that the dire economic situation in which the church of Castile found itself in the thirteenth century drove many individual clergymen into the arms of Jewish creditors. Indeed, the unequal distribution of rents among canons and the meagerness of income from some parishes left many members of the clergy on the brink of poverty.[49] However, many of the clerics whose debts to Jews are reflected in the extant documentation appear to have been men of considerable property. In an early example in the twelfth-century, Archdeacon Tomás of León enjoyed income from the parish churches of Castroverde, Valdeunco, Valdefuentes, and Malillos. In addition, he held an orchard in Castroverde and a plot of land in Valdeunco in tenancy from King Fernando II, who apparently favored the archdeacon with special friendship. Nevertheless, at the time the king donated Tomás's possessions to the church of Santa María de León, in 1162, with an understanding that the archdeacon would continue receiving his rents for as long as he lived, his prestimony (priestly annuity) was mortgaged to the Jew Abolphazan.[50] Although the amount of the loan is unknown, in all likelihood it was a large sum of money the archdeacon needed to further his economic well-being—perhaps by acquiring more real estate.

More than a hundred years later, another cleric with extensive business interests also borrowed money from the Jews. In 1291, Martín Domínguez, a canon at the cathedrals of León and Astorga, left a testament in which he willed his many possessions to the cathedral chapters and a handful of other individuals and religious orders. The canon apparently combined

---

47. William Chester Jordan, "Women and Credit in the Middle Ages: Problems and Directions," *Journal of European Economic History* 17, no. 1 (1988): 57.
48. Assis, *Jewish Economy*, 56.
49. Linehan, *Spanish Church and the Papacy*, 32–33.
50. Archivo de la catedral de León [ACL], no. 1036; CDACL, 5:335–38.

his religious duties with being a wine merchant, because he owned at least two wineries in León, stocked with barrels of wine and sacks of wheat. He was also the owner of "vineyards, and lands, and meadows, and houses." Yet the canon also had debts: some of the wheat was purchased on a loan, and various sums were borrowed from several individuals. Among them was an unnamed Jew to whom twenty *maravedís* were owed "on a cloak."[51] Still, the canon's confident account projects an overall picture of fiscal health. For a prosperous, business-minded individual like canon Martín Domínguez, loans represented not an economic necessity, but a strategy employed to acquire greater wealth.[52]

High dignitaries in the Northern Castilian ecclesiastical hierarchy also sought occasional "convenience loans" from Jews. It is possible that they maintained ties with Jewish financiers who could provide them with unusually high lines of credit.[53] For example, don Juan, bishop of Burgos and chancellor to King Fernando III, claimed in his 1246 testament that he owed a debt of "205 *maravedís* and 54 *kafices* [measures] of wheat" to Gascon, a Jew of Medinaceli.[54] In her 1321 testament, doña Blanca of Portugal, the abbess of the royal monastery of Las Huelgas de Burgos, revealed what appears to have been her personal debt to *rab don Yuçaf*: an astonishingly large sum of three thousand *maravedís*. She warned the convent that don Yuçaf had pledges to guarantee the loan, as well as letters of obligation.[55] A purveyor of large loans to an abbess of royal blood, don Yuçaf was certainly not in the same league as the anonymous Jew of León who made a petty loan of twenty *maravedís* to Martín Domínguez.

Once again, one should keep in mind that the evidence is heavily

51. ACL, cod. 40, f.16r.; CDACL, 10:396–99. Rodríguez Fernández mentions another canon's debt to Jews: sometime in the thirteenth century (the exact date is unknown), Martín Pérez, a canon at the Cathedral of León, owed to the Jews 300 "moropetinos per suas cartas"; Rodríguez Fernández, *La judería de la ciudad de León*, 135.

52. Compare this to the Toledan case described by Nina Melechen: between 1288 and 1291, a priest of the church of Santa Justa in Toledo and his mistress borrowed at least 3,000 *maravedís* from various Jewish lenders. The mistress likely invested most of it in real estate; see Melechen, "Jews of Medieval Toledo," 220.

53. Baer, *History of the Jews*, 1:122.

54. Baer, *Die Juden*, 2:28. Don Juan also claims a debt of 500 *maravedís* to the wife and children of *alfaquim* (physician) Don Yucef, probably for the latter's services. The original is said to be at the cathedral archive of Burgos, but I was unable to locate it.

55. DMHB, 5:328. Doña Blanca also mentions seven hundred *maravedís* owed to "don Çag"—perhaps also a debt; ibid., 5:327.

skewed in favor of larger loans provided to relatively prosperous members of the clergy. When the Castilian economy took a downward turn in the second half of the thirteenth century, the church was beset with financial woes, exacerbated by the reduction in royal grants and the Crown's demands for support in carrying out its expensive projects.[56] Since smaller loans rarely left records, the impact of this crisis on the rank-and-file clergymen is almost entirely hidden from view. One suspects, however, that they shared the fate of lay small proprietors, who were falling deeper into debt and losing their properties to creditors.[57] By chance, a document survives that provides a glimpse into the fate of one such unfortunate clergyman. In 1330, Pedro de San Esteban, a priest at Quintana de la Cuesta, had rural holdings in San Esteban, Hoscrispe, Muneo, and other places. Having contracted debts with several Jews from Medina de Pomar, he was nevertheless unable to pay from the income of his property. The Jews then presented their contracts to their *portero* (debt collector) in Medina de Pomar, who determined that Pedro owed forty-eight *almudes* (*almud* = about 4.6 liters) of wheat to Çag Farach, thirteen *almudes* of wheat to Çag Amiel, and thirteen and a half *almudes* of wheat to Yago Farach.[58] To pay off Pedro's debts and to compensate the *portero* for his efforts, all of the priest's lands were sold to the monastery of Santa María de Rioseco for five hundred *maravedís*.[59]

The growing institutional indebtedness of the church in Northern Castile and León is easier to trace in the records. By the middle of the thirteenth century, many religious institutions in the region found themselves burdened by unpaid debt.[60] In 1247, don Rodrigo, the bishop of Palencia, was even granted a half of the *tercias* of his diocese by the pope in order to satisfy some of his church's creditors. Most frequently, the

---

56. On the "Castilian crisis," see Ruiz, *Sociedad y poder real in Castilla* (Barcelona: Editorial Ariel, 1981), 13–48; and his recent reevaluation of his earlier thesis in *Crisis and Continuity*, 289–313. On the economic problems of Castilian church, see Linehan, *Spanish Church and the Papacy*, 101–27.

57. Ruiz, *Crisis and Continuity*, 306–7; "Trading with the 'Other,'" 72.

58. I am following the glossary in Ruiz, *Crisis and Continuity*, 327. Ruiz thinks that these could be monetary loans expressed in grain measures; see ibid., 313n42.

59. AHN, clero, Burgos, Rioseco, carp. 355, no. 5; published in de Moxó, "Los judíos castellanos en el reinado de Alfonso XI," *Sefarad* 35 (1975): 72–74.

60. As was not unusual for religious establishments in thirteenth-century Europe; Jordan, "Women and Credit in the Middle Ages," 53.

prelates turned to the banking houses of Florence and Pistoia for credit.[61] However, the overall increase in the availability of Jewish credit in Castile after about 1250 apparently led many monastic houses to seek credit from the Jews.[62] In the first half of the fourteenth century, there is a sudden upsurge—by Castilian standards—of records documenting indebtedness of monastic houses to the Jews. Northern Castile-León was in the zone of military operations during the civil war of the late 1290s, occasioned by the disputed succession of Fernando IV, and many religious institutions in the region suffered considerable losses. In 1302, the abbess of Santa María de Otero in León alluded to her convent's misfortunes in a grant of a house to Alfonso Núñez, a royal judge in León. He was rewarded for rendering many services to the monastery during the recent war, including a loan of three thousand *maravedís* that the nuns needed to pay off their debts to the Jews.[63]

After 1300, more and more monastic houses abandoned direct farming of their estates in favor of leasing them to tenants. It has been argued that the demographic crisis and the ensuing labor shortages forced many monastic houses to alter their economic policies.[64] The evidence suggests that at least in some cases rental agreements were prompted by the monasteries' need for ready cash to satisfy their Jewish creditors. For example, in 1319, the monastery of San Pedro de Arlanza, in the Burgos province, had to sign a rental agreement with García Sánchez de Maderuelo and his wife. For the next twenty-six years, the couple would collect all the agricultural produce from the village of Casuar, its vineyards, gardens, meadows, and pastures and have jurisdiction over the monastery's vassals residing there. The agreement specified that the six thousand *maravedís* the monastery received in advanced rent would go toward paying the debt the abbot and the convent owed to don Yago, a Jew of

61. Linehan, *Spanish Church and the Papacy*, 131, 149.
62. Eleazar Gutwirth, "Jewish Moneylending in 14th Century Castile: The Accord of the Puebla de Alcocer," in *Proceedings of the Tenth World Congress of Jewish Studies, Division B*, vol. 2, *The History of the Jewish People* (Jerusalem: World Union of Jewish Studies, 1990), 152. Nina Melechen estimates that the percentage of Toledan loans made by Jews reached 81 percent of all loans between 1251 and 1300, and 94 percent during the first half of the fourteenth century; see Melechen, "Jews of Medieval Toledo," 229.
63. Rodríguez Fernández, *La judería de la ciudad de León*, 204, 148.
64. Ruiz, *Crisis and Continuity*, 110.

Aranda.⁶⁵ An analogous case comes from the province of Palencia, where the monastery of San Zoilo de Carrión, in 1325, was forced to lease the entire barrio of San Martín in Frómista for the duration of ten years to Juan de Padilla for thirty thousand *maravedís*. The agreement, which rings with genuine desperation, states that the monastery owed "a great quantity of money" to the Jews of Carrión, who have taken virtually all of the monastery's possessions, including a certain "golden vessel," as sureties to guarantee the loan.⁶⁶ Finally, in 1362, the monastery of Santa María la Real de Aguilar de Campóo had to pawn its properties in Villadiego to Moses Cidycaro for eight hundred *maravedís*.⁶⁷

The full extent of the Jews' credit operations among the clergy of Castile-León will never be known. Nevertheless, enough evidence survives to reveal that indebtedness to Jews was not confined to any single level of the religious hierarchy. There were enough Jewish lenders to satisfy the credit needs of enterprising canons and impoverished priests, ecclesiastical dignitaries and monastic houses struggling to live off their diminishing rents. Undoubtedly, for some well-to-do churchmen, the easy availability of Jewish credit was a boon that enabled them to raise cash quickly on demand or to acquire additional real estate. But for most monasteries, cathedral chapters, and individual churchmen affected by the economic difficulties that plagued the kingdom from the 1260s on, a failure to repay debts to Jews could mean a loss of property and further impoverishment. Their plight mirrored that of artisans, merchants, and small landholders who found themselves in dire financial straits at the turn of the fourteenth century.⁶⁸ As we have seen, for the Castilian clergy, indebtedness to the Jews presented not only an economic, but also an ideological problem. Borrowing money from the Jews even at the legal

---

65. AHN, clero, Burgos, San Pedro de Arlanza, carp. 371, no. 12; published in de Moxó, "Los judíos castellanos en el reinado de Alfonso XI," *Sefarad* 36 (1976): 47–49.

66. Cited in María Luisa Palacio Sanchez-Izquierdo, "El monasterio de San Zoilo de Carrion: Jurisdiccion, franquezas y privilegios," in *Actas del I Congreso de historia de Palencia*, vol. 2, *Fuentes documentales y edad media* (Palencia: Diputación Provincial de Palencia, 1985), 68. This case illustrates the difficulty of working with the widely dispersed Northern Castilian sources: the author references the document's provenance as the Archivo del Colegio de los Jesuitas de León.

67. Baer, *Die Juden*, 2:191–92; AHN, clero, Palencia, Aguilar de Campóo, carp. 1675, no. 11. The document is illegible in places.

68. Ruiz, *Crisis and Continuity*, 297.

rate of 33.3 percent, which well exceeded the so-called "moderate" rate of 20 percent allowed in Aragon and approved by Pope Gregory IX, meant condoning and even helping perpetuate the practice of "immoderate usury" forbidden by Lateran IV.

Yet the apparent ubiquitousness of Jewish credit in ecclesiastical affairs suggests that the need for borrowed money far outweighed any scruples the Castilian clergy might have had in abetting the "sin" of usury. Gregory IX's 1229 mandate to the bishops of Burgos and Palencia to proceed against Jewish usurers "in accordance with canonical sanctions" failed to elicit any perceptible reaction from among the Castilian episcopate. Only in 1312–13, at the Council of Zamora, did the Castilian prelates insert a small paragraph in the constitutions that forbade Jewish usury. The paragraph stated that the measure was intended to fulfill the edicts of the Council of Vienne, which had prohibited usury in general, though not Jewish usury specifically, and equated usurers with heretics.[69] The Castilian church councils, whether legatine or non-legatine, would not address the issue of Jewish moneylending again in the fourteenth century. In any event, conciliar legislation meant little in a kingdom where the Jews and their commercial activities fell under the purview of royal jurisdiction. The failure of the papal reforms aimed at the Jews of Castile shows that only the king could provide effective redress for grievances stemming from the activities of Jewish moneylenders.

As it turns out, the men and women of the Castilian church did appeal to the king in an attempt to alleviate the burden of debt that threatened their livelihood. However, when they lodged complaints with the king, it was not over Jewish moneylending per se or the high interest rates

---

69. "Item quod non exerceant usuras cum christianis, nec eas seu aliquid pro eis extorqueant illo modo cum hoc sit prohibitum per constitutionem Domini Papae Clementis V. editam in dicto concilio Vienensi"; Tejada y Ramiro, *Coleccion de canones y de todos los concilios de la iglesia de España y de America,*, 5:1170; see Decrees of the Council of Vienne, no. 29, in *Decrees of the Ecumenical Councils*, vol. 1, *Nicaea I to Lateran V*, edited by Norman P. Tanner, 384–85 (London: Sheed and Ward; Washington, D.C.: Georgetown University Press, 1990). Constable has argued that the Council of Vienne's anti-Muslim rulings "mark the early fourteenth century as a moment of heightened anxiety and tension between Christians and Muslims in the Mediterranean World" and manifest a change in attitudes toward minority populations; see Olivia Remie Constable, "Regulating Religious Noise: The Council of Vienne, the Mosque Call and Muslim Pilgrimage in the Late Medieval Mediterranean World," *Medieval Encounters* 16 (2010): 66, 95.

involved (*immoderata usura*), but over the established procedure for collecting debts owed to Jewish moneylenders. As we shall see in part 3, this emphasis on regulating the collection of bad debts mirrored precisely the efforts of urban representatives at the Castilian representative assembly—the cortes. Until the Council of Zamora, Castilian clergy did not advocate a wholesale prohibition on Jewish usury, and even after 1313, the focus remained less on banning usury than on protecting ecclesiastical debtors who had fallen behind in their payments to Jewish moneylenders.

Like so many town councils (*concejos*) throughout Castile, ecclesiastical dignitaries objected to the activities of *entregadores*—professional collectors of old debts to Jews. In Toledo, a long-drawn-out conflict ensued in the last decade of the thirteenth century between the archbishop and the Jews of Toledo over the archbishop's right to appoint his own *entregadores* in the territories under his jurisdiction.[70] From the letter exchange between Sancho IV and Gonzalo García Gudiel, the archbishop of Toledo, it is evident that the king's order, which stipulated that only the judges appointed by the archbishop could do *entregas*, faced resistance from the Jews and the *concejo* of Toledo.[71] The conflict persisted well into the fourteenth century and spread beyond the boundaries of the diocese of Toledo. Apparently following the lead of urban representatives, prelates aired their grievances at the meetings of the Castilian cortes. At the cortes convened in Burgos in 1315, the prelates raised the issue of *entregadores*, and at their bidding Alfonso XI confirmed that no royal official could violate ecclesiastical privileges by entering their properties to collect debts to Jews.[72] It appears that the royal officials in Burgos contin-

---

70. For details, see Nieto Soria, "Los judíos de Toledo en sus relaciones financieras," *Sefarad* 42 (1982): 81; Melechen, "Jews of Medieval Toledo," 198–99.

71. BN, mss. 13089, ff. 35–36v, 38–39r, 51r–51v. The January 13, 1294, letter of Sancho IV states, "Por facer honra a Don Gonzalvo Arzobispo de Toledo tengo por bien que en las sus villas del e del Cabildo de la Eglesia de Toledo que non ayan y entregador nenguno que fag alas entregas de las debdas judios sinon los alcalles o los otros apontellados que estuvieren y por ellos, onde mando, et defiendo firmemientre que nenguno non sea osado daqui adelante de faser entrega en las villas et en los logares del Arzobispo e del Cabildo dela Eglesia sobredicha en rason de las debdas de los Judios si non los alcalles o los otros apontellados que estubieren y por ellos, si non qualquiera que lo fisese a el et aquanto que oviese me tornaria por ello."

72. "Otrossi, al que me pidieron que en los sus logares que son priuiligiados en que los mios merynos nin los mios ofiçiales non deuen entrar nin merynear nin a fazer entrega,

ued to evade the king's regulations, for in 1329 the abbess of Las Huelgas and the *comendador* of the Hospital del Rey were still complaining about the *entregadores* entering their properties to collect debts to Jews and to conduct investigations.[73]

The struggle against nonecclesiastical *entregadores* appears to have been the Castilian church's roundabout way of dealing with the problem of indebtedness to Jews. The church's evident intention was to keep debt collection on ecclesiastical territories under its own control in order to soften the impact the growing indebtedness to Jews was having on the members of the church and their lay vassals. Ecclesiastical *entregadores* were more likely to negotiate terms of payment that were favorable to the Jews' debtors. The fight against Jewish usury was thus subsumed into a much broader struggle to protect ecclesiastical privileges against the encroachment of royal power. It was a struggle the clergy shared with the kingdom's townsmen, who also decried the royal *entregadores'* impingement on the privileges of local *concejos*. In view of the vocal and persistent attacks on Jewish moneylenders by the urban representatives at the cortes, the clergy added little to the growing anti-Jewish discourse in late thirteenth- and early fourteenth-century Castile.[74] This lack of a distinctive clerical voice becomes even more apparent from an evaluation of the Castilian prelates' dealings with the Jewish tax collectors.

Dignitates a regibus non assumant: The Clergy and the Jewish Tax Collectors

The prohibition against Jews occupying public offices and exercising power over Christians was one of the most ancient restrictions on Jewish life in Christendom. Already in 418, Emperor Honorius expelled Jews from some branches of the government, and soon the imperial administration was

---

que mandasse que non entrassen y contra los sus priuilegios nin contra los sus buenos vsos que ouieron, tengolo por bien e otorgogelo, pero en tal manera que las entregas de las debdas que lo que los christianos deuen a los iudios o deuieren que las fagan los mios merynos e los mios ofiçiales en aquellos logares do los suelen fazer e en los sos logares dellos que son priuilegiados e que non ouieron de huso nin de costumbre de los fazer y nin ofiçial mio non deue y entrar, mando que sea guardado que las non fagan y"; DCB, 347.

73. AMB, no. 1845; published in CDCB, 316.

74. For more on the anti-Jewish petitions presented by the urban procurators at the cortes, see chapter 8.

almost entirely closed to Jews.[75] The Augustinian doctrine of Jewish witness stipulated that the Jews' "servitude" to Christians was a precondition for their toleration, and it followed that Jews could not take advantage of their hosts and rule over Christians.[76] As we have seen in chapter 2, in reconquest Castile, the employment of Jewish notables at the royal court was a deeply entrenched tradition. King Alfonso VI used the services of Jewish physicians, diplomats, and tribute collectors—a practice that attracted the attention of Pope Gregory VII, who had issued a sharp rebuke to the king in 1081.[77] Lateran IV declared it to be "absurd" for Jews to hold power over Christians and expressed concern that they might use the authority of their office to injure Christians.[78] Despite the church's prohibition, Castilian kings would not relinquish the services of their Jewish *almojarifes* and tax collectors and continued to employ Jews in public positions until the expulsion of 1492.[79] In fact, by the second half of the thirteenth century, it became increasingly likely that a Jew and not a Christian would undertake the unpopular task of channeling revenues into the seemingly bottomless royal purse. Jewish tax farmers, who depended entirely on the king's will and served at his mercy, were ideal, if greatly resented, instruments of royal power. Their number increased in the second half of the thirteenth century, with some influential Jewish families in Toledo forming "companies" specializing in collecting certain types of taxes.[80] The kings of Castile clearly liked the convenience, efficiency, and speed of this method: in 1287, for instance, Sancho IV entrusted Abraham el Barchilón with collecting taxes from the entire kingdom for the period of two years.[81]

75. Amnon Linder, "The Legal Status of the Jews in the Roman Empire," in *The Cambridge History of Judaism*, vol. 4, *The Late Roman-Rabbinic Period*, edited by Steven T. Katz, 160–61 (Cambridge: Cambridge University Press, 2008).

76. Jeremy Cohen, *Living Letters of the Law: Ideas of the Jew in Medieval Christianity* (Berkeley and Los Angeles: University of California Press, 1999), 29–30, 361.

77. Baer, *Die Juden*, 2:5; Simonsohn, *Apostolic See and the Jews*, 7:148.

78. "Since it is quite absurd that any who blaspheme against Christ should have power over Christians, we, on account of the boldness of the transgressors, renew what the Council of Toledo already has legislated with regard to this. We forbid that Jews be given preferment in public office since this offers them the pretext to vent their wrath against the Christians." Grayzel, *Church and the Jews*, 311.

79. Simonsohn, ed., *Apostolic See and the Jews*, 7:154.

80. José Manuel Nieto Soria, "Los judíos de Toledo en sus relaciones financieras," *Sefarad* 41 (1981): 309; Ladero Quesada, *Fiscalidad y poder real en Castilla*, 259.

81. Nieto Soria, "Los judíos de Toledo en sus relaciones financieras," 308.

Jewish financial agents could and did test the patience of Northern Castilian prelates when sent by the king to ecclesiastical estates to conduct investigations or to collect taxes. In the frequent clashes between the *realengo* (royal lands) and the *abadengo* (ecclesiastical lands), any zealous agent of the royal power—whether Jewish or Christian—could become a lightning rod for rising tensions. When in 1294 the monastery of San Salvador de Oña, in the Burgos province, claimed an exemption from the *fonsadera* tax (payable in lieu of military service), it was two Christians who emerged as the villains of the entire affair. During an inquiry conducted by a royal *alcalde* (judge), witness after witness stepped forward to affirm that despite having worked as collectors of *fonsadera* for the king, they never demanded the tax from San Salvador. The only Jew in the group, Samuel of Belorado, responded with a diplomatic statement that a demand of *fonsadera* from San Salvador would have violated the royal privileges granted to the monastery. Like the other witnesses, Samuel pointed a finger at Pero Ferrandez of Oña and Iohan Mathe of Burgos as the two officials who had collected *fonsadera* from the vassals of San Salvador "by force." When asked, Pero Ferrandez acknowledged "forcibly" levying the tax on the abbot and his vassals, while Iohan Mathe denied any wrongdoing.[82]

Yet it was not always possible for the Jewish officials of the king to preserve a mien of cool impartiality. In some cases, their activities on behalf of the king thrust them directly into the middle of the controversy, making them the target of the prelates' lawsuits or, alternatively, of the king's wrath. By all appearances, the Jewish officials' problems with the *abadengo* stemmed from their all-too-faithful attempts to carry out the king's policies. For instance, the 1288 lawsuit brought by the abbot of Santa María de Aguilar de Campóo against Çag de Haro, a Jewish official of the king, was part of the rising wave of protests against Sancho IV's campaign to reclaim the royal lands that had passed from the *realengo* to the *abadengo*. Initiated by Sancho in 1286, shortly after his ascent to the throne, the inquiry aimed at identifying and bringing back the royal lands that had been acquired by the church as a result of unauthorized donations, purchases, and exchanges of land.[83] Çag de Haro was acting on the king's or-

---

82. DMSSO, 212–16.
83. Nieto Soria, *Iglesia y poder real en Castilla*, 138–41.

ders when he charged that some houses in the barrio of *molinillo de Aguilar* had been illegally obtained by the monastery of Aguilar. The abbot countered that claim by filing a lawsuit with the royal *alcalde* in Aguilar, which cited royal privileges and testimonies of witnesses as the evidence supporting the monastery's right to the disputed properties. Mindful of the delicate nature of the monarch's relations with the church, Çag hastened to assure the court that the investigation was not intended to violate the monastery's privileges and that the investigators respected the abbot's rights.[84] After hearing Çag's conciliatory testimony, the *alcalde* decided the case in the abbot's favor. Being present during the judge's announcement, the Jewish official made no objection.[85] In fact, in August of 1288, only six months after this February decision, Sancho IV had to suspend his inquiry indefinitely.[86]

It was not the only time that a Jewish official found himself in the crossfire of church-state tensions in Northern Castile. Minding the royal interests but not the complex web of local ecclesiastical privileges, Jewish and Christian tax collectors often flouted much-cherished exemptions by demanding taxes where they were not due. At least that was the charge advanced in numerous lawsuits brought by the prelates against royal officials. In a 1340 case, also from Aguilar de Campóo, the bishop of Burgos complained to King Alfonso XI about the illegal collections of *fonsadera* from his vassals in Aguilar. The lawsuit alleged that a Christian, Gil García, and a Jew, Abraham Cordiella, collectors of *fonsadera*, took sureties from the bishop's vassals in the *merindad* (district under the jurisdiction of a *merino*) of Aguilar for nonpayment of the tax, despite the vassals' claim of immunity. After examining the letters of privileges duly shown by the bishop's representatives, the *alcalde* of Aguilar ruled that the bishop's vassals were exempt from paying the *fonsadera*.[87] In 1363,

---

84. "[O]ydo a don çag lo que el quiso dezir, falle quela pesquisa quelos dichos pesquisidores fizieren, que non empesçia al abbat et al Conuento en esta rrazon, e los priuilegios e los testimonios que el prior aduxo, quell aprouechauan."

85. "[D]on çag de faro estando presente non diziendo ninguna cosa contra esto, e amas partes recibiendo esta sentencia"; AHN, clero, Palencia, Aguilar de Campóo, carp. 1661, no. 18; Mercedes Gaibrois de Ballesteros, *Historia de reinado de Sancho IV de Castilla* (Madrid: Tip. de la Revista de archivos, bibliotecas y museos, 1928), 3:110–11.

86. Nieto Soria, *Iglesia y poder real en Castilla*, 141.

87. ACB, no. 1363. See an analogous case, also involving an allegedly illegal collection

a Jewish collector of taxes for the Infante Alfonso treated the abbot of the monastery of Santa María de Carracedo in the province of León with even less consideration, seizing thirty head of livestock from the monastery's farm against the abbot's will as a surety for nonpayment of taxes. When asked to explain his actions in court, the collector, Zag Garzon, did not deny the charges, but claimed that he held the abbot's flocks in lieu of the 1800 *maravedís* owed by the monastery to the Infante in arrears for three years. Once again, the royal charters, expediently presented by the abbot and proving special royal protection for the monastery, decided the outcome of the case, and the Jew was ordered to reunite the abbot with his herd.[88]

In at least one instance, Jewish tax collectors received a sharp rebuke from the king for disregarding a royal privilege given to the church of Burgos. Since the late twelfth century, the bishop and the cathedral chapter of Burgos had been enjoying income from the so-called *diezmos de los puertos* tax (a tithe on all imported and exported goods) in several ports on the Bay of Biscay.[89] In 1323, Alfonso XI (or his regents, since the king did not reach majority until 1325) gave the church of Burgos an additional privilege: an extra tithe (*rediezmo*) in the ports of Castro-Urdiales, Laredo, Santander, San Vicente de la Barquera, and Rioturbio. A year later, Bishop García wrote to the king, complaining about the conduct of the three Jewish tax farmers entrusted with collecting the *rediezmo* for the church of Burgos. The bishop alleged that the king's physician Rabbi Yuçaf Abenguinano, Yuçaf, son of Todros El Leui, and Yafiel Abenguinano, son of Rabbi Yuçaf, despite having received a charter signed by the king in Valladolid, refused to begin charging the extra tithe in mid-March of 1323, thereby violating the king's express wishes. In April of 1324, the royal chancellery issued another order. Citing the bishop's complaint that the three Jews had been hiding the truth about an early start of the rediezmo, the king issued what appears to be a thinly veiled warning. A timely receipt of their tithes by the bishop and the chapter, the king re-

---

of *fonsadera* from the vassals of San Benito de Sahagún by Yuçef Cordilla—possibly a relative of Abraham; CDMS, 7:66.

88. Rodríguez Fernández, *Las juderías de la provincia de León*, 363–64.

89. D. Mansilla Reoyo, ed., *Catálogo documental del archivo catedral de Burgos (804–1416)* (Madrid and Barcelona: CSIC, 1971), 89, 182.

minded his Jewish tax farmers, was a *condition* for their continuing in the king's service.[90]

In short, church dignitaries in Northern Castile had numerous run-ins with the king's Jewish officials. Nevertheless, like the issue of Jewish moneylending, tax farming by Jews never elicited a cogent and distinct response from the Castilian church, the stern condemnations issued from Rome notwithstanding. At Lateran IV and throughout the thirteenth century, the papacy continued to argue in the strongest terms against the practice of entrusting Jews with public offices. In 1233, Gregory IX wrote to the archbishop of Compostela, asserting that the presence of Jews in positions of public authority presented danger to Christians.[91] The pontiffs' many missives sent to the rulers of Portugal, Castile, and Aragon did not specifically mention tax collecting, but the public nature of that office undoubtedly met the criteria of positions forbidden to Jews.[92] However, the popes' efforts appear to have made little impact on the attitudes toward Jewish tax farming in Castile. In fact, some monasteries did not hesitate to employ Jewish tax farmers on their own estates. In one example, the monastery of San Miguel de Escalada in León hired Abraham Ruvielo to collect rents from two of its villages for twenty-six years. The monastery evidently had a change of heart over this arrangement, because in 1336 the abbot was complaining that in the more than five years since the start of Abraham's duties, the Jew not only collected the five thousand *maravedís* he had paid to the monastery, but also earned "much more." In the meantime, the mon-

---

90. "[L]e fue despues tomado por la dicha carta que vos ganastes callada la verdad como dicho es desde mediado el dicho mes de Marco que vos comnçastes la dicha renta fasta que les mandamos dar la dicha carta sellada con sello de plomo.... Y bien sabedes que los dichos diezmos que los arrendastes denos con condicion que fincase a saluo a los dichos Obispo y cauillo el rediezmo que ouiese a auer delos dichas puertos"; ACB, no. 1205. The original is barely legible, but there is a more recent copy; described in Cantera Burgos, "La judería de Burgos," 70–71.

91. "Et cum in concilio fuerit Toletano statutum et in generali nihilominus innovatum ne Judei publicis officiis preponantur, quoniam sub tali pretextu christianis plerumque nimium sunt infesti, cum sit nimis absurdum ut Christi blasphemus in Christianos vim exerceat potestatis"; Grayzel, *Church and the Jews*, 204–6.

92. For an overview of papal decrees on the subject see Simonsohn, *Apostolic See and the Jews*, 7:147–54. On the conflict between the papacy and the kings of Hungary over the issue of officeholding by non-Christians, see Berend, *At the Gate of Christendom*, 152–63; and Michael Lower, *The Barons' Crusade: A Call to Arms and Its Consequences* (Philadelphia: University of Pennsylvania Press, 2005), 77–82.

astery had grown poor, as a number of Jews and Christians in the vicinity of León had usurped rights over its possessions.[93]

Even though the evidence shows some prelates' palpable dissatisfaction with the king's officials who happened to be Jewish, none of it appears to have translated into concerted calls to end tax farming by Jews. This lack of response seems especially striking when compared to the efforts of urban procurators at the cortes to get Jewish officials dismissed from royal service. Starting at the end of the thirteenth century, the complaint that the Jewish tax farmers were enriching themselves at the expense of local elites formed the basis of numerous petitions presented to the king at the gatherings of the cortes. Beginning with the cortes of Palencia (1286), urban procurators sought to keep revenue collection in the hands of local oligarchs (hombres buenos) and to prevent royal officials, nobles, and Jews from participating in this potentially lucrative activity.[94] Appearing alongside this petition, albeit with less frequency, was a more general request to prevent the Jews from occupying positions of authority at the royal court.[95] The petitions of urban representatives seemingly show little interest in the theological implications of putting Jews in charge of Christians, requesting simply that such positions be limited to men of their own class.[96] Still, the failed but concerted effort by the urban oligarchs to prevent the king from employing Jewish officials dwarfed the altogether feeble reaction of the Castilian church. In 1279, a group of Castilian and Leonese prelates submitted a list of complaints about Alfonso X to Pope Nicholas III, which included an accusation that the king was employing Jewish officials and tax collectors and putting Jews in positions of power over Christians.[97] The

---

93. "[D]e los quales veynte et seys annos dize que son van passados mas de çinco annos, e que en estos dichos çinco annos que alleuado el dicho judio de las dos aldeas los dichos çinco mill mrs e mucho mas"; AHN, clero, León, Escalada, carp. 833, no. 17; described in Baer, Die Juden, 2:160.

94. Monsalvo Antón, Teoria y evolucion de un conflicto social, 174; Ladero Quesada, Fiscalidad y poder real en Castilla, 250–52; Isabel Beceiro Pita, "La vinculación de los judíos a los poderes señoriales castellanos (siglos XII–XV)," in Xudeus e Conversos na Historia, edited by Carlos Barros, 2:98 (Santiago de Compostela: Editorial de la Historia, 1994).

95. Monsalvo Antón, Teoria y evolucion de un conflicto social, 173.

96. Cortes of Valladolid, 1295; Cortes I, 131.

97. "Item judei christianis in officiis et exactionibus preponuntur, ex quo perveniunt multa mala inter que id est principuum [sic], quod christiani multi ut favorem habeant judeorum subiciuntur eis et eorum ritibus et traditionibus corrumpuntur"; Linehan, "The Spanish

issue came up again at the Council of Zamora (1312–13), and at the legatine Council of Valladolid (1322), when the prelates stated that Jewish officeholders were causing harm to Christians.[98] None of the other fourteenth-century provincial councils in Castile addressed the question of Jews in positions of authority.

It is tempting to assume that it was the "elite" clergy who found the Jews' presence mostly beneficial to their interests, whereas the "lower" clergy saw them as the cause of their slide into poverty and consequently espoused strong anti-Jewish sentiments. However, the reality was more complicated. As we have seen, clergymen with extensive properties could be forced to sell their land in order to pay off debts contracted with Jewish moneylenders. Entire monastic houses, favored with royal privileges and exemptions, could fall on hard times and pawn their lands to Jews. This is precisely what happened to the monastery of Santa María de Aguilar—incidentally, one of those "elite" institutions that received a royal grant of Jewish taxes.[99] Prelates objected to the supposed violations of ecclesiastical privileges by Jewish tax collectors, and no religious institution liked to see *entregadores* of old debts to Jews enter its properties. In other words, while dissatisfaction with the operations of Jewish moneylenders and tax collectors touched every level of ecclesiastical hierarchy, the clergy had become so habituated to deriving advantage from the Jews' presence that it would require a remarkable shift in mentality for them to take an unequivocally anti-Jewish stance.

If one is looking for evidence that fanaticism and ideological rigid-

---

Church Revisited: The Episcopal *Gravamina* of 1279," in *Authority and Power: Studies on Medieval Law and Government Presented to Walter Ullmann on His Seventieth Birthday*, edited by Brian Tierney and Peter Linehan, 135–36, 146 (Cambridge: Cambridge University Press, 1980).

98. The Council of Zamora: "Item ut de cetero dignitates seu aliqua officia a regibus seu quibuscumque aliis principibus secularibus non assumant et dimittant etiam intra dictum terminum jam assumptum"; Tejada y Ramiro, ed., *Coleccion de canones*, 5:676; the Council of Valladolid: "Absurdam et irrationabilem corruptelam, quae in Christianae Fidei vergit opprobrium, et jacturam, quae contra Canonicas Sanctiones Judaei, et Sarraceni Christianis in publicis perficiuntur (*praeficiuntur*) officiis sub quorum praetextu Christianis plurimum sunt infesti, exstirpare volentes, universis Ecclesiarum Praelatis sub interminatione Divini judicii praecipimus, et mandamus, ut Sanctorum Patrum statute super hoc edita per excommunicationis sententiam, et aliarum poenarum appositionem faciant inviolabiter observari"; Tejada y Ramiro, ed., *Colección de canones*, 3:500.

99. On the royal grant of taxes from the Jews of Aguilar to Santa María de Aguilar, see Huidobro y Serna and Cantera Burgos, "Los judíos en Aguilar de Campóo," 337.

ity always prompted the clergy to spread anti-Jewish feelings throughout the entire society, Castile is not a good case study.[100] Surprisingly, it is the lay society that took the lead in attacking the Jews, leaving the ecclesiastics to emulate the strategies employed by the urban representatives at the sessions of the Castilian cortes. The local episcopate never brought forth a figure like that of Bishop Ramon Despont of Valencia, who relentlessly harangued Jewish moneylenders and threatened to tear down synagogues, and even in the church of Aragon he was a bit of a maverick.[101] The arrival in Castile of the mendicant friars in the first quarter of the thirteenth century could provide a catalyst for a change in ecclesiastical attitudes toward the Jews. In fact, it has been argued that a change was indeed afoot at this time, as Iberian cities were becoming the scene of the "increasingly vigorous" proselytizing campaign by the mendicants to convert nonbelievers to Christianity.[102] It would seem that from the practical standpoint, the friars were much better positioned to undertake such a task than the members of the older ecclesiastical institutions: the nascent mendicant communities in Castile had no longstanding economic ties with the Jews, and they were not receiving subsidies of Jewish taxes from the Crown. In fact, a historian of the Dominican order in Castile, Francisco García-Serrano, has argued that "[i]n the cities, as well as along the frontiers of the reconquista, the friars were committed to their main goal of preaching and converting non-Christians."[103] Looking for signs of this commitment is no easy task in Castile. Documentation on proselytizing activities of the friars among non-Christians in thirteenth-century Castile is lacking, rendering García-Serrano's argument largely speculative. In the absence of a better alternative, we turn to the case study of a Northern Castilian city that at the end of the century had both a significant Jewish population and a Dominican convent. A close examination of the political situation in Palencia will show why a mission to the Jews would face serious obstacles in the kingdom.

100. Amador de los Ríos, Historia social, política y religiosa de los judíos, 30.
101. Meyerson, "Bishop Ramon Despont and the Jews of the Kingdom of Valencia," Anuario de estudios medievales 29 (1999): 641–53. On the lack of "episcopal action" in the Crown of Aragon, see also Barton, Contested Treasure, 191–92.
102. Chazan, Daggers of Faith, and more recently, his Jews of Western Christendom, 1000 1500, 100–101.
103. García-Serrano, Preachers of the City, 117.

FIVE ⁓ Tamquam domino proprio

THE BISHOP AND HIS JEWS
IN MEDIEVAL PALENCIA

My focus in this chapter is the city of Palencia and the surrounding smaller municipalities, located in the Tierra de Campos region of Northern Castile-León.[1] At the end of the thirteenth century, the lords of this episcopal city faced a drawn-out jurisdictional challenge from the *concejo* (city council) regarding the extent of the bishop's seigniorial rights, which included lordship over Palencia's Jewish and Muslim *aljamas*. At the same time as the bishops were defending their episcopal patrimony against the rebellious *concejo*, the city's newly established Dominican convent was feuding with the secular clergy over lay donations. In an atmosphere of intense competition for revenues, Palencia's wealthy Jewish *aljama* was more likely to be seen as a coveted source of income than a target of missionary proselytism.

Palencia barely registers in the historiography of Jewish-Christian relations in medieval Iberia.[2] This, in itself, is a telling fact, considering that it had a significant Jewish population and was a city where St. Dominic founded, in 1219, one of the first Dominican convents in Spain. Ar-

---

1. Some of the material in this chapter previously appeared in Maya Soifer Irish, "Tamquam domino proprio," 534–66. Works on the history of Palencia in the Middle Ages include Germán Delibes de Castro, Francisco Javier Pérez Rodriguez, ed., *Historia de Palencia*, vol. 1, *De la prehistoria a la época medieval* (Palencia: Ediciones Cálamo, 2002); Julio González, *Historia de Palencia*, vol.1, *Edades antigua y media* (Palencia: Excma. Diputación Provincial de Palencia, 1984); and Julián Clemente Ramos, "Estructuras dominales castellanoleonesas: Palencia en los siglos XII y XIII," *Studia Zamorensia* 7 (1986): 433–45.

2. See, however, Amador de los Ríos, *Historia social, política, y religiosa de los judíos*, 1:341–43; León Tello, *Los judíos de Palencia*; Julio Valdeón Baruque, "Judíos y mudéjares en tierras Palentinas (siglos XIII–XV)," in *Actas del II congreso de historia de Palencia*, vol. 2, *Fuentes documentales y edad media* (Palencia: Excma. Diputación Provincial de Palencia, 1990), 359–75; Fernando Suárez Bilbao, "Algunas noticias sobre Judíos en la provincial de Palencia," in *Actas del II congreso de historia de Palencia*, 2:609–25.

cheological evidence indicates that the Jews were present in the vicinity of Palencia by the end of the eleventh century.[3] During the turbulent reign of Queen Urraca, the Jews living in the diocese of Palencia suffered assaults at the hands of local Christians. In 1127, King Alfonso VII issued a pardon to the inhabitants of Saldaña, Cea, Carrión, and several other towns, forgiving the perpetrators for killing Jews and taking their property, and accepted a fine of two silver coins from each perpetrator's household.[4] The first direct evidence that a well-established Jewish community existed in Palencia in the second half of the twelfth century comes from King Alfonso VIII's 1175 charter entrusting forty Jewish families—likely the town's entire Jewish population—to the lordship of don Raimundo, the bishop of Palencia.[5]

Very little is known about the local Jews' economic activities over the next one hundred years. Like other Jews who had migrated to Northern Castile-León from Southern Spain in order to take advantage of the economic opportunities created by the urban boom along the road to Santiago de Compostela, the Jews of Palencia must have engaged in trade. A royal charter of 1296 included Jews among the groups exempt from the payment of *portazgo*—a tax paid on goods brought within cities—throughout most of the kingdom of Castile.[6] Moneylending was also a popular pursuit among the Jews living in the towns and villages of Tierra de Campos and the nearby Burgos province. The Jews from the village of Aguilar de Campóo, north of Palencia, were well known for providing small consumption loans to Christians, who were occasionally forced to sell land and other property in order to repay their debts.[7] The Jews' credit operations in the diocese of Palencia brought them enough prosperity and notoriety to provoke a harsh response from Pope Gregory IX, who, as we know, wrote a letter in the spring of 1229 to the papal legate in

3. Gravestones with Hebrew inscriptions found in Monzón de Campos, eight miles from Palencia, date to 1097; León Tello, *Los judíos de Palencia*, 6.
4. AHN, carpeta 894, no. 3; León Tello, *Los judíos de Palencia*, 37–38.
5. DCP, 153–54.
6. AMP, Pergaminos, no. 10; Rafael del Valle Curieses, "Archivo municipal de Palencia: Privilegios y cartas reales concedidos a la ciudad en la Edad Media (regesta y comentarios)," in *Actas del I congreso de historia de Palencia*, vol. 2, *Fuentes documentales y edad media* (Palencia: Excma. Diputación Provincial de Palencia, 1985), 121.
7. AHN, clero, Palencia, Aguilar, carp. 1667, no. 14; cited in Huidobro y Serna, and Cantera, "Los judíos en Aguilar de Campóo," 338.

Spain, accusing them of extorting "immoderate usury" from Christians and violating the statutes of general councils by constructing new and expensive synagogues.[8] At the end of the thirteenth century, the *aljama* of Palencia counted among the most affluent and populous Jewish settlements in Old Castile. The royal tax records indicate that in 1290 the Jews of Palencia paid more than 33,000 *maravedís* in taxes annually, second only to the tribute collected from the Jews of Burgos and Valladolid.[9]

The size and prominence of the Palentine *aljama* and of the Jewish communities located in the surrounding towns and villages could theoretically make them a prime target of the Dominican missionizing. As Pope Gregory's letter indicates, the town was already under the radar of the reform-minded papacy, and the pontiff had grounds to entertain high hopes that his requests would be heeded in Palencia. Ecclesiastical presence was stronger in Palencia than in most other Castilian cities with a significant Jewish population. The town was the seat of the bishop of Palencia, who earlier in the century still commanded enough power and influence to question the primacy of the archbishop of Toledo in the Spanish church.[10] Not only did the bishop reside in Palencia, but also, as the town's overlord, he exercised jurisdiction over Palencia and other towns and villages of the Palentine *señorío*, appointing municipal officials and even giving the town its charter of privilege (*fuero*) in 1180.[11] Besides being the only episcopal city on the northern *meseta*, the town also had a prominent cathedral chapter whose canons were given the status of knights and enjoyed many privileges and exemptions from royal taxation.[12] In addition, Palencia was an important intellectual and theological center. The cathedral school founded there in 1184 was granted the status of a university in 1212. It was at this school that the future St. Dominic studied to become an Augustinian canon. The presence of a university was a major draw for the Dominicans.[13] In 1218–19, Dominic

---

8. RAH, ms. 9-24-5/4558, f. 194v.

9. Partición de Huete; see Hernández, *Las rentas del rey*, 1:140.

10. Juan Francisco Rivera, "Notas sobre el episcopologio palentino en los siglos XIII y XIV," *Anuario de Estudios Medievales* 9 (1974–79): 407–24.

11. González Diez, "Formacion y desarrollo del dominio señorial de la iglesia palentina," *Actas del I congreso de historia de Palencia*, 2:275–308.

12. Del Valle Curieses, "Archivo municipal de Palencia," 132.

13. Guillermo Nieva Ocampo, "Los dominicos de Castilla: La genesis de una corpo-

returned to his native kingdom and founded six Dominican houses in Castile, including the convent of San Pablo in Palencia.[14]

In reality, despite being a hub of ecclesiastical activity, proselytizing was no more likely to take place in Palencia than in any other city in Castile. The complexity of Palentine politics ensured that the local Jewish *aljama* would become contested ground in the conflict between the town's ecclesiastical and secular powers. Starting in the late twelfth century, the city was mired in a controversy that pitted the bishop of Palencia against the city's burgesses, who challenged the bishop's right to interfere in the affairs of the city council (*concejo*) and attacked the exempt status of the cathedral chapter's many members and vassals (*excusados*).[15] The dispute was not unique to Palencia. Only about forty miles away, in Sahagún, the burgesses were also engaged in a protracted battle against the seigniorial rights of the town's ecclesiastical lord, the bishop of the monastery of San Benito.[16] Throughout it all, the revenues from the Jewish community of Palencia consistently remained one of the bishop's most coveted possessions, as both the city council and the Crown tried to wrest them away from ecclesiastical control. Thus, it was the Jews' taxation—not their salvation—that seemed to occupy the attention of the city's elites.

The Jewish *aljama* was first thrust into the controversy in 1192, when King Alfonso VIII acquiesced to the demands of the *concejo* and rescinded the Jews' earlier privilege (1177) that had exempted them from the *fonsadera* (a tax paid in lieu of military obligation) and other royal taxes. Now the city's religious minorities had to join the burgesses in the payment of these taxes, as well as to contribute to the maintenance of the city's

---

ración privilegiada en la baja edad media," in *Servir a Dios y servir al Rey: el mundo de los privilegiados en el ámbito hispánico, ss. XIII–XVIII*, edited by Guillermo Nieva Ocampo, Silvano G. A. Benito Moya, and Andrea Navarro, 22 (Salta: Mundo Editorial, 2011).

14. García-Serrano, *Preachers of the City*, 25–26.

15. María Asunción Esteban Recio, *Palencia a fines de la edad media: Una ciudad de señorío episcopal* (Valladolid: Universidad de Valladolid, 1989), 127–29.

16. Gautier-Dalché, *Historia urbana*, 214–21; José M. Fernández del Pozo, "Razones económicas de un conflicto en el Camino de Santiago," in *El Camino de Santiago: La hospitalidad monástica y las peregrinaciones*, edited by Horacio Santiago-Otero, 211–16 (Valladolid: Junta de Castilla y León, 1992). Jurisdictional disputes between citizens and lords of towns were not unique to Castile; see, for example, Barton, "Jurisdictional Conflict, Strategies of Litigation and Mechanisms of Compromise in Thirteenth-Century Tortosa," *Recerca* 14 (2012): 201–48.

fortifications.[17] The king's "compromise" created a situation fraught with tension. With the *concejo* in a state of almost constant rebellion against the bishop, refusing to pay him homage on many occasions, it was only a matter of time before the members of the council would attempt to challenge the bishop's right to collect taxes from Jews and Muslims.[18] A good opportunity finally arrived in 1282, when the bishop of Palencia, don Juan Alfonso, decided to abandon the camp of King Alfonso X and join his rebellious son, Sancho. Both sides had something to gain from the alliance. Juan Alfonso hoped that the new king would be more sympathetic to his interests in the ongoing conflict with the *concejo*. Sancho needed the bishop's political and financial support.[19] Apparently it was at this point in time that Juan Alfonso and the Infante came to an agreement that each would receive one-half of the *pechos* from the Jews and Muslims of Palencia. In addition, Sancho confirmed the bishop's lordship over the city and granted him further privileges.[20]

The king's fateful decision to divide Jewish and Muslim *pechos* between the bishop and the Crown fueled the *concejo*'s ambitions for a royal takeover of the *aljamas* and even created some doubts in the king's own mind. Did not the bishop's claim to the *aljamas* somehow violate the royal prerogative? After 1282, Sancho vacillated between confirming the bishop's rights over Palencia's religious minorities and invalidating any of the bishop's letters of privilege that infringed on the rights of the *concejo*.[21]

17. AMP, *Pergaminos*, no. 2; Baer, *Die Juden*, 2:22.
18. González Diez, "Formacion y desarrollo del dominio señorial de la iglesia Palentina," 303–4; Gautier-Dalché, *Historia urbana*, 285–87.
19. Nieto Soria, *Iglesia y poder real en Castilla*, 176–77.
20. The concession most insulting to the *concejo* was the bishop's right to name the *alcaldes* of the Hermandad; see Esteban Recio, *Palencia a fines de la edad media*, 156.
21. During the cortes in Palencia in 1286, the council's representatives apparently did their best to stoke the monarch's regalian ego until they persuaded him to defend the royal rights being usurped by the cunning bishop. In January 1287, Sancho sent a charter to the *concejo*, asserting that it was never his intention to diminish the rights of the Crown or of the *concejo* by giving the bishop his privileges. The letter stopped just short of revoking the bishop's lordship over the *judería* and *morería* of Palencia, but it asserted that the *concejo*'s share in the Jewish and Muslim taxes was not to be denied. If any of the bishop's letters of privilege, including those concerning Jews and Muslims, infringed on the Crown's or the council's rights, they were declared invalid; AMP, *Pergaminos*, no. 13; Gaibrois de Ballesteros, *Historia de reinado de Sancho IV de Castilla*, 3:89; Esteban Recio, *Palencia a fines de la edad media*, 158. The bishop complained, and a royal investigation concluded that the bishop and his successors could enjoy half of the Jewish and Muslim *pechos* "completely" (*conplidamientre*). In addition,

A new opportunity for the city council to advance its agenda arrived in 1296. By then Castile had an underage king, Fernando IV, whose rights to the throne were being disputed by the Infantes Juan and Alfonso de la Cerda. The city of Palencia lay in the middle of the war zone, and its support was of crucial importance to the young king and María de Molina, his mother and regent. Although both the *concejo* and the cathedral chapter came out on the king's side, it was the *concejo* that could mobilize the *vecinos* to fight on the king's behalf.[22] After the city's military brigade had captured the castle of Tariego, at the end of June 1296 the grateful monarch and his council showered the *concejo* of Palencia with favors, giving the city new landholdings and tax exemptions and confirming its old privileges, even if they trumped those of the bishop.[23]

However, the city council was unable to capitalize on its gains. A few months before these events, the relations between the bishop and the *concejo* had reached a nadir when the men of the council and their followers assassinated the bishop's *merino* and several servitors of the cathedral chapter and burned a tower belonging to the bishop.[24] The council secured a royal pardon, but Palencia's Dominican bishop, Fray Munio, worried about the possible implications of the *concejo*'s newly found favor with the king, insisted that his privileges, in turn, be confirmed. On August 9, 1296, about a month after the men of the *concejo* had left Valladolid in triumph carrying a new royal charter, the king's chancery issued a proclamation admonishing the council to respect the bishop's rights. The Jews were still the bishop's, just as they had been in the past.[25]

To no one's surprise, the royal decision failed to satisfy the recalcitrant *concejo*. In 1297, after Pope Boniface VIII had forced Fray Munio to resign from his post for committing an unspecified "iniquity," the *concejo* refused to pay homage to the new bishop, Alvaro Carillo, and another

---

Muslims and Jews had to pay their taxes separately from the council, with the exception of their contributions to communal works (*fazenderas*); ACP, no. 335; described in León Tello, *Los judíos de Palencia*, 104.

22. Esteban Recio, *Palencia a fines de la edad media*, 160–61.

23. AMP, *Pergaminos*, nos. 8, 9, and 10; described in León Tello, *Los judíos de Palencia*, 105–106; del Valle Curieses, "Archivo municipal de Palencia," 121–22; AMP, *Pergaminos*, no. 13; described in León Tello, *Los judíos de Palencia*, 106; del Valle Curieses, "Archivo municipal de Palencia," 122–23.

24. Esteban Recio, *Palencia a fines de la edad media*, 161.

25. ACP, no. 339; Leon Tello, *Los judíos de Palencia*, 43–44.

round of conflict and litigation ensued.[26] In May 1298, representatives of the *concejo* were summoned to the royal court in Valladolid to answer the charges brought against them by the bishop. Throughout the hearing, the men of the council of Palencia maintained an assertive attitude, reminding the king of the services the *concejo* had rendered him in the past. The king's and the council's interests were linked, the representatives suggested, as evidenced by the many charters of privilege received by the *concejo*. When asked if the bishop's allegation that the council had been collecting the taxes of Jews and Muslims for the past three years was true, the representatives made no effort to deny it. On the contrary, they argued that the royal privileges allowed them to collect *pechos* from all the Jews and Muslims who qualified as *vecinos* of Palencia.[27]

The representatives' argument at the royal court was an admirable exercise in rhetoric, but it soon became clear that the *concejo's* finest hour had passed. Fernando IV and his regents finally decided that the royal power in Palencia was better represented by the bishop than by the unruly *vecinos*. Bishop Alvaro, who happened to be the king's relative, moved quickly to consolidate his power in the city.[28] When the royal court issued a judgment in the bishop's case in January 1300, it was not favorable to the council. In fact, the bishop had all of his wishes and demands granted. The *concejo* was ordered to desist from interfering with the bishop's right to appoint *alcaldes*, to select *excusados*, and to collect various taxes, among them the *pechos* of Jews and Muslims. Moreover, the *vecinos* had to restore the bishop's burned tower and to beg forgiveness from their lord in a public procession.[29]

26. Sancho IV's pivotal role in the election of Fray Munio is the reason most often cited; see Rivera, "Notas sobre el episcopologio Palentino," 418; Alvarez Reyero, *Crónicas episcopales palentinas*, 115–16. Linehan thinks that Fray Munio was the same person as "Munio of Zamora," who was involved in the sexual scandal more than a decade earlier at the convent of S. María de Zamora; see his *The Spanish Church and the Papacy*, 224–25, or his *The Ladies of Zamora* (Manchester: Manchester University Press, 1997); see also Esteban Recio, *Palencia a fines de la edad media*, 162.

27. "Et alo otro que nos preguntados ssi tomamos el pecho delos moros e delos judios a esto uos dezimos que nos que non leuamos dellos pecho ninguno ssaluo ende que [unless] nos ffazen vesindat segund quelo auemos por priuilegios delos reyes por que non deuen pechar nin ffazer tributo apartado ssinon con el conçeio de Palencia"; AMP, Pergaminos, no. 39; described in León Tello, *Los judíos de Palencia*, 107.

28. Nieto Soria, *Iglesia y poder real en Castilla*, 179–80.

29. "Et lo que mandamos sobrello es esto que en esta carta sera dicho, quelo que pidio

As one might have expected, this court decision did not put an end to the *concejo*'s fight against the bishop's seigniorial power in the city of Palencia. In late 1300 there was another violent confrontation as the representatives of the council threatened to assassinate the bishop and his entourage during a meeting after the bishop had named the *alcaldes* without consulting the council.[30] If the *concejo* never again obtained a royal decision favorable to them on the issue of Jewish and Muslim *pechos*, it was not for lack of trying. In 1305, they made another attempt, urging the monarch to protect royal prerogatives. According to the letter Fernando IV later sent to the bishop, "when we were in Palencia ... some men told us that the Jews and Moors of this place were ours, as were the Jews and Moors who live in other towns and villages of our domain." The king was easily persuaded and issued an order to "take" some of the Jews in the belief that they were his. Bishop Don Alvaro quickly registered his protest, and the king was made to realize his "mistake." Fernando dispatched a new confirmation of the bishop's privileges, which reaffirmed Alvaro's dominion over Palencia's religious minorities. Echoing King Alfonso VIII's original donation, the charter stated that the Jews and Muslims had to answer to the bishop "as to their own lord."[31] No other lord—not even the king—had the right to retain them in his service. The only valid claim the king had in the Jewish and Muslims communities of Palencia had been spelled out in the agreement between King Sancho and Bishop Juan Alfonso, and that was the right to collect one half of all the Jewish and Muslims taxes.[32] The bishop and the cathedral chapter could enjoy the other half. Fernando's charter thus was a deliberate attempt to recreate as closely as possible the situation as it had existed at the end of the twelfth century. It was as if the intervening years of complex negotiations and battling charters were erased from memory.

---

el obispo que le diessedes vos el conçeio la martiniega et que le dexassedes los moros et los judios commo los ouieren los otros obispos en tiempo del rey don Sancho et que le dexassedes fazer los alcalles de la villa et los escriuanos et tomar los escusados a el e alas personas et canonigos de su eglesia et que le desenbargasedes el portazgo commo dizen las cartas de la conpusiçion que auedes en vno, la vna mia et la otra del rey don Sancho mio padre que fue fecha en Çamora"; ACP, no. 344; León Tello, *Los judíos de Palencia*, 45–48.

30. Esteban Recio, *Palencia a fines de la edad media*, 163–64.

31. "Commo a su sennor propio"; the 1177 charter used the formula "tamquam domino proprio."

32. ACP, no. 348; León Tello, *Los judíos de Palencia*, 107.

The events of 1305 show that the conflict between the two main players—the bishop and the *concejo*—went beyond one town's struggle for political autonomy. It touched on such a pivotal issue for the monarchy as the Crown's jurisdiction over the Jews of Castile. At a time when the flow of taxes to the royal treasury was diminishing, any exceptions to the *servi regis* principle, such as the bishop of Palencia's lordship over the Jews and Muslims in his city, were damaging to the monarchy's interests. This was likely the essence of the argument made by the *vecinos* of Palencia in an attempt to persuade the king to take a stronger stance in protecting the interests of the Crown. The fact that they almost succeeded further underscores the point. Fernando's purported lack of knowledge regarding the situation of the Jews and Muslims in Palencia belies the fact that only several years earlier his chancery had produced a sentence confirming the bishop's rights. Perhaps the king was led to believe that as long as he received half of the *pechos* from the *aljamas* of Palencia, he had jurisdiction over half of their inhabitants. It is also plausible that the king welcomed the opportunity to claim these taxes for the royal treasury, as his father had attempted to do earlier, and only the strong objections from Bishop Alvaro, an important ally, stayed his hand.

The episode also raises intriguing questions about the group whose interests and concerns were never registered in the script of the ongoing drama—the Jews of Palencia. There are reasons to believe that they would have welcomed an opportunity to shed the bishop's lordship in favor of the king's. Indeed, when "some men" suggested to King Fernando that the Jews and Moors of Palencia were "his," a group of Jews—but not of Muslims—immediately materialized under the leadership of Çag Nihoray to accept the king's protection. One wonders if they acted according to a prior agreement between them and some *vecinos*. When fifty years prior to these events in Palencia the Christian burgesses of Sahagún rebelled against their ecclesiastical lord, the abbot of San Benito de Sahagún, the Jews there also sided with the *concejo*.[33] There is no evidence

---

33. See chapter 6. See also the case of the Jews of Albelda (1285, 1292), who preferred the king's jurisdiction to that of the bishop of Calahorra; Baer, *Die Juden*, 2:74–76; Nieto Soria, "Los Judíos como conflicto jurisdiccional," 247. On the Jews' support of the Christian citizens of Tortosa against their lords (the Templars and the Montcada family), see Barton, *Contested Treasure*, 113.

to suggest that having a religious dignitary for a lord made the Jews an enhanced target of discriminatory treatment.[34] It is likely, however, that ecclesiastical Jews had considerably less leeway in the matters of self-rule than the royal *aljamas*. As we are going to see, the Jews of Sahagún complained about the lack of communal autonomy, and a similar situation probably existed in Palencia, as well. In addition, the Jews of Palencia had good reasons to be unhappy about the double burden of taxation imposed on their community. Alfonso VIII's 1192 charter in effect split the authority over Jews and Muslims between the *concejo* and the bishop, ordering religious minorities to pay taxes to both the king and their immediate overlord. It is not beyond the realm of possibility that the Palentine Jews worked behind the scenes with the Christian *vecinos* to be removed from the bishop's lordship and placed under the royal jurisdiction.[35]

The bishop's struggle tested the limits of the Crown's willingness to tolerate ecclesiastical jurisdiction over the Jewish *servi* of the king. The bishop had to depend for confirmation of his privileges on the very sovereign who counted income from the Jewish *aljamas* among one of his largest and most reliable sources of revenue.[36] Even though the bishop was able to prevail in the last round of the town council's challenge to his authority, the king's eagerness to accept the argument that Palencia's Jews and Muslims were "his," after decades of contentiousness that produced

---

34. Paul Freedman found that, in general, ecclesiastical style of lordship was very similar to the lay one; see his *Origins of Peasant Servitude*, 142–43.

35. In 1300, representatives of the *concejo* wanted Jews and Muslims to participate in the communal restitution to the bishop for burning his tower, "because the evil deed was done by all," but Fernando turned down their request; ACP, no. 344. Contrary to what Amador de los Ríos has claimed, there is no evidence that the Jews took part in the assault on the tower. His claim is probably based on an erroneous interpretation of one sentence in Fernando IV's August 1296 letter to the bishop: "Otorgo que por los priuilegios que yo di al concejo de Palencia et las mercedes queles fiz en razon delos judios et del perdonamiento dela Torre del Obispo que fue de maestre Andres *que ellos quemaron* et delos omnes del Obispo *que y mataron*" [emphasis added]. The letter refers to the members of the council, not to the Jews; ACP, no. 339.

36. In 1311, Bishop Gerardo, don Alvaro's successor, found himself in a difficult situation with the *vecinos* and was forced to ask Fernando IV for a new confirmation of his privileges, including the right to collect one half of the Jewish and Muslim taxes; ACP, no. 367; León Tello, *Los judíos de Palencia*, 108; Esteban Recio, *Palencia a fines de la edad media*, 165. As far as one can tell from the evidence, there was no other serious attempt to dispute the bishop's right of jurisdiction over the *aljamas* of Palencia.

numerous royal charters affirming the opposite, highlights the precariousness of the bishop's seigniorial rights over the town's religious minorities. Everyone involved in the dispute seemed to recognize that the bishop's status as the Jews' and Muslims' overlord was an anomaly in the kingdom of Castile, revocable at the king's will. Indeed, by the last quarter of the thirteenth century, King Alfonso X had taken from the abbot of Sahagún his authority over the local Jewish *aljama* along with the right to collect tribute from them.[37] The bishops of Palencia spent decades defending their privileges from the unruly *concejo* and the king, whose support for Palencia's prelates was checkered and halfhearted.

As the seemingly interminable conflict dragged on, the conversion of the Jews was probably the furthest thing from everyone's mind. After all, the parties involved in the dispute had a vested interest in letting the Palentine Jews remain Jews. Only the friars of the Dominican convent of San Pablo, relative newcomers to the city, could realistically entertain such hopes, having no privileges or money to lose in the event of the Jews' conversion. But even if the friars had intended to preach to the Jews, it is difficult to see how they could carry out their plans. Suffice it to say that the Jews remained under the bishop's jurisdiction, and the bishop was no friend of the Dominicans, as evidenced by the fact that the friars had to wage a battle of their own with the bishop and the rest of Palencia's ecclesiastical establishment. A major controversy had unfolded in the 1240s and 1250s after Pope Innocent IV authorized the Dominicans to have conventual churches, thus channeling away donations that otherwise would go to the parish churches and the cathedral. At one point, the bishop excommunicated the Dominicans of Palencia for their failure to pay fines.[38] For several decades, the Dominicans struggled to overcome a bitter opposition from the secular clergy over lay donations.[39] The reconciliation finally came in 1294, when the Dominican Fray Munio of Zamora became the bishop of Palencia.[40]

37. See chapter 6.

38. García-Serrano, *Preachers of the City*, 62.

39. On the arrival of the mendicant orders in Castile, see also Teofilio Ruiz, *From Heaven to Earth: The Reordering of Castilian Society, 1150–1350* (Princeton University Press, 2002), 25–26.

40. Fray Munio, however, was soon removed by Pope Boniface VIII; see García-Serrano, *Preachers of the City*, 40; Francisco Rivera, "Notas sobre el episcopologio Palentino," 418.

The city's tense political landscape was thus hardly propitious for proselytism among the Jews. How much one can extrapolate from Palencia's case is a matter of conjecture. One suspects, however, that the task of pursuing converts among the Jews would run into similar difficulties in other towns, in both Castile and Aragon. The crucial decades between 1240 and 1270, which supposedly saw an intensification of the friars' proselytizing campaign among the Spanish Jews, was the time when the newly arrived mendicant orders faced fierce opposition from the elite and secular clergy.[41] Peter Linehan has vividly described the smoldering tensions between the Dominicans of Burgos and the local cathedral chapter.[42] Robin Vose has argued that "the mid-thirteenth century was a crucial period for the Dominican Order in the Crown of Aragon—a time in which friars struggled to establish a viable place for themselves in various cities of the realm and stretched their human resources to the limit by founding a whole series of new convents."[43] His observation is also true for Castile. It may be that the friars were too preoccupied with establishing their presence in Castilian towns and attending to the spiritual needs of the townspeople to pay much attention to the Jews. Besides, almost anywhere the friars went they were likely to encounter a Jewish community bound by ties of financial obligation to a monastery, a cathedral chapter, a bishopric, or, in most cases, to the Castilian Crown itself. The friars would have to risk impinging on many privileges and claims of jurisdiction in order to proselytize among the Jews.

Thanks to the patronage of the king and the nobility, the mendicant orders were remarkably successful at quickly becoming a part of the Castilian ecclesiastical hierarchy.[44] It did not take very long for the friars to gain popularity and influence at the royal court. In the mid-1260s, Alfonso X was openly professing his admiration for the mendicant fri-

---

41. García-Serrano, *Preachers of the City*, 81; Chazan, *Daggers of Faith*, 3.

42. Peter Linehan, "A Tale of Two Cities: Capitular Burgos and Mendicant Burgos in the Thirteenth Century," in *Church and City: Essays in Honour of Christopher Brooke*, edited by David Abulafia, Michael J. Franklin, and Miri Rubin, 81–110 (Cambridge: Cambridge University Press, 1992).

43. Vose, *Dominicans, Muslims and Jews*, 137.

44. On the royal patronage of the Dominican Order in Castile, see Nieva Ocampo, "Los dominicos de Castilla," 21–41.

45. Linehan, *The Spanish Church and the Papacy*, 222.

ars.[45] His son and successor, King Sancho, was particularly close with the Dominicans, appointing Friar Munio of Zamora to the bishopric of Palencia against the pope's wishes. Soon, they began to reap the benefits of their lucrative situation, which included large monetary donations from the royal *aljamas*. In 1308, King Fernando IV assigned 800 *maravedís* to the Dominicans of Toro from the revenues of the *judería* of that town.[46] Mendicants had the ear of the Castilian monarchs, but showed no apparent interest in using their influence to mount a missionizing campaign directed at the Jews. The Biblioteca Nacional preserves a curious document—a 1344 agreement between the Dominicans and the Franciscans of Toro regarding the appropriate times and places for preaching, probably intended to avert potential conflicts between the two orders. The document includes a long list of churches and other locations where the friars are expected to preach. Predictably, there is no mention of the town's *judería*, synagogue, or the Jews.[47]

A reasonable objection can be raised that not enough evidence survives from Castile to determine the full extent of the friars' conversionary preaching among the Jews. There were almost certainly individual preachers, some of whom may have been mendicants, who made earnest attempts to convert the Jews, but their efforts did not leave any trace in the records. Yet even in the much-better-documented Crown of Aragon there is little evidence of a sustained drive by the Dominicans to proselytize among Jews and Muslims. Vose has questioned the notion that the Barcelona Disputation of 1263, instigated by the learned Dominican friar Raymond Penyafort and inspired by a convert's zeal of a former rabbinical student, Pablo Christiani, was only "the tip of an iceberg of widespread missionary work."[48] In 1242, King James I of Aragon passed an edict that expressed support for mendicant proselytizing and ordered Jews and Muslims to attend the friars' sermons. The order was reissued in 1263, but in response to the complaints from the Jewish communities, the Aragonese rulers subsequently tempered its effects by stipulating that the Jews could not be forced to attend the sermons and forbidding the friars to enter synagogues with large retinues. Partly because of the

46. Baer, *Die Juden*, 2:114.
47. BN, mss 11170, f. 30–33.
48. Vose, *Dominicans, Muslims and Jews*, 134.

kings' protective measures and partly because the friars were mainly occupied with instructing Christians in the orthodox doctrines, by the end of the thirteenth century the missionizing efforts in Aragon had stalled. Moreover, the preaching episodes that did take place appear to have been special initiatives of a few enterprising individuals, rather than a strategy systematically employed by the Dominican order as a whole.[49]

Postscript

In the late 1370s, the Jewish *aljama* of Seville complained to the king that there was a preacher in their town whose inflammatory sermons were inciting the populace to attack the Jews. This cleric was claiming that he would help defend any Christian who wounded or killed a Jew and that the king and queen would be amenable to pardoning the attacker. He also sent letters to the city councils in Alcalá de Guadaíra and other towns in the diocese of Seville, threatening them with excommunication if they allowed Jews to live among Christians and have any business or social relations with them. This man was no ordinary priest: he was Ferrán Martínez, canon at the Cathedral Chapter of Seville, archdeacon of Écija, and vicar of the archbishop of Seville. In response to the Jews' complaints, kings Enrique II and Juan I both wrote letters to the members of the city council that urged them to protect the royal Jews, but no effective measures were taken, and Martínez was allowed to continue his preaching campaign.[50] After King Juan and the archbishop of Seville died within a few months of each other in 1390, Martínez sent orders to the clergy of several towns in the diocese to demolish the "illegally" built synagogues in their communities. Some of them complied, and a number of synagogues were destroyed.[51] Greatly perturbed by these events, in January 1391 the regents for the child-king Enrique III threatened to hold

49. Ibid., 135–63.

50. The royal letters are preserved in AHN, sección clero, Toledo, catedral, carp. 7215 (previously 7218), no. 1–7; they were published by Amador de los Ríos, *Historia social, política y religiosa de los judíos*, 2:579–89.

51. Martínez's order to demolish the synagogues is discussed in the letter by Pedro Tenorio, archbishop of Toledo, to the clergy of Écija, and in their reply to the archbishop (1396); Martinez's order to the clergy of Santa Olalla is enclosed; AHN, sección clero, Toledo, catedral, leg. 7215 (7218), leg. 634; Amador de los Ríos, *Historia social, política y religiosa de los judíos*, 2:610–14.

the Cathedral Chapter financially responsible for any attack on the Jews if they did not restrain Martínez.[52] But by then it was probably already too late. In March of 1391, the people nearly assaulted the Jewish quarter in Seville. On June 6, the riot began anew, leaving hundreds of Jews dead and many more forcibly converted to Christianity.[53] From Seville, the violence spread to Cordoba and Toledo and then into the lands of the Crown of Aragon. The deaths and conversions of so many Jews permanently altered the physical and spiritual landscape of Jewish life in Spain.[54]

In the histories that attempt to explain the massacres of 1391, Ferrán Martínez is often presented as an archetype of the Christian preacher whose charismatic sermons helped translate the audience's inchoate anti-Jewish attitudes into violent action.[55] We should not forget, however, that Martínez was an exceptional figure among the Castilian clergy, and his decision to take a sweeping action against the Jews in the diocese of Seville had no precedent in the history of the relations between the Castilian church and the Jews. It is true that his anti-Judaism, though particularly intransigent, was not unusual in late fourteenth-century Castile. The archdeacon's mature years coincided with the Civil War of the 1360s, when Enrique Trastámara openly used anti-Jewish propaganda in his bid for the Castilian throne.[56] The anti-Jewish discourse at the cortes hardened significantly during those years, and even King Juan I called the Jews "bad

---

52. BN (Burriel), mss. 13089, f. 78; Henry Charles Lea, "Acta Capitular del Cabildo de Sevilla," *American Historical Review* 1, no. 2 (1896): 220–25.

53. Pero López de Ayala, *Crónicas*, ed. José-Luis Martín (Barcelona: Planeta, 1991), 713, 738–39.

54. On the pogroms of 1391, see Lea, "Ferrand Martinez and the Massacres of 1391," *American Historical Review* 1, no. 2 (1896): 209–19; Philippe Wolff, "The 1391 Pogrom in Spain: Social Crisis or Not?" *Past and Present* 50 (1971): 4–18; Benzion Netanyahu, *The Origins of the Inquisition in Fifteenth Century Spain* (New York: Random House, 1995), 127–83; Benjamin Gampel, "'Unless the Lord Watches Over the City': Joan of Aragon and His Jews, June–October 1391," in *New Perspectives on Jewish-Christian Relations: In Honor of David Berger*, edited by Elisheva Carlebach and Jacob Schacter, 65–89 (Leiden: Brill, 2012); Isabel Montes Romero-Camacho, "Antisemitismo sevillano en la baja edad media: El pogrom de 1391 y sus consecuencias," in *Actas del III colloquio de historia medieval andaluza: La sociedad medieval andaluza; Grupos no privilegiados* (Jaén: Duputación Provincial de Jaén, 1984), 57–75.

55. Montes Romero-Camacho, "Las minorías étnico-religiosas en la Sevilla del siglo XIV: Mudéjares y judíos," in *Sevilla, siglo XIV*, edited by Rafael Valencia, 149 (Seville: Fundación José Manuel Lara, 2006); Emilio Mitre Fernández, *Los judíos de Castilla en tiempo de Enrique III: El pogrom de 1391* (Valladolid: Universidad de Valladolid, 1994), 36.

56. See chapter 8.

and wicked" in his correspondence with the Cathedral Chapter of Seville in 1388.[57] That said, Martínez's hard-line measures throw into sharp relief the inertia of the kingdom's ecclesiastical authorities. In justifying his actions and opinions at the Tribunal del Alcázar in Seville in February 1388, the archdeacon repeatedly stressed his intention to enforce the existing secular and ecclesiastical legislation on the Jews. That the Jews were allowed to mingle with Christians and build new synagogues without any authorization was "against God and law" (*contra Dios é contra la ley*), Martínez claimed, undoubtedly referring to the conciliar legislation and secular laws like *Las siete partidas* (officially promulgated in 1348).[58] In other words, Martínez was trying to accomplish in his diocese what the church and the king had been unwilling to do in the kingdom as a whole. Alone (as far as we know) among the Castilian priesthood, the archdeacon challenged the Crown's traditional monopoly on the Jews and even circumvented his ecclesiastical superiors, earning several reprimands from the king and incurring an investigation into his views and activities by the office of Pedro Gomez Barroso, archbishop of Seville.[59]

In essence, Ferrán Martínez's campaign in the diocese of Seville challenged the very legitimacy of the Jews' place in the medieval Castilian political order, in which the king controlled the Jews, and the church generally acquiesced to this arrangement. It set in motion a chain of events that had disastrous consequences for the Jewish communities in Castile and Aragon. However, the role played in the pogroms of 1391 by the infamous Castilian clergyman should not obscure the fact that the Castilian church generally lagged behind the rest of society in building a coherent anti-Jewish discourse. When a forceful argumentation against Jewish moneylenders and tax collectors made its appearance in Castile, it did not come from the church. At the meetings of the kingdom's representative assembly, the cortes, urban procurators used their forum to mold disparate grievances of lay townspeople into an enduring and virulent anti-Jewish discourse. It was this discourse that ultimately paved the way for Ferrán Martínez and the great catastrophe of Spanish Jewry.

57. Diego Ortiz de Zuñiga, *Análes eclesiasticos y seculares* (Madrid: 1795), 2:230.
58. AHN, sección clero, Toledo, catedral, carp. 7215 (7218), no. 7; Amador de los Ríos, *Historia de los judíos*, 2:588–89.
59. Amador de los Ríos, *Historia de los judíos*, 2:592–94.

PART 3

Jews and Christians in Northern Castile

(CA. 1250–CA. 1370)

SIX ∾ The Jews of Castile at the End of the *Reconquista* (Post-1250)

CULTURAL AND COMMUNAL LIFE

By the middle of the thirteenth century, the successes of Christian armies against the Almohads in Andalusia marked the beginning of a new era in the history of Castile and its Jewish minority. After the victory at Las Navas de Tolosa (1212) and the capture of Córdoba (1236) and Seville (1248) by Fernando III, the military frontier moved farther south, beyond the Guadalquivir Valley. With the remaining Muslim kingdom of Granada now under the Castilian protectorate, the most active phase of the reconquest came to an end.[1] For the Jews of Castile, the Christian colonization of Andalusia meant, first and foremost, the opening up of new settlement opportunities in the south. The frequent appearance of Jewish names in the *Libros de Repartimiento* (land registers) indicates a deliberate royal policy to attract Jews to the new Andalusian frontier. Jewish notables and officials at the royal court, many of them from Toledo, received significant land holdings in southern Castile.[2] Among the new Jewish settlements in Christian Andalusia, the *aljama* of Seville underwent a particularly rapid growth, eclipsing most older centers and by the end of the century becoming the second-largest Jewish community in Castile (after Toledo).[3]

As for the earlier period, documentation that would shed light on the inner life of Jewish communities is scarce for Toledo and virtually non-

1. González Jiménez, "Frontier and Settlement in the Kingdom of Castile," 64–67.
2. Ray, *Sephardic Frontier*, 20.
3. Ibid.; Montes Romero-Camacho, "La aljama judía de Sevilla en la baja edad media," in *El Patrimonio hebreo en la España medieval*, edited by Alberto Villar Movellán and María del Rosario Castro Castillo, esp. 25–29 (Cordoba: Universidad de Cordoba, 2004); Wiebke Deimann, *Christen, Juden und Muslime im mittelalterlichen Sevilla* (Münster: Lit, 2012), 175–206.

existent for Northern Castile. Enough information can be culled from various sources, however, to surmise that Jewish life in the region was undergoing major changes between the mid-thirteenth century and the first decade of the fourteenth century. The transformations in cultural and religious life are the most apparent. During this period, the Castilian Jewry began to pull away from its Andalusian heritage and to be drawn into the European cultural orbit—Ashkenazi Jewish as well as Christian. By the middle of the century, a distinctive mystical tradition, the Kabbalah, had emerged in Castile and Aragon in response to Maimonidean rationalism. In the 1290s, Moses de León and a group of kabbalists based in Toledo and Northern Castile produced the most influential work of medieval Castilian mysticism—the Zohar (The Book of Splendor). Other developments are much harder to trace. Scholars of Jewish communities in Castile and the better-documented Crown of Aragon have argued that factionalism and social tensions intensified within the aljamas in the thirteenth century. The evidence is more conclusive for Aragon, but there was at least one attempt to institute communal reforms in Toledo. Finally, the trend toward a tighter control of Jewish communal affairs by the monarchy accelerated in both kingdoms. The royal interference strengthened the aljamas' autonomy and was generally welcomed by the Jews themselves, but in the long run it was not without negative economic and political consequences, which will be addressed in chapter 7.

Describing the cultural landscape of Jewish communities in Castile and Catalonia in the first half of the thirteenth century, Bernard Septimus speaks of "the increasing detachment of Spain from the Islamic world and its new attachment to Europe."[4] In Castile, he associates the beginning of this cultural shift with the career of Rabbi Meir ha-Levi Abulafia (ca. 1165–1244), also known by his Hebrew acronym the Ramah, a major Talmudist and halakhic authority, and for several decades the leader of the Jewish community in Toledo. Born in Burgos, R. Abulafia moved to Toledo as a young man but maintained close ties to his native city and the family members he left behind.[5] He belonged to one of the old upper-class families whose members had ruled the Jewish commu-

---

4. Septimus, Hispano-Jewish Culture in Transition, 39.
5. Ibid., 7–9.

nity of Toledo for generations and served at the Castilian royal court as *almojarifes*, physicians, and diplomats.⁶ Unlike their counterparts in Catalonia, the *nesi'im* of Barcelona, however, R. Abulafia's circle viewed the rationalism of Moses Maimonides with some suspicion and emphasized the primacy of Torah study over the "foreign wisdom"—philosophy. After Maimonides's *Mishneh Torah* first became known to the European Jews in the 1190s, this "philosophically knowledgeable anti-rationalism" led R. Abulafia to seek allies among the French Tosafists against Maimonides's nontraditional stance on the bodily resurrection of the dead (before the sage clarified his position in *Treatise on Resurrection*).⁷

The Castilian Jews' reorientation toward the Franco-German *halakhic* tradition was a slow process that continued throughout the thirteenth and into the fourteenth century.⁸ In the 1230s, the controversy over the works of Maimonides broke out in earnest in Provence and Spain. The *nesi'im* of Barcelona sided with the rationalists in Provence, while the group challenging their rule, whose principal leaders were R. Moses ben Nahman (Nahmanides) (1194–1270) and R. Jonah Gerondi (c. 1200–63), supported the anti-rationalist camp of R. Solomon ben Abraham of Montpellier.⁹ Both sides appealed to the Jewish leadership in Burgos and Toledo for support, but even though R. Abulafia refused to organize a joint effort with the anti-rationalists, neither did he support the rationalists' excommunication (*herem*) of R. Solomon. When R. David Kimhi, a respected Provencal

6. Elka Klein, when describing the *nesi'im* of Barcelona, gives convincing reasons that they should not be called an "aristocracy," or a "courtier class." I believe her argument is valid for Castile, as well; see Klein, *Jews, Christian Society, and Royal Power in Medieval Barcelona* (Ann Arbor: University of Michigan Press, 2006), 53, 85.

7. Septimus, *Hispano-Jewish Culture in Transition*, 48, 62. On the Tosafists (Talmudic scholars in France and Germany who created "additions," *tosafot*, to Rashi's glossaries on the Talmud) see, for example, Avraham (Rami) Reiner, "From Rabbenu Tam to R. Isaac of Vienna: The Hegemony of the French Talmudic School in the Twelfth Century," in *The Jews of Europe in the Middle Ages*, edited by Christoph Cluse, 273–82.

8. Abraham Grossman, "Relations between Spanish and Ashkenazi Jewry in the Middle Ages," in *Moreshet Sepharad: The Sephardi Legacy*, edited by Haim Beinart, 1:220–39 (Jerusalem: Hebrew University Press, 1992).

9. The literature on the Maimonidean controversy is extensive; see, for example, Daniel Jeremy Silver, *Maimonidean Criticism and the Maimonidean Controversy, 1180–1240* (Leiden: Brill, 1965), and Septimus, "Piety and Power in Thirteenth-Century Catalonia," in *Studies in Medieval Jewish History and Literature*, edited by Isadore Twersky, 1:197–230 (Cambridge, Mass.: Harvard University Press, 1979). On Nahmanides, see among others, Nina Caputo, *Nahmanides in Medieval Catalonia*; Isadore Twersky, ed., *Rabbi Moses Nahmanides (Ramban): Explorations in His Religious and Literary Virtuosity* (Cambridge, Mass.: Harvard University Press, 1983).

rationalist scholar, came to Toledo and Burgos to muster support for the *herem*, the local leaders, convinced of the corrosive effects of rationalism, gave him a cold reception. R. Abulafia's brother, who was living in Burgos, even had R. Kimhi expelled from the city.[10]

Throughout the controversy and beyond, anti-rationalists clearly held sway in Burgos and Toledo, but this does not mean that they remained unchallenged by those more sympathetic to the study of philosophy. Toledo, in particular, remained steeped in Arabic learning and the traditions of the Andalusian Jewish culture. In 1305, R. Asher ben Yehiel (Rosh) (c. 1250–1328), the head of the German Jewry, came to Toledo after fleeing his native land because of the fear of persecution.[11] R. Asher's arrival in Toledo and his work as the head of the city's *beit din* (Jewish court) and the *yeshiva* (Talmudic school) and as the leading rabbinic authority in Castile have been called a "peak of Ashkenazi influence in Spain." Communities and individuals throughout the kingdom sought his legal opinion in difficult and controversial cases.[12] Despite spending many years of his life in Castile, R. Asher remained steadfast in his preference for the Ashkenazi customs over the native Spanish ones and in his rejection of rationalist thought and the study of philosophy.[13] Not surprisingly, some local rabbinic leaders pushed back against R. Asher's insistence on following "foreign" customs and disputed his interpretations of the *halakhah*. Toward the end of R. Asher's life, R. Israel Israeli of Toledo, a rationalist scholar, challenged his qualifications to interpret an old Toledan ordinance on the grounds that the Ashkenazi rabbi did not have the necessary command of literary Arabic and the proper training in philosophy and logical reason-

10. Septimus, *Hispano-Jewish Culture in Transition*, 65–69.

11. The year of his death is unclear. Most scholars favor 1327 or 1328, but Judah Galinsky sees 1320–21 as more likely; see Galinsky, "An Ashkenazic Rabbi Encounters Sephardic Culture: R. Asher b. Jehiel's Attitude towards Philosophy and Science," ed. Dan Diner, in *Jahrbuch des Simon-Dubnow-Instituts/Simon Dubnow Institute Yearbook* 8 (2009): 191–211; Baer, *History of the Jews*, 1:316–25; Israel Ta-Shema, "Between East and West: Rabbi Asher b Yehiel and His Son Rabbi Ya'aqov," in *Studies in Medieval Jewish History and Literature*, edited by Isadore Twersky and Jay M. Harris, 3:179–96 (Cambridge, Mass.: Harvard University Press, 2000).

12. On R. Asher ben Yehiel's involvement in a criminal case in Córdoba, see Ray, *Sephardic Frontier*, 119–23.

13. Ta-Shema, "Between East and West," 182–83; Galinsky, "Ashkenazic Rabbi Encounters Sephardic Culture," 194–97. Galinsky argues, however, that Rabbi Asher may have adjusted his personal opinion to fit the local realities and held that the study of non-Jewish wisdom was permitted as long as it remained subordinated to the study of the Torah.

ing. In response, R. Asher argued that his qualifications rested on "the true reasoning of the Torah" and stressed the dangers of using philosophy in interpreting the Jewish law.[14] After R. Asher's death, his son, R. Judah ben Asher, led the Toledan community until the middle of the fourteenth century and continued his father's work of transforming the religious life in the city in accordance with the Ashkenazi pietistic ideals.[15] The Toledan *yeshiva* produced a steady supply of motivated young scholars, able to spread their knowledge among the less-educated Jews and raise the level of religious observance in their communities.[16]

The success of the Talmudic school in Toledo was only one factor behind the revival of lay Jewish religiosity in Castile. The popularity of the kabbalistic teachings was another. In cities and villages, marketplaces and private homes, streets and synagogues, itinerant mystics were exhorting the people to follow the commandments and be prepared for the imminent arrival of the Messiah.[17] Begun as a domain of knowledge accessible only to a small and secretive fraternity of scholars, over the course of the thirteenth century the Kabbalah was transformed into a popular tradition.[18] The origins of kabbalistic thought in Castile are obscure. It appears that the first kabbalistic circle in Spain appeared in Gerona (Catalonia), and was composed of the pupils of R. Isaac the Blind (1160–1235), a famed Provencal mystic. The Geronese circle may have helped spread the kabbalistic doctrine to Castile. By the middle of the thirteenth century, two brothers-kabbalists were active in Soria—R. Jacob and R. Isaac ha-Cohen—whose student, R. Moses ben Simeon of Burgos, taught the doctrine to R. Todros ben Joseph ha-Levi Abulafia (c. 1220–98), the nephew of Ramah, who was born in Burgos and became a major scholar and communal leader in Toledo.[19]

---

14. Galinsky, "Ashkenazic Rabbi Encounters Sephardic Culture," 200; Baer, *History of the Jews*, 1:318–19.

15. On the role of R. Judah ben Asher in preserving his father's legacy and influence, see Galinsky, "On the Heritage of R. Yehudah ben ha-Rosh, Rabbi of Toledo: A chapter in an Exploration of the Responsa Literature of Christian Spain," *Pe'amim* 128 (2010–11): 175–210 [Hebrew].

16. Judah Galinsky, "On Popular Halakhic Literature and the Jewish Reading Audience in Fourteenth-Century Spain," *Jewish Quarterly Review* 98, no. 3 (2008): 313.

17. Baer, *History of the Jews*, 1:267–70.

18. Harvey Hames, *The Art of Conversion: Christianity and Kabbalah in the Thirteenth Century* (Leiden: Brill, 2000), 81.

19. Moshe Idel, "Jewish Thought in Medieval Spain," in *Moreshet Sepharad: The Sephardi*

The intellectual sources of kabbalistic mysticism are complex (far too complex to be discussed here in detail), but specialists are unanimous in stressing the influence of the contemporary cultural and religious environments—both Jewish and Christian. The majority of Spanish kabbalists belonged to the so-called "theosophical-theurgical" school, which focused on the connection between God and his creation via the *sefirot* (attributes or emanations), and stressed the need for strict religious observance and performance of the biblical commandments.[20] Like Ramah's "philosophically knowledgeable anti-rationalism," at its core the Kabbalah was a reaction by the traditionalists ("kabbalah" means "tradition") to the spread of philosophical speculation. They sought to shield Judaism against the infiltration of foreign ideas and revitalize Jewish belief and practice.[21] The kabbalists believed themselves to be the guardians and transmitters of ancient mystical thought, and some elements of the Spanish Kabbalah may have dated to the ancient times. However, scholars trace its more immediate origins to the traditions of the eleventh- and twelfth-century *Hasidei Ashkenaz*, transmitted to Spain through Provence. The Cohen brothers of Soria studied mysticism in France, and one of the main sources of the Spanish Kabbalah—the *Book of the Bahir*—originated in Germany.[22]

Much of the discussion of Christian influences on the Kabbalah centers on the principal text of Castilian mysticism—the *Zohar*. Written in an archaic Aramaic, the work was first circulated in the 1290s and presented

---

Legacy, edited by Haim Beinart, 1:272–75(Jerusalem: Hebrew University Press, 1992); Scholem, *Major Trends in Jewish Mysticism*, 3rd ed. (New York: Schocken, 1995), 175. For biographical information on R. Todros ben Joseph ha-Levi Abulafia, I relied on the entry in the *Encyclopedia Judaica*, ed. Fred Skolnik and Michael Berenbaum, 2nd ed. (Detroit: Keter, 2007), 1:343–44.

20. Idel, "Jewish Thought," 1:277–78; Hames, *Art of Conversion*, 50–51. Scholem distinguishes between "the two opposing schools of thought in Spanish Kabbalism": "the ecstatic and the theosophical"; *Major Trends*, 124. The ecstatic or prophetic Kabbalah is exemplified in the thought of R. Abraham Abulafia (from 1239 to after 1291). His ideas, however, did not gain wide popularity among his contemporaries in Spain. On Abulafia, see Harvey J. Hames, *Like Angels on Jacob's Ladder: Abraham Abulafia, the Franciscans and Joachimism* (Albany: State University of New York Press, 2007).

21. Hames, *Art of Conversion*, 32–33.

22. Idel, "Jewish Thought," 1:272–73, 276; Hames, *Like Angels on Jacob's Ladder*, 35; Yehuda Liebes, *Studies in the Zohar*, trans. Arnold Schwartz, Stephanie Nakache, and Penina Peli (Albany: State University of New York Press, 1993), 197n28.

as the creation of R. Simeon ben Yohai, who lived in the second century, but it has been proved beyond a doubt that the Zohar is essentially a medieval work.²³ Several scholars have noted the convergence of Jewish and Christian mystical speculation in the thirteenth century, and the Zohar serves as a prime example of this process. The messianic prophecies contained in the Zoharic texts bear an uncanny resemblance to the apocalyptic visions of the Spiritual Franciscans inspired by the ideas of Joachim of Fiore, a twelfth-century Christian mystic.²⁴ Moreover, traditional Christian symbols and teachings may have influenced several key concepts in the Zohar. For example, the threefold division of the ten *sefirot* and the description of the Godhead as a threefold unity evoke the Christian doctrine of the Trinity.²⁵ The active interaction between the human and divine through the mystical emanations can be seen as the Jewish mystics' answer to the Christian belief in the intercessory role of the saints.²⁶

Whether these ideas were direct borrowings from Christianity or developed in response to spiritual challenges common to both religious communities, it is hard to avoid the conclusion that the blossoming of Jewish mysticism in Castile was the result of an ongoing adaptation to the new cultural milieu. Thirteenth-century Castile is well known as the scene of an intense collaboration between Christian and Jewish scholars under the auspices of the learned King Alfonso X. Their work was largely confined to the translation of scientific works from Arabic into Castilian. The inquisitive king did, however, request translations of the most important Jewish texts: the Torah, the Talmud, and even some pre-Zoharic

---

23. Gershom Sholem believed that the entire work was composed by R. Moses de León (ca. 1250–1305), a Kabbalist who was born in Guadalajara, maintained close ties to the Kabbalistic circle in Toledo headed by R. Todros ben Joseph Abulafia, traveled a great deal, and spent the last years of his life in Ávila; Scholem, *Major Trends*, 186–87, 193. More recently, Yehuda Liebes and others have maintained that while R. Moses de León was the principal author of the Zohar, it was the product of a whole group of scholars active in Castile during the second half of the thirteenth century; Liebes, *Studies in the Zohar*, 88.

24. Baer, *History of the Jews*, 1:249. The influence of Joachimism and the Franciscans on the thought of Abraham Abulafia, a Catalan Jewish mystic and a self-proclaimed messiah, is the focus of Hames's *Like Angels on Jacob's Ladder*. On Joachim's relatively tolerant portrayal of the Jews and their role in the divine plan for history, see Robert E. Lerner, *The Feast of Saint Abraham: Medieval Millenarians and the Jews* (Philadelphia: University of Pennsylvania Press, 2000).

25. Liebes, *Studies in the Zohar*, 140.

26. Chazan, *Jews of Medieval Western Christendom*, 105.

kabbalistic works. The ostensible purpose of such translations was to demonstrate the truth of the Christian faith presumably revealed in these texts.[27] Even though no evidence exists to substantiate an analogous interest in an alien faith on the part of the kabbalists, it is not inconceivable that they, too, found certain elements of the Christian doctrine to be useful for elucidating Zoharic mysteries. They may have even discussed these esoteric matters with mendicant friars, whose numbers grew substantially in the northern part of the kingdom over the course of the thirteenth century.

The spread of mystical and apocalyptic ideas produced a variety of responses in the Castilian Jewish community. One of its most immediate consequences was the appearance of messianic movements in Ávila and Ayllón in the early 1290s. From Jewish and Christian sources we know that two self-proclaimed prophets created a great stir among the people with their announcements that on the last day of Tammuz, 1295 (5055 A.M.), the Messiah would blast his horn and summon the Jews out of exile. According to Abner of Burgos, who later converted to Christianity and became Alfonso of Valladolid but was at the time a physician in Burgos, the people assembled in their synagogues, dressed in white garments and anxiously awaiting the arrival of the Messiah. Suddenly, crosses appeared on their clothing, and when they returned home, they found that the garments there were marked with crosses, as well. Abner relates that some people were so traumatized by the experience that they turned to him for medical help. Some were deeply shaken in their beliefs and embraced Christianity. Abner claims that the year 1295 was the beginning of the spiritual journey that led to his own conversion around 1320.[28]

27. "Furthermore he ordered translated the whole law of the Jews, and even their Talmud, and other knowledge which is called *qabbalah* and which the Jews keep closely secret. And he did this so it might be manifest through their own Law that it is all a [mere] representation of that Law which we Christians have; and that they, like the Moors, are in grave error and in peril of losing their souls"; cited in Norman Roth, "Jewish Collaborators in Alfonso's Scientific Work," in *Emperor of Culture: Alfonso X the Learned of Castile and His Thirteenth-Century Renaissance*, edited by Robert I. Burns, 60 (Philadelphia: University of Pennsylvania Press, 1990). On the translation project and the Jews' participation in it, see also Jose S. Gil, *La escuela de traductores de Toledo y los colaboradores judíos* (Toledo: Instituto Provincial de Investigaciones y Estudios Toledanos, 1985), esp. 57–87.

28. The events are mentioned in the responsa of R. Solomon ben Adret of Barcelona, who placed a ban on the false prophet in Ávila (he also placed a ban on Abraham Abulafia,

Did the similarities between some kabbalistic concepts and Christian teachings, especially when coupled with disappointed messianic expectations, ease some people's passage from Judaism to Christianity? As far as Abner of Burgos is concerned, Baer suggests that they did, but in the absence of any significant body of evidence on Jewish conversions in Castile prior to 1391, it would be difficult to answer this question definitively.[29] Paola Tartakoff's study of Jewish conversion in the Crown of Aragon has shown that many Jews converted out of pragmatic considerations, usually to escape personal difficulties: poverty, intracommunal violence, romantic complications, and criminal convictions.[30] Moreover, even if the spread of mystical teachings caused some Jews to waver in their commitment to the faith, on the whole the Zoharic doctrine was more likely to strengthen than to loosen their attachment to Judaism. The *Zohar* and other kabbalistic texts propagate a highly negative view of Christianity and other "idolatrous" faiths. Non-Jews are portrayed as inferior beings, whose "souls are from the side of impurity" and who are not fully human.[31] According to the *Zohar*, if a Jew crosses the bound-

---

who thought himself to be the Messiah and adopted 1290 as the year of redemption; see Hames, *Like Angels on Jacob's Ladder*, 7, 45). Abner's account in *Book of the Wars of the Lord* has not survived, but it is quoted in the writings of Pablo de Santa María and Alfonso de Espina, as well as alluded to in Abner of Burgos's *Mostrador de Justicia*, ed. Walter Mettmann (Opladen: Westdeutscher Verlag, 1994), 1:13–14. On Abner of Burgos/Alfonso of Valladolid, see Baer, *History of the Jews*, 1:277–81, 1:327–54; Moshe Lazar, "Alfonso de Valladolid's *Mostrador de justicia*: A Polemical Debate between Abner's Old and New Self," in *Judaísmo Hispano: Estudios en memoria de José Luis Lacave Riaño*, edited by Elena Romero, 1:121–34 (Madrid: CSIC, 2002); Ryan Szpiech, "Polemical Strategy and the Rhetoric of Authority in Abner of Burgos/Alfonso of Valladolid," in *Late Medieval Jewish Identities: Iberia and Beyond*, edited by Carmen Caballero-Navas and Esperanza Alfonso, 55–76 (New York: Palgrave Macmillan, 2010); and Szpiech, *Conversion and Narrative: Reading and Religious Authority in Medieval Polemic* (Philadelphia: University of Pennsylvania Press, 2013), esp. 143–73.

29. "There can be no doubt that the streams of mystical thought then meandering through Spanish Jewry had a decisive influence upon Abner's thinking in the course of the intellectual crisis which he resolved by his conversion to Christianity"; Baer, *History of the Jews*, 1:335.

30. Paola Tartakoff, *Between Christian and Jew: Conversion and Inquisition in the Crown of Aragon, 1250–1391* (Philadelphia: University of Pennsylvania Press, 2012).

31. "These [sefirotic] lights form an image below to establish the image of everything that is contained within Adam, for the inner form of all inner forms is called by this name, and from here [we know that] every form that is contained in this emanation is called 'Adam,' as it is written, 'for you are men' [Ez 34:31], you are called men but not the rest of the nations, for they are idolaters ... The spirit that emanates on the rest of the idolatrous

ary separating the "holy seed" from other nations by eating non-kosher foods or by having sexual intercourse with a non-Jewish woman, he commits an act of idolatry that renders him impure and essentially nonhuman. Some passages go as far as to argue that to avoid being contaminated, a Jew must eschew all contact with non-Jews.[32] Christian secular and canon law set similar limitations on social interaction with Jews and Muslims, also with the aim of preserving the believers' spiritual purity.[33] This was the ideal: religious leaders in both communities were aware that transgressions were a regular occurrence.[34] However, by infusing the Jews' traditional claim to special status vis-à-vis the divine with a new meaning, the authors of the Zohar gave the Jews a fresh rationale to observe the commandments and maintain the lines of separation from the gentile world. The proliferation of works on religious topics aimed at popular audiences in the fourteenth century serves as indirect evidence that the kabbalists' prescriptions were having at least some effect on religious observance.[35]

The kabbalists' concern with raising the pietistic standard of the Jewish community is readily apparent, but some scholars perceive a radical aspect in their avowedly conservative and traditionalist stance: a call for social reform. In the thirteenth century, social tensions flared up in several communities in the lands of the Crown of Aragon.[36] In Barcelona during the 1230s, a group of the nouveau riche—commercial Jewish families mostly

---

nations, which derives from the side that is not holy, is not considered [to be in the category of] humanity ['adam]"; Zohar 1:20b, cited in Elliot Wolfson, "Ontology, Alterity, and Ethics in Kabbalistic Anthropology," *Exemplaria: A Journal of Theory in Medieval and Renaissance Studies* 12, no. 1 (2000): 139, 142 (Zohar 1:131a–b). Some Christian polemicists similarly questioned the Jews' humanity on the grounds that had the Jews possessed the capacity for reason, they would have embraced Christianity; see Anna Sapir Abulafia, *Christians and Jews in the Twelfth-Century Renaissance* (New York: Routledge, 1995).

32. Wolfson, "Ontology, Alterity, and Ethics," 146–49; see also Barry R. Mark, "Kabbalistic *Tocinofobia*: Américo Castro, *Limpieza de Sangre* and the Inner Meaning of Jewish Dietary Laws," in *Fear and Its Representations in the Middle Ages and Renaissance*, edited by Anne Scott and Cynthia Kosso, 152–86 (Turnhout: Brepols Publishers, 2002).

33. See the edicts of the IV Lateran Council (1215) in Grayzel, *Church and the Jews*, 309; *Las siete partidas*, Partida 7.24.7–11 (see chapter 7).

34. On the setting of sexual boundaries, see Nirenberg, "Conversion, Sex, and Segregation: Jews and Christians in Medieval Spain," *American Historical Review* 107, no. 4 (2002): 1065–93.

35. Galinsky, "On Popular Halakhic Literature," 325.

36. Ray, *Sephardic Frontier*, 131–32.

engaged in moneylending—successfully challenged the entrenched authority of the courtier-*nesi'im*, who had monopolized the power in the city for several generations.[37] The conflict in Barcelona was mainly between the old and the new elites, but in other cities, the challenge came from the economically disadvantaged members of the community. Yom Tov Assis, who has studied the revolt in Zaragoza, argues that the poor mounted an organized opposition to the rule of the wealthy oligarchs, demanding representation in the communal government and a more equitable tax distribution. He believes that class tensions extended to other Jewish communities in Spain. As evidence, he cites the pressure from below to establish communal charity funds—the *hekdesh*—to alleviate the plight of the poor.[38]

Whether a similar situation existed in Toledo and Northern Castile is hard to know because of the scattered nature of the evidence. The works of Castilian mysticism (the *Zohar* itself and the later additions to it, the *Ra'aya Mehemna* and the *Tikkunim*) fill in some of the missing pieces. For Baer, the message contained in these writings amounts to nothing less than a "revolutionary eschatology": a belief in the "imminence of revolutionary changes" that will occur upon the arrival of the Messianic age.[39] Woven into the discussion of mystical and ethical concepts is the critique of the contemporary Castilian Jewish society. The anonymous author of the *Ra'aya Mehemna* is unflinching in his criticism of the wealthy, power-hungry, and morally corrupt Jewish elites, "who are 'resplendent in their outer attire but are rotten within." He contrasts this picture of spiritual

---

37. Klein, *Jews, Christian Society, and Royal Power*, 116–41; Septimus, "Piety and Power," 1:201–13.

38. Assis, "Welfare and Mutual Aid in the Spanish Jewish Communities," in *Moreshet Sepharad*, 1:318–45. In Toledo, R. Asher ben Yehiel established a *hekdesh* when he arrived in the city. The testament of R. Judah ben Asher, son and successor of R. Asher, states, "My lord, my father of blessed memory, ordained in his city in Germany that every member of the congregation should pay a tithe of his whole income, and in the district of Toledo he likewise ordained that he and his children should follow the same course. And after his death, I and all my brethren resolved to maintain the practice and to add to its terms"; Israel Abrahams, ed., *Hebrew Ethical Wills* (Philadelphia: Jewish Publication Society of America, 1954), 192. Judah Galinsky has shown that the practice of establishing *hekdesh* trusts became widespread in northern Spain in the second half of the thirteenth century; Galinsky, "Jewish Charitable Bequests and the Hekdesh Trust in Thirteenth-Century Spain," *Journal of Interdisciplinary History* 35, no. 3 (2005): 431.

39. Baer, *History of the Jews*, 1:250, 277.

degradation with the pietistic ideal embodied by the wandering, poor mystics, "who are 'beautiful within though their dress is shabby." The kabbalists praise poverty as a sanctified condition that draws one closer to God and enjoin the wealthy to abandon the pursuit of riches and dedicate their lives to the study of the Torah.[40]

To what extent can the Zoharic texts be read as a reflection of the actual class conflict between the poor and the rich in the Castilian Jewish society? There is little doubt that social and economic stratification proceeded apace in the Jewish communities in Castile, just as it did in the Christian ones. Like the non-noble knights (*caballeros villanos*) in the Christian municipalities, members of the Jewish elite obtained tax exemptions from the monarchy while the lower-class Jews were forced to bear the brunt of the royal impositions, sliding further and further into poverty. According to the complaint lodged with the king at the cortes of Valladolid in 1312, there were more than five thousand such tax-exempt, affluent Jews in the kingdom.[41] The impoverishment of the lower-class Jews may explain the kabbalists' profound concern with the morality of poverty and wealth. Yet it is far from certain that the Zoharic corpus reflects revolutionary aspirations of the common people. For Baer, who associates the Jewish courtier aristocracy with philosophical rationalism, religious relativism, and moral corruption, it is a given that the Castilian pietists came from the lower classes, but most modern scholars reject Baer's portrayal of the elites as too simplistic.[42] Septimus and others have shown that the Castilian rabbinic leadership was fairly conservative and had a long history of opposing the more extreme forms of rationalism. Very little biographical information is available on the authors of the Zohar and other kabbalistic works, but while they did not necessarily hold official posts, they were experts in Talmudic law and thus belonged to an elite group of scholars.[43] R. Moses

40. Ibid., 272, 265.

41. *Cortes* I, 220; Francisco Ruíz Gómez, "Aljamas y concejos en el Reino de Castilla durante la Edad Media," *Espacio, Tiempo y Forma*," *Historia medieval* 6, series 3 (1993): 63–64. Compare this with the situation in Aragon, where wealthy Jews, rabbis, halakhic authorities, and Jews who rendered special services to the Christian elites (doctors, merchants, diplomats et al.) were granted exemptions from taxes. Many aljamas objected vigorously to such arrangements; see Assis, *Jewish Economy in the Medieval Crown of Aragon*, 221, 228.

42. Klein, *Jews, Christian Society, and Royal Power*, 71.

43. Wolfson, "Ontology, Alterity, and Ethics," 130. On the dichotomy between crown rabbis and rabbinic scholars, see Ray, *Sephardic Frontier*, 113–19.

de León, the principal author of the Zohar, was part of a kabbalistic circle based in Toledo that included R. Todros ben Joseph Abulafia and his son, R. Joseph, to whom he dedicated several of his books.[44] R. Todros Abulafia was both a kabbalist and a courtier, an acknowledged leader of the Castilian Jewish community who was also close to Alfonso X and performed diplomatic functions for the king.[45]

The ideas expressed in the Zoharic writings did, however, play a part in the communal reforms that R. Abulafia attempted to implement in Toledo in the early 1280s. Baer has thought that the reforms were intended to correct the wayward behavior of the courtier class, but Marc Saperstein has successfully argued against this interpretation.[46] In fact, there is no extant evidence of an open conflict in Toledo between courtier-rationalists and their opponent-pietists, similar to the anti-*nesi'im* revolt in Barcelona during the 1230s. By that point, R. Abulafia's family had dominated Jewish communal leadership in Northern Castile and Toledo for several generations. The stimulus for the reforms came from outside of the Jewish community. In 1279, during the revolt of Infante Sancho against his father, Alfonso X, one of the royal Jewish tax collectors, Çag de la Maleha, misappropriated the money intended by the king for the siege of Algeciras. The king accused Çag and other Jewish tax collectors of treason and had them publicly executed. In January 1281, Alfonso ordered that "all the *aljamas* of the Jews" (probably the Jewish communal leadership) be imprisoned and held until they agreed to pay an enormous tribute.[47] The same month, R. Abulafia, who apparently was spared incarceration, delivered a sermon (or sermons) to his community, urging them to embark on the path of moral and religious reforms.

There is an obvious connection between the harsh punishment in-

44. Scholem, *Major Trends*, 187; Liebes, *Studies in the Zohar*, 136.

45. Liebes even hypothesizes that the personage of R. Simeon ben Yohai in the Zohar was modeled on R. Abulafia; *Studies in the Zohar*, 136–37. Septimus notes that the Catalonian kabbalists who led the revolt against the *nesi'im* in the 1230s "hardly seem plebeian. And Nahmanides is thoroughly courtly"; Septimus, "Piety and Power," 1:215.

46. Marc Saperstein, "The Preaching of Repentance and the Reforms in Toledo of 1281," in *Models of Holiness in Medieval Sermons*, edited by Beverly Mayne Kienzle, 171 (Louvain-la-Neuve: Fédération Internationale des Instituts d'Études Médiévales, 1996).

47. Cayetano Rosell, ed., *Crónicas de los reyes de Castilla* (Madrid: Atlas, 1953), 1:55, 58; *Chronicle of Alfonso X*, trans. Shelby Thacker and José Escobar (Lexington: University of Kentucky Press, 2002), 225, 235–36. For additional details, see chapter 7.

flicted on the Jews of Castile by the king and R. Abulafia's stern admonitions. Scholars have assumed that the reforms were a spontaneous reaction by a community in the throes of a spiritual crisis, eager to assuage God's anger at their transgressions by pledging to adopt more rigorous standards of behavior. As Baer puts it, "[t]he hearts, contrite and repentant, were now amenable to reform in the pietist spirit."[48] That a lot of soul-searching took place in Toledo is probably true, but I believe there is more to the story. It seems very likely that R. Abulafia was urged, if not required, to crack down on religious and moral violations in the Jewish community by his lord—the king. Alfonso had just imposed a collective penalty on the Jews of Castile, and it would be logical for the king to see the implementation of an internal reform in the Jewish community as a natural extension of his drive to set the affairs of the royal *aljamas* in order.

Some remarkable parallels between the changes proposed by R. Abulafia and King Alfonso's own legislative initiatives support this hypothesis. Like the king's famous legal corpus—the *Fuero real*, the *Espéculo*, and *Las siete partidas*, R. Abulafia's reforms are directed at the entire Jewish community, not just a small spiritual or courtly elite.[49] To be sure, they reflect the particular concerns of the Jewish community and are informed by the rabbi's own kabbalistic orientation. Backing his points with extensive citations of Talmudic passages, R. Abulafia enjoins his audience to observe the rules prescribed by the *halakhah*: attend daily services, refrain from talking during public worship, be more fastidious in the observance of the Sabbath and the festivals, and stop ordering Christian and Muslim servants to perform tasks during the Sabbath that are forbidden to Jews. The sermon also censures the practice of using gentile servants to skirt the prohibition of taking interest from a fellow Jew.[50] Usury also happened to be one of King Alfonso's top concerns: in 1268, he forbade Christians to lend money at interest and then included the prohibition in

---

48. Baer, *History of the Jews*, 1:257.
49. Saperstein, "Preaching of Repentance," 173. On Alfonso X's legislative program, see chapter 7.
50. Saperstein, "Preaching of Repentance," 162, 165. Abulafia's sermon is preserved in the responsa collection of Judah ben Asher, *Zikhron Yehudah* (Berlin: 1846), 43a–45b. On the discussion by the Ashkenazi halakhists of the legality of using gentile intermediaries in intra-Jewish loans, see Soloveitchik, "Pawnbroking," 203–68.

Las siete partidas.[51] Even more significant is the rabbi's focus on maintaining the lines of separation between Jews and non-Jews and especially between the Jews and their Muslim female servants. In a passage that bears a strong imprint of kabbalistic views on Jewish sexuality and holiness, R. Abulafia condemns such interfaith sexual liaisons: "Regarding the Muslim women with whom Jews are accustomed to behave licentiously, this too is forbidden ... Jews, who are a holy people, must not profane their seed in the womb of a gentile woman, thereby fathering offspring for idolatry."[52]

The usual explanation for the prominence of this theme in R. Abulafia's sermon is the laxity of morals in Toledo, where Jewish men frequently pursued sexual relations with Christian and Muslim women.[53] Another way to approach the sermon, however, is to view it as an extension of the Alfonsine reform project, endorsed and promoted by the Toledan *aljama*'s spiritual leadership. The king and the rabbi both focus on the household—the place where informal interactions between members of different faiths could easily lead to illicit relations. R. Abulafia's sermon betrays a particular anxiety over the presence of Muslim and Christian women in Jewish homes. So grave is the rabbi's concern with upholding the demarcation lines between Jews and gentiles that in a departure from the usual judicial procedure, he orders anyone who becomes aware of another Jew's sexual relations with a Muslim or Christian woman to come forward and report the violation to the judges. The punishment for this transgression is "a great ban of excommunication." Perhaps to reduce temptation, servant women should be commanded to wear distinctive clothing—"black garments made of a coarse material."[54] Tellingly, King Alfonso's legislative initiatives also sought to curb interfaith commingling, especially within the household. In particular, he wanted

---

51. *Cortes* 1, 80; *Las siete partidas*, Partida 5.11.31.

52. Saperstein, "Preaching of Repentance," 166.

53. Baer, *History of the Jews*, 1:237–39; Ray, *Sephardic Frontier*, 172–73. The sensual poetry of Abulafia's nephew, Todros ben Judah Abulafia (from 1247 to after 1298), is often cited as evidence of the Jewish courtiers' predilection for non-Jewish women; see, for example, one of his poems in the recent translation by Peter Cole: "There's nothing wrong in wanting a woman / and loving girls is hardly a sin—/ but whether or not they're pretty or pure, / Arabia's daughters are what you should look for"; Cole, ed. and trans., *The Dream of the Poem: Hebrew Poetry from Muslim and Christian Spain, 950–1492* (Princeton: Princeton University Press, 2007), 260.

54. Saperstein, "Preaching of Repentance," 169–70.

Christians and Jews to stop the practice of employing wet nurses of another faith and issued stipulations to that effect on several occasions throughout his reign.[55] Alfonso's most important legal code, *Las siete partidas*, forbade Jews to keep Christian servants, strictly prohibited them to engage in sexual intercourse with Christian women ("who are spiritually the wives of Our Lord Jesus Christ"), and mandated the wearing of distinguishing marks by Jews to prevent illicit sexual relations.[56]

The kabbalist rabbi and the Christian king thus shared a vision of a well-ordered society in which the social, and especially sexual, boundaries between religious communities were clearly marked and meticulously observed.[57] Possibly urged on by King Alfonso, R. Abulafia saw the crisis in the aftermath of the terrible events of 1281 as a propitious moment to reform the Jewish community in accordance with the ideas popular in the kabbalistic circles as well as the Castilian courtly circles.[58] If my hypothesis is correct and Alfonso played a role in the communal reform advocated by R. Abulafia, the king's actions continued a long tradition of royal interference in the internal Jewish affairs that went back at least to the twelfth century, when (as we have seen in chapter 2), Alfonso VII helped the Jewish communal leaders suppress Karaites in Castile. A hundred years later, the Jewish leaders continued to welcome the king's involvement in the *aljamas*' affairs and to view the monarchy as their most reliable ally. The exorbitant taxes Alfonso imposed on the Jews of Castile in the 1280s did not visibly undermine their respect for the king. R. Abulafia's successor, R. Asher ben Yehiel, could still argue that the taxes were a fair price to pay for royal protection: "It seems to me that all types of taxes must be considered defense expenditures. For it is they that preserve us among the gentiles. For what purpose do some of the gentile nations find in preserving us and allowing us to live among them if not the benefit that they derive from Israel in that they collect taxes and extortions from them?"[59]

Several scholars have recognized the trend toward a greater involvement by the kings of Castile and Aragon in the Jewish communal affairs

55. *Fuero real*, IV.ii. IV; *Cortes* 1, 62, 77, 227.
56. *Partida* 7.24.7–11.
57. See also Nirenberg, *Communities of Violence*, 127–65.
58. See Mark, "Kabbalistic *Tocinofobia*," 165.
59. Asher ben Yehiel, *Commentary on the Babylonian Talmud, Baba Bathra*, 1:29; cited in Septimus, *Hispano-Jewish Culture in Transition*, 13 (translation is Septimus's).

during the second half of the thirteenth century, even if some disagreement exists over whether this involvement strengthened or weakened the *aljamas'* autonomy. Most often, royal intervention entailed the appointment of monarchy-backed Jewish officials whose task was to adjudicate disputes within the community in accordance with the Jewish law, the *halakhah*. In one well-known and well-studied example, after the *nesi'im* had been ousted from power in Barcelona, King James I of Aragon gave the community a charter in 1241, which authorized the election of two or more "honest and worthy men" (*probos homines et legales*) who would investigate and resolve disputes and impose penalties payable to the royal bailiff of Barcelona. At the same time, the Aragonese Crown encouraged the use of royal courts for adjudicating internal affairs of the Jewish communities.[60] For Jonathan Ray, the growing number of appeals submitted by Jewish individuals and communal leaders to the royal courts is evidence of the monarchy's efforts to exert greater control over the *aljamas* and to undermine the authority of Jewish institutions.[61] Elka Klein argues, however, that this development "went hand in hand with increased support of internal [Jewish] judicial structures" and points out that a Jewish self-government controlled by the monarchy ("autonomy by design") was the best option available to the *aljamas*.[62] The reaction by rabbinic authorities to the use of Christian courts was generally negative, but even they held royal justice in high regard.[63] Halakhic experts like Solomon ben Adret accepted royal appointments to serve as judges and communal secretaries and even participated in the royal courts as plaintiffs.[64]

In Castile, starting in the mid-thirteenth century, there was a similar

60. Klein, *Jews, Christian Society, and Royal Power*, 128, 153.
61. Ray, *Sephardic Frontier*, 143.
62. Klein, *Jews, Christian Society, and Royal Power*, 143, 161. On the efforts by the king of Aragon to publicize the benefits of the royal "autonomy by design" among the Jews still controlled by seigniorial regimes (such as the one in Tortosa), see Barton, *Contested Treasure*, 102–4.
63. See, for example, R. Jonah Gerondi's interpretation of a mishnaic passage: "The simple sense of this *mishnah* would [seem to] speak to the discredit of kings. But Heaven forbid, Heaven forbid, this thing cannot be nor can it stand! For it is through them that the whole world is preserved. They execute judgment and justice. And there is no man on earth who can be as truthful as they. For being unafraid, they need not fawn upon people. And nothing prevents them from following a straight path"; cited in Septimus, "Piety and Power," 1:212–13.
64. Klein, *Jews, Christian Society, and Royal Power*, 153–54, 159–61.

drive by the king to attain a greater control over internal Jewish affairs. The evidence from Sahagún, in Northern Castile, shows that at least in some cases, royal interference could be beneficial for the *aljamas* and was welcomed by the Jews. The Jewish community in this small municipality was one of the few ecclesiastical *aljamas* in the kingdom, controlled by the abbot of the monastery of San Benito de Sahagún. Since the early twelfth century, the Christian burgesses in Sahagún had been engaged in a protracted struggle for greater economic and political autonomy from their ecclesiastical lord, and the Jews eventually joined their cause.[65] In 1255 there was a new outbreak of hostilities between the abbot and the *concejo* when a royal judge accused the abbot of infringing on the king's rights and persuaded several groups, including the Jews, to send their representatives to the king with a list of complaints.[66] According to the anonymous chronicler of Sahagún, when the Jews arrived in Alfonso X's presence, they asserted "that in no way did they belong to the jurisdiction of the abbot, but that *they were servants [siervos] of the lord King, and were obligated to serve the royal power in all things*. They also said that the lord Abbot had oppressed them without reason and in various ways" (emphasis added).[67] The Jews of Sahagún were already paying most of their taxes to the king, and this gave them grounds for challenging the jurisdiction of the abbot. They were evidently aware of the declaration in the *Libro de los fueros de Castilla* that even the Jews under the jurisdiction of private lords "ought to be the king's, under his protection and for his service," and quoted it almost verbatim in support of their case.[68]

The Jews of Sahagún reminded the king that they were ultimately

65. For more details on this conflict, see Maya Soifer Irish, "Tamquam domino proprio," 534–66.

66. Antonio Ubierto Arteta, ed., *Crónicas anónimas de Sahagún* (Zaragoza: Universidad de Zaragoza, 1987), 150; Martínez Liébana, El dominio señorial del monasterio de San Benito de Sahagún en la baja edad media (siglos XIII–XV) (Ph.D. diss., Universidad Complutense de Madrid, 1990), 621–25.

67. "Los judíos aún eso mesmo afirmavan que en ninguna manera pertenesçía[n] a la jurisdiction del abad, ca siervos heran del señor rei e eran thenudos en todas las cosas de servir al poderío real. Deçían aún qu'el señor abad los agraviaba a sin raçón en muchas maneras"; Ubierto Arteta, *Crónicas anónimas*, 152.

68. "The Jews are the king's; although they might be under the jurisdiction of magnates or their knights or other men, or under the jurisdiction of monasteries, all of the Jews ought to be the king's, under his protection and for his service"; Sánchez, ed., *Libro de los fueros de Castiella*, 54; see also Alvarado Planas and Oliva Manso, eds. *Los fueros de Castilla*, 291.

royal Jews and implored him to give them the kind of autonomy already available to most other *aljamas* in Castile. Alfonso X apparently did not need much persuading and soon arrived in Sahagún to promulgate a new *fuero*. The 1255 document recognized the abbot's claim to lordship over the Jewish community and required the Jews to pay an annual tribute and pecuniary damages to their ecclesiastical lord. At the same time, Alfonso granted the *aljama* a much greater degree of judicial autonomy than it had hitherto enjoyed under the ecclesiastical rule. The Jews of Sahagún received a model of governance commonly found in the royal *aljamas* of Northern Castile. They now had the same *fuero* as the Jews of Carrión, and the rabbis of Burgos were allowed to appoint "elders" (*adelantados*) to judge cases within the *aljama* according to Jewish law (*segund so ley*). In mixed litigation, testimonies of one Christian and one Jew were now required, in line with the customary law of Northern Castile, but in contradistinction to an earlier disposition of the local *concejo*. As in the lands of the *realengo*, a Jewish official, *albedi*, would represent the lord's—in this case, the abbot's—authority in the *aljama*.[69] The subsequent documentation shows that the abbot's authority over the Jewish community of Sahagún became largely nominal, and the king treated it as any other royal *aljama*.[70]

Alfonso's interest in the governance of Jewish communities was the corollary of his attempts to expand royal power and reshape the kingdom's institutions in accordance with his ideal of active governance. The Jewish leaders welcomed the royal involvement when it strengthened the *aljamas*' privileges and protections, but even they could not fail to see that the king's favors came at a high price. Strong royal power was good for the Jews, but helping maintain it resulted in a huge economic and human cost to the Jewish communities. As we are going to see in chapter 7, not only did the drive to obtain greater revenues from the Jewish communities damage their fiscal health, but the royal assistance with debt collections also drove a wedge between the Jews and their Christian clients and damaged interfaith relations in the kingdom.

69. AHN, clero, Sahagún, carp. 917, no. 13; CDMS, 5:325–26; see Sanchez, *Libro de los fueros*, 113–14.

70. The Partition of Huete in 1290 listed the Jews of Sahagún among other royal *aljamas* paying tribute to the king, but made no mention of the abbot's portion (as it did for the bishop of Palencia); see Francisco J. Hernández, *Las rentas del rey*, vol. 1, *Estudio y documentos*, 140, and Carrete Parrondo, "El repartimiento de Huete de 1290," 130.

SEVEN ∾ Jews, Christians, and Royal Power in Northern Castile

Seeing that it is our duty to support and protect [the Jews], like the kings our predecessors had done, and for the great service that [the Jews] rendered us in the form of large quantities of *maravedís* they have just given us, and also for other amounts of *maravedís* that they have to give us every year, in addition to the *cabeça de pecho* that they have been paying us—a service that is intended for the maintenance of our maritime frontier—we think it well to show them our favor in the following manner.

This frank acknowledgment of the Jews' large contribution to the revenues of the Castilian Crown prefaced a charter of privilege given to the Jews of the kingdom by King Alfonso XI in 1335.[1] Over eighty years had passed since the death of Alfonso's great-great-grandfather, Fernando III, the conqueror of Córdoba and Seville. Yet the charter dwelt on the same themes that had been part of the official royal lexicon since the time of Fernando and other great warrior-kings: the Jews' financial importance to the Castilian Crown and the link between the king's protection of the Jews and the continuation of Castile's military successes. Even the circumstances of Alfonso's reign were reminiscent of the times of his illustrious ancestor. Castile was once again in the throes of a conflict with a brazen Muslim enemy—the Marinids of Morocco. Having dealt the Muslims decisive blows at Salado and Algeciras, Alfonso XI might have captured Gibraltar and even invaded North Africa had not the Black Death carried him off in 1350 at the age of thirty-nine.[2] However, Castile's maritime frontier was safe, in part thanks to the unceasing flow of Jewish capital into the royal treasury.

Alfonso XI's charter to the Jews can be taken as a palpable demon-

---

1. AMME, no. L-H0190-008; Cantera Burgos, "La judería de Miranda de Ebro," *Sefarad* 1 (1941): 132–37.
2. O'Callaghan, *History of Medieval Spain*, 408–14.

stration of the stability and continuity of royal policies.³ However, one should not forget that Alfonso XI's Castile was not quite the same kingdom inherited by Alfonso X in 1252. With the death of Fernando III, the active phase of the reconquest in Castile was over, and except for the brief surge of crusading energy under Alfonso XI, the reconquest would not resume in earnest until Fernando and Isabel began their final push against the Nasrid kingdom of Granada in 1484. Moreover, reading the rest of Alfonso's 1335 charter, one is struck by a sense of disquiet that permeates the letter's description of the Jews' situation in Castile and of their relations with Christians. From the representatives of the Jewish communities the king has learned that the Jews are "poor and ruined" (*pobres e estragados*). Christian debtors put numerous obstacles in the collectors' way in order to avoid paying back their loans. One complaint is directed squarely at the king himself: Alfonso has granted Christians numerous extensions on the repayment of debts. The Jews also hint darkly that they have been subjected to "violence and oppression" (*fuerças y premias*), and they ask the king to protect the *aljamas*' rights.⁴

Because Castilian kings continued to avow their support for the Jews and employ them as *almojarifes* and tax collectors (in the neighboring Aragon, Jewish bailiffs were dismissed in the 1280s), it is often assumed that Jewish-Christian relations in the kingdom did not undergo any significant changes until well into the fourteenth century. Even Yitzhak Baer, whose lachrymose narrative of Jewish-Iberian experience is framed by persecutions and punctuated by disasters, contends that "[t]he spirit of the Reconquest," his other name for toleration, continued unabated in Castile down to the civil war of the 1360s.⁵ But the evidence tells a different story. The records hail from different corners of Northern Castile and range from a handful of property transactions to formal appeals to the king by the urban procurators. In many of them, the signs of tensions between Jews and Christians are difficult to miss. A few examples should suffice. The cornerstone of Jewish-Christian coexistence in Cas-

3. Ray, *Sephardic Frontier*, 96.
4. AMME, no. L-H0190-008.
5. Baer, *History of the Jews*, 1:307. For a critique of the "lachrymose school," see Nirenberg, *Communities of Violence*, 9, 228. Norman Roth is dismissive of Baer as somebody who was "constantly looking for evidence of oppression of the Jews in Spain"; Roth, "The Civic Status of the Jew in Medieval Spain," 147.

tile, spelled out in many *fueros*, had long been the legal principle that in mixed cases testimony by witnesses from each religious community was required.[6] By the end of the thirteenth century, the townsmen of many Northern Castilian locales were successfully challenging this principle, along with the right of the Jews to have separate judges (*alcaldes*).[7] In 1219, Fernando III could talk his way out of Pope Honorius III's order that the Jews of his kingdom wear distinguishing signs. In 1313, a call for such signs came from Alfonso XI's own subjects.[8] Before the 1270s, there were no restrictions in Castile on Jewish ownership of real estate. In 1293, the prohibition of Jews buying land from Christian taxpayers entered the cortes legislation after two decades of lobbying by the *vecinos* of Burgos.[9]

These worrisome attacks on the rights of the Jewish *aljamas* began within the twenty years that followed the end of "the age of the great reconquest."[10] Baer's observation that the conditions of the reconquest were favorable for the Jews, while its cessation weakened Jewish communities in Spain, remains essentially valid.[11] He did not, however, take into consideration the immediate consequences of the hiatus in the reconquest after the 1260s because he mistakenly believed that Castilian society hardly changed in the second half of the thirteenth century.[12] In reality, the changes were dramatic and even painful. After the incorporation of Andalusia into the Castilian kingdom, a redistribution of population led to a decline in agricultural production in Northern Castile. The expulsion of the *mudéjars* after the revolt of 1264 exacerbated the economic crisis in the kingdom because the Christian settlers who replaced them did not have adequate knowledge of the agricultural techniques peculiar to the South. Alfonso X's monetary policies could not stop the out-of-control inflation plaguing the kingdom. His three successive attempts

6. See chapter 2.
7. In Miranda de Ebro and Burgos, as well as in the cortes petitions; Cortes 1, 227.
8. Cortes 1, 227.
9. Cortes 1, 115.
10. O'Callaghan, *History of Medieval Spain*, 358.
11. Novikoff, "Between Tolerance and Intolerance in Medieval Spain," 26; Valdeón Baruque, *Judíos y conversos en la Castilla medieval* (Valladolid: Universidad de Valladolid, 2000), 41. Mark Meyerson has challenged the idea that the Jews' position in Spain declined "unremittingly from this period [late thirteenth–early fourteenth centuries] until the expulsion of 1492"; see his *Jews in an Iberian Frontier Kingdom*, 6, and *Jewish Renaissance in Fifteenth-Century Spain*.
12. Baer, *History of the Jews*, 1:307.

to stabilize the currency (in 1264, 1271, and 1277) only led to a debasing of coinage and a rapid increase in prices. Adverse economic conditions, high taxation, and widespread indebtedness continued to afflict Castilians for generations, negatively affecting Jewish-Christian interaction and fostering anti-Jewish attitudes.[13]

Another momentous development that altered the dynamics of Jewish-Christian relations was the political realignment in Northern Castilian towns after the rise to prominence of a new group of oligarchs. At the height of the reconquest, *caballeros villanos*, or urban knights, were members of the urban militia wealthy enough to be able to afford their own horse, weapons, and armor. Because of their important role in the reconquest, urban knights began to accumulate privileges, monopolize municipal offices, and gain political influence, so much so that by the late twelfth century, their representatives were summoned by the king to participate in the royal court (*curia*). This was the origin of Castile's representative assembly—the cortes.[14] The real change in the urban knights' fortunes came during the reign of Alfonso X, whose alliance with the wealthy urban elites was intended to buffer the Crown against the antagonism of the powerful nobility. Starting in 1255, Alfonso granted generous tax exemptions and other privileges to the *caballeros villanos* in Northern Castile, completing their control of political and economic life in towns.[15] Representatives of the *concejos* dominated by urban knights became frequent visitors at Alfonso's court, carrying mandates from their towns to petition the king for a confirmation of privileges or a resolution of some matter of great importance to city councils.[16] More and more frequently, these petitions included requests to restrict and regulate the activities of Jewish property owners and moneylenders. The *caballeros villanos* of Northern Castile's largest city—Burgos—led the way with a series of complaints, starting in the

13. Ruiz, *Crisis and Continuity*, 293–307, and *Spain's Centuries of Crisis*, 28–36, 141; O'Callaghan, *Learned King*, 124–26.

14. O'Callaghan, *Cortes of Castile-León*, 16; José María Mínguez, "La transformación social de las ciudades y las cortes de Castilla y León," in *Las Cortes de Castilla y León en la edad media: Actas de la primera etapa del congreso científico sobre la historia de las cortes de Castilla y Leon, Burgos, 1986* (Valladolid: Cortes de Castilla y León, 1988), 2:15–43; Lourie, "Society Organized for War: Medieval Spain," 54–76; Ruiz, *Crisis and Continuity*, 238.

15. Ruiz, *Crisis and Continuity*, 239–42.

16. See O'Callaghan, *Cortes of Castile-León*; Evelyn Procter, *Curia and Cortes in León and Castile, 1072–1295* (Cambridge: Cambridge University Press, 1980).

1260s, about the Jews' purchases of taxable properties (*heredades pecheras*) in the city. Beginning with the cortes of Valladolid (1293), attacks on the Jews became a regular feature of collective petitions submitted for the king's consideration during the gatherings of Castile's representative assembly. Whether the petitions were the consequence of the urban elites' economic competition with the Jews or a reflection of popular attitudes with a much broader social base, it is undeniable that the urban procurators became the voice of anti-Jewish hatred in Castile, creating a powerful political discourse with grave repercussions for the kingdom's Jews.[17]

Perhaps the most consequential transformation to affect the Jews of Castile in the thirteenth century was the change in their relationship with the monarchy. The argument in this chapter seeks to provide a more nuanced alternative to the conventional approach, which sets up a dichotomy between the protective power of the royal policies and the antagonism of the Christian masses.[18] As one historian of medieval Burgos put it, "Two factors ... characterize the life of Hebrew communities in Castile: on the one hand, royal protection ... and, on the other hand, popular hostility."[19] I am not suggesting that the kings of Castile reneged on their role as protectors of the *servi regis*: the chapter began with Alfonso XI's reaffirmation of his support for the Jews. However, the relationship between the Crown and the Jews could not remain static when the Castilian monarchy itself was undergoing major changes in the second half of the thirteenth century. The kings of Castile had traditionally derived their authority from their military prowess and ability to win land and fame for their retainers in battles against the Muslim enemy.[20] With the start of an extended hiatus in the reconquest, the old alliances forged during the long march south faltered, and the Crown was forced to search for new sources of authority to counteract the kingdom's particularistic tendencies and the growing belligerence of the magnates.[21]

---

17. See chapter 8.

18. This view, expressed in Baer, *History of the Jews*, 1:51, has been recently challenged by Ray, *Sephardic Frontier*, 82–84, who argues that the Jews frequently found protection by establishing ties with lords other than the king.

19. Juan Bonachía Hernando, *El concejo de Burgos en la baja edad media (1345–1426)* (Valladolid: Universidad de Valladolid, 1978), 52.

20. Ruiz, "Une royauté sans sacré: La monarchie castillane du bas moyen âge," *Annales* (May–June 1984): 429–53.

21. Ruiz, *Crisis and Continuity*, 298–99.

The policies adopted by the enterprising Alfonso X to accomplish this goal had negative consequences for the kingdom's Jews. First, the attempt to ground royal authority in the Roman and Visigothic imperial legislative traditions and replace an assortment of local customs with a uniform code of law resulted in an infusion of ideologically rigid language from Roman and canon law into the kingdom's legal discourse on the Jews. Even though Alfonso's legislation on the Jews in the *Fuero real* and *Las siete partidas* did not immediately change the Jewish minority's situation in Castile, some of the statutes were promulgated during Alfonso's reign, while others had a more long-term impact. Most importantly, it heralded the king's contention that it was his duty not only to protect and tolerate the Jews and their religious worship, but also to safeguard the Christian community against the purported dangers of social intercourse between Christians and Jews. Second, the *concejos*' political alliance with the monarchy came at a price—the extension of royal authority into towns and the king's unwelcome meddling in municipal affairs. The Jews were caught in the tug-of-war between the centralizing tendencies of the Crown and the town councils' attempts to preserve local *fueros* and privileges.[22] Municipal officials resented the intrusions of royal tax collectors and tax farmers (some of whom were Jewish), but they reserved their special ire for *entregadores* and *porteros*—royal agents entrusted with collections of outstanding debts to Jewish moneylenders. The tensions over loan enforcement became one of the main reasons behind the growing estrangement between Jews and Christians in Northern Castile, and the royal policies were largely to blame for this state of affairs.

Finally, the financial crisis enveloping the kingdom and the high expenses of the monarchy left Alfonso X habitually strapped for cash. One of his solutions was to tap more aggressively into one of the Crown's most traditional and reliable sources of revenue—the Jews. During the latter part of his reign, the Jews of Castile experienced fiscal pressure from the Crown that surpassed anything they had seen before. Besides imposing unusually heavy taxes, the king began to encourage Jewish moneylending by prohibiting Christians to engage in it in the hopes that the profits from the Jews' credit operations among Christians would be a financial boon to the Crown. It was an indirect way to increase the royal

---

22. Ladero Quesada, *Fiscalidad y poder real en Castilla*, 72.

income from towns, and that is why the activities of the *entregadores* were crucially important in ensuring that the money wound up in the royal treasury. The townsmen undoubtedly saw through the royal stratagem, but that understanding did nothing to alleviate the anger directed at the Jews, who were ultimately blamed for the royal trampling on local privileges and the impoverishment of Christian debtors.

King Alfonso X and his successors thus adhered to the traditional policy of protecting the Jews, but they anchored it to the exploitative fiscal demands of the monarchy.[23] The Jews of Castile did not escape a fiscal squeeze of the kind also experienced in the thirteenth century by the Jews of France, England, and the Crown of Aragon.[24] Yom Tov Assis has described in detail how the "insatiable demands" of the royal treasury led the kings of Aragon to create a "system of extortion" that allowed them to profit from the Jews' financial activities through confiscations of debts, usury investigations, exorbitant taxes, and extraordinary subsidies.[25] As in Aragon and elsewhere, in Northern Castile the king's demands for money forced the Jews to call in debts and attempt to collect loans from Christians with assistance from royal justices or special officials, who could take insolvent debtors to court, imprison them, and confiscate their property.[26] Assis has argued that in the Crown of Aragon reliance on Jewish money led to tensions between Jews and Christians, and his observation is also true for Castile.[27] In fact, the evidence from Northern Castile reveals a situation that closely resembles the state of affairs in Valencia after 1283 as described by Mark Meyerson: "As long as Jewish and Christian taxpayers were caught up in the seemingly perpetual cycle of moneylending, royal taxation, and debt collection, the litigation and ill will generated by Jewish usury could at best subside to a low level; at worst it cast a pall over relations between Jews and their Christian neighbors."[28]

23. See Meyerson, *Jews in an Iberian Frontier Kingdom*, 100–101.
24. On France, see Jordan, *French Monarchy and the Jews*. On England, see Robin R. Mundill, *The King's Jews: Money, Massacre and Exodus in Medieval England* (London: Continuum, 2010). On Aragon, see Meyerson, *Jews in an Iberian Frontier Kingdom*.
25. Assis, *Jewish Economy*, 35, 73, 133, 160.
26. Jordan, *French Monarchy and the Jews*, 134; Stacey, "Jewish Lending and the Medieval English Economy," 97–98; Assis, *Jewish Economy*, 60–61.
27. Assis, *Jewish Economy*, 22.
28. Meyerson, *Jews in an Iberian Frontier Kingdom*, 194.

Castile was certainly not the only kingdom in medieval Europe where royal piggybacking on Jewish moneylending wreaked havoc on interfaith relations, but it was unique in having a cogent legislative and political anti-Jewish discourse whose evolution can be traced until the end of the fourteenth century and the pogroms of 1391.[29] Time and again, urban procurators gathered at the cortes to complain that the Jews were extorting excessive taxes and charging exorbitant interest rates, taking property away from Christians, violating local *fueros*, giving the king "evil counsel," and generally ruining the kingdom.[30] The townsmen had fresh motivation to remember that it was an insult to call somebody a "Jew" and that the Jews were considered greedy and unscrupulous.[31] Gradually, the preexisting stereotypes and the new grievances coalesced into an anti-Jewish discourse that grew progressively harsher. Eventually, at the cortes meeting in Toro in 1371, the procurators submitted a petition that scornfully described the Jews as "insolent, wicked people, enemies of God and of the entire Christendom."[32]

David Nirenberg has argued persuasively that broader ideological narratives about religious minorities acquire their potency within specific local contexts and "are contingent upon a host of other structures and ideas, many of which have quite local meaning."[33] In Castile, the local contexts and the collective discourse were locked into a mutually reinforcing relationship. Enhanced by ancient religious stereotypes, anti-Jewish attitudes grew more potent in the specific configuration of local concerns and controversies, but found a receptive wider audience when the urban representatives gathered to draft collective petitions before the upcoming meetings of the cortes. The bitingly anti-Jewish petitions and the accompanying royal ordinances were then recorded in special book-

---

29. Ruiz, *Spain's Centuries of Crisis*, 149.

30. See especially León Tello, "Legislación sobre judíos en las cortes de las antiguos reinos de León y Castilla," in *Papers of the Fourth World Congress of Jewish Studies* (Jerusalem: World Union of Jewish Studies, 1968), 55–63; and Monsalvo Antón, *Teoria y evolucion de un conflicto social*, 167–81.

31. The fueros of Coria, Cáceres, and Usagre assign the same fine for calling somebody a "Jew," a "cuckold," a "traitor," or a "leper"; Suárez Bilbao, *El fuero judiego en la España cristiana*, 58; see also *Cantar de mío Cid*, any edition.

32. La real academia de la historia, *Cortes de los antiguos reinos de León y de Castilla* (Madrid: 1863), 2:203–4.

33. Nirenberg, *Communities of Violence*, 12.

lets, *cuadernos*, and carried home by the urban representatives, disseminating these ideas kingdom-wide and solidifying the narrative of Jewish greed and harmfulness to the Christian community. Luckily, enough documentation survives for Northern Castile to show how a confluence of local crises and discourses could affect the ideas about Jews in the entire kingdom. It also gives a glimpse into some of the pressures and frustrations experienced by Christian and Jewish communities as they struggled to find a workable mode of coexistence at a time of major change and upheaval.

The Jews and Alfonso X's Legislative Program

In the second half of the thirteenth century, rapid changes in the Castilian society and a sense of growing crisis began to test the durability of interfaith coexistence on the northern *meseta*. During the decades that followed Fernando III's triumph over the Muslims in Córdoba (1236) and Seville (1248), the kingdom of Castile entered a period of painful adjustments that negatively affected virtually every sector of the Castilian society. The Jews, now more than ever considered indispensable by the cash-hungry monarchy, were hit hard by royal policies that managed to be simultaneously protective and contemptuous, permissive and exploitative. Alfonso X, on whom posterity bestowed the honorific title *el Sabio* for his scholarly and literary talents, was a sovereign whose high ambitions could be matched neither by the state of his finances nor by his political and administrative abilities. Lauded by some as the embodiment of Spanish religious tolerance for his collaboration with Muslim and Jewish scholars and for his sponsorship of a multilingual corpus of translators, Alfonso nevertheless ordered expulsions of Muslims from large swaths of Andalusia and subjected the Jews to fiscal pressure, adopting some of the less savory tactics from the arsenal of Castile's northern neighbors.[34] The kingdom as a whole suffered from demographic imbal-

---

34. Norman Roth, "Jewish Collaborators in Alfonso's Scientific Work," 59–60; John Tolan, "Une *convivencia* bien précaire: La place des juifs et des musulmans dans les sociétés chrétiennes ibériques au Moyen Âge," in *La Tolérance: Colloque international de Nantes, mai 1998, Quatrième centenaire de l'édit de Nantes*, edited by Guy Saupin, Rémy Fabre, and Marcel Launay, 386–90 (Rennes: Presses Universitaires de Rennes, Centre de Recherche sur l'histoire du Monde Atlantique, 1999). H. Salvador Martínez has argued that Alfonso promoted *convivencia cultural*, but also did everything in his power to impede *convivencia social*; see his *La con-*

ance, high inflation, and economic destabilization. It may be, as Teofilo Ruiz suggests, that Alfonso was "as much a victim of circumstances as of his own limitations as a ruler," but few doubt that his unsuccessful and financially ruinous bid for the imperial throne drove his kingdom even further into the ground.[35]

Alfonso's policies toward the Jews have received mixed reviews from historians, but the evidence suggests that his legislative and administrative activities had a negative overall effect on Jewish-Christian relations in the kingdom of Castile.[36] Even during the early "tolerant" period of his reign (before the mudéjar rebellion of the mid-1260s), the king signaled his intent to bring the status of the kingdom's Jews in line with the ideologically restrictive requirements of Roman and canon law. In this, he was following the initiative of his father, Fernando III, who had ordered a translation of the old Visigothic code, Forum iudicum, into Castilian under the name Fuero juzgo, and subsequently granted it to Toledo, Córdoba, Seville, and other towns in Andalusia and Murcia.[37] In the fuero accompanying the concession of the Fuero juzgo to Córdoba, Fernando III reiterated one of its central precepts, ordering that "to fulfill the teachings of the Holy Fathers," no Jew should occupy positions of authority over Christians.[38] Alfonso's ambitious program to replace the kingdom's diverse legal norms, articulated in the fueros, with a uniform code of law led to the writing of the king's two

---

vivencia en la España del siglo XIII: Perspectivas alfonsíes (Madrid: Ediciones Polifemo, 2006), 16. For an overview of the Alfonsine policies on the Jews, see David Romano, "Alfonso X y los judíos: Problemática y propuestas de trabajo," Anuario de Estudios Medievales 15 (1985): 151–77.

35. Ruiz, Crisis and Continuity, 294–98.

36. Note, however, his efforts to strengthen the communal autonomy of some aljamas; see chapter 6.

37. O'Callaghan, "Alfonso X and the Partidas," in Las siete partidas, vol. 1, The Medieval Church, edited by Robert I. Burns, xxxii (Philadelphia: University of Pennsylvania Press, 2001).

38. "Item ut sanctorum patrum precepta impleantur quibus obedire volumus et debemus, iubeo ut nullus iudeus vel nuperrenatus habeat mandamentum super ullum xristianum in Corduba nec in suo termino nisi esset Almonxifus meus"; Victoriano Rivera Romero, ed., La carta de fuero concedida á la ciudad de Córdoba por el rey D. Fernando III (Córdoba: Imprenta, librería y litografía del Diario, 1881), 16.

Fuero juzgo, book XII, title II, law 14: "establecemos en esta ley, que vala por siempre daquí adelantre, con todos ls varones de nuestra corte, que ningund judío desdel primer anno que nos regnamos adelantre ningun cristiano libre, nin siervo, nin mancebo non aya en su poder, nin en su servicio, nin aya ningun criotiano por mercendero [servant], nin gelo consentamos, que los alleguen á sí en ninguna manera"; Joaquín Ibarra y Marín, ed., Fuero juzgo en Latin y Castellano (Madrid: La Real Academia Española, 1815), 181.

best-known legislative works—the *Fuero real* and *Las siete partidas*. Inspired by contemporary political theology and influenced by late Roman legal sources (such as the recently discovered Emperor Justinian's *Corpus iuris civilis*) and the main works of canon law, Alfonso's codes stress the monarch's responsibility to protect "the common good" of the realm against potential violations of the Christian public order by non-Christian minorities.[39] Even though some dismiss the *Fuero real* and the *Partidas* as merely "theoretical" codes written by churchmen (the *Partidas* was not "explicitly promulgated" until 1348), the *Fuero real* remained in force at least until 1272 and perhaps beyond.[40] In addition, Alfonso personally promulgated a few of the provisions from the *Fuero real* during the meetings of the kingdom's representative assembly—the cortes. Other stipulations reminiscent of those found in Alfonso's codes reappeared in the cortes legislation early in the fourteenth century.

The *Fuero real* was one of the earliest products of Alfonso X's legislative program and, according to some historians, the only one of Alfonso's legal codes promulgated during his lifetime.[41] Granted to numerous Castilian towns starting in 1255, it was intended by the king as a municipal code that would supplement or supplant the older customs and *fueros*.[42] There exists considerable disagreement regarding the date of its completion and

39. O'Callaghan, "Alfonso X and the *Partidas*," xxxvii–xxxviii; Burns, "Introduction to the Seventh Partida," 5:xxvi. Jurists trained in ecclesiastical and Roman law first appeared in Castile in the second half of the twelfth century, and by the middle of the thirteenth century they were already actively participating in the writing of Alfonso X's legal codes; see Martínez Díez, "Los comienzos de la recepción del derecho Romano en España y el fuero real," in *Diritto commune e diritti locali nella storia dell'Europa: Atti del Convegno di Varenna (12–15 giugno 1979)* (Milan: A. Giuffre, 1980), 259; Antonio García y García, "En torno al derecho Romano en la España medieval," in *Estudios en homenaje a don Claudio Sanchez Albornoz en sus 90 años* (Buenos Aires: Instituto de Historia de España, 1985), 3:59–72.

40. O'Callaghan, "Alfonso X and the *Partidas*," xxxviii. He argues that Alfonso "probably did not consider that the *Partidas*, as the amended text of the earlier code [*Espéculo*], required a separate promulgation," and that "[i]n that sense, the *Partidas* already had the force of law during the reign of Alfonso X"; O'Callaghan, *Learned King*, 37; see, however, Norman Roth, "The Civic Status of the Jew," 149.

41. Palacios Alcaine, ed., *Alfonso X el Sabio*, xvi. Other historians believe that both the *Fuero real* and *Espéculo* were promulgated in 1255; see O'Callaghan, "Sobre la promulgación del Espéculo y del Fuero real," in *Estudios en homenaje a don Claudio Sanchez Albornoz en sus 90 años*, 3:168; Jerry R. Craddock, "La cronología de las obras legislativas de Alfonso X el Sabio," AHDE 51 (1981): 371, 380; and Aquilino Iglesia Ferreirós, "Fuero real y Especulo," AHDE 52 (1982): 111–91.

42. O'Callaghan, *Learned King*, 32.

promulgation, but according to the most common opinion, Sahagún and Aguilar de Campóo received it in 1255, whereas Burgos, Palencia, Soria, Alarcón, Peñafiel, Atienza, Buitrago, and some other towns accepted it a year later.[43] After 1256, Alfonso X continued the process at a somewhat slower pace, granting the Fuero real to a number of towns in Extremadura and Murcia until 1272, when the rebellion of Castilian nobility forced the king to restore the old fueros.[44]

The Fuero real owes little to the earlier fuero legislation, instead borrowing heavily from the Fuero juzgo and canon and Roman law.[45] At first glance, the departures from the tone and the content of the fueros are not as drastic as might be expected.[46] The original Visigothic anti-Judaism of the Fuero juzgo shows little impact on the precepts of the Fuero real. Most notable is the absence of a prohibition of the Jews occupying positions of power over Christians, found in Fernando III's fuero to Córdoba. Nor is there any mention of the Fourth Lateran Council's recent (1215) decrees for the Jews to wear distinguishing signs, to pay tithes, or to abstain from walking outside on Christian holidays.[47] Following the principle tacitly articulated in the fueros and officially acknowledged by the contemporary

43. Martínez Díez thinks that FR was written before 1252, perhaps as early as 1249; see Martínez Díez, "Los comienzos de la recepción del derecho Romano en España y el Fuero real," 259, 261. Alfonso García-Gallo, on the other hand, believes that the Espéculo was the royal code promulgated in 1256, whereas FR was not written until after Alfonso X's death; see, for example, his "La obra legislativa de Alfonso X: Hechos e hipotesis," AHDE 54 (1984): 97–161. For the generally accepted opinion, see Palacios Alcaine, Alfonso X el Sabio, and Antonio Pérez Martín, "El fuero real y Murcia," AHDE 54 (1984): 55–96.

44. Teofilo Ruiz believes that FR remained valid after 1272 in some towns of Old Castile, such as Burgos; see Ruiz, "El siglo XIII y primera mitad del siglo XIV," 114. Not all towns returned to their old fueros, and Alfonso's successors granted FR to some towns; see Pérez Martín, "El fuero real y Murcia," 88.

45. Martínez Díez, "Los comienzos de la recepción del derecho Romano en España y el fuero real," 260; Pérez Martín, "El fuero real y Murcia," 67–70. Gálo Sánchez argued earlier that the only municipal fuero from which FR had borrowed heavily was the fuero of Soria; see Sánchez, ed., Fueros castellanos, 259. However, Martínez Díez challenged his view, arguing that, instead, FR was the source for the fuero of Soria; see his "El fuero real y el fuero de Soria," AHDE 39 (1969): 545–62.

46. I am following the edition of FR published by Palacios Alcaine, ed., Alfonso X el Sabio. Another recent edition of FR is Martínez Diez, ed., Leyes de Alfonso X, vol. 2, Fuero real: Edicion y analisis critico (Ávila: Fundacion Sánchez Albornoz, 1988).

47. Grayzel, Church and the Jews, 307–9; David Romano, "Marco jurídico de la minoría judía," in De historia judía hispánica (Barcelona: Publicacions de la Universitat de Barcelona, 1991), 272. Las siete partidas, on the other hand, would later include most of these provisions.

papal legislation, the *Fuero real* protects the Jews' freedom of worship. The Jews are allowed "to read and to possess all of the books of their Law, given to them by Moses as well as by other prophets."[48] They can celebrate the Sabbath and other festivals, and nobody can prevent them from doing so by forcing them to go to court, by taking sureties, or in any other way.[49]

Aside from this basic principle of toleration, there is little in the *Fuero real* to suggest an affinity with the tone, language, or content of the earlier *fueros*. The whole approach to the issue of the Jews' presence in Castilian society has changed. The *fuero* legislation accepts as a given the distinctiveness and separateness of the Jewish community, but it is not concerned with enforcing this separation as a means of protecting the dominant Christian society from Jewish influence. Granted, many *fueros* discourage social interaction between religious groups—Jews, Christians, and Muslims—ordering them to attend public bathhouses on different days and banning sexual intercourse of Jewish and Muslim men with Christian women.[50] But never prior to the promulgation of the *Fuero real* are the Jews singled out as a special threat to Christendom. For the first time in Castilian legislation, the Jews—but not the Muslims—have an entire chapter dedicated to them (*De los iudíos*). The chapter on the Jews is found in the Fourth Book of the *Fuero real*—the book dedicated to criminal acts and their punishment.[51]

---

48. "Mas otorgamos que puedan leer et tener todos los libros de su Ley assí como les fue dado por Moysén et por los otros prophetas"; FR, IV.ii. I.

49. "Non deffendemos que los iudíos non puedan guarder sos sábados et las otras fiestas que manda su Ley et que usen todas las otras que an otorgadas por Sancta Eglesia et de los reyes. Et ninguno non sea osado de gelo toller nin de gelo contrallar. E ninguno non los constrinnga que uengan, nin que embíen a iuyzio en estos días sobredichos, nin les faga pendra, nin afincamiento ninguno por que fagan contra su Ley" ; FR, IV.ii. IX. Compare to the papal bull *Sicut judeis*: "while they [Jews] celebrate their festivals, no one shall disturb them in any way by means of sticks and stones, nor exact forced service from any of them other than such as they have been accustomed to perform from ancient times"; see Grayzel, "The Papal Bull Sicut Judeis," in *Essential Papers on Judaism and Christianity in Conflict*, edited by Jeremy Cohen, 232 (New York: New York University Press, 1991).

50. Most famously, in Cuenca: James Powers, trans., *The Code of Cuenca*, 13.

51. In this sense, FR foreshadows *Las siete partidas*, where the chapter on the Jews is also placed in the *partida* dedicated to criminal law; see Burns, "Introduction to the Seventh Partida," 5:xxvi. Antonio Pérez Martín notes that this organization mirrors that of the Decretals collections: *iudex, iudicia* (with *clerus* omitted to include royal law), *connubia*, and *crimen*; Pérez Martín, "El fuero real y Murcia," 71.

Several laws in the chapter speak of specifically Jewish crimes against Christianity. The very first law forbids Jews to own books that aim to destroy Christianity (*nuestra Ley*). The books in question are most likely anti-Christian polemical treatises such as *Toledot Yeshu*, although it is possible that Alfonso X also has the Talmud in mind.[52] Another law "firmly" (*firmemietre*) prohibits Jews from attempting to draw Christians away from their law (*su Ley*); death and confiscation of property await those who dare to violate this prohibition.[53] There is no parallel prohibition for Muslims to attract Christian apostates, even though Christians are forbidden, under the threat of death, to convert or to permit their children to convert to Judaism or Islam.[54] Every time a Jew utters blasphemy against God, St. Mary, or any other saint, he is to receive a fine of five *maravedís* and five lashes.[55] This law might have been taken directly from the *Fuero juzgo*, although similar measures had long been a staple in ecclesiastical legislation, including the canons of the Fourth Lateran Council.[56] The next law prohibits Jews (but not Muslims) and Christians from raising or nursing (*criar*) each other's children.[57] Once again, the source of this law is found in church legislation. The Council of Rouen (1074),

---

52. "[d]efendemos que non lean nin tengan libros a sabiendas que fablen en nuestra Ley et que sean contra ella pora desfazerla"; FR, IV.ii.I. FR also prohibits Jews to own books that speak against their own religion; FR, IV.ii.I. Jeremy Cohen has argued that this is an anti-Talmudic measure; Cohen, *Friars and the Jews*, 81. Larry Simon disagrees: "Jews in the Legal Corpus of Alfonso el Sabio," 81–82.

53. "Firmemietre defendemos que ningun iudío non sea osado de sosacar christiano ninguno que se torne de su Ley nin de lo retaiar; et el qui lo fiziere muera por ello et todo lo que ouiere sea del rey"; FR, IV.ii. II.

54. "Ningún christiano non sea osado de tornarse iudío, nin moro, nin sea osado de fazer su fijo moro o iudío. Et si alguno lo fiziere, muerra por ello. Et la muerte deste fecho sea atal aue sea de fuego"; FR, IV.i. I.

55. "Si el iudío dixiere denuesto ninguno cotra [sic] Dios, o contra Sancta María, o contra otro Sancto, peche V morabedís por cada uegada que lo dixiere et fágal el rey dar cinco açotes"; FR, IV.ii. III. Some manuscripts of FR say X morabedís and diez açotes; see Martínez Diez's edition of FR, *Leyes de Alfonso X*, vol. 2, *Fuero real*, 407.

56. Comp. to *Fuero juzgo*: "Nengun judío non blasme, ni en ninguna manera dexe la santa fée de los cristianos ... nin nenguno nonla contralle, nin de fecho, ni de dicho"; *Fuero juzgo*, 237. The IV Lateran Council: "We most especially forbid anyone to dare to break forth into insults against the Redeemer"; Grayzel, "Church and the Jews," 309.

57. "Ningún iudío nin iudía non sea osado de criar fijo de christiano, nin de Christiana, nin de dar so fijo a criar a christiano nin a Christiana. Et qui quier que lo fiziesse, peche I morabedís al rey et non lo faga más"; FR., IV.ii. IV. Martínez Diez's edition says L morabedís; *Leyes de Alfonso X*, vol. 2, *Fuero real*, 407.

the Third Lateran Council (1179), the Council of Montpellier (1195), the Council of Paris (1213), and the Council of Terragona (1239), among others, forbade employment of Christian wet-nurses by Jews.[58] Originally conceived as an extension of the prohibition for Jews to employ Christian slaves, this precept undergoes further transformation in the *Fuero real*, setting additional limitations on social intercourse between Jews and Christians.[59]

Although they are few in number, these laws reflect a dramatic reassessment by the Castilian monarchy of its responsibilities toward religious minorities. The *Fuero real* strives to portray the king, first and foremost, as the champion of Christian orthodoxy.[60] The Jews may be singled out as the greatest threat to Christian doctrine, but other non-Christians fare only slightly better. Scattered throughout the four books of the *Fuero real* are laws that include Jews, Muslims, heretics, diviners, and excommunicates in the list of persons whose rights are circumscribed in judicial procedures and property laws. Jews, Muslims, and heretics cannot serve as advocates for Christians in the court of law, and they are not allowed, except in certain cases, to bring lawsuits against anyone.[61] In addition, the *Fuero real* seeks to prevent religious minorities from acquiring Christian property through inheritance. It places Jews in the category of persons (among others, Muslims, heretics, women, children, the mad,

---

58. Bernhard Blumenkranz, "The Roman Church and the Jews," in *Essential Papers on Judaism and Christianity in Conflict* (New York: New York University Press, 1991), 203; Grayzel, "Church and the Jews," 25–26.

59. On the law prohibiting Jews to purchase and own Christian slaves, see the Theodosian Code, 16.9.2–3, in Clyde Pharr, ed., *The Theodosian Code and Novels and the Simondian Constitutions* (Princeton: Princeton University Press, 1952), 471–72. This prohibition on Jews and Christians employing each other's wet-nurses will have a long history in the cortes legislation, first appearing in the ordinances for 1258. It will reappear repeatedly in the cortes ordinances throughout the rest of the thirteenth and in the fourteenth century; see Monsalvo Antón, *Teoría y evolución de un conflicto social*, 171.

60. O'Callaghan, *Learned King*, 49.

61. "Mandamos que ningún hereie, nin iudio, nin moro non sea uozero por christiano contra christiano, nin sieruo, nin ciego, nin descomulgado], nin sordo, nin loco, nin omne que non aya edat complida"; FR, I.ix.IV. "Defendemos que ninguna mugier, nin omne sin edat cumplida, nin alcalde, nin merino, nin otro ninguno que tenga officio de iusticia mientre que el oficio touiere, nin ome que sea echado de la uilla o de la tierra mienter que fuere echado, nin omne que tomó auer pora acusar a otro o por non accusar, nin iudío, nin moro, nin erege, nin omne agorado [etc.] ... non puedan accusar a otro ninguno sobre cosa ninguna"; FR, IV.xx.II.

the deaf et al.) who cannot serve as executors of wills (cabeçales).⁶² Neither Jews, Muslims, heretics, nor any non-Christians can inherit property from Christians.⁶³ Those who become Jews, Muslims, or heretics can be disinherited by their parents.⁶⁴ The *Fuero real*'s inheritance laws betray an underlying desire to keep property within the Christian community. This "novel and increasing concern with property," in the words of Teofilo Ruiz, is characteristic of thirteenth-century Castile. As the *Fuero real* shows, the concern is not only with preserving property and using it in the interests of "the individual and the family," but also with keeping it in the hands of a larger "family"—the community of believers.⁶⁵ For the first time, the kingdom's economic interests are defined in religious terms, with the Christian community's well-being now of paramount importance.

The Alfonsine code *Las siete partidas*, the apex and the synthesis of the king's legislative efforts, was finished in 1265, but not officially promulgated during Alfonso's lifetime.⁶⁶ The *Partidas* contains an even fuller expression of Alfonso's vision of an ideal Christian society and the Jews' place in it, and it hews even closer to canon law and the writings of contemporary Christian theologians.⁶⁷ The Second *Partida* embraces an image common in medieval political theology—that of a king as the head directing the movements of the body—his subjects (body politic, *universitas*): "as from the head originate the feelings by which all the members of the body are controlled; so also by the commands which originate from

---

62. "Mandamos que ningún sieruo, nin religioso, nin mugier, nin omne que non sea de edat, nin loco, nin erege, nin moro, nin iudío, nin mudo, nin sordo, nin ome que sea dado por aleuoso o por traydor, nin omne que sea iudgado a muerte, nin omne que sea echado de tierra, que non puedan seer cabeçales en ninguna manda"; FR, III.iv.VII.

63. "Deffendemos que nigún clérigo nin lego non pueda, en iuda ni en muerte, iuidio, nin moro, nin herege, nin omne que non sea christiano fazer herdero. E si alguno lo fiziere, non uala et el rey herede todo lo suyo"; FR, III.v.xvi.

64. "Otrossí lo pueda desheredar sil yoguiere con la mugier, o con la barragana, o sil fiziere cosa por que deua morir, o prender lisión, o si por prisión de so cuerpo nol quisiere fiar, o si lo embargar o destoruar, de guisa que non pueda fazer manda, o si se fiziere erege, o si se tornare moro, o iudio, o si ioguiere en catiuo et non le quisiere quitar en quanto pudiere; FR, III.viii.II.

65. Ruiz, *From Heaven to Earth*, 55–56.

66. Craddock, "La cronología," 373–74; Salvador Martínez, *La convivencia*, 137.

67. Specifically, the *Decretales of Gregory IX* and Ramon de Penyafort's *Summa de Poenitentia*; see Simon, "Jews in the Legal Corpus of Alfonso el Sabio," 86.

the king, who is the lord and head of all the people of this kingdom, they should be directed and guided."[68] The duty of the king, who "occupies the position of God" in his kingdom, is to protect the body against internal and external enemies through the exercise of justice and law.[69]

The threats to this community of believers headed by a God-like figure are addressed in the Seventh *Partida*, and the Jews (Title 24, *De los iudios*, "Concerning the Jews") are found right after sorcerers and diviners and before Muslims, heretics, suicides, and blasphemers. Like the *Fuero real*, the Seventh *Partida* offers the Jews protection and toleration of their beliefs and worship, but only if they "pass their lives among Christians quietly and without disorder (*mansa mente e sin mal bolliçio*)," not blaspheming or trying to attract Christian converts.[70] Right after this traditional statement of toleration, the *Partida* makes its one deviation from the church's official position on the Jews by giving credence to the rumor (*oymos dezir*, "we have heard it said") that the Jews practice ritual crucifixion of Christian children on Good Friday to express their contempt for Christianity.[71] The rest of the *Partida* tries to strike a balance between extending to the Jews their customary protections and imposing penalties for crimes against the Christian order. The king guarantees the Jews' right to worship God in their synagogues, forbids anyone to violate the sanctity of their Sabbath, and prohibits forced conversions to Christianity.[72] But most of the laws in the *Partida* are concerned with protecting the spiritual integrity and physical safety of the Christian community. The Seventh *Partida* goes much further than the *Fuero real* in imposing strict limitations on social interaction between members of the two faiths. The Jews may not keep Christian servants in their houses, and eat, drink,

---

68. Partida 2.1.5. I am following Robert I. Burns's 2001 edition of Samuel Parsons Scott's translation of *Las siete partidas* and Suárez Bilbao's text of the titles in the *Partidas* related to Jews in *El fuero judiego en la España cristiana*, 255–66; see also Ernst H. Kantorowicz, *The King's Two Bodies: A Study in Mediaeval Political Theology* (Princeton: Princeton University Press, 1997), 314–16; O'Callaghan, *Learned King*, 18–20. The image of the Church as the body of Christ originates with St. Paul: 1 Cor 12:12–31; Col 1:18; 2:18–20; Eph 1:22–23.

69. Partida 2.1.7 and 2.10.2.

70. See the conclusion of Innocent III's bull *Sicut judeis* (1199): "We wish, however, to place under the protection of this decree only those (Jews) who have not presumed to plot against the Christian Faith"; Grayzel, *Church and the Jews*, 94–95.

71. Partida 7.24.2

72. Partida 7.24.4–6.

and bathe with Christians. Wine and medicine made by Jews are forbidden for Christian consumption. Jews are strictly prohibited from having sexual intercourse with Christian women, "who are spiritually the wives of Our Lord Jesus Christ." To prevent illicit sexual relations, the Jews are ordered to wear "some distinguishing mark upon their heads" (*sennal çierta sobre sus cabeças*) to make them easily recognizable.[73]

At the time of their creation, the *Fuero real* and *Las siete partidas* were more than legal codes; they were important political and ideological statements made by the king who brought new energy and zeal to the task of state-building. Many—if not most—of their stipulations on the Jews remained unenforced, and the dealings between Christians and Jews likely continued to follow the customary regulations outlined in local *fueros*. In fact, in 1254 Alfonso X confirmed the *fuero* given to the Jewish community of Haro, and his son, Sancho IV, followed suit in 1287.[74] The *fuero* of Cuenca was restored to a number of cities by 1272 after they had resisted the application of the *Fuero real*.[75] The *Fuero real* never became the general law of the kingdom, while *Las siete partidas* went through several redactions after Alfonso's death and was not explicitly promulgated until much later.[76] However, one should not underestimate the impact of the Alfonsine codes on the development of the anti-Jewish political and legal discourse in Castile. The codes revealed Alfonso's belief that the royal protection of the Jews and the king's protection of Christians *from* the Jews were two sides of the same coin. Just as it was the king's prerogative to control the Jews and benefit from their presence in the kingdom, it was also his responsibility to discipline them and to impose penalties for their crimes and transgressions against Christians and Christianity.

His legal pronouncements notwithstanding, Alfonso never relin-

---

73. Partida 7.24.7–11.

74. León Tello, "Nuevos documentos," 163, 157–58. In 1288, however, the *judería* of Haro was robbed by the troops of Sancho IV, who sacked the village after the murder of its lord and his former favorite, Lope Díaz de Haro. According to the Partition of Huete (1290), the king later compensated the Jews of Haro for their losses by forgiving them half of their tribute. Sancho's successor, Fernando IV, confirmed the *fuero* of Haro; see León Tello, "Nuevos documentos," 155; León Tello, "La estancia de judíos en castillos," 462; Hernández, *Las rentas del rey*, 140.

75. Powers, *Code of Cuenca*, 23.

76. See Romano, "Marco jurídico de la minoría judía," 274; Palacios Alcaine, *Alfonso X el Sabio*, xvi; Simon, "Jews in the Legal Corpus of Alfonso el Sabio," 84.

quished the services of his Jewish physicians, tax farmers, and financiers.[77] He did, however, take a few steps toward implementing some of the provisions of his legislation on the Jews. The main stipulation in the *Fuero real* limiting social interactions between Jews and Christians was the prohibition against employing wet-nurses (or nannies) of another faith. Alfonso first enacted this provision even before the promulgation of the *Fuero real*, in 1252, at the cortes of Seville. Later, the law reappeared in the legislation of the cortes in Valladolid (1258) and in Jerez (1268).[78] Even though submission of collective petitions became the rule at the cortes in the last decade of the thirteenth century, the ban on interfaith childcare did not reappear in the cortes legislation until 1313—a good indication that the law was Alfonso X's special initiative.[79] Alfonso's attempts to enact social barriers between Jews and Christians evidently paved the way for the cortes's legislation on the same matter. In the decades to follow, representatives of *concejos* would ask the king to ban the Jews' use of Christian names, to require their wearing of distinguishing signs, and to compel them to reside in separate neighborhoods.[80]

Once the king signaled his willingness to correct Jewish "errors" through public law, it became a standard practice among the urban representatives to arrive at the cortes bearing anti-Jewish petitions. Between 1252 and 1350, thirty-two cortes were convened in Castile, and twenty eight of them issued ordinances that mentioned Jews.[81] The overwhelming majority of these petitions asked the king to legislate on the matter of Jewish moneylending. Traditionally, the Jews' credit operations fell under the purview of the king. Many old *fueros* (*fuero* of Haro, *Libro de los fueros de Castilla*) included rules for lending money at interest, but Alfonso X was the first king to issue regulations of Jewish moneylending that were intended to be universally applicable in the kingdom of Castile. In 1255, Alfonso's *Fuero real* set the legal interest rate at *tres por quatro*, and in

77. Salvador Martínez, *La convivencia*, 165.
78. Palacios Alcaine, ed., *Alfonso X el Sabio*, 109; Georg Gross, "Las cortes de 1252: Ordenamiento otorgado al concejo de Burgos en las cortes celebradas en Sevilla el 12 de Octubre de 1252 (según el original)," *Boletín de la Real Academia de la Historia* 182 (1985): 112; *Cortes* 1, 62, 77.
79. Procter, *Curia and Cortes in León and Castile*, 208; O'Callaghan, *Cortes of Castile-León*, 123; *Cortes* 1, 227.
80. See chapter 8.
81. Romano, "Marco jurídico de la minoría judía," 281.

1258 the regulation was already included in the legislation promulgated at the cortes of Valladolid.[82] Subsequently, no king failed to reaffirm the permissible interest rate (usually *tres por quatro*, or 33.3 percent) at the cortes as a manifestation of what had become, since the times of Alfonso X, a royal prerogative to regulate usury in the kingdom.[83]

The Jews and Moneylending in Northern Castile

In the last quarter of the thirteenth century, the growing fiscal pressure on the Jews drove more of them into moneylending, causing lasting damage to Jewish-Christian relations in Northern Castilian towns. The worsening economic conditions in the kingdom and an inefficient management of finances left the Castilian Crown perpetually short on funds. Alfonso's expensive campaign, beginning in 1257, to obtain the crown of the Holy Roman Empire made the king's search for additional sources of revenue even more urgent.[84] Taxing the Jews was one of the Castilian kings' tried and true solutions to fiscal problems, but Alfonso gave it a new twist. Banning Christian moneylending and transforming it into a type of royal monopoly in which only Jews and Muslims were allowed to participate, Alfonso put in place a mechanism that would allow him to profit from what essentially amounted to an indirect taxation of his Christian subjects.[85] The Crown's quest for a drastic increase in revenues forced Jewish creditors to become more aggressive in pursuing debt collections. By assisting them in this endeavor, the monarchy heedlessly cut through the fabric of local privileges, agreements, and relations, doing irreparable damage to the fragile culture of interreligious negotiations and raising the level of mutual distrust that could spill into physical violence against the Jewish minority.

Moneylending was not always considered a predominately Jewish occupation. It is difficult to pinpoint the precise moment when the perception of moneylending as an essentially Jewish activity first surfaced in Northern Castile. The *Cantar de mío Cid*, which dates to the late twelfth or

---

82. FR, 109; Cortes 1, 60.
83. For a good summary of the usury regulations at the cortes, see León Tello, "Legislación sobre judíos en las cortes," 58–60.
84. Ruiz, *Crisis and Continuity*, 302–3; O'Callaghan, *Learned King*, 205.
85. See Assis, *Jewish Economy*, 19.

early thirteenth century, rather unceremoniously poked fun at two greedy but hapless moneylenders from Burgos (assumed to be Jewish)—Raquel and Vidas—and praised the cleverness of the gallant Cid, who never had the slightest intention of repaying his debt. This poetic justification for not fulfilling one's credit obligations to Jews curiously foreshadowed the all-too-real problem of collecting old debts faced by the Jews of Castile later in the century.[86] The *Libro de los fueros de Castilla* contained numerous clauses regulating Christians' indebtedness to Jews. Some chapters that dealt with Jewish moneylenders even cited judicial decisions (*fazañas*) made in real court cases. However, Christians' participation as creditors in loan operations was also acknowledged, and many chapters dealt with hypothetical situations in which Christians and Jews lent money or pawned various objects to one another (*cristiano a judio o judio a cristiano*).[87] The *Fuero real* tellingly placed usury (*usuras*) regulations in the chapter dedicated to Jews (*De los iudios*), but included a caveat that the same laws applied to all creditors, whether Jews, Christians, or Muslims.[88] The ordinances of the cortes convened early in Alfonso X's reign continued to deal with the matter in a similar vein, reflecting the king's pragmatic belief that members of all three faiths were engaged in lending money at interest. The cortes of Valladolid (1258) restated the *Fuero real*'s prohibition of interest rates higher than 33.3 percent (*tres por quatro*), addressing the injunction specifically to Jewish usurers, but not overlooking "all those who engage in usury"—Christians, Moors, and Jews.[89] If these legal sources are to be taken at face value, the Jews were a group most firmly associated with moneylending, but they were in all likelihood greatly outnumbered by Christian usurers.

However, a sudden shift in royal policy in the late 1260s had major implications for the Jews' role as purveyors of credit to Christians. At the cortes of Jerez in 1268, Alfonso X forbade Christians from engaging in usury.[90] The origins of this prohibition are obscure, but it was likely re-

---

86. *Cantar de mío Cid* (*The Poem of the Cid*), trans. Rita Hamilton (Manchester: Manchester University Press, 1975), 24–29.

87. Sanches, ed., *Libro de los fueros de Castiella*, chapters 19, 33, 34, 61, 73, 92, 96, 221, 234, 249, 306.

88. Palacios Alcaine, ed., *Alfonso X el Sabio*, 408.

89. *Cortes* 1, 60.

90. "Ca tengo quelos cristianos non deuen dar a vsuras por ley nin por derecho"; *Cortes* 1, 80.

lated to the king's desire to promulgate laws worthy of the Holy Roman Emperor, for whose throne Alfonso was making a passionate bid.[91] It is no coincidence that Las siete partidas also banned usury, defining it as any interest accumulated beyond the principal.[92]

In line with the prohibition of Christian usury, all the subsequent cortes legislation, starting with the cortes of Valladolid in 1293, described and regulated usury as a domain of Jews and Muslims. Of course it would be a mistake to assume that all Christian lending at interest was eliminated with the stroke of the legislator's quill pen, although the official prohibition might have deterred some Christians from getting involved in it while forcing others to operate clandestinely through an intermediary of Jewish or Muslim partners.[93] The ineffectiveness of the ban was so transparent that many decades later, in 1348, Alfonso XI had to reissue the prohibition at the cortes of Alcalá de Henares, along with a stern admonition that usury presented a grave danger to the soul and was harmful to the kingdom.[94] Nevertheless, for a time, Alfonso X took his campaign against Christian usury quite seriously, no doubt in part because it held the promise of financial rewards in the form of fines imposed on communities whose members were caught engaging in usurious practices.[95] In May of 1278 Burgos found itself the subject of a usury inves-

91. Callaghan, Learned King, 198–213.

92. Partida 5.11.31 defines as legal only those loans that involve repayment of a sum equal to or less than the principal.

93. The cortes legislation contains occasional injunctions against Christians lending money in the name of Jews or Muslims—for example, the cortes of Burgos (1315): "Otrossi no pidieron que daqui adelante ningun judio non ffaga debda nin obligaçion en nonbre de christiano"; Cortes 1, 280. On the tactics used by Christian lenders in the small Catalan town of Santa Coloma de Queralt to avoid the appearance of charging interest, see Gregory B. Milton, "Christian and Jewish Lenders: Religious Identity and the Extension of Credit," Viator 37 (2006): 301–18. Milton argues that although the majority of lenders in the town were Christians, they preferred to state their loans in measures of wheat. On the role of Jewish moneylenders in Santa Coloma, see also Milton, Market Power: Lordship, Society, and Economy in Medieval Catalonia (1276–1313) (New York: Palgrave Macmillan, 2012), 82–91.

94. "La cobdiçia que es rrayz de todos los males en tal manera çiega los coraçones delos cobdiçiosos que non temiendo a Dios nin auiendo verguenna alos omes, desuergonnada miente dan avsuras en muy grant peligro de sus almas e danno de nuestros pueblos; et por ende mandamos que qual quier christiano ochristiana de qual quier estado ocondiçion que sea que diere avsura, que pierda todo lo que diere oprestare e que sea de aquel que rresçibio el enprestido"; Cortes 1, 531.

95. In addition to Burgos, fines were imposed on Alba de Tormes and Alcalá de Henares; see O'Callaghan, Learned King, 247, and 341–42n51.

tigation when Infante Sancho turned down the *concejo*'s request for intervention on its behalf, claiming that the pope himself had urged King Alfonso to stem this sinful practice that was causing the "loss of souls." In the course of the next several months, Sancho and Alfonso competed to collect the fine of 60,000 *maravedís* imposed on the city for the sin of usury. Sancho evidently prevailed in the struggle, pocketing the fine by October, even as Alfonso continued to press the *concejo* for payments.[96]

With Christian usury banned and Muslims as far as we can tell not actively participating in moneylending, the Jews were in effect officially designated as the royal usurers. After 1268, usury had essentially become a royal prerogative, with only the king's *servi*, the Jews (and, nominally, the Muslims), allowed to practice it. This development was part and parcel of the royal policies, which—although they were not necessarily planned and rationally carried out—had the cumulative effect of pushing the Jews into moneylending in greater numbers than ever before. The reasons for this transformation lay with the growing fiscal appetite of the Castilian Crown and the king's realization that a ready source of capital had been close at hand all along and only needed an extra squeeze to produce greater financial rewards.

It took several decades, but gradually a mechanism fell into place that allowed the king to profit from Jewish usury in several ways. The Crown could expect to receive income from the fines imposed on Christians violating the ban as well as to collect handsome revenues from the lawsuits brought against Christians for nonpayment of debts to Jews. The royal officials responsible for collecting such debts, as well as for bringing debtors to court, had existed at least since the time of Fernando III and were variously known as *porteros* and *entregadores*.[97] In 1231, the king gave a *portero* to the Jews of Villadiego dependent on the Hospital del Rey (Burgos), whose duties included collecting sureties for "manifest" debts and taking disputes over all other debts to court.[98] Little is known about the

---

96. CDCB, 141–57; Ruiz, "Burgos: Society and Royal Power, 1250–1350" (Ph.D. diss., Princeton University, 1973), 269–71.

97. A late-fourteenth-century document indicates that *porteros* and *entregadores* had different functions: the former ratified letters of obligation, while the latter carried out the confiscations of property; see Ruiz Gómez, "Aljamas y concejos en el Reino de Castilla durante la Edad Media," 66. In the documents that I examined, however, there seems to be no clear distinction between the two types of officials.

98. DHR, 137.

origins or the nature of the so-called *entregas de los judíos*—most likely a portion of each recovered debt, part of which was used to pay for the services of the *entregador*, with the rest going straight to the royal treasury. The recently discovered Accounts Book of 1290–92 listed income from the *entregas* among the "regular" (as opposed to "extraordinary") royal revenues. Only the *entregas* from the Jewish *aljamas* of the Extremadura were listed in detail, ranging from 200 to 1,000 *maravedís* per community, and distributed to various servitors of the Crown. The only entry for Old Castile indicated that the *entregas* from the region's *aljamas* would go to the *merino mayor*, the main royal representative in the region.[99]

The king also sought to benefit from Jewish usury indirectly by pressing the *aljamas* for more taxes. In the last years of Alfonso's reign the amount of the Jewish tax, *cabeza del pecho de los judíos*, jumped to an all-time high as the king struggled to finance his various expensive projects. The excuse for demanding higher contributions from the Jews came in 1279, when one of the Jewish tax collectors, Çag de la Maleha, directed the money intended by the king for the siege of Algeciras to Infante Sancho, who used it to pay for the return to Castile of his mother, Queen Violante. According to the royal chronicler, Alfonso retaliated against his son and the treasonous Jews by arresting Çag along with other Jewish tax collectors and then, in September 1280, having Çag brought to the Infante's residence in Seville and afterward dragged through the streets of the city until he died. In January 1281, Alfonso issued an order that "all the *aljamas* of the Jews be imprisoned on the Sabbath day" and held until they agreed to pay the enormous sum of 12,000 *maravedís* a day for a year.[100] Nor was

99. Hernández, *Las rentas del rey*, cxxxviii, 135–37; Ladero Quesada, *Fiscalidad y poder real en Castilla*, 78.

100. "[é] vino á Valladolid ... é libraron cartas para todo el reino en grand poridad, en que envió mandar que todas los aljamas de los judíos fuesen presos en un dia de sábado. É desque fueron presos todos, pleiteó con ellos el rey don Alfonso por doce mill maravedís cada dia de aquella moneda que corria"; Rosell, ed., *Cronicas de los reyes de Castilla*, 1:55, 58; *Chronicle of Alfonso X*, trans. Shelby Thacker and José Escobar, 225, 235–36. There is some confusion as to whether other Jews were also executed that day. Baer claims that Çag was hanged and another Jew, "an intimate of Sancho," was dragged through the streets of Seville. A third Jew converted to Christianity; Baer, *History of the Jews*, 1:130. Norman Roth contradicts Baer by (1) asserting that Çag de la Maleha should be identified with don Zag, the son of Mair Ibn Susan (Shushan), and not with Isaac, the son of Solomon Ibn Sadoq, and (2) claiming that Isaac was executed (also by dragging) by Alfonso "years" before the death of Çag de la Maleha. Roth relies on the *Chronica* of Alfonso X and on an undated eulogy (also

the imposition of this "fine" a one-time affair. Francisco Hernández, the discoverer and publisher of the Accounts Book, speculates that the Jews were made to pay the same amount (12,000 maravedís a day or 4,320,000 maravedís a year) the next year (1281). Subsequently, the sum was reduced every year by 1,000 maravedís a day, probably in reaction to the Jews' desperate entreaties to stop this fiscal bloodletting of Jewish communities. According to the Partition of Burgos, in 1286 and 1287, respectively, the aljamas handed over to the king 7,000 and 6,000 maravedís a day. By 1290, the amount was less than half of what the Jews were forced to pay in 1280: 5,275 maravedís a day, or 1,925.366 maravedís a year. Still, according to Fernández's calculations, in 1292, almost half of all the regular revenue of the Crown came from the taxes imposed on Jewish communities.[101]

Predictably, the relentless fiscal pressure to which the aljamas were subjected in the last two decades of the thirteenth century had an adverse effect on their economic health. In 1312, Fernando IV wistfully remarked that in the days of his father and grandfather, Sancho IV and Alfonso X, the Jewish aljamas were paying the king 6,000 maravedís a day, whereas he only received from them one-fifth of the former amount (or about 1,200 maravedís a day).[102] By then it was already becoming apparent that the Crown's strategy of turning Jews into royal moneylenders, regulating usury in minute detail, and providing assistance to Jewish creditors with collecting old debts was not bringing in the desired results. In 1348, at the cortes in Alcalá de Henares, Alfonso XI would drastically change the course by banning Jewish usury and attempting to revive the aljamas' economy by allowing them to purchase inheritable estates.[103]

Until this happened, however, the Castilian Crown had openly counted on the success of the Jews' usurious operations as a way of boosting royal revenues. Only three years before the ban on Jewish usury, in 1345, Alfonso XI tried to impress on his Christian subjects the importance of repaying their debts to Jews by declaring that unless the Jews collected

---

apparently used by Baer) penned by Todros ben Judah Abulafia; Norman Roth, "Two Jewish Courtiers of Alfonso X Called Zag (Isaac)," Sefarad 43 (1983): 75–85.

101. Hernández, Las rentas del rey, cxxxvi–cxxxvii, 337.

102. "Otrossi me ffiçieron ssaber quelas mis aljamas delos judios delos mios rreynos ssolian pechar al Rey don Alfonso mio auelo e al Rey don Sancho mio padre, sseys mill mr. cada dia, e desto non sse escusaua ningun judio, que me pechauan ami el quinto"; Cortes 1, 220.

103. Cortes 1, 532–33.

the debts promptly, they could not meet their fiscal obligations to the Crown. Almost fifty years earlier, his grandfather, Sancho IV, made a very similar statement, laying bare the connection between Christians' debts to Jews and the *aljamas*' ability to pay their *pechos*.[104]

The double thrust of the royal policies—banning Christian usury and imposing staggering rates of taxation on the Jewish *aljamas*—all but made certain that the Jews would be driven to rely on moneylending to a much greater degree than ever before. In Castile, as in Aragon, by the last quarter of the thirteenth century, Jewish usury had become "a nearly inescapable livelihood that the Jews' fiscal servitude to the monarchy required."[105] Only by lending money to Christians at high interest rates and collecting the debts in a timely manner could the Jews hope to accumulate enough capital to satisfy the cash-hungry monarchy. One should note, however, that moneylending never became the Jews' exclusive occupation. Artisanal pursuits continued to be open to the Jews of Northern Castile and León, although some Jewish artisans—as Samuel the carpenter of Astorga did in 1317—also provided loans to Christians on the side.[106] Despite the prohibitions on buying inheritable estates, the Jews continued to do so, as evidenced by occasional mentions of Jewish landowners in the records.[107] Still, options were dwindling as the Jews found themselves compelled to focus more intently on funneling any surplus wealth into the royal treasury. As references to Jewish moneylenders increase in frequency toward the end of the thirteenth century, so do, tellingly, the accounts of tensions between Jewish creditors and their Christian clients. The Crown's fiscal policies pitted *aljamas* against *concejos*, leaving behind a legacy of antagonism and resentment.

104. Alfonso XI: "por quelos judios estan muy pobres e non pueden conprar los pechos que nos an adar e avn nos deuen algunas quantias dellos, que por esto non podemos dar la espera mas de un anno." Sancho IV wanted usury cases to move quickly through courts, so that "non rreçiban los iudios alongamiento por que sse detenga el pecho que me ouieren adar"; *Cortes* 1, 486, 115.
105. Meyerson, *Jews in an Iberian Frontier Kingdom*, 8.
106. Gregoria C. Domínguez, César A. Álvarez, and José A. Martín Fuertes, eds., *Colección documental del archivo diocesano de Astorga* [CDADA] (León: Centro de Estudios e investigación "San Isidoro," 2001), 304–5.
107. A Jew by the name of Mose bought some land in la Nava near Aguilar de Campóo in 1315 (see note 59). Don Arsento, a Jew, owned an estate near Belorado in 1356; Huidobro y Serna and Cantera Burgos, "Juderías burgalesas," 47.

The Problem of Old Debts

Although some scholars have argued that routine interfaith social and economic interaction bred familiarity and even friendship, there is plentiful evidence that such contacts could cut both ways.[108] This was certainly the case in medieval Northern Castile, where economic relations between Jews and Christians occasioned friendly exchanges, but were also often the cause of friction and discord.[109] Whenever disagreements arose, intercommunal contacts, especially negotiation of agreements (official and informal), intended to anticipate or smooth over friction and conflicts, were crucial to stabilizing interfaith relations. In Northern Castile, these negotiations were a source of constant preoccupation for both Jews and Christians, especially in the latter part of the thirteenth century, when disputes over taxation, judicial autonomy, and especially moneylending increased in both frequency and intensity. One suspects that in most cases, the two communities were able to arrive at mutually acceptable terms. However, the Crown's assistance with debt collections, seen by the *concejos* as a violation of local privileges, upended the traditional mechanisms of conflict resolution and elicited a strong backlash against the Jews and their credit operations.[110]

Since the royal chancery routinely handled appeals from Jewish and Christian communities and issued charters outlining the king's decisions, intercommunal contacts left behind the lengthiest documentary record. These documents show that interfaith property sales and loan agreements

---

108. Joseph Shatzmiller, *Shylock Reconsidered: Jews, Moneylending, and Medieval Society* (Berkeley: University of California Press, 1990), 123; Klein, *Jews, Christian Society, and Royal Power*, 162; however, see also Nirenberg, *Communities of Violence*, esp. 30–40, and William Chester Jordan, "Jews on Top: Women and the Availability of Consumption Loans in Northern France in the Mid-Thirteenth Century," *Journal of Jewish Studies* 29 (1978): 39–56. Olivia Remie Constable has argued that Christian, Muslim, and Jewish merchants in the Mediterranean tended to form business networks with members of their own religious group; see Constable, "Merchants and Cross-Cultural Commerce in the Medieval Mediterranean World," in *History as Prelude: Muslims and Jews in the Medieval Mediterranean*, edited by Joseph V. Montville, 136 (Lanham, Md.: Lexington, 2011).

109. Ruiz, "Trading with the 'Other,'" 76.

110. Parts of this section and the following section, "Belorado and Miranda: *Concejo* vs *aljama*," were previously published in Maya Soifer Irish, "The Problem of Old Debts: Jewish Moneylenders in Northern Castile (Belorado and Miranda de Ebro, ca. 1300)," *Sefarad* 74, no. 2 (2014): 279–302.

were rather elaborate affairs that brought together not only the parties directly involved in the transaction, but also witnesses from both religious communities, as was required by Castile's customary law. More intriguing and perhaps suggestive of the normalcy that characterized most interfaith encounters are records of transactions between Christians that list Jews among the witnesses, even though there is no apparent reason for their inclusion. For instance, a 1222 sale of a few properties by one Christian family to another, in Sahagún, was witnessed by "Benaito, Iudeo," whose name appeared at the end of a long list of Christian witnesses, among them several priests and chaplains.[111] Similarly, in 1233, a group of artisans witnessed a sale of a house in the city of León. The group included a bridle-maker (*frenarius*), a girdler (*corrigiarius*), a shoemaker (*zapatarius*), a skinner (*pellicier*), a buckle-maker (*fiblilero*), and a scabbard-maker (*vaginarius*). Unlike the Christians, the two Jews who appeared among the witnesses—"Iaques, iudeus" and "Cide, iudeus"—did not have their professions appended to their names, although they were probably also artisans.[112] The two documents conjure a picture of cohesive neighborhoods whose Christian and Jewish residents were on friendly enough terms with each other to come together as witnesses when called upon to do so by their neighbors.

Whenever an interfaith transaction was about to take place, a group of Jews and Christians appeared before a public notary or a scribe of the town council and had the contract recorded and certified by a scribe, who affixed his signature below those of witnesses of both faiths. One such transaction took place in Astorga (León) in 1262, when Abrafan Pardal and his wife, Ouroduena, went to the town's public scribe with a group of Christians and Jews to record a property transaction that stemmed from a debt owed to them by Yuan (Juan) Marcos, a Christian. In lieu of the debt, Abrafan seized Juan's estate and pawned it to two Christian brothers, Juan and Miguel Rodríguez, for 22 *maravedís*, with a stipulation that Juan Marcos or his heirs retained the right to recover the estate. To make the agreement "more binding" (*mais firme*), Abrafan signed his name in Hebrew letters. The archdeacon of Astorga, a judge (*alcalde*), a knight (*ca-*

---

111. AHN, clero, Sahagún, carp. 912, no. 8; CDMS, 5:138–39.
112. ACL no. 6130; CDACL, 8:24–25.

vallero), and a royal merino, as well as three Jews, were among those who were present during the transaction and acted as witnesses.[113]

The presence of witnesses from both faiths not only satisfied a long-standing custom, but also smoothed over a conflict-prone situation in which a Jewish moneylender's right to collect the debt was pinned against the insolvency of the Christian debtor, whose loss of an estate was likely to become permanent. This and other similar documents underscore the fact that communal cooperation and approval were essential for the success of interfaith transactions, especially those that involved the sensitive issue of Christians' debts to Jews. The importance of communal consent was amplified in the late thirteenth and early fourteenth centuries as a growing number of Christians could not or would not meet their credit obligations to Jews. A proliferation (by Northern Castilian standards) of records during this period documenting Christians' inability to pay their debts to Jews and the loss of land or other property that stemmed from their insolvency indicates a problem that quickly transcended interpersonal relations, becoming a communal issue.

It goes without saying that most debts contracted by Christians with Jews were small consumption loans that were repaid quickly and left few traces in the documentation.[114] Even in cases when debts could not be collected on time, it made good business sense for the Jews to renegotiate payment deadlines instead of antagonizing clients by having the *entregadores* take them to court and seize their property.[115] Popular hostility was also an important factor to consider, as some clients were unscrupulous enough and powerful enough to defy the royal protection of the Jews and attack them over a business deal gone awry.[116] Nevertheless, conflicts

---

113. CDADA, 121–22; Rodríguez Fernández, *Las juderías de la provincia de León*, 357.

114. Jordan, "Women and Credit in the Middle Ages," 37, 57.

115. Meyerson, *Jews in an Iberian Frontier Kingdom*, 200; Nina Melechen, "Loans, Land, and Jewish-Christian Relations in the Archdiocese of Toledo," in *Iberia and the Mediterranean World of the Middle Ages*, edited by Larry Simon, 1: 205 (Leiden: E. J. Brill, 1995).

116. Consider, for example, the episode that transpired in Abelgas, near the city of León, in the mid-thirteenth century (precise date is unknown). The canons of Santa María de Abelgas complained that the son of Domingo García de Luna had imprisoned several Jews and swore to hold them until they paid him a ransom, saying he cared nothing for the royal authority ("Filio Dominico García de Luna tenía elos iudeos presos e díxoles Iohannes Castellano ke los soltás, ke pesaría al re e a don Gundisaluo, e ille respón ke non daría por lo re nada e non dimisit eos donec pectauerunt de suos denarios"); ACL no, 598; CDACL, 8:172–73.

could and did arise over the issue of unpaid debts. Given the delicacy of the situation in which Jewish creditors found themselves if they chose to take the matter to court, communal legislation regulating such cases was of immense importance in helping diffuse potential tensions. The *Libro de los fueros* contained several articles that addressed the problem of contested loans. One *fuero* stipulated that if a Christian debtor denied the validity of the contract presented by his Jewish creditor, an inquiry was to be conducted by the *alcalde* (judge): if the contract was found to be valid, the debtor was fined 60 *sueldos* on top of repaying the loan; otherwise, the Jewish creditor lost the loan and had to pay the same amount in fines.[117] Another *fuero* stated that a Christian with a "manifest" unpaid debt to a Jew could be seized and physically held until the loan was repaid.[118]

Of course, such communal legislation could do little to dispel resentment of a Christian debtor who lost freedom or property over an unpaid debt to a Jew. It did, however, give a measure of legitimacy to the idea that loans contracted with Jewish moneylenders had to be repaid and even provided a mechanism—effective or not is another matter—for collecting old debts to Jews. However, communal consent was essentially rendered irrelevant when the enforcement of loan repayment was taken away from local control and placed in the hands of outsiders—royal bureaucrats. The *Libro de los fueros* reflected Old Castile's customary law as it existed in the first half of the thirteenth century. When Alfonso X attempted to replace local *fueros* with a unifying code of law—the *Fuero real*—the issue of local control over old debt collections was left unaddressed. It appears that the king had made a surreptitious decision that henceforward the royal *entregadores* would be entrusted with this function, bypassing officials of the *concejos*. Facing protests from the urban procurators at the 1293 cortes in Valladolid, Sancho IV half-heartedly reassured them that local *alcaldes* would still be in charge of collecting old debts to Jews, except, the sly king

---

117. *Libro de los fueros*, 34 (title 61): "Esto es por fuero: que sy judio demanda a cristiano deuda por carta et dise el cristiano que non le a de dar nada, deue el alcalle tomar la carta, et deue sacar los pesquiridores. Et sy el judio pudier prouar, deuel dar la deuda el cristiano; et peche sesenta sueldos. Et sy judio non prouar la carta, deue perder la deuda e pechar sesenta sueldos."

118. Ibid., 49 (title 96): "Esto es por fuero de todo omne que deua deuda manifiesta a judio o non auyere de quela pagar: quel prendan el cuerpo fasta que page al judio la deuda, asy commo fuero es; et non le saque dela villa."

added, in places where the royal *merino* was already collecting them.[119] What Sancho "forgot" to mention was the fact that the *merino mayor* was responsible for the *entregas* in the entire region of Old Castile.[120]

One imagines that the town representatives were none too pleased with the king's answer. Not only were the moneylenders in question members of a minority group whose religious beliefs, supposed wealth, and privileged position with the Crown all rendered them suspect in the eyes of Christian townsmen, but also *entregadores* impinged on local privileges at a time when Castilian communities faced multiple economic and political pressures. Unlike local judges, royal collectors of debts to Jews were not likely to be sympathetic to the plight of the less-fortunate debtors who had fallen behind on their payments and faced losing land or other property as a consequence of the *entregas*. A dozen or so surviving documents from the late thirteenth and early fourteenth centuries provide an eloquent testimony to this growing problem.

It comes as no surprise that the great majority of these records illustrate the difficulties faced by single women—most of them widows—whose indebtedness to Jewish moneylenders exacerbated their already precarious economic position. The cases have a wide geographical and chronological span. Between 1290 and 1295 the abbot of the Cistercian monastery Santa María de Rioseco made several purchases of land from individuals in the village of Horna who had to sell their properties in order to satisfy Jewish moneylenders from the nearby Medina de Pomar. Two of the sellers were women: in 1290, Sancha Alvarez sold her cereal-producing lands, vineyards, and pastures for 150 *maravedís*, and in 1295, doña Elvira followed suit, selling her lands in Horna for 250 *maravedís*. A royal official, the *portero* of the Jewish community in Medina, was prob-

---

119. *Cortes* I, 111: "Otrossi alo que nos dixieron en razon delas entregas delas debdas delos iudios, que dizen que fazen los porteros delos iudios en las nuestras villas e en los nuestros logares, lo que dizen que non fue en tienpo del Rey don Ferrando nuestro auuelo nin del Rey nuestro padre, etque nos pidan merçed quelas entregas quelas fagan por mandado delos alcaldes assi commo solian seer en tienpo delos otros rreyes que fueron ante que nos; a esto tenemos por bien que en los logares do el nuestro merino mayor deue fazer las entregas delos iudios quelas faga, et en los otros logares quelas fagan por mandado delos alcaldes, assi como se solian fazer en tienpo del Rey don Fferrando nuestro auuelo e del Rey don Alfonso nuestro padre."

120. According to the Accounts Book of 1290–1292; see Hernández, *Las rentas del rey*, cxxxviii, 135–37.

ably involved in the transactions, confiscating the properties and putting them up for sale to liquidate the debts owed to his Jewish clients.[121]

Whether prosperous or humble, widows faced the prospect of having a large portion of their income eaten away by debts bequeathed to them by their late husbands. After Martín López, resident of Cristóbal de Polentera in León, had died, his debts to Jewish moneylenders passed on to his widow, Marina Pérez, and to his sons. The family evidently possessed extensive properties, but the debt was large, as well. In 1312, they were forced to sell their lands to the abbot of Santa María de Carracedo for 800 *maravedís* and 8 *sueldos*.[122] Doña María of Aguilar de Campóo, the widow of Per Abbat, was left with a much smaller debt of 15 *maravedís*. Even so, in 1315, she had to cede a plot of land in La Nava to her late husband's Jewish creditor, Mose.[123] Another widow, María Alfonso, probably struggling to maintain her cereal-growing fields after the death of her husband, was forced to borrow grain—wheat, rye, and barley—from three Jews: Abrafan Royuelo of León, doña Çara (herself a widow), and Saul of Mansilla. In 1324, unable to meet her obligations, María had to let go of the lands she and her late husband had been renting from the monastery of San Miguel de Escalada. In return, the canons took on María's debts to the Jews.[124]

Widows may have been particularly vulnerable, but they were not the only ones suffering a loss of property as a direct result of indebtedness to Jews. Occasionally one has to look between the lines of property sale agreements for the telling signs of an unpaid debt behind the transaction. For instance, when in 1259 Mosse Aramas and his wife, Cinfa, declared themselves paid for all the rights in the meadows bought by a can-

---

121. AHN, clero, Burgos, Rioseco, carp. 354, nos. 6, 9; the *portero* is mentioned in the third transaction, the sale of land by Muño García (carp. 354, no. 7); see also Ruiz, "Trading with the 'Other,'" 72: instead of "Homa," it should be "Horna"; in fact, the village still exists today.

122. Rodríguez Fernández, *Las juderías de la provincia de León*, 359.

123. AHN, clero, Palencia, Aguilar, carp. 1667, no. 14; cited in Huidobro y Serna and Cantera Burgos, "Los judíos en Aguilar de Campóo," 338.

124. AHN, clero, Escalada, carp. 833, no. 10; Rodríguez Fernández, *Las juderías de la provincia de León*, 360–61. Yet another case comes from Astorga (1317), where María Martínez, widow of Juan Pérez, owed a certain quantity of grain to Samuel, a Jew of Astorga. María was at least able to keep her property in the family, selling some land to her daughter, Juana, for 25 *maravedís*; CDADA, 304–5.

on of the Cathedral of León from Pedro Lobónez of Valdelafuente, they must have been referring to a debt that Pedro owed them and was forced to repay by selling his land.[125] In addition to fields, meadows, and vineyards, families could lose houses or other property because of unpaid debts. In 1294, Tel Gutiérrez and his wife, Teresa Pérez, were forced to move out of their house in Quintanilla and into a much smaller house in Quintana Palaçio in an exchange of properties with the monastery of San Salvador de Oña. As their old house cost considerably more than their new dwelling (*porque valie mas la nuestra casa de Quintaniella*), the difference of 4,000 *maravedís* was meant to be a repayment of the couple's debt to Abraham, a Jew of Briviesca.[126]

It is important to note that not all sales of property that stemmed from indebtedness to Jews were the consequence of desperate circumstances. Large-size loans were usually taken for business rather than subsistence purposes. As examples from other parts of Castile show, some well-to-do borrowers took the risk of delaying the repayment for years beyond the original deadline, betting on the judges' reluctance to award creditors the full amount they were owed. They could lose property as a result of *entregas*, but in the meantime they enjoyed a long-term loan at what ended up being a very low interest rate.[127] The reasons behind the Christians' disinclination to repay their debts to Jews on time may have been many, but the end result was the same: more and more debt liquidation cases landed in courts, raising the level of mutual distrust between the Jewish and the Christian communities. It is impossible to pinpoint the exact time—even the right decade—when the issue of old debts first became a matter of contention. One early sign was the dispute that arose in the 1270s in Burgos over the appointment of separate judges (*alcaldes apartados*) to hear cases between Christians and Jews.

Castilian Jews had long enjoyed the privilege of having special judges in mixed litigation. The late-twelfth-century *fuero* of Cuenca required two *alcaldi* from each religious community, while other *fueros* called for a mix

125. ACL, no. 581; CDACL, 8:341–42; Rodríguez Fernández, *La judería de la ciudad de León*, 196. The document is notable for its inclusion of the signatures of six Jewish witnesses and a Jewish scribe ("Bención, escriuán de aliama").
126. AHN, clero, Burgos, Oña, carp. 302, no. 6; DMSSO, 3:220–21.
127. Melechen, "Loans, Land, and Jewish-Christian Relations," 199.

of royal and local judges.[128] In Burgos, the Jewish community secured a privilege from Alfonso X that two royal *alcaldes* be appointed to hear mixed cases. One of the appointees was a vassal (*criado*) of doña Berenguela, the king's sister.[129] Since a great deal of mixed litigation dealt with disputes over Christians' debts to Jews, the *concejos* had a clear preference for their own judges to be in charge of hearing and deciding such cases. Like the universally despised royal *entregadores*, judges appointed directly by the king equated the interests of Jewish creditors with those of the king, for whose treasury the Jews' profits were ultimately bound. Therefore, they were more likely to side with the Jewish creditors and award them the full amount they claimed as their due.

Such considerations were probably behind the attempts by the *concejo* of Burgos to deny the city's Jews their right to have separate judges. In 1278, the Burgos *aljama* sent representatives to Alfonso X, complaining that the *concejo* had falsely asserted having reached an agreement with the Jewish community, according to which the *aljama* agreed to have *alcaldes* jointly with the *concejo* and even to contribute a yearly sum of 333⅓ *maravedís* for the maintenance of these judges. The *aljama* denied ever entering into such an agreement and asked the king to restore their right to separate judges. King Alfonso sided with the Jews, ordering the *concejo* to respect the privileges conferred on the *aljama* by himself and his father, Fernando III.[130] But the issue simply would not go away. The *concejo* of Burgos was determined to gain control over the pleading of debt cases brought by Jewish moneylenders against Christian borrowers. Representatives from Burgos were probably in charge of drafting a petition presented to the king at the 1286 cortes in Palencia that once again assaulted the Jews' right to separate *alcaldes*. The new king, Sancho IV, proved to be more sympathetic to the idea than was his predecessor: he abolished the

---

128. See chapter 2.
129. AMB, no. 4125; *CDCB*, 150–51.
130. Ibid.: "Agora el aliama enbiaronseme querellar e dizen que por rrazón que omes de uuestro Conçeio venieron a mi e me dixieron que el aliama eran abenidos convusco que non ouiesen alcaldes apartadamiente así commo lo yo mandé por mis cartas, et que estimaran convusco de dar cada anno por gualardón de alcaldía ellos e uuestra alfoz trezientos e XXXIII e terçia de la moneda nueua.... Et el aliama dizen que non fizieron tal abenençia convusco nin estimaron convusco de uos dar gualardón a uos los alcaldes, así commo los omes de uuestro Conçeio me dixieron. Etc."

office of special judges, but stipulated that cases involving Jews had to be judged separately, thus laying bare the Crown's interest in having debt cases pass quickly through the courts so that, the king asserted, "the Jews do not get a delay [in collecting debts] that would detain the *pecho* they owe me."[131]

In the end, the *aljama* of Burgos proved unable to preserve its right to *alcaldes apartados*. In 1295, the tutors of Fernando III gave in to the *concejo's* request to get rid of all additional judges (*que tirase de las alcaldías los otros alcaldes que y son agora*) beyond the four who were entrusted with hearing the cases between Christians, Jews, and Muslims.[132] The Burgos council's thinly disguised attack on the Jews' right to separate judges followed on the heels of the legislation issued by the cortes in 1293 in Valladolid, which reiterated the 1286 prohibition of *alcaldes apartados*.[133] Even so, some *aljamas* apparently held on to their separate judges, because at the 1307 cortes in Valladolid, the urban procurators complained bitterly that Jewish usury was ruining the land and blamed the problem on the office of separate judges. The king once again agreed to abolish it.[134] But for as long as the king realized that special judges were more likely to move the Jews' money quickly out of courts and into the royal coffers, the procurators faced an uphill battle.[135]

The conflict in Burgos over *alcaldes apartados* also highlights the challenges faced by the Jewish communities caught between the fiscal demands of the Castilian Crown and the needs of their Christian clients. The mad hike in the amount of Jewish *pechos* instigated by Alfonso X in the 1280s must have put a considerable strain on the *aljamas'* resources

---

131. "Otrossi tengo por bien quelos judios non ayan alcaldes apartados assi commo les agora auian, mas que el vno de aquellos ommes buenos enque yo ffiar la justiçia dela villa les liure sus pleytos apartada mientre, en manera quelos cristianos ayan su derecho, e los judios el suyo, e que por su culpa daquel quelos ouier a judgar *non rreçiban los judios alongamiento por quesse detenga el pecho que me ouieren adar* [emphasis added]"; Cortes 1, 99.

132. AMB, no. 125; CDCB, 247–49.

133. Cortes 1, 115.

134. "Otrossi alo que me pidieron por merced en fecho delas vsuras delos judios, que touiesse por bien de auer mio acuerdo en guisa que non venga dellos tanto mal commo viene nin se astrague dellos [nin se astrague por ellos] la tierra commo se astraga. Et que fuesse la mi merced que non ouiessen juezes apartados, mas quelos juezes e los alcaldes del ffuero que estudieren por mi en los logares librassen las contiendas que acaesçiessen entre los christianos e ellos"; Cortes 1, 195.

135. At the cortes of 1351, Pedro I defended the Jews' right to a separate judge; Cortes 2, 40.

and forced Jewish moneylenders to press harder for repayment of debts by relying more extensively on the services of royal *entregadores* and special judges. The souring of business relations between Jews and Christians was the inevitable outcome of the Crown's reckless fiscal policies, aggravated by the fact that the towns, too, were subjected to extraordinary taxation (*servicios*) and forced loans, many of them collected by Jewish tax farmers.[136]

One can easily imagine the consternation of Christian borrowers, who previously could count on having their payment deadlines extended by sympathetic Jewish moneylenders, but who were now inundated with demands for repayment and dragged to court by debt collectors. Yet, it is no less important to consider the frustrations of Jewish lenders, who had little choice but to try and salvage what they could from old letters of obligation. At the 1293 cortes of Valladolid, the urban procurators complained that the Jews were trying to collect debts "from a long time ago" (*debdas de luengo tienpo*), thereby causing "many errors" (*muchos engannos*) to occur. Sancho IV agreed that the Jews should be allowed no more than six years to collect debts.[137] But even that seemed too long for the procurators, who tried, unsuccessfully, to reduce the period to four years.[138] During the civil war, the royal guardians, apparently prompted by the pleas of the *aljamas*' representatives, extended the period to nine years, but the legislation promulgated at the 1301 cortes in Zamora moved it back to six years.[139] The six-year cap became a standard one for the kingdom of Castile, although some Jewish communities succeeded in securing privileges from the Crown that prolonged it to ten and even thirty years.[140]

The controversy over the collection of old debts therefore struck at the heart of several critically important issues. Not only was the economic livelihood of both communities at stake in the conflict, but also it set the rights and privileges of the *aljamas* on the collision course with those of

136. O'Callaghan, *Cortes of Castile-León*, 131–41.
137. "Otrossi las cartas delas debdas quelas demanden fata daquiadelante seys annos, et dend adelante quell non rrepondan por ellas"; *Cortes* 1, 114–15.
138. At the cortes of Valladolid in 1299; *Cortes* 1, 144.
139. *Cortes* 1, 154.
140. The decisions of the 1329 cortes in Madrid mention the period of ten years for Valladolid and that of thirty years for Toledo; *Cortes* 1, 423.

the *concejos*. In the negotiations that ensued, the Crown usually played the role of an arbitrator at the later stages, but the initial bargaining occurred at the local level during face-to-face meetings between representatives of Jewish and Christian communities. By a lucky chance, records of such negotiations have survived to permit a detailed examination of how they were conducted, what goals were pursued by either side, and what impact these local controversies may have had on the state of Jewish-Christian relations in Northern Castile. The records hail from two small towns in the Burgos province—Belorado and Miranda de Ebro.

Belorado and Miranda: *Concejo* vs. *Aljama*

Both Belorado and Miranda de Ebro had well-established *juderías* that traced their origins to at least the early twelfth century.[141] A royal town only about thirty miles east of Burgos, Belorado nevertheless was not part of the Burgalese *señorío* and remained independent despite being ruled by a succession of royal servitors.[142] At the end of the thirteenth century, Miranda was part of the diocese of Calahorra, but was later given by the king to the bishop of Burgos before passing, in the late 1360s, under the control of the Burgalese *concejo*.[143] Of the two Jewish communities, the *aljama* of Belorado was clearly the more affluent one, with a tribute of 8,500 *maravedís* to Miranda's 3,312 *maravedís*, according to the 1290 Partition of Huete. The prosperity of the *aljama* of Belorado stemmed in part from the involvement of its members in moneylending and in part from its strategic location on the Camino de Santiago in a town with a major market that attracted traders from towns and villages miles away. Several important

---

141. Several studies are dedicated to the Jews of Belorado and of Miranda de Ebro; see Fidel Fita, "La aljama hebrea de Belorado: Documentos históricos," BRAH 29 (1896): 338–45; Huidobro y Serna and Cantera Burgos, "Juderías burgalesas," 35–59; Inocencio Cadiñanos Bardeci, "Los judíos de Belorado y sus contornos," Sefarad 54 (1994): 227–51; Cantera Burgos, "La judería de Miranda de Ebro," Sefarad 1 (1941): 89–140; and Sefarad 2 (1942): 325–75; Cadiñanos Bardeci, "Precisiones sobre la sinagoga de Miranda de Ebro," Sefarad 54 (1994): 41–45; José Luis Lacave, "Un testamento hebraico fragmentario de Miranda de Ebro," Sefarad 46 (1986): 271–79.

142. Don Lope Días de Haro in the thirteenth century and don Sancho, brother of Enrique II, in the latter part of the fourteenth century; Cadiñanos Bardeci, "Los judíos de Belorado," 231, 233.

143. Juan Antonio Bonachía Hernando, *El señorío de Burgos durante la Baja Edad Media (1255–1508)* (Valladolid: Universidad de Valladolid, 1988), 34.

Jewish tax collectors and financiers came from Belorado; among them, Samuel of Belorado, who was regularly mentioned in the royal Books of Accounts as a collector of royal tribute.[144]

Yet, the affluence of the Belorado's Jews did not provide an adequate safeguard against the financial squeeze affecting *aljamas* throughout Northern Castile. Like the Jewish moneylenders elsewhere, the town's Jewish creditors were forced to pursue debt collections more aggressively, provoking an outcry from the Christian community. The first documented sign of tensions came in 1301, when the *concejo* of Belorado obtained a privilege from Fernando IV that required the *aljama* to be responsible for the maintenance of the royal castle's tower of Homenaje, thus considerably increasing the Jewish community's tax burden. Even more tellingly, the Jews of Belorado and its surroundings were banned from entering the town on market day (Monday) and making purchases there.[145] In attacking the Jews' economic livelihood, the *concejo* was likely responding to the Jews' redoubled efforts at collecting debts from the disaffected Christians, who accused the Jews of being driven by greed and resented the wealth built, they thought, on the backs of Christian debtors.[146]

Fernando IV's concession to the *concejo* could not resolve the simmering tensions over the issue of outstanding loans. Only one year later, in 1302, the *concejo* and the *aljama* began negotiations to address the problem more directly. In March of that year, representatives of both communities gathered in the presence of Garçi Ferrandez de Villamayor, Castile's *adelantado mayor* (royal governor), and after many deliberations drafted an agreement, which was then signed by about two dozen Jewish and Christian witnesses.[147] The agreement reveals a great deal about the conflict-

144. Baer, *Die Juden*, 2:90–91.
145. RAH, ms. 66.981.O–16, ff. 403v–4; Huidobro y Serna and Cantera Burgos, "Juderías Burgalesas," 52–53; see also Ruiz Gómez, "Aljamas y concejos," 74–75.
146. This was an ongoing theme in the complaints presented against the Jews at the cortes.
147. Two versions of this agreement survive, both preserved at the Biblioteca de la real academia de historia in Madrid, in sixteenth-century copies; RAH, mss. 66.977. O–16, ff. 400v–401v, and 66.974. O–16, ff. 399v–400. The shorter version appears to be a derivative of the longer version, despite having a different date (March 3 instead of March 13 of the longer version), and different Jewish witnesses. The longer version is also found at the Belorado municipal archive and was published by Huidobro y Serna and Cantera Burgos in "Juderías burgalesas," 44–46, and by Cadiñanos Bardeci, in "Los judíos de Belorado," 244–46.

prone nature of the Jews' credit operations in small-town Castile. Behind the formalized language of the accord, one detects two communities at loggerheads over their conflicting objectives, as the Jews' determination to collect their debts as promptly as possible was matched by the Christians' equally strong determination to delay the payments for as long as possible.[148] According to the text of the agreement, Jewish creditors had complained that Christian debtors were trying to extend their payment deadlines by offering the Jews *señales*, best translated as "earnest money."[149] In all likelihood, *señales* were small payments intended to buy debtors more time to settle their obligations while preventing creditors from seizing their property. If the Jews chose to accept *señales*, year after year, they faced the danger of never getting the full amount due to them, since the cortes legislation only allowed them six years to collect debts. On the other hand, the pressure must have been considerable for the Jews to accept *señales*, because a refusal to do so carried the risk of antagonizing their Christian clients. Confronted with this no-win situation, the Jews of Belorado presented their case to the *concejo*, who accepted their reasoning and agreed that henceforward the payment of debts could not be delayed on account of *señales* (*que las debdas de los judios non se demoren por señales*).

The *concejo* did not make this concession simply out of the goodness of their hearts. In return, the town council received complete control over collection of debts. Making no mention of royal *entregadores*, the agreement gave the officials of the *concejo* the power to assist the Jews at every stage of the *entregas*. If a Jew or a Jewess wanted to demand a debt from a resident of Belorado, he or she had to present their letter of obligation to a judge or a *merino* of Belorado, who would appoint a council to look into the matter. Its representatives would then go to the house of the debtor

---

148. A similar situation existed in the lands of the Crown of Aragon, where Jewish moneylenders also encountered grave difficulties with collecting outstanding debts; see Assis, *Jewish Economy*, 39.

149. See Title V, Law VII of the Fifth Partida (*Las siete partidas*): "Señal dan los homes unos a otros en las compras, et acaesce que se repiente despues alguno dellos . . . etc." Samuel Parsons Scott translates "señal" as "earnest money" and adds in a footnote that "the *arrha*, or earnest money of the Romans, was merely a penalty imposed for nonperformance of the contract of sale by the purchaser"; Scott, *Las siete partidas*, vol. 4, *Family, Commerce, and the Sea*, ed. Robert I. Burns (Philadelphia: University of Pennsylvania Press, 2001), 1029. William C. Jordan suggested the alternative definition, more appropriate for the context of the Belorado agreement.

or the guarantor and seize the property in the amount of the debt indicated in the letter of obligation. The debtor had three days to either pay off the debt or to increase the value of the surety, after which period the officials sold the debtor's movable property in nine days and real estate in thirty days. It was the officials' task to ensure that a Jew or a Jewess collected debts "without any delay." If help was needed in enforcing this agreement, the judges (*alcaldes*), members of the town councils, and the *prestamero* (priest-in-training) were to go with the Jews and ascertain that the debts were paid to them in full (*conplidamiente*).[150]

Was the agreement enforced, and if so, did it help ease tensions between the two communities of Belorado? Only circumstantial evidence exists, and it points toward negative answers to both questions. The royal control and interference in the economic and political fortunes of Belorado was too pervasive to allow for communal agreements to make a difference. In the several years following the 1302 agreement, Fernando IV's chancery issued several letters that could potentially upset the delicate balance of intercommunal relations in the town. First, at the end of 1303, the king responded to the town council's petition to appoint a scribe, conceding the privilege on the condition that the scribe record the "debts" (*deudas*) the Jews owed him. Belorado's *aljama* must have been in arrears on the payment of *pechos* to the king, which in itself is an indirect testimony to its continued difficulties in collecting unpaid debts from Christians.[151] The subject of Jewish *pechos* from Belorado elicited the chancery's interest at least twice during these years. In 1303, Fernando allowed the *concejo* to collect the tax from the Jewish community in order to compensate the town for the loan it had given the king to repair the walls of Zamora. But only two years later, in 1305, the king issued an unequivocal demand that the town's Jews were to pay their *pechos* separately from the Christians by dividing the taxes equitably among themselves and bringing the money to town in order to give it directly to the royal officials.[152]

Given the Crown's concerns over the timely payment of *pechos* by the *aljama* of Belorado, it is not unreasonable to suppose that the king, possi-

---

150. RAH, ms. 66.974. O-16, ff. 399v-400; Cantera Burgos, "Juderías burgalesas," 44-45; Cadiñanos Bardeci, "Los judíos de Belorado," 244-45.
151. RAH, ms. 66.976. O-16, f. 400; Cantera Burgos, "Juderías burgalesas," 54.
152. Cantera Burgos, "Juderías burgalesas," 54-55.

bly after receiving a plea from the town's Jews, chose to rely on the services of *entregadores* to collect debts from Christians, ignoring the communal agreement of 1302. If that was indeed the case, then the privilege given to the town at the 1325 cortes in Valladolid by the young Alfonso XI was in step with the Crown's decision to exert greater control over the Jewish finances in Belorado. The privilege stated that the Jews would be given a separate judge to decide their cases. The description of the privilege is too laconic to determine whether the judge in question was appointed to hear cases between Jews and Christians. Since by all appearances that was indeed his task, the royal order was in direct violation of the 1302 agreement, which had assigned this function to the *alcaldes* of the *concejo*. The privilege also reveals further evidence of intercommunal friction in Belorado. The Jews were once again forbidden to trade with Christians at the Monday market, because of their propensity for "fraud" and "roguery" (*fraudes y bellaquerias*).[153] The prohibition was reiterated in 1333.[154]

Therefore, it seems likely that the intercommunal negotiations of 1302 failed to normalize the state of Jewish-Christian relations in Belorado. The agreement's existence shows that had they been left to their own devices, the two communities could find common ground and perhaps even resolve their differences to mutual satisfaction. However, the pull of the triangular relationship between the Jews, the *concejos*, and the Crown was as strong in Belorado as it was in the rest of Northern Castile, and it bent local interfaith relations out of shape by harnessing the Jews' credit operations among Christians to the financial needs of the Crown.

An even more vivid example of the powerful influence exerted by the monarchy over local politics comes from the town of Miranda de Ebro. A series of documents preserved in the town's municipal archive and published over seventy years ago by Francisco Cantera Burgos show a richness of detail rarely found in Northern Castile and allow one to follow the many twists and turns of the drama that unfolded in this northeastern corner of the kingdom beginning in the last years of the thirteenth century.[155] The

---

153. RAH, ms. 66.972. O–16, ff. 398–99; Cantera Burgos, "Juderías burgalesas," 55–56.
154. RAH, ms. 66.997. O–16, ff. 408v–9; Cantera Burgos, "Juderías burgalesas," 56; Baer, *Die Juden*, 2:102.
155. As of 2009, the documents were still housed at the municipal archive of Miran-

drama spanned several decades and involved many protagonists with conflicting interests and agendas. On the one side, there were Jewish creditors from Miranda, Haro, and Pancorbo whose livelihood and ability to meet their tax obligations to the Crown depended on collecting debts in a timely manner from the inhabitants of Miranda. Their efforts were countered by Christian debtors who hid letters of obligation in order to evade payments and by the *concejo* of Miranda that tried to protect its *vecinos* from creditors by evoking the town's immunity from the intrusion of *entregadores*. The king played the role of a mediator, walking a thin line between the need to have the debts collected and deposited into royal treasury in the form of Jewish *pechos* and the fear of antagonizing the *concejo* by trampling its privileges.

Strictly speaking, the drama was another case of negotiations between the local *concejo* and the Jewish *aljama*. However, the case exemplifies the process through which local tensions could feed into the kingdom-wide malaise that began to affect Jewish-Christian relations in the early fourteenth century. On March 8, 1294, the *alcalde* (judge) of Miranda, García Martínez, accompanied by two *jurados* (representatives of the town council) and a number of *omes buenos* from Miranda and the environs, held a meeting at the graveyard of the church of Santa María with ten Jewish representatives. During the meeting, the Jews were asked if they had obtained "illegal letters" from the king that authorized the royal *merino* to appoint a *portero* in Miranda who would collect the debts owed by local Christians to Jews. The *alcalde* had raised this issue with Rabbi Çaguy, Çaguy Pardo, and other Jews before, in January of the same year, but now he wanted assurances from the Jewish creditors that they would no longer use letters that so blatantly violated the privileges listed in the town's *fuero*. The Jewish representatives categorically denied receiving such letters from the king or the *merino* and promised never to obtain them in the future. Moreover, they declared themselves perfectly satisfied with the assistance provided by the *concejo* and the *alcalde* in the matter of collecting old debts (*entregas*). Their only complaint concerned the admissibility of testimony of two Christians against a Jew, which they considered unjust. The *alcalde* then re-

---

da de Ebro. Francisco Cantera Burgos's transcripts and the commentary were published in two installments in the two inaugural issues of the journal *Sefarad*; see Cantera Burgos, "La judería de Miranda de Ebro (1099–1350)," *Sefarad* 1, 1941, 89–140, and "La judería de Miranda de Ebro" (1350–1492), *Sefarad* 2 (1942): 325–73.

sponded that no injustice was being committed, since a testimony of two Jews against a Christian, as well as that of two Christians against a Jew, was valid. He failed to persuade the Jewish representatives on this point, but they did sign a memorandum acknowledging their satisfaction with the *concejo's* management of the *entregas*.[156]

The presence during the meeting of two Jewish witnesses from the neighboring towns (David of Haro and Mose of Pancorbo) signaled that the matter of collecting old debts in Miranda concerned not only the town's Jews, but also a much wider network of Jewish creditors catering to Miranda's Christian *vecinos*. The sincerity of the *concejo's* commitment to facilitating the *entregas* was tested only two years later when the tensions in Miranda exploded into a major controversy involving several *aljamas*, an eminent royal servitor, and the Crown. The chronology of the events is difficult to reconstruct, but it appears that sometime in the summer of 1296, Diego López de Haro, lord of Vizcaya, who had recently entered the Castilian king's service, complained that he had not received a tribute from the Jews of Haro and the bishopric of Calahorra he was assigned as Fernando IV's servitor.[157] In response, Polo Pérez, the royal tax collector in the bishoprics of Burgos and Calahorra, acknowledged that he was unable to collect tribute from the Jews of Haro. They had locked themselves up in their *judería* and refused him entry, arguing that they could not pay until Christian debtors in the town of Miranda fulfilled their credit obligations.[158] The royal chancery then dispatched an urgent

---

156. AMME, no. L-H0213-053; Cantera Burgos, "La judería de Miranda de Ebro (1099–1350)," 112–13. Ten Jews are mentioned in the Castilian text as being present at the meeting; eight of them are from Miranda: Sento [Shem Tov] the *alfaquin* [physician or sage], his sons Çagui [Isaac] and Hamuy, Çagui (son of Ordoña), Hazibuena (widow of Barzilay), Alazar the *alfayate* [tailor], his brother Çagui, and Juçe [Jusef]; and two are from nearby towns: David of Haro and Mose of Pancorbo. Five of those present affixed their signatures, in Hebrew, at the end of the document. One of the signatures is barely legible. [Çagui, son of Sento] משה בר יסף [Mose of Pancorbo] דוד בר יהודה ולהה [David of Haro] ר יוסף (?) יצחק בר שם טוב [Sento] שם טוב בר יצחק

157. According to the Partition of Huete (1290), many royal servitors were assigned tribute from specific Jewish *aljamas*. Among those receiving compensation from the *aljama* of Haro in 1290 were Infante Alfonso, the king's son, and Samuel of Belorado, the royal tax collector; Hernández, *Las rentas del rey*, 153–54.

158. Only six years prior to these events, in 1288, the *judería* of Haro was sacked by the troops of Sancho IV. According to the Partition of Huete, the king later forgave the Jews of Haro half of their tribute as a compensation for their losses; Hernández, *Las rentas del rey*, 138.

letter to the *alcalde* and the *concejo* of Miranda, upbraiding them for disobeying the king's orders and demanding immediate action.[159]

The letter alleged that the *alcalde*, the town council, and the public scribe of Miranda had done everything in their power to prevent the collection of debts owed to the Jews of Haro. This information came from two royal servitors, residents of Burgos, who had been sent to Miranda to conduct investigation.[160] According to their version of the events, a Jew named Varon came to Miranda bearing letters of obligation that belonged to other Jews (most of them probably from Haro) and intending to plead cases with local Christians. Instead, he was seized together with the letters and held against his will on the orders of the *alcalde*. When the investigators went to see Diago Pérez, the town's public scribe, to get information on the debts owed to the Jews of Haro, the scribe flatly refused to show them the town's financial records. In fact, the investigators suspected that the scribe hid the loan contracts in conspiracy with two prominent men of Miranda, don Martín Martínez and don Yuanez de Vitoria, who owed the Jews a certain sum of money. The two men had promised to repay the debt after collecting the revenue from their landed estates, but now with the contracts safely put away they were denying ever borrowing money from the Jews. Moreover, the complaint went on, Fernant Martínez, son-in-law of Martín Martínez, and Johan Urtiz, had promised to give the royal investigators 6,000 *maravedís* in *entregas*, but later denied ever making such a promise.

Upon receiving the investigators' report, the royal chancery's officials expressed surprise at the happenings in Miranda and the disservice done to the monarch by the town's prominent citizens. They ordered that the Jew Varon be released and handed over to the royal representatives together with the contracts and that Fernant Martínez and Johan Urtiz pay

159. AMME, no. L-H0039-031. The long parchment contains the report of Polo Pérez, written down by his scribe, which includes the letter from the chancery of Fernando IV (dated August 11, 1296) and the copies of four loan contracts between Diago Martínez and Juzme of Haro (dated March–December 1294). Virtually no records of lending agreements between Jews and Christians in Northern Castile are extant, making this document exceedingly rare and valuable. The report itself is dated October 20, 1296. It was published by Cantera Burgos, in "La judería de Miranda de Ebro (1099–1350)," 118–23.

160. The servitors' names are listed as don Esias and Garçía González [or Gutiérrez or Garcéz] of Burgos.

the promised 6,000 *maravedís* in *entregas*. And while the citizens of Miranda were now held accountable for their debts, or at least a portion of them, the money did not go to the Jewish creditors. As soon as they obtained the records of old debts from the scribe, the investigators were to collect only the *principal* from every debt owed by men and women of Miranda and then claim the money for the king. The chancery forgave the accumulated interest (*tan bien del logro commo de la ganançia*) and declared as invalid all the subsequent letters of obligation if the Jews were to present them.

In essence, the royal chancery's order in the summer of 1296 constituted a *captio* on a local scale: the Jews of Haro lost the interest portion of the loans, and the principal was confiscated in lieu of their outstanding taxes to the king.[161] It may have been the first instance of direct royal interference with the Jews' outstanding loans in Northern Castile. Not until 1315 would the regents to Alfonso XI execute a kingdom-wide *captio* by canceling one-third of every debt owed to Jews and allowing the rest to be repaid in installments.[162] The Jewish creditors from Haro likely suffered great financial loss as a result of this affair. This much is clear from the four surviving letters of obligation included in the report written by Polo Pérez (the tax collector). The letters document the loans taken by Diago Martínez, son of the archpriest, from don Juzme of Haro in 1294. The total amount of the four loans reached at least 368 *maravedís*, not counting the cost of the two *fanegas* of wheat Diago had borrowed from the Jew. Nevertheless, when Polo Pérez showed Diago the contracts and demanded payment, Diago claimed that he had never received from Juzme more than 332 ½ *maravedís* in principal and that the rest of the debt represented the built-in interest. Polo decided to take Diago's word for it (*yo falle en uerdad que era assi*) and accepted the 332 ½ *maravedís*, citing the king's privilege canceling interest on all loans.[163] There is no indication that Juzme or his representative was present during the transaction to challenge Diago's assertions.

The events of 1296 left a residue of frustration and resentment among Miranda's residents. True, Christians saw parts of their debts significantly reduced, but they still had to pay, losing the freedom to postpone

---

161. On *captiones* in France, see Jordan, *French Monarchy and the Jews*, 9–31.
162. Cortes 1, 284.
163. AMME, no. L-H0039-031; Cantera Burgos, "La judería de Miranda de Ebro (1099–1350)," 122–23.

payments for months or years on end. The *concejo* hated to see their decisions overridden by strangers—royal officials sent from Burgos. But the Jews lost the most from the affair. Not only did they suffer financial losses, but also they could no longer hope that the *concejo* would uphold the letter of the 1294 agreement and give them a helping hand in collecting outstanding loans. Now that royal interference had dealt a fatal blow to the spirit of the 1294 agreement, debt collection in the town of Miranda became a particularly daunting task for the Jews, regardless of whether they came from Miranda or Haro. It is no wonder, then, that the Jewish creditors of Miranda, Haro, and Pancorbo banded together to try and get royal *entregadores* to perform this unpleasant duty for them. Sometime in late 1303 or early 1304, they sent representatives to Garçi Ferrandez de Villamayor, the *adelantado mayor* (royal governor), who were able to get an authorization to put a royal official, *portero*, in Miranda who would be responsible for collecting outstanding loans from the town's Christians.

It was this move by the Jews that precipitated a new chapter in the drama. Garçi Ferrandez sent his officials (*merinos*) to Miranda who descended on the town and "took everything they could find" (*les tomaron todo quanto les fallaren*), thereby violating the town's privileges and *fueros*. This was the essence of the complaint the *concejo* of Miranda took to the royal court in the spring of 1304.[164] The council's representatives who appeared before the king were the town's *alcalde*, Garçi Martínez, as well as Diago Pérez and Ferrant Martínez—probably the same individuals who were involved in the 1296 events. The Jews sent their own representative, Haui Moreno, who was joined by two guarantors—Rabi Çahagui (Çagui) and Çahagui Pardo. Ten years previously, these two Jews of Miranda had participated in negotiating the agreement with the *concejo*. The old spirit of cooperation was now all but dead as the opponents faced each other over the divide of broken promises and unfulfilled obligations, made only wider by the official setting of the royal court. Haui Moreno brought letters of representation (*personeria*) from four Jews of Haro, one Jew of Pancorbo, and fifteen Jews of Miranda (among them five women).[165]

164. AMME, no. L-H0190-022. The text has faded in the folds of the parchment, making it difficult to read in some places. Cantera Burgos, "La judería de Miranda de Ebro (1099–1350)," 123–29.

165. Haro: Yhuda, son of Juezme; Fazen [Juzme?], son of Santo; Daui, son of Rabbi Çahat; Salamon son of Samuel. Pancorbo: Rab Don Esua. Miranda: Rabi Çahat [?], son of

When it was Haui Moreno's turn to answer the *concejo*'s complaint, his words contradicted the Jews' claim, made during the meeting at Miranda's cemetery in 1294, that they had never received privileges from the king authorizing them to have a *portero* in the town. Alfonso X was the first monarch to grant such letters to the Jews of Miranda, and the charters were later confirmed by Sancho IV and the current monarch, Fernando IV. Haui brought the charters along to be examined by the king. It appears that the *aljama* had been denying their existence in the hopes of obtaining the town council's cooperation. Now that such hopes had dimmed, Haui dropped all pretenses and openly declared that the *concejo* was refusing to accept the validity of the Jews' privilege. In response, the representatives of the *concejo* vehemently objected to the Jews' petition to allow a *portero* administer the collection of outstanding loans in Miranda. They asserted that their town's privileges and *fueros* were much more ancient, having been first granted by Emperor Alfonso VI (*emperador don Alfonso que la villa poblo*) and confirmed by "other kings" and by King Fernando himself. These charters prohibited royal *merinos* from officiating in Miranda and its surroundings and stated that only *jurados* appointed by the *alcalde* had the authority to collect old debts in the town.[166] They demanded that the Jews' privileges be destroyed (*ronper*) and that the *concejo* be compensated for damages stemming from the violation of the town's *fuero*.

Two opposing sets of privileges lay in front of the royal officials entrusted with resolving the suit, a vivid testimony to the duplicitous royal policy. Publicly, the monarchy had been reiterating its support for local officials doing the *entregas* and prohibiting the use of special *entregadores* (at the cortes of 1293, 1299, and 1301).[167] Away from the limelight, however, the Crown continued to encourage the employment of royal officials in collecting outstanding loans and, it turns out, even granted some *aljamas* letters of privilege authorizing the placement of *entregadores* in their com-

---

Hanini [or Hamui]; Yhuda, son of Çahagui de Suzana; Çahagui Pardo; Juze, son of Barzelay; Samuel his brother; Mosse, son of Juziel; Alazar his brother; Samuel, son of Çahagui; Daui son of Çagui; Juezme son of Çagui; Sol Uellida, daughter of Barzelay; Oro wife of Çidiello; Dona Venda, wife of [?]; Sol Uellida, wife of Mosse; Lunbre, wife of Santo. Some names have faded beyond recognition; AMME, no. L-H0190-022; Cantera Burgos, "La judería de Miranda de Ebro (1099–1350)," 124–25.

166. Christian representatives cited the *fueros* of Miranda and Logroño: "segund que lo an de fuero et assi que lo ussauan en Logroño donde ellos an fuero."

167. *Cortes* I, III, 144, 149, 153.

munities. Now the court had to pick sides and decide which side's privileges it was going to uphold. The outcome of the case was easy to predict. Fernando IV, a young king who had only recently come of age, needed all the support he could muster. Alienating the *concejo* of Miranda was not a good option. Hence, the court declared that the Jews' letters of privileges violated the town's *fuero* and could not be carried out. Into the fire, therefore, the Jews' letters went. At the same time, the royal court made sure that the king got what was due to him, ordering that all the debts contracted since the reign of Fernando's father, Sancho IV, had to be collected by the *alcalde* of Miranda with no further delay (*sin otro alongamiento ninguno*).[168]

The court's decision appears to have brought to an end the central chapter in the drama that drove a permanent wedge between the Jewish and the Christian communities of Miranda. Assuming the decision was indeed enforced, one can only speculate on how the Jews of Haro, Pancorbo, and Miranda managed to continue collecting outstanding loans from the residents of Miranda. It is fair to assume that they faced an uphill battle. It was a battle fought on a daily basis not only by the three Jewish *aljamas* in this small northeastern corner of Castile, but also by Jewish creditors throughout the kingdom. On the Christian side, too, the issue of old debt collection continued to affect every community whose residents contracted loans with the "king's usurers." Disaffections born of local conflicts found their way to the halls where the urban procurators gathered for the meetings of the cortes or *ayuntamientos* aired their grievances and compiled petitions they intended to present to the king. The Jews, too, came together occasionally to exchange opinions and draft collective plans for action. Not much is known about these assemblies, but it is indisputable that they sent their own representatives to petition the king and try to counteract the influence of the Christian procurators.[169]

Although the Jews of Haro had reasons to despair of ever obtaining a royal *portero* for Miranda, their spirits might have been raised by a royal privilege they, along with other Castilian *aljamas*, received from King Alfonso XI in August 1335.[170] The privilege was a response to a petition

---

168. AMME, no. L-H0190-022; Cantera Burgos, "La judería de Miranda de Ebro (1099–1350)," 127–29.
169. Valdeón Baruque, *Judíos y conversos en la Castilla medieval*, 36.
170. AMME, no. L-H0190-008; this is a 1363 copy of Alfonso XI's charter from 1335. Cantera Burgos, "La judería de Miranda de Ebro (1099–1350)," 132–37.

composed at a Jewish intercommunal assembly and delivered by its representatives to the royal court in Valladolid.[171] The very first issue addressed by the petition was that of *entregadores*. The Jews complained that they had been driven to poverty and ruin (*pobres e estragados*) by the many obstacles that prevented them from collecting debts from Christians in a timely manner. The king responded by detailing the procedures the *entregadores* were to follow in collecting outstanding loans and by authorizing them to seize property in lieu of debts. He did not directly address the delicate issue of who would be responsible for appointing *entregadores*, but from the context it is clear that the king expected local *alcaldes* to be in charge of their operations and to impose a fine of 60 *maravedís* on debtors who refused to pay off their loans.[172] Only on private and ecclesiastical estates did Alfonso reserve the right to appoint *entregadores* if the local officials failed to do so. Four years later, at the cortes of Madrid (1339), the king issued a decision that was less favorable to the *concejos*. It appeared to be a compromise that was unlikely to please either the town council or the Jews. *Entregadores*, the king stated, were to be appointed by the royal official, the *merino mayor* of Castile, but they had to be Christian and come from among the local *omes buenos*.[173]

There is other evidence indicating that in the latter part of his reign Alfonso XI began to give his tacit approval to the royal officials' interference in the collection of outstanding loans. Once again, in 1347, the simmering conflict in Miranda drove the *concejo's* representatives to the royal court, where they complained bitterly about the supposed violation of their *fuero* by the *merino mayor*, who was presumably conducting his own *entregas* in the town. The *omes buenos* asked that the 1304 decision by Fernando IV's court be upheld. Alfonso obliged, imposing a fine of 600 *maravedís* on violators of his father's charter, but it is by no means clear how

---

171. "Sepades que los procuradores de las aljamas de los judios de nuestros regnos nos vinieron a nos, aqui a Valladolit, sobre fecho de las sus heredades que les nos mandamos agora entrar e nos mostraron en como son pobres e estragados por muchas daños e perdidas que an reçebido en sus faziendas, señaladamente en las sus deudas, non lo podiendo cobrar de aquellos que gelas deuen por muchos enbargos que ouieron, assy en razon de las esperas que nos mandamos dar a los christianos commo en las otras maneras de fuerças e de premias que les fueron fechas en los tiempos pasados"; AMME, no. L-H0190-008.

172. "[e]l alcalle del lugar que lo constrenga e le ponga pena de sessenta *maravedís* que fasta plazo quieto faga la entrega"; AMME, no. L-H0190-008.

173. Cortes 1, 462.

committed he was to enforcing his decision.[174] The tensions between the Jewish and the Christian communities in Miranda showed no sign of abating, and a satisfactory resolution to the conflict was nowhere in sight.

The drama had a sad and violent postscript. In 1360, during Enrique Trastámara's invasion of Castile, Christian residents of Miranda took advantage of the anarchy to settle scores with the Jews by attacking the local *judería*. According to the Chronicle of Pedro I (*Crónica del rey don Pedro Primero*) written by Pero López de Ayala, after Enrique's troops had entered Castile through the Rioja and advanced toward Miranda, local residents took his side and began to kill and despoil the Jews.[175] Pedro I soon reclaimed the Rioja and punished those directly involved in the attacks on royal property during the invasion. Even so, two years later, in 1362, the royal *merinos* were still harassing residents of Miranda and confiscating their property in retaliation for killing their town's Jews. Pedro ordered all authorized seizures of persons and property to stop and imposed a penalty of 600 *maravedís*.[176]

All the while, Jewish creditors continued to do business among Miranda's Christians. Neither the seven-decade-long controversy over the status of *entregadores* nor the civil war—not even the physical violence directed at local Jews—could disrupt the painful process put in motion each time Jewish creditors loaned money to Christians, then waited, more often than not past the deadline, to collect their debts, and finally received a slow

---

174. The privilege was confirmed by Pedro I on October 18, 1351. Pedro's letter contains copies of Fernando IV's original charter and of Alfonso XI's confirmation, dated November 10, 1347. The *concejo* of Miranda asked Pedro for a confirmation because Alfonso's letter "was written on paper and got torn" ("esta dicha carta era escripta en papel e se ronpia"); AMME, no. L-H0039-029. Enrique II confirmed it on February 5, 1367. AMME, no. L-H0190-021; Cantera Burgos, "La judería de Miranda de Ebro" (1350–1492), *Sefarad* 2 (1942): 341–43, 350–51.

175. "E otro dia fué a Miranda de Ebro, por quanto avian robado alli á los Judios, é tenian la parte del Conde, é fizo y Justicia de omes de la villa. " *Crónica abreviada*: "E otro dia fué á Miranda de ebro, por quanto avian robado é muerto alli los Judios, é tenian la parte del Conde, é fizo y justicia de dos omes de la villa, é al uno decian Pero Martinez, fijo del Chantre, é al otro Pero Sanchez de Bañuelos; é al Pero Marinez fizo cocer en un caldero, é al Pero Sanchez fizo asar estando el Rey delante, e fizo matar otros de la villa"; Rosell, ed., *Crónicas de los reyes de Castilla*, 1:504; López de Ayala, *Crónicas*, 240–41; Valdeón Baruque, *Los judíos de Castilla y la revolución Trastámara*, 34.

176. Pedro's letter is dated May 2, 1362. AMME, no. L-H0039-040; Cantera Burgos, "La judería de Miranda de Ebro (1350–1492)," 330, 348.

trickle of payments. For as long as the *aljamas* were connected by chains of financial obligations to the Crown and the Christians needed consumption loans, the cycle that had proved so damaging to Jewish-Christian relations would persist. In 1367, representatives of Miranda's *concejo* visited Enrique II's court, which happened to be passing through Haro, bringing letters that described the disastrous state of affairs in their town. Christian residents had borrowed "great quantities of money" (*grandes quantias de maravedís*) from the Jews and now risked losing their property (*perder lo que han*) because of their inability to pay. Enrique granted the *concejo* an extension of two years on all loans contracted with the Jews and waved all penalties and interest (*non corran penas ... nin logros*) accumulated during that time.[177] There is no way to gauge the effect of this order on the economic well-being of local *aljamas*, but chances are Jewish creditors were soon back in Miranda, trying to solicit new loans and seek compensation on the existing ones. They had no choice: their livelihood, their reputation with the Crown, their very right to remain on the Castilian soil depended on it.

To conclude, negotiations between religious communities were an essential if often overlooked component of the Northern Castilian coexistence. Jews and Christians made efforts to generate intercommunal consensus on such controversial issues as appointment of special judges for mixed litigation and collection of outstanding loans. Unfortunately, negotiations often collapsed due to a combination of internal and external pressures. The breakdown in local relations had serious implications. What began as relatively benign negotiations over local issues paved the way for renegotiation of the Jews' very position in relation to the kingdom's Christian community. A fateful combination of the royal policies and the cortes legislation spurred by petitions of urban procurators led to the formation of a potent anti-Jewish discourse that threatened to undermine the very foundation of Castilian religious coexistence.

---

177. Pedro added a caveat that the order did not apply to debts that affected royal "rentas e pechos e derechos." The letter is dated January 3, 1367; AMME, no. L-H0039-037; Cantera Burgos, "La judería de Miranda de Ebro (1350–1492)," 349–50.

EIGHT ⁕ "Insolent, Wicked People"

THE CORTES AND ANTI-JEWISH
DISCOURSE IN CASTILE

The Cortes Petitions as an Anti-Jewish Discourse

When, in the spring of 1366, Enrique de Trastámara invaded Old Castile through the Rioja, intending to capture the throne of his half-brother, Pedro I, he sent proclamations to the local *concejos*, striking a theme that had never before characterized epistolary productions of the royal chancery. Condemning the lawful king of Castile as an "evil tyrant, enemy of God," Enrique accused Pedro of favoring Jews and Muslims and enriching them even as his Christian subjects throughout the kingdom grew poor through excessive taxation—an act, the challenger asserted, that amounted to the abasement of the Christian faith. The future Enrique II pledged to liberate the kingdom from such subjugation and captivity, seemingly signaling the end of the protective relationship between the Castilian monarchy and the Jews.[1] Much has been written about the first Trastámara king's innovative use of anti-Jewish propaganda as a way of mobilizing public opinion against the reigning monarch.[2] However, far

---

1. "[a]quel tiranno malo enemigo de Dios e de la su santa Madre Eglesia fizo e fazia en ellos continuada miente, acreçentando sienpre en maldat e en crueldat, destruyendo las eglesias e los ... dellas, matando e desastrando los fiiosdalgo e desterrandolos e faziendolos pecheros, e despechando los çibdanos e los labradores de toda la tierra, e acreçentando e enrrequiçiendo los moros e los iudios e en señorandolos e abaxando la fe catolica de nuestro Señor Jhesu Christo, oviemos de venir á sacar e librar estos regnos de tanta sujecçion e de tanto desafu[e]ro e de tanta cativdat"; Serrano, ed., *Fuentes para la historia de Castilla*, vol. 2, *Cartulario del Infantado de Covarrubias*; Valdeón Baruque, *Los judíos de Castilla y la revolución Trastámara*, 39.

2. Valdeón Baruque, *Los judíos de Castilla y la revolución Trastámara*; Monsalvo Antón, *Teoria y evolucion de un conflicto social*, 235–38; Isabel Montes Romero-Camacho, *Los judíos en la edad media española* (Madrid: Arco Libros, 2001), 48; Belnart, *Los judíos en España*, 168–70; Pedro I was also accused of being a "Jewess's son"; see, for instance, Nirenberg, "Figures of

less attention has been paid to the fact that the success of his rhetoric depended on his audience's receptiveness to the anti-Jewish message.

Enrique's opportunistic propaganda hit the mark precisely because by the mid-fourteenth century, the kingdom of Castile was already saturated with anti-Judaism and possessed a full-fledged anti-Jewish discourse, disseminated in part through the legislation of Castile's representative assembly—the cortes. As a matter of fact, Enrique's central claim—that the Jews were driving Christians to poverty and profiting from their misery—had made repeated appearances in the petitions of urban procurators presented at the cortes throughout the first half of the fourteenth century. The Jews had been accused, among other things, of ruining the land through their usury (1307), employing deceitful tactics to extort excessive taxes from Christians (1313), charging double interest (1329), and causing Christians to lose all their property (1339).[3] It is my contention that the language of the *cuadernos* (booklets containing the cortes legislation) both expressed and fostered the swell of public sentiment in Castile that had become harshly anti-Jewish by the 1360s. All Enrique had to do was dip into its biting rhetoric for inspiration.

Numerous *cuadernos* survive from the second half of the thirteenth century and from the fourteenth century. They were booklets that contained the texts of petitions and the king's responses, drawn up by the royal chancery and carried home by urban procurators after the conclusion of cortes sessions. These *cuadernos* remain our only source on the cortes legislation, since the copies kept in the Castilian royal chancery have been destroyed. Most of them appeared in the collection prepared by the Real Academia de la Historia in the nineteenth century, although additional *cuadernos* have been found and published since.[4] The preparation of the *cuadernos* essentially began when the representatives of towns came to-

---

Thought and Figures of Flesh: 'Jews' and 'Judaism' in Late-Medieval Spanish Poetry and Politics," *Speculum* 81, no. 2 (April 2006): 421.

3. *Cortes* I, 195, 241, 421, 464.

4. O'Callaghan, *Cortes of Castile-León*, 6; *Cortes* I; *Cortes* 2; see also Gross, "Las cortes de 1252," 95–114; for the *cuadernos* of the cortes of Seville (1261), see Matías Rodríguez Díez, *Historia de la ciudad de Astorga*, facsimile edition (León: Editorial Celarayn, 1981), 2:715–20; Joseph O'Callaghan, "Las cortes de Fernando IV: Cuadernos ineditos de Valladolid 1300 y Burgos 1308," in *Alfonso X, the Cortes, and Government in Medieval Spain* (Aldershot: Ashgate, 1998), 13:1–14.

gether to exchange opinions, consult the records of previous cortes, and draft petitions to be presented to the king at an upcoming meeting of the cortes.[5] The sharing of grievances and the writing of collective petitions gave the procurators a better shot at getting a favorable response from the king.[6] The king then rejected or approved their requests, in whole or in part, but the petitions themselves, which often contained sharp criticism of the Jews, were duly written down in the *cuadernos* and taken by the procurators to their hometowns.

The cortes' anti-Jewish *cuadernos* were therefore much more than legislation per se: they led to a textualization of interfaith tensions in Castilian towns, fashioning the scope, the thrust, and the language specific to expressions of anti-Jewish feelings in the kingdom of Castile. In effect, they shaped a discourse—a way of thinking, writing, and talking about the Jews—that became one of the hallmarks of Castilian anti-Judaism. Among the many anti-Jewish discourses pervading Christian exempla, drama, hagiography, imagery, and polemics in the Late Middle Ages, the Castilian urban procurators' legislative assault on the Jews has not yet attracted the attention it deserves or found its own historian.[7] In fact, it has never been characterized as a "discourse" at all, despite having many of its classic features. Like the much-studied accusations of ritual murder and host desecration, the *cuadernos* created and perpetuated hostile stereotypes whose potency was predicated on the myth of grave danger the Jews posed to the Christians of Castile.[8] One *cuaderno* after another consistently emphasized the alien status of Jewish officials, tax collectors, and moneylenders and lamented the damage their supposed malice and greed were inflicting on the Castilian kingdom. The charges were repeated in an almost ritualistic manner, drawing upon the language of

---

5. O'Callaghan, *Cortes of Castile-León*, 72–73.
6. Procter, *Curia and Cortes in León and Castile*, 207–8.
7. However, Monsalvo Antón comes close to being one; see his "Cortes de Castilla y León y minorías," in *Las cortes de Castilla y León en la edad media: Actas de la primera etapa del congreso científico sobre la historia de las cortes de Castilla y León, Burgos, 1986* (Valladolid: Cortes de Castilla y León, 1988), 2:145–91; and his earlier *Teoría y evolución de un conflicto social*, 168–81. Pilar León Tello dedicated an article to the cortes' treatment of the Jews, but it is no more than a topical arrangement of its anti-Jewish petitions; see León Tello, "Legislación sobre Judíos en las cortes," 2:55–63. O'Callaghan has a section on the Jews in his *Cortes of Castile-León*, 180–83.
8. Rubin, *Gentile Tales*, 4.

the earlier *cuadernos* and using a formalized set of epithets, accusations, and demands. In essence, the discourse on the Jews' harmfulness to the Christian community was reenacted every time the procurators gathered at the cortes and released a barrage of anti-Jewish petitions intended to evoke the misery allegedly inflicted on the towns by the Jews.

One may raise an objection that the *cuadernos* lacked the proper structure of a narrative anti-Jewish discourse. They did not create a "story" in the strictest sense of the word, with an involved plot, recognizable protagonists, and vivid, even fantastic, details.[9] But it compensated for what it lacked in intricacy with a blunt straightforwardness of the message. With stunning readiness, Castile's woes were blamed on the Jews and their malevolent intent to harm Christians by acquiring power over them and cheating their way to greater riches. Spain's preeminent historian and the myth's modern proponent, Claudio Sánchez-Albornoz, distilled the message to its core when he asserted that the Jews "tried to dominate, or at least, exploit, the nation that had given them refuge" and "enriched themselves at the expense of the misery of the people."[10]

Another possible objection to reading the anti-Jewish petitions as a discourse is the lack of explicitly theological or sacramental language in the *cuadernos*. True, most of the procurators' complaints against the Jews had economic underpinnings, and their talk of taxation, indebtedness, interest rates, payment schedules, and corruption of Jewish officials seemingly had little to do with the deicidal Jews of the traditional Christian narrative. However, the ostensibly mundane language of material gain and loss easily fed into theological clichés and became infused with religious imagery. The association between usury and murder was an ancient theological trope. The book of Ezekiel lists usury among other iniquitous acts—adultery, theft, oppression of the poor, and idolatry—for which "a robber, a shedder of blood" deserves to die ("his blood shall be

---

9. On the structure of the Eucharist desecration narratives see ibid., especially chapter 2. On the appearance and spread of the ritual murder accusation, see Langmuir, "Thomas of Monmouth: Detector of Ritual Murder," in *Toward a Definition of Antisemitism* (Berkeley: University of California Press, 1990), 209–36; and John M. McCulloh, "Jewish Ritual Murder: William of Norwich, Thomas of Monmouth, and the Early Dissemination of the Myth," *Speculum* 72 (1997): 698–740.

10. Claudio Sánchez-Albornoz, *Spain, a Historical Enigma*, trans. Colette Joly Dees and David Sven Reher (Madrid: Fundacion Universitaria Española, 1975), 2:773, 777.

upon himself") (Ez 18:10–13). As Kenneth Stow points out, in the Middle Ages, "Jewish lending ... was repeatedly and internationally identified with Jewish acts of homicide against Christian society." The figure of a Jewish moneylender was the perfect representation of the harm the Jews in positions of power could inflict on Christians. In the host desecration narratives, the perpetrator of the crime was often a male Jewish usurer, who persuaded his (female) Christian client to steal the consecrated host (the body of Christ) for him to abuse. These stories created a tight chain of powerful associations, linking together the bleeding host, the Jews' ancient crime of deicide, and the contemporary Jewish usurers' economic abuse of Christian debtors.[11]

Castilian literary texts employed religious imagery to warn Christians against the dangers of Jewish power. In one example, the courtier and writer Pero López de Ayala (1332–1407), drew an evocative parallel between crucifixion and the imposition of high taxes on the people by the Jewish tax collectors. In his *Rimado de palacio*, he likened the overtaxed kingdom of Castile to a sufferer who did not notice blood coming out of his side (*e non cata el cuitado que toda esta sangre sale del su costado*). Another verse seemed to conjure the dark shadow of the ritual murder accusation: Jewish collectors of revenues, Ayala wrote, were "ready to drink the blood of the poor sufferers" (*están aparejados para bever la sangre de los pobres cuitados*).[12] Because the theme of Jews' greediness and penchant for unsavory financial practices jibed so well with the stereotype of Jewish materiality and refusal to see beyond the "bodily sense" of the scripture, it became a standing trope in Christian devotional literature. *Cantiga* 25 in the *Cantigas de Santa María*, a collection of songs in praise of St. Mary attributed to Alfonso X, depicted an avaricious Jewish moneylender who accepted Jesus Christ and St. Mary as his Christian debtor's "guarantors," only to try and charge the debtor twice by denying that he had already received a payment. At the end of the *cantiga*, through the intervention of the Virgin, who condemned the "wretched Jew" for his falsehoods, the truth

11. Stow, "Good of the Church, the Good of the State," 240–41; Rubin, *Gentile Tales*, 72.
12. López de Ayala, *Rimado de Palacio*, ed. Hugo O. Bizzarri (Madrid: Real Academia Española, 2012), 44, 42. Ayala was a courtier, writer, and royal chronicler who served Pedro I, Enrique II, Juan I, and Enrique III; see Constance Wilkins, *Pero López de Ayala* (Boston: Twayne, 1989), 1–7, 116.

was exposed, and the Jew converted to Christianity.[13] The image of Jews as greedy, treacherous, mendacious usurers found in the *Cantigas* was also a regular refrain in the petitions of urban procurators. As if echoing the Marian tale, on more than one occasion the *cuadernos* accused the Jews of "maliciously" (*maliçiosamiente*) doubling the charges found in the letters of obligation.[14]

In other words, the absence of openly doctrinal vocabulary in the *cuadernos* should not lead one to discount the significance of ideological motivation in the actions of urban procurators.[15] Behind the procurators' complaints lay the assumption, present in legal and theological discourse since the early centuries of the church, that if given access to positions of power the Jews would inexorably use it to harm Christians and their faith. It is in the light of this supposition that one should interpret procurators' incessant protests against the alleged financial exploitation of townsmen by Jewish tax collectors and moneylenders and the "evil counsel" of the king's Jewish advisers. The same thinking underlined Enrique's claim that by empowering the Jews Pedro degraded Christianity and his kingdom. In the *cuadernos*, as well as in Enrique's propaganda, the traditional stereotype of Jews as greedy, treacherous, and inherently antagonistic figures was seamlessly woven into the tale of Castile's recent economic, social, and political woes.[16]

---

13. Albert Bagby, "The Jew in the Cantigas of Alfonso X, el Sabio," Speculum 46, no. 4 (1971): 681–84. For a different take on the Jews' role in the *Cantigas*, which emphasizes "grudging tolerance toward Jews," see Angus MacKay and Vikki Hatton, "Anti-Semitism in the Cantigas de Santa Maria," in Society, Economy and Religion in Late Medieval Castile, edited by Angus MacKay, ix (London: Variorum Reprints, 1987); see also Dwayne Carpenter, "Social Perception and Literary Portrayal: Jews and Muslims in Medieval Spanish Literature," in Convivencia: Jews, Muslims, and Christians in Medieval Spain, edited by Vivian Mann, Thomas Glick, and Jerrilynn Dodds, 61–81 (New York: Jewish Museum, 1992). In a new study that analyzes representations of Jews in the Iberian visual culture, Pamela Patton argues that polemical imagery criticizing the Jews' involvement in moneylending begins to develop in Iberia (in Aragon to a greater extent than in Castile) during the latter part of the thirteenth century under the influence of northern European models; see Patton, Art of Estrangement: Redefining Jews in Reconquest Spain (University Park: Pennsylvania State University Press, 2012), 54–62, 76–77, 162–64.

14. Cortes 1, 421 (Madrid, 1329), 486 (Burgos, 1345).

15. As does Monsalvo Antón in his Teoría y evolucion de un conflicto social, 169. Benzion Netanyahu denies any religious underpinnings of the townsmen's opposition to the Jews; see Netanyahu, Origins of the Inquisition, 82.

16. On the association between royal power, materialism, and "Jewish" fiscality, see

Given the potency of the stereotypes cultivated in the *cuadernos* during a span of over fifty years, one may wonder why no significant outbursts of violence against the Jews occurred in Castile until a political crisis gripped the kingdom in the middle of the fourteenth century. It may be that unlike the narratives prevalent in northern Europe, the cortes' anti-Jewish discourse did not contain inflammatory stories or images of Jews inflicting physical harm on Christ or Christians and consequently was less likely to result in retaliatory violence. The fact remains that it took Enrique's propaganda and a vacuum of authority created by the civil war to incite anti-Jewish violence on a large scale.

There is little doubt that the cortes' hostile legal discourse had primed Castile for Enrique's anti-Jewish message, which quickly caught fire. Already during the early stages of his rebellion, in 1355, Enrique had local helpers when his troops assaulted the lesser of Toledo's *juderías* (el Alcaná), and killed numerous Jews—"men and women, old and young."[17] By 1360, when the Trastámara forces invaded the Rioja, the rebel forces' attacks on local Jews had become part of a deliberate strategy to attract more supporters. As explained by Pero López de Ayala, Enrique ordered his troops to kill the Jews in Nájera because the local residents would willingly (*de buena voluntad*) join the massacre, and the deed would cause them to fear retaliation from King Pedro and take the count's side.[18] As

---

Nirenberg, *Anti-Judaism: The Western Tradition* (New York: W. W. Norton, 2013), 194–201; and Nirenberg, "Deviant Politics and Jewish Love: Alfonso VIII and the Jewess of Toledo," *Jewish History* 21 (2007): 25–26.

17. "E el conde e el maestre, desque entraron en la cibdad, asosegaron en sus posadas; pero las sus compañas comenzaron a robar una judería apartada que dicen el Alcana, e robáronla, e mataron los judíos que fallaron fasta mil e docientas personas, omes e mujeres, grandes e pequeños"; López de Ayala, *Crónicas*, 145–46. King Pedro later pardoned the Toledans who had sided with Enrique, but excluded those who had participated in the assault on the royal Jews, including "the Moors of Toledo," and several Christians, some of whom were probably converts from Islam; Baer, *Die Juden*, 2:185–86; Valdeón Baruque, "La judería toledana en la guerra civil de Pedro I y Enrique II," in *Symposio "Toledo judaico," Toledo 20–22, Abril 1972* (Toledo: Publicaciones del Centro, 1973), 119–20; Rica Amran, *Judíos y conversos en el reino de Castilla: Propaganda y mensajes políticos, sociales y religiosos (siglos XIV–XVI)* (Valladolid: Junta de Castilla y León, 2009), 52–53; Clara Estow, *Pedro the Cruel of Castile, 1350–1369* (Leiden: Brill, 1995), 179.

18. "[e]l conde don Enrique, e don Tello, e el conde de Osona, e los otros caballeros ... llegaron a Nájara, e ficieron matar a los judíos. E esta muerte de los judíos fizo facer el conde don Enrique, porque las gentes lo facían de buena voluntad, e por el fecho mesmo tomaban miedo e recelo del rey, e tenían con el conde"; López de Ayala, *Crónicas*, 239.

we have seen, violent attacks on the Jews by their Christian neighbors also took place that year in Miranda de Ebro.[19] More violence followed in 1366, this time at the hands of foreign mercenaries fighting on Enrique's side, when "free companies" commanded by Bertrand du Guesclin attacked the Jews in Briviesca. Soon after Enrique was crowned the king of Castile in April 1366 he dropped anti-Jewish language from his propaganda, but attacks on the Jews continued.[20] In 1367, King Pedro's mercenaries, the English troops led by Edward, Prince of Wales (the Black Prince) assaulted the Jews in Aguilar de Campóo and Villadiego.[21] Even in the absence of foreign troops, however, and despite the fact that Enrique had toned down his anti-Jewish message, local Christians in the towns that took the rebel's side turned their wrath on the Jews. The Jews were attacked and their homes and synagogues sacked in Valladolid, Segovia, Ávila, Paredes, and Jaén.[22]

Once in power, Enrique did an about-face and put Jews in charge of the royal finances, but his wartime propaganda and his harsh treatment of the Jews during and after the civil war left an indelible mark on the subsequent rhetoric of the cortes petitions.[23] Despite reverting to the poli-

19. See chapter 7.
20. It may be that Enrique thought that the victory was near and realized that he would need Jews in his service once he took over; Amran, Judíos y conversos, 55; Valdeón Baruque, Los judíos de Castilla y la revolución Trastámara, 39–40. On the Castilian civil war as a new theater of operations in the Hundred Years' War, see Carlos Andrés González Paz, "The Role of Mercenary Troops in Spain in the Fourteenth Century: The Civil War," in Mercenaries and Paid Men: The Mercenary Identity in the Middle Ages, edited by John France, 331–43 (Leiden: Brill, 2008); L. J. Andrew Villalon, "'Seeking Castles in Spain': Sir Hugh Calveley and the Free Companies' Intervention in Iberian Warfare (1366–1369)," in Crusaders, Condottieri, and Cannon: Medieval Warfare in Societies around the Mediterranean, edited by L. J. Andrew Villalon and Donald J. Kagay, esp. 315–25 (Leiden: Brill, 2003).
21. Valdeón Baruque, Los judíos de Castilla y la revolución Trastámara, 47–48.
22. Valdeón Baruque, Los judíos de Castilla y la revolución Trastámara, 48; Valdeón Baruque, Judíos y conversos, 72–73; Netanyahu, Origins of the Inquisition, 115–17; León Tello, Los judíos de Palencia, 16. Samuel Zarza, the author of Mekor Hayyim (Mantua: 1559), mentions attacks on the Jews in Briviesca, Aguilar, Villadiego, Segovia, Ávila, and Paredes; he claims that in Valladolid, eight synagogues were destroyed; Baer, Die Juden, 2:200–201.
23. Valdeón Baruque, Los judíos de Castilla y la revolución Trastámara, 64–69. Enrique imposed exorbitant tributes on the Jews of Burgos (1366 and 1367) and Palencia. The Jews of Toledo (1369) were subjected to tortures and deprived of food and drink, and their property was sold until the king could obtain 20,000 gold doblas; Valdeón Baruque, Los judíos de Castilla y la revolución Trastámara, 44–46; Amador de los Ríos, Historia de los judíos de España y Portugal, 571–73.

cies of his predecessors, the king still found anti-Judaism quite expedient for drumming up popular support. The charters issued by Enrique II's own chancery routinely bullied the Jews into paying their annual tribute by threatening them with imprisonment, confiscation of property, and even starvation if they did not comply.[24] The anti-Jewish climate of the postwar years emboldened the procurators to attack the Jews in more expressly ideological terms. At the 1371 cortes in Toro, the upsurge in rhetoric marked not a new departure, but rather an addition to a discourse that had been almost a century in the making. The anti-Jewish petition submitted by the procurators had a harsh, unstintingly hostile tone:

> Because of the great liberty and power that was given to the enemies of the Faith, especially the Jews, in all of our kingdoms, in the [royal] house, as well as in the houses of barons, nobles, knights, and squires, and because of the great offices and honors that [the Jews] received there, all the Christians had to obey and fear them and pay them the greatest respects possible, so that the *concejos* of cities, towns, and villages of our kingdoms, as well as individuals, were all slaves and subjects kowtowing to the Jews, ... and as a result the Jews, being as they are an insolent, wicked people, enemies of God and of all Christendom, with great audacity committed many wicked deeds and briberies, in such a way that all our kingdoms, or the greater part of them, were destroyed and despoiled by the Jews, ... and they did it while scorning Christians and our Catholic Faith.[25]

The infusion of theological vocabulary completed the logical progression of the charges leveled at the Jews by urban representatives. Long singled out as a grave threat to the well-being of Castilian communities, the Jews had now been labeled as the enemies of the "entirety of Christendom."

---

24. See, for example, Enrique's 1366 grant of Jewish tribute to the convent of Santa Clara de Burgos. The Jews of Burgos are to pay an annual tribute of 3,000 *maravedís* to Santa Clara, and if they fail to fulfill their obligation, they are to be imprisoned and held captive without food or drink until the sum is paid; López Mata, "Morería y judería [de Burgos]," 370. The 1369 royal grant of 5,000 *maravedís* in Jewish *pechos* to the Dominican monastery of San Pablo de Palencia specifies that if the Jews are unwilling or unable to pay, the money would come from the sale of their property. In the meantime, they are to be incarcerated and deprived of food and drink; AHN, clero, Palencia, San Pablo, carp. 1725, nos. 13 and 15. Enrique II's 1371 confirmation is published in León Tello, *Los judíos de Palencia*, 49–51. Similar language is contained in the 1375 concession of 6,000 *maravedís* to the cathedral of León from the Jews of the city of León; Rodríguez Fernández, *La judería de la ciudad de León*, 221–27.

25. *Cortes* 2, 203.

The procurators' petitions, therefore, fashioned a coherent and forceful anti-Jewish discourse, with grave repercussions for the fate of interfaith relations in Castile. However, it is not enough to merely focus on the ideological impact of the anti-Jewish *cuadernos* and gloss over their specific content, which provides a window into socioeconomic tensions between Jews and Christians in Castilian towns. In fact, these tensions were the driving force behind the discourse, and they were what lent it credibility and made its impact so dramatic. Even as they harbored and fostered negative stereotypes about the Jews, the procurators pursued time- and place-specific goals, intended to strip the Jews of their legal privileges and to gain advantage in economic and political spheres.[26]

The Social Origins of the Cortes Petitions

A number of possible approaches to interpreting the cortes petitions have been exemplified in the cortes' historiography. Much depends on how one chooses to answer the following question: what were the social origins of the anti-Jewish sentiments expressed in the petitions and in the cortes legislation in general? The answer hinges on the broader issue of the genesis, composition, and functions of the Castilian representative assembly. Scholars trace the beginning of the cortes to the first recorded instance of the townsmen's participation in the royal *curia* (court) in 1188, in León.[27] Most tie the development of the representative assembly to the commercial rebirth of the twelfth century, the revival of towns, and the advent of townsmen as an important economic and political force. The rise of urban aristocracy, or non-noble knights (*caballeros villanos*), in particular, and their monopolization of political power in towns are said to be the primary reason behind the royal invitation to the *curia*.[28] The central debate in the cortes historiography has focused on whether the assembly represented a real restraint on the royal exercise of legislative power. While some historians have characterized the cortes as an expression of the sovereign will of the people, others have stressed its role as an

---

26. Monsalvo Antón, "Las cortes de Castilla y León y minorías," 163–64; Ruiz, "Trading with the 'Other,'" 66–67.

27. O'Callaghan, *Cortes of Castile-León*, 16.

28. Mínguez, "La transformación social de las ciudades," 2:15–43; Lourie, "Society Organized for War," 54–76.

instrument of royal power.[29] The latest assessments reject both positions as extreme and tend toward a middle ground.[30]

Both of these historiographic issues—the relative weight of the royal power and the estates in the legislative process, as well as the role played in the cortes by the *caballeros villanos*—have a direct bearing on the ways one might approach the cortes' anti-Jewish legislation. Given the crucial role of urban knights in the politics of the *concejos* in the thirteenth century and in the selection of representatives (*personeros*) for the cortes, it seems reasonable to conclude that anti-Jewish feelings were emanating from this select group of urban oligarchs. Indeed, as a number of scholars have pointed out, by the mid-thirteenth century, the Castilian *concejos* had long ceased being democratic institutions as control over municipal offices came to rest in the hands of non-noble urban knights—members of the tax-exempt elite, who had sufficient income to serve in the royal army with their own horses, weapons, and armor.[31] In most cities, the argument continues, the urban oligarchs selected *personeros* from among their own ranks, and Castile's representative assembly ended up being not very representative, although a "fiction" of representation was maintained.[32] It goes without saying, then, that the grievances urban procurators took to the cortes, including those that concerned the Jews, were expressions of their class interests.

29. Francisco Martínez Marina, *Teoría de las Cortes o grandes juntas nacionales de los reinos de León y Castilla*, vols. 1–3 (Madrid: 1913); Manuel Colmeiro, *Introducción a las Cortes de los antiguos reinos de Leon y Castilla*, vols. 1–2 (Madrid: 1883–84); Wladimir Piskorki, *Las Cortes de Castilla en el período de tránsito de la edad media a la moderna*, trans. Claudio Sánchez Albornoz (Barcelona: Ediciones Albir, 1977); see also Gaines Post, *Studies in Medieval Legal Thought: Public Law and the State, 1100–1322* (Princeton: Princeton University Press, 1964), 163–64: "consent according to the Roman law was not a democratic expression of the sovereign will of the people. Rather, it was a procedural kind of consent given in the assembly as the king's high court and council; and it was, although based on the lawful rights of all individuals represented, finally subject to the decision of the king in his capacity of supreme public authority in the realm."

30. O'Callaghan, *Cortes of Castile-León*, 5. See also his fine overview of the historiography in ibid., 2–5.

31. Ruiz, *Sociedad y poder real en Castilla*, 147–98.

32. Ruiz, "Judíos y Cristianos en el ambito urbano bajomedieval," 2:80–82; Teofilo Ruiz, "Oligarchy and Royal Power: The Castilian Cortes and the Castilian Crisis 1248–1350," *Parliaments, Estates and Representation/Parlements, états et representation* 2, no. 2 (1982): 96–97; Mínguez, "La transformación social de las ciudades," 38–42; Bonachía Hernando, *El concejo de Burgos*, 114.

The nature of these grievances, too, has been adduced as further evidence of the urban knights' particular animosity toward the Jews. Teofilo Ruiz has argued that the urban mercantile elites seeking to curb competition from the minority groups used the cortes petitions to launch a frontal attack on Jews' and Muslims' economic activities. Specifically, they wanted to eliminate Jews from trade, the real estate market, tax collecting, and usury—all areas in which *caballeros villanos* were particularly active.[33] However, one can raise an objection that the grievances in the petitions were too heterogeneous to be easily attributable to a single social group, even one as influential as the urban knights. Some of the demands may have come from the oligarchs, while most betray more complex origins.

For example, the efforts to ban Jews from tax collecting and to entrust the office to local *hombres buenos*, initiated at the cortes of Haro in 1288 and subsequently repeated on numerous occasions, might have been motivated in part by the oligarchs' desire to profit from this lucrative activity.[34] However, the wish to safeguard local autonomy against the centralizing tendencies of the Crown was at least as big a factor in the procurators' drive against Jewish tax-collectors.[35] Similarly, the habitually reiterated petitions to forbid the Jews' purchases of taxable properties (*heredades pecheras*) from Christians had less to do with competition for real estate between the Jews and the urban oligarchs and more with the complaints from the towns' taxpayers (*pecheros*) that their burden of taxation increased as a result of such purchases. *Caballeros villanos*, it must be stressed, were exempt from taxes, while the Jews paid them separately from Christian *pecheros*.[36]

The most frequent grievance that appeared in the cortes petitions was undoubtedly the cluster of issues associated with Jewish moneylending. Not only were these complaints numerous and most insistent, but they also involved a great variety of related concerns. The procurators appealed to the king to cap the official interest rate at 33.3 percent, to keep

33. Ruiz, "Trading with the 'Other,'" 66–67.
34. *Cortes* 1, 104; some of the other occasions: 110 (Valladolid, 1293); 131 (Valladolid, 1295); 149 (Burgos, 1301); 163, 176 (Medina del Campo, 1302, 1305); 191 (Valladolid, 1307); 224, 241 (Palencia, 1313); 275 (Burgos, 1315); *Cortes* 2, 150–51 (Burgos, 1367).
35. Ladero Quesada, *Fiscalidad y poder real en Castilla*, 72.
36. *Cortes* 1, 115 (Valladolid, 1293); 136 (Cuellar, 1297); 176 (Medina del Campo, 1305).

collections of outstanding loans and litigation over them in the hands of local officials, to reduce the length of allowable loan-collection period, to postpone repayment of loans, and to enact partial cancellations of debts. This litany of complaints notwithstanding, the one request that *never* appeared among them was a demand to ban Jewish moneylending altogether. In fact, after Alfonso XI attempted to do just that, at the cortes of Alcalá de Henares in 1348, the procurators registered their protest.[37] It is doubtful that the urban oligarchs sought to squeeze the Jews out of moneylending in order to secure their control over the trade.[38] Rather, the complaints should be taken at their face value, as evidence of angst over Jewish usury that originated in the conflicts over small consumption loans taken out by middling members of urban communities who were never very far from impoverishment—a phenomenon also well-known from other parts of Europe.[39]

As will be shown, the procurators' complaints about the Jews reflected concerns that were not limited to urban knights, but reflected community-wide anxieties over local autonomy, the inability of their poorer members to repay outstanding loans in times of economic crises, and the desire to curb what was perceived as the Jews' excessive power. I agree with José Monsalvo Antón that anti-Jewish feelings expressed in the petitions permeated the entirety of urban society, from the oligarchs to the poorest of the *pecheros*.[40] Perhaps instead of trying to pinpoint the precise social origin of the anti-Jewish petitions, it should be emphasized that the *caballeros villanos* was the group most responsible for channeling and shaping the anti-Jewish sentiments emanating from a broad cross-section of the urban population of Castile.[41]

Furthermore, in a discussion of the social origins of the cortes' anti-

---

37. Alfonso XI banned Jewish usury in 1348, allowing the Jews to buy *heredades pecheras*, but in 1351 the procurators asked Pedro I to rescind the prohibition on Jewish usury and to forbid their purchase of taxable properties; Cortes 1, 532; Cortes 2, 39.

38. Ruiz, "Trading with the 'Other,'" 67.

39. See chapter 7. For northern Europe, see Jordan, "Jewish-Christian Relations in Mid-Thirteenth Century France: An Unpublished Enquête from Picardy," Revue des études juives 138 (1979): 47–54; and Jordan, "An Aspect of Credit in Picardy in the 1240s: The Deterioration of Jewish-Christian Financial Relations," Revue des études juives 142 (1983): 141–52.

40. Monsalvo Antón, "Las cortes de Castilla y León y minorías," 150.

41. In my opinion, it is unhelpful to view the *procuradores* sent to cortes through the narrow prism of what is presumed to be their class interests. Such an approach confuses

Jewish legislation, one should not forget that the cortes were, first and foremost, a royal court that had no juridical independence from the king.[42] Before we rush to interpret the presentation of petitions at the cortes as an expression of direct, unfiltered voice of the people—whether *caballeros villanos* or other groups—it is necessary to consider the active role played by the Crown in the promulgation of laws at the assembly. By the time procurators took home their *cuadernos* containing the results of the cortes' efforts, the petitions will have gone through several rounds of a complex legislative dance involving the estates, the king's advisers (*curia*), and the king himself.[43] A dialogue of sorts took place whose outcome depended in large part on the political strength and acumen of the reigning monarch.[44] Strong, ambitious kings, most notably Alfonso X and Alfonso XI, did not hesitate to use the cortes to advance their own vision of a monarchy in which the reins of legislative, jurisdictional, and administrative powers were placed firmly in the hands of the king.[45]

In fact, anti-Jewish legislation first entered the cortes legislation not by way of petitions, but through the legislative program of Alfonso X, some of whose laws on Jews and Muslims adopted at the cortes of Seville (1252) and Valladolid (1258) closely resembled provisions set in the *Fuero*

---

democratic representation in the modern sense of the word with the concept of representation as it was understood in the thirteenth century based on Roman law. It is true that the Castilian *concejos* were not democratic institutions and that the process of selecting *procuradores* was heavily skewed in favor of the urban oligarchs. But this is not a valid reason to deny their role as representatives of the communities from which they came. When the procurators were picked, they were given the so-called *cartas de personería*, or legal mandates, that authorized them to plead their town's case at the royal court, or at the cortes. They also carried detailed instructions on matters of importance to the community. By all indications, they took their roles seriously. It is an oversimplification to dismiss their activities as a fiction or mockery of representation; see Procter, "The Towns of Leon and Castile as Suitors before the King's Court in the Thirteenth Century," *English Historical Review* 74, no. 290 (January 1959): 21–22; Procter, *Curia and Cortes in León and Castile*, 162–64; Mínguez, "La transformación social de las ciudades," 40.

42. O'Callaghan, "Las cortes de Castilla y León," 1:159.

43. Jean Gautier-Dalché, "L'organisation des cortes de Castille et León," in *Las cortes de Castilla y León en la Edad Media*, 1:281–82.

44. Adeline Rucquoi, "Pouvoir royal et oligarchies urbaines d'Alfonso X à Fernando IV de Castille," in *Genesis medieval del estado moderno: Castilla y Navarra (1250–1370)* (Valladolid: AMBITO Ediciones, 1987), 176.

45. Benjamín González Alonso, "Poder regio, cortes y regimen politico en la Castilla Bajomedieval (1252–1474)," in *Las cortes de Castilla y León en la edad media*, 2:213.

real, Alfonso's municipal law code promulgated in about 1255.[46] For example, the much-repeated prohibition against Jewish, Christian, and Muslim women serving as wet-nurses in families of a different faith made its first appearance in 1252 at the cortes of Seville. After the *Fuero real* reiterated it around 1255, the law found its way into the legislation of the cortes in Valladolid (1258) and in Jerez (1268).[47] Even though submission of collective petitions became the rule at the cortes in the last decade of the thirteenth century, the ban on interfaith nursing did not reappear in the cortes legislation until 1313—a good indication that the law was Alfonso X's special initiative.[48]

An even more crucial and ubiquitous piece of the cortes legislation—regulation of interest rates—also came from the *Fuero real*. In 1255, Alfonso's municipal code set the legal rate at *tres por quatro*, and in 1258 the regulation was already included in the legislation promulgated at the cortes of Valladolid.[49] Subsequently, no king failed to reaffirm the permissible interest rate (usually 33.3 percent) at the cortes as a manifestation of what had become, since the times of Alfonso X, a royal prerogative to regulate usury in the kingdom.[50] The Crown's aim to assert this prerogative through the cortes legislation, just as much as the procurators' own interest in the issues related to Jewish moneylending, should be held responsible for the predominance of usury regulations in the *cuadernos*. Some of the ordinances (*ordenamientos*) on moneylending and pawnbroking issued by the chanceries of Alfonso X and Sancho IV were cited *in toto* by the cortes legislation year after year, the last time late in the minority of Alfonso XI, in 1322.[51]

This does not mean that the procurators were left out of the loop or that their petitions regarding usury and other issues went unheeded. How-

---

46. Joseph O'Callaghan, "Sobre la promulgacion del *Especulo* y del *Fuero real*," in *Estudios en homenaje a don Claudio Sánchez Albornoz en sus 90 años* (Buenos Aires: Instituto de Historia de España, 1985), 3:168.

47. Palacios Alcaine, ed., *Alfonso X el Sabio*, 109; Gross, "Las cortes de 1252," 112; *Cortes* 1, 62, 77.

48. Procter, *Curia and Cortes in León and Castile*, 208; O'Callaghan, *Cortes of Castile-León*, 123; *Cortes* 1, 227.

49. *Fuero real*, 109; *Cortes* 1, 60.

50. For a good summary of the usury regulations at the cortes, see León Tello, "Legislación sobre judíos en las cortes," 2:58–60.

51. *Cortes* 1, 352.

ever, it is probably fair to say that the king and his advisers exercised the power to screen and select petitions worthy of royal attention as well as to deny requests seen as damaging to the Crown's interests. When the royal power was weakened by royal minorities or political unrest, the procurators' petitions showed considerably less restraint. For example, during the minority of Alfonso XI, the cortes legislation was flooded with anti-Jewish petitions, such as the request, unprecedented for Castile, to force the Jews to wear a special distinguishing yellow sign, "as in France." Even though Infante Juan turned down the procurators' demand with an evasive promise to seek advice from the prominent men of the realm, the mere fact of its appearance in the *cuadernos* testifies to the inadequacy of the royal tutors in the role of defenders of the Jews' customary privileges.[52] In contrast, Alfonso XI could afford to pick and choose which petitions he wished to answer. Only the existence of a prescreening mechanism can explain why none of the Jews-related petitions presented during his reign's cortes dealt with the "social" issues of separation and segregation, even as the king addressed numerous requests of economic and jurisdictional nature, the great majority of them being regulations of Jewish usury.[53]

Finally, it is necessary to bear in mind that the presentation of petitions at the cortes by urban procurators and the promulgation of royal legislation in response to these petitions emulated the traditional confirmation of privileges, or *fueros*, by the king.[54] It is no wonder that cortes-issued *cuadernos* were sometimes mistaken by historians for local privileges.[55] In a very real sense, many of the cortes' anti-Jewish laws *were* privileges awarded by the king to towns, and they were seen as such by the procurators. Year after year, the *concejos*' representatives came to the cortes asking the king to confirm various laws, such as restrictions on the actions of *entregadores* (collectors of old debts to Jews) or the prohibition on the Jews' purchases of taxable properties. This need for reconfirmation of privileges, born out of centuries-long practice, accounts for the ritualistic manner in which the requests were repeated.[56] In other words,

---

52. Cortes 1, 227.
53. Cortes 1, 378–79, 415–18, 421–25, 462–88, 515–16, 531–34, 594, 598, 611–13, 631–34.
54. Antonio Linage Conde, "El paralellismo jurídico-político entre las cortes y los fueros: A propósito del de Sepúlveda," in *Las cortes de Castilla y León, 1188–1988*, 1:219–21.
55. O'Callaghan, *Cortes of Castile-León*, 6.
56. Ruiz, "Judíos y cristianos en el ambito urbano bajomedieval," 2:81.

much of the cortes' legislative output was the sum total of the towns' efforts to obtain new privileges or confirmations of old *fueros* and the king's response to these efforts. Although the Crown was usually receptive to the towns' requests, local ordinances and *fueros* were occasionally sacrificed on the altar of the king's legislative powers.[57] The cortes' anti-Jewish legislation was therefore a multilayered political, legal, and discursive phenomenon, a product of the triangular relationship that bound the king, the Christian urban communities, and the Jews.

The Jews' Response

How did Castile's Jewish community respond to the stream of hostile petitions submitted to the king by town representatives at cortes? The evidence is scarce, since the Jews, as a special property of the royal treasury, were never invited to the cortes. One has to read between the lines of the *cuadernos* to detect glimpses of the Jews' reaction to the cortes legislation and the policies of the *concejos*. There is little doubt that most *aljamas* maintained direct communication with the king by sending representatives to the royal court who, like the Christian *personeros*, carried letters of *personería* that entitled them to speak for their communities, participate in lawsuits, and negotiate with the king and the Christian *concejos*.[58] Surviving documentation preserves several examples of such negotiations arbitrated at the royal court. The controversy in Burgos over the naming of special judges (*alcaldes apartados*) has been described previously.[59] The conflicts usually revolved around letters of privilege that the Jews obtained from the king to protect their interests against the political maneuvering of Christian *concejos*.

"Battles of privileges" between *aljamas* and *concejos* were a routine occurrence throughout Castile. In the last years of the thirteenth century and in the first decade of the fourteenth century, one such battle unfolded in the city of León between the local Christian and Jewish communities. In 1291, the *concejo* complained to King Sancho IV about the Jewish artisans working in the city. According to the report of the Christian *veci-*

---

57. González Alonso, "Poder regio, cortes y regimen politico," 223–26.
58. See chapter 7 for an example of Jewish *personeros* from Haro and the surrounding towns.
59. See chapter 7.

nos, the Jews refused to observe the council's ordinances regulating the making of shoes and the preparation of hides. Claiming a special exemption from the king of Castile, they allegedly refused to let the council's inspectors oversee their work and declined to use a special mold (*tabra*) for making shoes provided by the council. The king sided with the *concejo*, ordering the Jews to obey the council's ordinances.[60] However, the tensions stretched into the next decade, with the *concejo* attempting to deny the Jews separate *alcaldes* and demanding that the *aljama* contribute to the salary for a new royal official in the city, *juez de salario*. Once again, the Jews produced royal letters of privilege that appeared to counter the council's claims. The result of the ensuing negotiations was a compromise: the Jews agreed to pay the new judge, as the *concejo* acknowledged their right to *alcaldes apartados*.[61] For the Jews, letters of privilege issued by the royal chancery were the best line of attack and defense on everything from the *aljamas*' communal rights to recovery of bad debts by Jewish moneylenders. By all indications, they did not shirk from using such letters aggressively whenever the need arose. The town representatives even complained at cortes about the Jews' effective application of these privileges, claiming that they were doing "great damage" (*gran danno*) to Christians.[62]

The Jews' voice was never openly heard during the cortes sessions, and yet it was implicitly present in the Christian representatives' complaints, as well as in the occasional remarks the kings made in reply to procurators' petitions. For example, in 1322, the regents forbade Christians to register debts with vicars and archpriests. It is plausible that the original complaint came from the Jews.[63] One can speculate that *aljamas* sent their representatives to the king between the cortes sessions to try and sway the monarch's opinion on matters important to them. At the 1325 cortes, Alfonso XI seemingly referred to one such meeting when he quoted the Jews' complaint about the difficulties they were encountering

60. Archivo municipal de León, no. 40; José Antonio Martín Fuertes, María del Carmen Rodríguez López, and María Jesús Pradal García, eds., *Colección documental del archivo municipal de León* [CDAML] (León: Centro de Estudios e Investigación "San Isidoro," 1998), 63; Rodríguez Fernández, *La judería de la ciudad de León*, 203–4.
61. Rodríguez Fernández, *La judería de la ciudad de León*, 204–7.
62. *Cortes* I, 144, 331.
63. *Cortes* I, 357.

in collecting bad debts from Christians. According to Alfonso, the Jews told him (los judios me dixieron) that after the death of King Fernando IV, their efforts at collecting outstanding loans had been impeded by powerful individuals, as well as by moratoriums on payments issued by the regents. In addition, the Jews complained to the king (los judios me querellaron) about their debtors' practice of obtaining excommunication letters from the pope and the prelates to avoid paying off debts.[64] Before the start of the 1345 cortes in Burgos, Alfonso might have received another delegation from the aljamas of the kingdom. When the procurators put forward their request for a three-year moratorium on the payment of debts, the king cited his information that the Jews were very poor (muy pobres) and unable to fulfill their tax obligation to the Crown as the reason for declining their petition and offering a much shorter, one-year moratorium. The king's information probably came from the Jewish delegates who had tried to anticipate and neutralize the procurators' request by convincing the king of the aljamas' poverty.[65]

Shut out of Castile's representative assembly, aljamas' representatives likely came together for meetings that in some ways may have resembled the Christian cortes.[66] In the Crown of Aragon, where the evidence documenting such meetings is much more abundant, Jewish representatives from Catalonia, Aragon, and Valencia occasionally met to discuss common issues. More frequently, the delegates from each of the three kingdoms met separately, mainly to negotiate the distribution of royal taxes between the different aljamas.[67] There are scattered references to intercommunal assemblies in the Castilian documentation. The extant privilege addressed by Alfonso XI in 1335 to the "procurators of the Jewish aljamas of our kingdoms" (procuradores de las aljamas de los judios de nros. regnos) shows that the Jews might have adopted some of the methods and procedures employed by the Christian cortes. After discussing their common concerns and drafting petitions, Jewish representatives submitted them to the king. Even though the monarch was not present at such assemblies, he received Jewish representatives at his court and sent back detailed replies. Like Christian procurators, on whose consent the king counted to levy his

64. Cortes 1, 378–79.
66. Valdeón Baruque, Judíos y conversos, 36.
67. Assis, Jewish Economy, 139–43.

65. Cortes 1, 486.

extraordinary taxation (*servicios*), the *aljamas* tried to get a redress of their grievances by emphasizing their financial usefulness to the Crown and enumerating the past services they rendered the king. As we have seen, in the 1335 privilege, Alfonso XI acknowledged the receipt of a "great quantity of money" (*vna grand quantia de mr.*) from the Jews as a special *servicio* for the maintenance of the sea frontier (*frontera de la mar*), in addition to the yearly contributions in *pechos* from the Jewish communities of the realm. The Jewish procurators left the royal court carrying tangible evidence of the king's appreciation for their services—a royal charter that granted the Jews various privileges, among them, regulations of debt collections by royal *entregadores*.[68]

In other words, using Christian *concejos*' own weapons, the Jews of Castile put up a struggle to fend off the cortes' legislative assault. By petitioning the king and receiving royal charters favoring their cause the *aljamas* hoped to deflect the barrage of anti-Jewish petitions constantly directed at them by the disaffected Christian townsmen. But try as they might, the time and circumstances were not on their side. Only five years after the issuance of the privilege to the Jewish *aljamas*, Alfonso XI heeded the Christian procurators' plea and cancelled one-fourth of every debt owed to Jews at the *ayuntamiento* (non-plenary cortes) of Llerena in 1340.[69] In truth, the monarch tried to placate the towns because he wanted to obtain their consent for more taxes needed to finance his military campaign.[70] The Crown's financial ambitions and vacillating policies, economic crises, and political instability all conspired to roll back the Jews' privileges, a process that began in the latter part of the thirteenth century and continued apace in the first half of the fourteenth century.

The Legislative Attack on the Jews

In analyzing the cortes petitions, it is particularly important not to reduce their legislative assault on the Jews to any single line of attack. The *cuadernos* talk about removing the Jews from positions of power, taking away their tax exemptions, and regulating Jewish moneylending, but their full

---

68. See chapter 6; AMME, no. L-H0190-008; Cantera, "La judería de Miranda de Ebro," 132–37.
69. Cantera Burgos, "La judería de Miranda de Ebro," 138–140.
70. O'Callaghan, *Cortes of Castile-León*, 38.

impact can only be appreciated when all of these complaints and demands are studied *in toto* as a discourse that developed and matured over a period of time. The anti-Jewish petitions fall into two broad categories: those that include the Jews among other distrusted "outsiders," usually clerics and nobles, whose special privileges place them beyond the purview of the *concejos*; and those that are directed squarely and unequivocally at the Jews. In the first category are petitions that ask the king to strip members of privileged groups who are not *hombres buenos* of their tax-exempt status and block them from acting as tax collectors and other high public officials in towns. The second type of appeals presented at the cortes encompass numerous anti-usury petitions. These *cuadernos* treat moneylending as a specifically Jewish activity and articulate the procurators' demand that it be tightly controlled and regulated, lest the kingdom suffer irreparable damage.

My approach is to treat the two types of petitions as part of a single discourse in which these seemingly heterogeneous complaints coalesced into a mutually reinforcing set of stereotypes that fed into the townsmen's resentment of the Jews. Indeed, the image of an unscrupulous Jewish moneylender aligned perfectly with the procurators' contention that the privileged status of the Jews outside the jurisdiction of the *concejos* gave them an unfair advantage over Christians and endowed them with powers that were detrimental to the well-being of the urban communities and the kingdom as a whole.[71] In fact, the portrayal of the Jews as the ultimate outsiders with excessive and dangerous powers over Christians emerged as the linchpin of the Castilian anti-Jewish discourse.

No other single matter involving the Jews received as much attention at the cortes as the subject of usury. Complaints about the damaging effects of Jewish moneylending on the Castilian society surfaced at virtually every gathering of the cortes—a sign that the issue carried a lot of weight with the procurators. As I have shown, regulations of Jewish moneylending first entered the cortes legislation through the ordinances

71. Netanyahu concludes that the cortes' petitions targeted the Jews, the nobility, and the clergy equally, and should not be seen as directed "against the Jews qua Jews." However, he focuses almost exclusively on the petitions pertaining to tax exemptions, the holding of public offices, and property acquisitions, ignoring the vast majority of the procurators' complaints about Jewish usury; see Netanyahu, *Origins of the Inquisition*, 75–91.

of Alfonso X. However, it did not take the procurators long to take the initiative in petitioning the king to stem the alleged abuses perpetrated by Jewish moneylenders and their agents. At the cortes of Valladolid in 1293, the town representatives submitted to Sancho IV's attention several grievances that would become a regular fixture in the cortes petitions, forming the basis for the running commentary on the evils allegedly brought upon the kingdom by the Jews' greed, unscrupulous business tactics, and disregard for the well-being of Christian communities. One of the 1293 petitions targeted *porteros* (also known as *entregadores*)—royal officials put in charge of collecting outstanding loans for Jewish moneylenders. Fearing royal encroachment on local privileges, the *concejos* wanted these loans collected by town officials (*alcaldes*).[72] An even stronger objection to the activities of these collectors of bad debts would be made almost two decades later, in 1307, when the procurators gathered in Valladolid condemned them on moral grounds, arguing that *entregadores* were abusing Christian debtors and inflicting great damage on the land. In another petition submitted at the same cortes, Jewish usury was denounced as the cause of the kingdom's ruin.[73]

Other anti-usury petitions of 1293 also struck a theme destined to be embraced by the subsequent generations of urban representatives. The petitions alleged that Jewish moneylenders were engaging in illicit activities and using various subterfuges to bypass royal legislation and take advantage of hapless Christian debtors. In one ploy, the procurators charged, the Jews were breaking Alfonso's ordinances and charging a much greater rate of interest than the 33.3 percent allowed in the kingdom of Castile.[74] Another tactic involved pressuring debtors for repayment of loans that could no longer be collected legally because the six-year win-

72. *Cortes* 1, 111. In the next several decades, the demand was frequently repeated at the cortes: in 1299, 1300, 1301, 1307, 1313, 1315, 1329, 1339, 1351; *Cortes* 1, 144, 153, 191, 242, 285, 418, 462; *Cortes* 2, 39.

73. "Otrossi alo que me dixieron que por quelos entregadores delas debdas delos judios fazian muchas cosas desaguisadas e sin rrazon, et ffazian mucho agrauiamientos alos debdores, por que vinie muy grand danno alos dela tierra.... Otrossi alo que me pidieron por merced en fecho delas vsuras delos judios, que touiesse por bien de auer mio acuerdo en guisa que non venga dellos tanto mal commo viene nin se astrague dellos [nin se astrague por ellos] la tierra commo se astraga"; *Cortes* 1, 191, 195.

74. The admonition not to exceed the legal interest rate was repeated in 1293, 1301, 1313, 1315, 1325, 1329, and 1349; *Cortes* 1, 114, 153, 229, 285, 378, 423, 631.

"INSOLENT, WICKED PEOPLE" 243

dow allowed for their collection had expired.[75] In 1329, the procurators added another accusation to the already lengthy list of illegal strategies supposedly employed by Jewish moneylenders: with a "malicious" intent (maliçiosamiente) to overcharge debtors, the Jews were writing letters of obligation in twice the amount of what Christians actually received from their creditors.[76]

Was there any reality behind these accusations, or were they simply trumped-up charges designed to drive the Jews out of moneylending and other economic activities where they faced competition from Christians?[77] As is often the case, these sweeping condemnations had points of intersection with reality, but presented it in a distorted, one-sided way. The nature of these accusations suggests that they had roots in the conflicts, common enough throughout Castile, over the collection of bad debts. Chapter 7 has described the difficulties faced by Jewish moneylenders in recovering outstanding loans in the towns of Belorado and Miranda de Ebro. Even the cortes legislation could not avoid mentioning this problem. In 1325, at his very first cortes, Alfonso XI alluded to the Jews' complaint that town councils, prelates, noblemen, and even the pope, by means of letters of excommunication, did their best to prevent them from collecting outstanding loans from Christians.[78] It does not take a big leap of the imagination to suppose that Jewish moneylenders tried to cut their financial losses by evading the king's prohibition against collecting debts beyond the allotted six-year period and by employing built-in interest rates or late fees on overdue debts—practices that could account both for the accusation of illegal interest rates and the charge of writing cartas dobladas.[79] What was for Christian debtors the evidence of the Jews' malice and greed was for the

75. At the cortes of 1293, 1299, 1300, 1301, 1317, 1318, 1329, 1345, 1348, 1351; Cortes 1, 114, 144, 154, 312, 331–332, 423, 480, 486, 515–516, 598; Cortes 2, 38.
76. In 1329, 1345, and, a similar accusation, in 1348; Cortes 1, 421–22, 486, 532.
77. Ruiz, "Trading with the 'Other,'" 66.
78. "[q]uelos judios me dixieron que ovieron muchos enbargos en los tienpos passados despues que el Rey don Fferrando mio padre finó aca, assi por cartas de merçedes quelos tutores dieron de espera en general e en especial, commo de otras muchas fuerzas queles fiçieron los conceios e los perlados e los cavalleros e en otras maneras, porque non podieron auer sus cobdas entregadas.... Otrossi por quelos judios me querellaron que muchos del mio ssennorio, assi clerigos commo legos, que ganaron e ganan buldas del Papa e cartas delos perlados quelos descomunguen ssobre las debdas queles deuen"; Cortes 1, 379.
79. Melechen, "Jews of Medieval Toledo," 204–5.

Jewish moneylenders an attempt to stay afloat in an atmosphere openly hostile to their business.

In fact, resentment against Jewish usury grew steadily in Castile during the years leading to Alfonso XI's coming of age in 1325. The cortes of Palencia called together by Queen María and Infante Pedro in June 1313 adopted legislation that urged the faithful to uphold the constitutions recently issued by the provincial Council of Zamora (January 1313), reminding them that excommunication and damnation would befall any Christian who persisted in the sin of usury.[80] As the campaign against Christian usury gathered steam, the royal stance on Jewish usury increasingly came to resemble the policies carried out by the Capetian kings of France and the kings of the neighboring Aragon.[81] It was no coincidence that only two years after the cortes of Palencia, in 1315, the Jews of Castile suffered their very first kingdom-wide *captio*, when the cortes assembled in Burgos issued legislation canceling one-third of all outstanding debts owed to Jewish moneylenders and establishing a timetable for the repayment of the remaining two-thirds. To ensure the collection of the rest, and mindful of the needs of the royal treasury, the regents ordered that *entregadores* perform their duties and press debtors for payment.[82] In 1322, the cortes of Valladolid repeated the 1315 legislation, once again ordering a cancellation of one-third of every debt.[83]

With Alfonso XI reaching his majority in 1325, a new routine emerged at the cortes that transformed cancellations of debts or moratoriums on payments into a near-regular occurrence.[84] The procurators would come

80. "Otrossi nos pidieron que por rrazon que el Papa ffizo agora nueva miente vna constitucion contra todos aquellos que dieron o dan a vssuras en que pone en ella muy grant pena de maldiçion e de descomunion contra los que ffueron en ffecho e en conseio de dar a vssuras e contra los que deffendieren quelas ossuras (sic) que sson dadas que non ssean tornadas, que nos que tengamos por bien et mandemos quela dicha costituçion ssea guardada en todo ssegund que en ella dize, e niguno no ssea osado de passer contra ello, porque sseria grande peligro delas almas e contra los mandamientos de ssanta eglesia. Tenemoslo por bien e otorgamos gelo"; *Cortes* I, 240. Don Rodrigo de Padrón, archbishop of Santiago de Compostela and one of the chief participants in the Council of Zamora, assisted in preparing the legislation issued by the cortes of Palencia; García y García, "Judíos y moros en el ordenamiento canónico medieval," 178; Ruiz, *Spain's Centuries of Crisis*, 154.

81. Jordan, *French Monarchy and the Jews*, esp. chapters 5–9. The first *captio* in Aragon was ordered by James I in 1257; see Assis, *Jewish Economy*, 25.

82. *Cortes* I, 284.

83. *Cortes* I, 355–56.

84. The kings of Aragon also regularly issued moratoriums on debts to Jews; see Assis, *Jewish Economy*, 36–37, 63–70.

to the cortes complaining bitterly of bad harvests, high taxes, and exploitation by Jewish moneylenders and petition the king to stave off a disaster. Alfonso and his successors (with the exception of Pedro I) would then try to earn moral capital by making some concessions, although never to the full extent desired by the procurators. It all began in 1325, when town representatives arrived at the cortes in Valladolid with a litany of complaints against the artful Jewish moneylenders, who, they said, were driving Christians into poverty. They proceeded by asking the king to forgive townsmen one-third of every debt, with the remaining two-thirds to be repaid in installments over a period of eighteen months. In response, the young king showed strong resolve and political acumen unusual for a newly minted monarch. Willing to appease the towns but weary of conceding too much, he canceled only one-fourth of the debts, dividing the rest into three installments, to be paid over a period of one year.[85] Alfonso XI remained equally cautious for the rest of his reign, scaling down the procurators' requests to cancel as much as one-half (in 1329, Madrid) of every debt owed by townsmen, to the more reasonable one-fourth (in 1329 and 1348).[86] On most occasions he eschewed debt reductions altogether, preferring to assuage the disgruntled townsmen by postponing repayment of debts (*esperas*) by a year, even after having been asked for a three-year delay.[87]

Nevertheless, it is indisputable that Alfonso XI was the first Castilian monarch to interfere with the Jews' credit operations on a regular basis over a long period of time. He must have kept the kingdom's Jewish moneylenders on edge throughout his reign, although it is impossible to determine the actual impact of his edicts on their business. He was certainly no friend of usury in general and Jewish usury in particular. At the cortes in Alcalá de Henares in 1348, Alfonso surprised even the procurators antagonistic to Jewish usury by declaring usury "a very grave sin" and the cause of "damages and tribulations" afflicting the kingdom and forbidding Jews and Muslims to lend money at interest. He also professed his intention to allow the Jews' settlement in his kingdom until the prophecies were fulfilled and the Jews converted to the true faith.[88]

85. Cortes 1, 378.
86. Cortes 1, 421–422, 532.
87. In 1339, 1335, and 1349; Cortes 1, 464, 479, 486, 634.
88. Alfonso's statement might have been, in part, a response to the 1339 proposal by Gonzalo Martínez de Oviedo to expel the Jews from Castile; Beinart, *Los judíos en España*, 165.

To ensure that the Jews could provide for themselves, Alfonso allowed them to purchase landed properties in certain regions of the kingdom.[89]

Alfonso's attempt to convert the Jews into agriculturalists certainly brings to mind the 1253 edict by Louis IX of France that ordered the Jews to live "by the honest labor of their own hands or by commerce" or else leave the kingdom.[90] While there were obvious parallels, the two orders, separated by almost one hundred years, had less in common than it might appear. Unlike Louis IX, Alfonso XI did not threaten his Jews with expulsion. Rather the opposite was true: the Jews were invited to stay until "the end of times." Moreover, Alfonso showed willingness to take care of their economic well-being by letting them purchase land from Christians— contrary to the earlier cortes legislation, and despite an active resistance of the *concejos*.

If any similarities are to be evoked, they can be found in the strength of anti-Jewish usury sentiment prevalent in both kingdoms on the eve of Louis's and Alfonso's legislation. In France, the royal *enquêtes* of the 1240s revealed a wave of resentment against Jewish moneylenders who "extorted or stole usury" and the royal officials who accepted bribes to enforce the collection of debts.[91] As we have seen, the cortes petitions constantly harped on the evils of Jewish usury, for many of the same reasons: illegal overcharges and the excesses committed by the royal *entregadores*. Alfonso XI was no saintly king, but even he might have been motivated, in part, by a sense of moral obligation to do justice.[92] Salvador de Moxó, however, has questioned this explanation, suggesting instead that Alfonso had been planning an administrative reform that included putting an end to Jewish usury and replacing Jewish fiscal agents with Christian officials.[93]

---

89. "Et por que nuestra voluntad es quelos judios se mantengan en nuestro sennorio; e asy lo manda sancta yglesia, por que aun se an atornar a nuestra fe e ser saluos segunt se falla por las profeçias, e por que ayan mantenimiento e manera de beuir e pasar bien en nuestro sennorio, tenemos por bien que puedan auer e conprar heredades para sy e para sus herederos en todas las çipdades e uillas e logares de nuestro rregalengo e en sus terminos en esta manera: de Duero allende fasta en quantia de treynta mill mr. cada vno desque ouier casa por sy; et de Duero aquende por todas las otras comarcas fasta quantia de veynte mill mr. cada vno commo dicho es"; *Cortes* 1, 532–34.

90. Jordan, *French Monarchy and the Jews*, 148–49.

91. Ibid., 156–58; Jordan, "Jews on Top," 40–41, 48; Jordan, "Jewish-Christian Relations in Mid-Thirteenth Century France."

92. Sanchez-Albornoz, *Spain, a Historical Enigma*, 2:788.

93. Salvador de Moxó, "Los judíos castellanos en la primera mitad del siglo XIV," in *Simposio "Toledo judaico"* (Toledo 20–22 Abril 1972) (Toledo: Centro Universitario, 1973), 1:101.

Alfonso's ban on Jewish usury turned out to be a half-hearted and failed effort, but it shed light on the intentions of the *concejos* with regard to the Jews. It turned out that they did not wish to get rid of Jewish moneylenders after all: they only wanted them regulated, restrained, and prevented from acquiring an unfair advantage over Christians. At the cortes of Madrid, in 1349, the king and the procurators were back to business as usual, regulating the interest rate and negotiating a delay in payment schedules.[94] Moreover, the year after Alfonso's death, at the cortes of Valladolid in 1351, the procurators came out in support of allowing the Jews to engage in usury. As far as the procurators were concerned, it was a much greater travesty to let the Jews compete with the urban oligarchs in the lucrative land market.[95]

In fact, the poverty of Christian debtors, while real, was only one of the motivating factors in the procurators' attack on Jewish usury. For all the talk at the cortes of the harmful effect of Jewish usury on the economic health of Castilian communities, the procurators' overriding anxiety lay with the special status of Jewish moneylenders, which not only put Jews in position of power over Christians, but also made their operations immune to the jurisdiction of the *concejos*.[96] The same concern applied to Jewish tax collectors and other Jewish officials and even to Jewish landowners who would not pay taxes on properties acquired from Christian *pecheros* (taxpayers) or share in the communal tax burden. The procurators were certainly aware that the Jews' real and supposed power ultimately came from their lord—the king. However, their attack on the Jews' privileges was not merely an attempt to resist the encroachment of royal authority.[97] The *concejos* genuinely resented the *aljamas*' privileges and sought to equalize the playing field by making them a relic of the past.

To some extent, they succeeded. The signs of power struggle within towns between *concejos* and *aljamas* appeared long before the procurators' political demands aimed at the Jews first entered petitions presented at cortes. By the 1260s, tensions developed in Burgos, as evidenced by a series of complaints sent to Alfonso X by the *aljama* and its Christian counterpart. The Burgos *concejo*'s efforts, in the 1270s, to deny the Jews' right

---

94. *Cortes* 1, 631, 634.
95. *Cortes* 2, 39; Estow, *Pedro the Cruel*, 166.
96. Jordan, "Jews on Top"; Meyerson, *Jews in the Iberian Frontier Kingdom*, 179.
97. Ruiz, "Trading with the 'Other,'" 71.

to separate judges (*alcaldes apartados*) were described in chapter 7. By 1286, the prohibition on separate judges for the Jews appeared in the cortes legislation.[98] Burgos took the lead on another issue that was to have serious implications for the economic and political standing of the Jewish community. The towns were famously resentful of tax-exempt groups, usually ecclesiastics, who did not contribute their fair share to the communal tax burden. In Palencia, for example, the townsmen of this episcopal city fought the exempt status of the Cathedral Chapter's and the bishop's *excusados* for most of the thirteenth century. The local *aljama* became entangled in the struggle when the city council attempted to collect taxes from the Jews and Muslims of Palencia.[99]

In Burgos, the *concejo* went on the offensive in the late 1260s, complaining to the king in 1268 that the city's clerics, moneychangers (*monederos*), residents of the barrio of San Felices, and the Jews abused their privileges by purchasing taxable estates (*heredades pecheras*) and refusing to pay taxes on them. As a result, the city found it difficult to meet its tax obligations to the king. Alfonso answered that he had already ordered the Jews to refrain from buying such properties or to pay taxes on them if they did so in the future.[100] In 1279, the *concejo* complained again, this time obtaining a mandate from the king to sell all the taxable properties belonging to Jews and other exempt groups and to keep the money in lieu of taxes.[101] There is little doubt that when an almost identically worded proscription had appeared in the legislation adopted by the cortes in Valladolid in 1293, the Burgalese procurators had been the moving force behind the petition.[102] As the Burgos *concejo* fought the *aljama*'s tax exemption in real estate, they also had their eyes set on the taxes paid by the city's Jewish community, and taxing or selling Jewish properties was a step toward achieving both goals. In 1301 their hopes were gratified when Fernando IV granted the *concejo* an annual income of 12,000 *maravedís* from the *cabeza de pecho* paid by the Jews of Burgos.[103]

The controversy in Burgos that spilled over into the cortes petitions was as much about political power of the *concejo* as it was about the control of economic resources in the city. In the same way, the Jews' economic

98. Cortes 1, 99.
99. See chapter 5.
100. AMB, no. 99; CDCB, 119–23.
101. AMB, no. 2505; CDCB, 167.
102. Cortes 1, 115.
103. AMB, no. 93; CDCB, 264–68.

and juridical privileges were closely intertwined, and a successful attack on one category of privileges often brought about a lessening of the other. The procurators' critique of the Jews' tax-exempt status had far-reaching implications, leading to what was for Castile the first cortes-legislated ban on Jewish ownership of landed estates. In the decades following the first prohibition on purchases of *heredades pecheras* by the Jews in 1293, the monarchs uniformly sided with the procurators in ordering the Jews not to purchase any inheritable estates in the royal domain and to sell those they already possessed, except for the houses in which they resided.[104] It is not known whether the ban was effective, but when in 1345 Alfonso reversed his decision and ordered the Jews to stop lending at interest and buy land instead, the change was met with protests from the procurators.[105] In any event, the very appearance of restrictions on property ownership by Jews was a chilling reminder of the erosion of their privileges and status in the kingdom.

The urban procurators were less successful in their efforts to stem the longstanding practice of employing Jews as tax collectors or *almojarifes* (financial officers) at the royal court. However, the stream of petitions reiterating this demand, one of the most common during this period, created a powerful propagandistic discourse later exploited by Enrique Trastámara in his war of words with Pedro I. Jewish officials attracted the *concejos'* ire for several reasons. Like the *entregadores* of debts, Jewish tax collectors were royal agents who cared little for local needs and local *fueros* and who pocketed the money that could have benefited local *omes buenos*.[106] The same considerations led town councils to oppose members of the titled aristocracy, noblemen, and clerics in the role of tax collectors.[107] The cortes petitions speak of these groups with distrust bordering on animosity, describing them repeatedly as "troublemakers" (*ommes rreboltosos*).[108] But in the procurators' eyes, no group could be trusted in the office of tax collector less than Jews—the ultimate outsiders—who, like Jewish money-

104. In 1297, 1300, 1305, 1329: *Cortes* 1, 136, 176, 425; O'Callaghan, "Las cortes de Fernando IV," 8.
105. *Cortes* 2, 39.
106. Tax collectors customarily received 2.3–3 percent of the amount collected in taxes; see Ladero Quesada, *Fiscalidad y poder real en Castilla*, 252.
107. *Cortes* 1, 155.
108. At the cortes of 1295, 1313, and 1315; *Cortes* 1, 131, 224, 275.

lenders, used their positions of power over Christians to do harm and to enrich themselves at the community's expense.

During the reign of Alfonso X, the issue of Jewish officials was never raised in the cortes petitions. It was not until 1288 that Sancho IV, at the cortes in Haro, while making several important concessions to towns, first replied in the affirmative to the procurators' request that Jews not be appointed as tax collectors. The king also promised to entrust the collection of taxes only to *omes buenos*—that is, to members of the urban nobility (*caballeros villanos*).[109] The king's ostensible validation of the procurators' distrust of Jewish officials carried certain symbolic weight. There may be a connection between Sancho's acceptance of the towns' request and his cancellation, at the same cortes, of all tax arrears (dating back to the early 1270s) that his chief tax farmer, a Toledan Jew named Abraham el Barchilón, had been contracted to collect under the direction of Lope Días de Haro, the former *mayordomo mayor*. Sancho was holding the cortes at the ancestral stronghold of his disgraced favorite, who had been killed during the previous month (June 1288).[110] The procurators may have thought that the king's rejection of Lope's fiscal policies was an opportune moment to request a dismissal of all Jewish tax officials, el Barchilón included. The Jew's association with Lope did not seem to affect him personally, but it likely further hurt the reputation of Jewish tax collectors, already damaged by Alfonso X's prosecution of Çag de la Maleha and weakened by conflicts between the Jewish agents of the king and municipal and ecclesiastical officials.[111]

Neither Sancho IV nor his immediate successors had any real intention of dispensing with the services of their Jewish *almojarifes* and tax collectors. But the town procurators continued to press the king to do so, repeatedly drawing up petitions that included the Jews in a group of "undesirables" such as clergymen, nobles, and other "outsiders" (*omes de ffuera*).[112] In 1295 a more ominous demand emerged in a petition submitted at the cortes in Valladolid: that all positions at royal court be reserved

---

109. *Cortes* I, 104–5.
110. O'Callaghan, *Cortes of Castile-León*, 27–28, 137; Baer, *History of the Jews*, 1:131–33.
111. See chapters 4 and 7.
112. In 1293, 1295, 1301, 1302, 1305, 1307, 1313, 1315, 1317, and 1322; *Cortes* I, 110, 131, 149, 155–56, 163, 175, 191, 224, 275, 305, 342, and 348.

for *omes bonos* of the towns and that no Jew be allowed at court.[113] It would be a number of years before another petition targeting exclusively Jewish officials would be presented at a cortes, but when it happened, during the minority of Alfonso XI, the petitions revealed a high level of animosity toward Jews in positions of power.

In 1313, at the cortes of Palencia, Infante Juan promised the procurators that Jews would be forbidden to occupy any office (*que aya otro offiçio ninguno*) at his own court or that of the king.[114] And at another cortes assembled the same year in Palencia, presided over by Queen María and Infante Pedro, the procurators urged the king and the royal tutors not to entrust the Jews with any offices, especially those of *almojarife* and tax collector. The reason for their request, they asserted, lay in the outrageous behavior of Jewish tax collectors, who deceived Christians (*ffizieron alos christianos muchos engannos*) in their single-minded pursuit of taxes for the king. If Christian taxpayers could not meet their obligations, the Jews demanded pledges in lieu of taxes, thereby driving taxpayers into debt and causing them to lose their property (*ssacauan a muchos christianos delos que auien*).[115] The charge against Jewish tax collectors echoed the allegations leveled at the same cortes against Jewish moneylenders. Even the same language (*ffazian engannos*) was employed to indict both groups, cementing the image of Jews as callous and treacherous outsiders who used their economic and political power to evil ends.

There is no doubt that the procurators' entreaties, while formally appeased by the king at cortes, had little practical effect. Tax collections and tax farming by Jews went on as before. Even though at the cortes of 1329 in Madrid the young Alfonso XI gave his general approval to the petition asking the king to prevent Jews from occupying positions at court, nothing was heard about the issue at cortes for the rest of his reign.[116] The

113. "Otrossi tenemos por bien quelos oficiales de nuestra casa sean omes bonos delas uillas de nuestros rregnos assi commo era en tiempo del Rey don Alffonso que vencio la batalla de Vbeda, e en tiempo del Rey don Alffonsso que vencio la batalla de Merida, e del Rey don Fernando; et que non ande y iudio"; *Cortes* I, 131.

114. *Cortes* I, 230.

115. *Cortes* I, 241.

116. The procurators' complaint in 1329 was directed specifically against Yuçaf de Écija, *almojarife mayor* of Alfonso XI, who lost the king's favor that year; Ladero Quesada, *Fiscalidad y poder real en Castilla*, 236; *Cortes* I, 415–16.

policies pursued by Alfonso's son and successor, Pedro I, created new fodder for the procurators' discontent. In relying on the services of Jewish financiers, especially Samuel Leví of Toledo, his *tesorero mayor*, Pedro made no grand departure from the practice of his predecessors, his father included. However, bluntly disregarding Castilian political decorum, he not only employed many Jews at court, but also failed to placate the procurators with sternly anti-Jewish language or to show his good will to towns by giving out meaningful concessions. At the cortes of Valladolid in 1351, Pedro even defended the Jews against the procurators' attacks, calling them "weak" people (*giente fraca*) who had a poor grasp of Castilian law and needed royal protection.[117] Pedro's reputation as a "Jew-lover," a monarch under the sway of Jewish advisers, or even, scandalously, a Jewess's son, had roots in these short-sighted policies.[118]

Pedro's supposed hobnobbing with the Jews created an ill repute that was almost too easy for his rival to exploit. Enrique Trastámara's anti-Jewish propaganda drew heavily on the growing public outcry against Jewish officials that had been so frequently expressed in the cortes petitions. In the accusation of despoiling and abusing Christians that Enrique leveled against Jewish tax collectors and other officials, one immediately recognizes echoes of procurators' complaints voiced at cortes in the course of the previous eighty years. In 1367, Enrique's rhetoric, infused with strong anti-Jewish sentiment permeating the kingdom, made its way back to the cortes to influence, in its turn, the procurators' verbal attack on Jewish officials. At the cortes of Burgos, where Enrique was recognized as king, the procurators dropped all restraint as they went on the offensive blaming Jewish royal officials for the iniquities perpetrated during Pedro's reign. As if copying from Enrique's script, the petition made the Jews' guilt and evil intent more explicit than ever before, claiming that the Jews deliberately plotted to harm Christians (*querien*

---

117. Cortes 2, 40, 44.

118. Valdeón Baruque, *Los judíos de Castilla y la revolución Trastámara*, 25–31; Luis Suárez Fernández, *Monarquía hispana y revolución Trastámara* (Madrid: Real Academia de la Historia, 1994), 18. Clara Estow argues that there was nothing particularly "pro-Jewish" in Pedro's policies and that the king simply adhered to the traditional Castilian royal policy of protecting the Jewish minority and employing Jewish financiers. Pedro's image as "judeophile," she argues, is the product of the Trastámaran propaganda, with little basis in reality; see Estow, *Pedro the Cruel*, 164–75.

mal e dapno delos christianos). Lamentably, they succeeded: "the evils and calamities, deaths and exiles happened in the past on the advice of Jews who were confidants and officials of previous kings." The procurators went on to demand that no Jew should occupy any office, including that of physician.[119]

Enrique's reply to the petition was noteworthy. He refused to honor the request, claiming, somewhat disingenuously, that no other king had ever been presented with such a petition. Lest some calamity befall the kingdom, he pledged not to allow any Jews on the royal council, but stood firm in his intention to continue employing Jewish tax collectors, since no Christians could be found to perform the task.[120] Anti-Judaism had been a convenient tool for mobilizing public opinion against Pedro, but once Enrique took the throne, he found that practical exigencies of running a kingdom dictated a more pragmatic approach to the issue of Jewish officeholders. Four years later, in 1371, at the cortes of Toro, called by one historian the "climax" point of medieval Castilian anti-Judaism, the procurators renewed their attack in even more vehement tones, describing the Jews as enemies of Christianity and accusing them of taking bribes and committing other crimes to the detriment of the kingdom.[121] Among other things, the procurators demanded that the Jews not be appointed to any offices whatsoever.[122] Once again, Enrique demurred, promising only to adhere to custom in dealing with this issue.[123]

The tangible results of the procurators' efforts might have been slow in coming, but their legislative attacks on Jewish officials, more than any

---

119. *Cortes* 2, 150–51.

120. "A esto rrespondemos que tenemos en sseruiçio lo que en esta rrazon nos piden, pero nunca alos otros rreyes que ffueron en Castilla ffue demandada tal petiçion. Et avnque algunos judios anden en la nuestra casa, non los ponemos en el nuestro Consejo nin les daremos tal poder, por que venga por ellos dapno alguno ala nuestra tierra.... A esto rrespondemos que verdat es que nos que mandamos arrendar la dicha rrenta a judios, por que non ffallamos otros algunos quela tomassen"; *Cortes* 2, 150–51.

121. Valdeón Baruque, *Los judíos de Castilla y la revolución Trastámara*, 62.

122. "[e]t otrosi que non ouiesen ofiçios ningunos en la nuestra casa nin de otro sennor nin cauallero nin escudero de nuestros rregnos, nin fuesen arrendadores delas muestras rrentas, por quanto fazian con ellas falsa mente muchos males e muchos cohechos"; *Cortes* 2, 203–4.

123. "[e]n rrazon de todo lo al que enla dicha petiçion se contiene, tenemos por bien que pasen segund que pasaron en tienpo delos rreyes nuestros anteçesores e del Rey don Alfonso nuestro padre"; ibid.

other anti-Jewish measure, succeeded in conceptualizing and reinforcing Christian hostility against the unpopular minority. It dovetailed with other negative stereotypes about the Jews, filling in with morbid colors between the lines of an image that suggested a dangerous outsider bent on doing harm to the community. As town representatives sought to curb the Jews' privileges and undercut their economic and political standing, they took aim at institutionalizing their outsider status through a series of measures intended to bring about separation between Jews and Christians.

Compared to most other anti-Jewish demands found in the cortes petitions, requests for limiting social intercourse and establishing symbolic and physical barriers between the two groups were relatively few in number and tended to appear in clusters during the periods of the monarchy's weakness. On various occasions, the cortes imposed a ban on the use of Christian names by Jews, forbade the Jews to employ Christian wet-nurses (and vice versa), required them to wear special fabrics, dress, or distinguishing signs, and relegated them to separate neighborhoods. Once again, it must be pointed out that along with some other regulations aimed at Jews, the separation clauses entered the cortes legislation on the initiative of Alfonso X. For example, the prohibition against Christian, Jewish, and Muslim nurses to serve employers of a different religious faith made its first appearance in the legislation promulgated by Alfonso at the cortes of Seville in 1252.[124] Soon after, the clause was included in Alfonso's municipal code, the *Fuero real* (circa 1255), and remained a staple of the wise king's cortes ordinances for the rest of his reign.[125] Alfonso also attempted to regulate Jewish dress by including Jews in his sumptuary legislation promulgated at cortes in 1258, 1261, and 1268. The Jews were told to abstain from wearing certain luxury items, bright colors, and clothes made of expensive materials.[126] However, these measures cannot be characterized as anti-Jewish, since they mainly sought to curb ostentatious display of riches by the Jewish elites.[127]

---

124. Gross, "Las cortes de 1252," 112.

125. The cortes of 1258, 1261, and 1268: *Cortes* 1, 62, 77; Rodríguez Díez, *Historia de la ciudad de Astorga*, 2:718.

126. *Cortes* 1, 59, 68–69; Rodríguez Díez, *Historia de la ciudad de Astorga*, 2:719.

127. Melechen, "Jews of Medieval Toledo," 121–22. See also Melechen's article on the

Following Alfonso's reign, these symbolic measures would be promulgated at cortes only sporadically, either during periods of royal minority or early in a monarch's reign. As anti-Judaism gathered steam in Castile, the procurators showed an increasing predilection for such measures, which politically vulnerable kings were all too eager to grant as an easy and noncommittal way of placating the towns. After 1268, when Alfonso's favorite separation clauses, along with a new prohibition on the Jewish use of Christian names, were adopted at the cortes of Jerez, the cortes legislation was silent on these issues for several decades, until a sudden outburst of activity during Alfonso XI's minority put them back on the agenda. As we have seen, the cortes of 1313, having taken place on the heels of the provincial church council in Zamora (1312–13), was a propitious occasion for adopting anti-Jewish legislation. The procurators demanded and received confirmations of Alfonso X's ordinances on the use of Christian names, interfaith nursing, and dress regulations for the Jews. But this time the representatives went even further, asking the royal regents to institute a Castilian equivalent of the Jewish badge used in France (ssinal de pano amariello ... ssegunt lo trayan en França)—and a radical innovation it would have been, if Infante Juan had dodged the custom and approved it.[128]

This latest attack revealed the townsmen's intention to challenge some of the Jews' most entrenched privileges. For the first time since the early thirteenth century, when Fernando III had firmly rejected the papacy's demand for distinguishing signs, the wearing of a Jewish badge was publicly endorsed in Castile.[129] In all likelihood, the procurators thought that this measure, along with other ordinances aimed at separating and humiliating the Jews, would serve as an antidote to the excessive power supposedly wielded by the Jews. Even so, the idea did not gain much traction with the next ruler, Alfonso XI, whose cortes sessions never once adopted any of the separation clauses. When Pedro I convened the one and only cortes of his reign, in 1351, the procurators jumped at the chance to

---

use of identification in Toledan documents to establish symbolic boundaries between Jews and Christians: "Calling Names: The Identification of Jews in Christian Documents from Medieval Toledo," in *On the Social Origins of Medieval Institutions: Essays in Honor of Joseph F. O'Callaghan*, edited by Donald Kagay and Theresa Vann, 21–34 (Leiden: Brill, 1998).

128. *Cortes* 1, 227, 244, 231. The regulations on nurses and the use of Christian names were again approved at the cortes of Valladolid in 1322; *Cortes* 1, 352.

129. See chapter 4.

get the anti-Jewish symbolic measures approved by the new monarch. In one petition, they argued that Christian women should be barred from conversing with Jews, nursing their children, and living in their households, because such situations created opportunities for sin (*ocasiones de pecar*). The king granted this petition, as well as the usual requests against the use of Christian names and the wearing of expensive clothes and jewelry by the Jews. The procurators' case was undoubtedly helped by the fact that the king expected to collect hefty fines from violations of these ordinances.[130]

One of the petitions presented at Pedro's cortes was quite unprecedented in the history of the institution. It showed that the Jewish quarters (*juderías*) were becoming more segregated as Jews and Christians set out to carve the urban space into separate neighborhoods for their coreligionists. Pedro was asked to approve the already existing agreements between *aljamas* and *concejos* that had reserved certain streets and neighborhoods for the Jews' exclusive use. The king supported the petition without making segregation a universal requirement for Castile.[131] The unimpeded mingling of Jews and Christians in the *juderías*, so common in the previous two centuries, was becoming a thing of the past.

With Enrique Trastámara on the Castilian throne, town representatives had every reason to expect a favorable reception of their anti-Jewish grievances. Not surprisingly, at the cortes of 1371, convened shortly after many Castilian *juderías* had fallen victim to the attacks instigated by Enrique's troops and carried out by many of the Jews' own neighbors, they unleashed a barrage of anti-Jewish petitions, using a language that was pointedly abusive and derogatory. The centerpiece of their submissions was a petition that accused the Jews of every manner of offense against Castile and Christianity. As if underlining the importance attributed to such measures by the procurators, the petition consisted mainly of calls for a total separation of Jews from the Christian community. The Jews were to live "marked and separated from the Christians, as ordained by God and mandated by laws and privileges, and wear signs, the way they do in other kingdoms, so that they are distinguished from the Christians and have no occasion to cause as much evil and harm as they do now." In

130. *Cortes* 2, 18, 19.
131. *Cortes* 2, 19.

addition, they were not to wear good clothes, ride mules, or call themselves by Christian names.[132]

However, the most extraordinary feature of this petition was not its language, its demands, or the fact that Enrique agreed with the procurators that the Jews should wear badges ("to honor God and us"). It was the townsmen's appeal, twice in the course of the petition, to the foreign ways of dealing with the Jews as preferable to Castile's own customs and traditions. Given the reverent treatment Castilians usually accorded their customary privileges and norms, there can be no mistaking the procurators' intentions. The townsmen were not yet ready to send the Jews into exile ("because they had to live and to give faith and testimony to the death of our Lord Jesus Christ"), but there was nothing oblique in the message sent by their petition: they wanted to undercut the very foundation of the Jews' status in the kingdom and destroy the specific privileges that had governed their life in the kingdom for several centuries.

Conclusion

One of the main observations that has emerged from my study of Jewish-Christian relations in Northern Castile is the variety of responses in the Christian community to the presence of a Jewish minority in the kingdom. Although there is little doubt that traditional anti-Jewish discourses continued to shape Christians' attitudes toward the Jews, the various groups and sectors in Castilian society viewed the Jews primarily through the lens of their own interests. The monarchy, the ecclesiastical institutions, and the municipal councils (*concejos*) all developed extensive ties with the Jews, and these relationships did not remain static but continued to develop throughout the period. Already by the late eleventh century, the king of Castile-León, his power boosted by his role as a military leader in the war against Muslims, began to lay claims of exclusive jurisdiction over the kingdom's nascent Jewish communities. At the same time, the monarchy was committed to distributing fiscal and jurisdictional shares in the Jewish communities among royal retainers, both lay and ecclesiastical, whose loyalty and military support were necessary in the ongoing process of war and colonization. By and large, the Castilian kings succeeded at establishing

---

132. *Cortes* 2, 203–4.

their jurisdictional claim to the Jews as the "property of the royal treasury" and by the middle of the thirteenth century strengthened their control over the *aljamas*, actively interfering in the Jewish communal affairs.

For their part, Northern Castile's numerous ecclesiastical institutions accepted lucrative donations of Jewish taxes from the king, and some even received jurisdiction over entire Jewish communities. The Castilian church's commitment to this arrangement and the Crown's vigilant control over the Jewish revenues made the papal initiatives to restrict the Jews' political and economic roles a hard sell in the kingdom. I have shown that while some Castilian clergymen were vehemently anti-Jewish, collectively they never developed a coordinated strategy on the Jews or even showed much interest in the issue.

The opposite is true about the Christian townsmen, whose relations with their Jewish neighbors vacillated between cooperation and conflict. In some communities, the Jews enjoyed a limited citizenship, contributed to communal projects, and even occasionally sided with the Christian *concejos* in revolts against ecclesiastical lords. In the late thirteenth century, however, the town procurators began to develop a common anti-Jewish strategy while drafting and submitting petitions to the king during the meetings of the Castilian cortes. I have argued that the Crown's heavy-handed tactics in enforcing the collection of outstanding debts to Jewish moneylenders led to the breakdown in the negotiations between the Jewish and Christian communities, creating a fertile ground for the intensification of anti-Jewish attitudes in Castilian towns.

Even though the Jews' attitudes toward the various powers in the Christian society are more difficult to trace in the extant sources, I have tried to show that the Jews were active players in the kingdom's politics. Throughout the period, and despite the oppressiveness of some royal policies, the Jews had a predominantly positive view of royal authority, regarding the king as their most reliable ally in the kingdom. The leadership of the Jewish communities readily accepted royal support and protection in exchange for the fiscal and administrative services they rendered the Crown. The Jewish elites relied on the king to suppress internal religious dissent and regulate communal affairs. In Sahagún and Palencia, the Jews supported the efforts to limit the temporal authority of the prelates who ruled over their cities, seeking to avoid excessive taxation and gain the type of communal autonomy available to the royal *aljamas*. When the Christian urban representatives led legislative attacks against the Jews at the cortes, aiming to curtail their privileges in towns, the Jews sent their own representatives to the king, reminding him of their usefulness to the Crown and urging him to protect their customary rights.

As much as possible, I have tried to avoid the dichotomous categories of tolerance and persecution, arguing instead that some degree of insecurity always characterized Jewish life in Northern Castile and León.[133] Jewish-Christian coexistence was most stable in this region between the third quarter of the twelfth century and circa 1260. The *fueros* and privileges granted by the kings of Castile to their fiscal servitors indicate an intention to treat the Jews as a special source of revenue for the Crown and to create for them a distinct legal and social status that set them apart from the Christian *vecinos*. While the actual degree of the Jews' participation in communal life of their municipalities varied from place to place, the surviving evidence suggests that during this period both ecclesiastics and lay Christians generally accepted the rules of engagement with the Jews that arose partly from royal policies and partly from local practice. Over time, however, these arrangements proved to be fragile. The worsening economic crisis, widespread indebtedness to Jewish moneylenders, political realignment in towns, and exploitative royal fiscal practices all paved the way for a sustained attack on Jewish privileges carried out by the representatives of urban elites. I have shown that despite the Jews' best efforts to deflect the *concejos*' attacks, in the century that separated Alfonso X's reign from the first Trastámara's ascent to the Castilian throne, the Jewish communities of Northern Castile experienced a deterioration in their juridical, economic, and political situation.

It remains an important task for the historians to explain why the problems present in Jewish-Christian coexistence since late antiquity became insurmountable toward the end of the Middle Ages and why by 1500 the Jewish minority disappeared from most parts of Western Europe.[134] In particular, a new study is needed to explore in detail whether the internal fissures that had developed in Jewish-Christian coexistence in

133. Ray, "Beyond Tolerance and Persecution," 1–18.
134. Jeremy Cohen, *Living Letters of the Law*, 13–17.

Castile by the mid-fourteenth century prepared the ground for the event that looms large in the history of Spanish Jewry—the violence of 1391.[135] We have all been warned against creating false continuities in Jewish history and joining ideas and events into a chain that invariably leads to the Holocaust.[136] But in this case the causal links are tangible and real. The conclusions reached in this book should shed light on the pivotal events of 1391 and, conversely, benefit from a long-term perspective. As Mark Meyerson and others have argued, the anti-Jewish violence set in motion in the summer of 1391 by the preaching of Ferrán Martínez started in Castile, and probably would not have occurred without the Castilian example.[137] Even though there was no direct link between the violence of 1366–67 and the events of 1391, and many of the Jewish communities affected by the Trastámara troops' attacks recovered and even blossomed in the intervening years, the strident anti-Jewish discourse that had reached its peak at the end of the civil war kept the public attuned to its grievances and prejudices. It is doubtful that the spark ignited by Martínez would have wreaked the havoc it did had Castilian Christians not been in the habit of viewing the Jews with a mixture of suspicion and animosity. The preexisting tensions between Jews and Christians in Castilian towns and the harsh rhetoric directed at the Jews by the procurators at cortes did not make 1391 inevitable, but they brought the possibility of violence into sharper relief.

One of the most influential Spanish medievalists, Luis Suárez Fernández, has suggested that the petitions submitted by the urban procurators at the cortes in Toro in 1371 and Enrique II's response to them read like a roadmap for the subsequent events in Castilian-Jewish history: the massacres of 1391 and, eventually, the expulsion of the Jews from the now unified Spanish kingdom in 1492.[138] Of course, the legislative attack of 1371 did not signal the end of Jewish-Christian coexistence; nor was it

---

135. The authoritative studies of the 1391 events include Wolff, "1391 Pogrom in Spain," 4–18; Mitre Fernández, *Los judíos de Castilla en tiempo de Enrique III*; and Netanyahu, *Origins of the Inquisition*, 127–67.

136. Nirenberg, *Communities of Violence*, 7–10, 245; see, however, his *Anti-Judaism*, 9.

137. Meyerson, *Jews in an Iberian Frontier Kingdom*, 279. Netanyahu believes that Ferrán Martínez masterminded the events in both Castile and Aragon; *Origins of the Inquisition*, 160–62.

138. Suárez Fernández, *Monarquía hispana y revolución Trastámara*, 59.

the beginning of the end. Even in the aftermath of the terrible events of 1391, some Castilian *aljamas* prospered, while others entered a period of decline. The communities of Belorado and Briviesca, for example, found themselves under the control of noble families and were better off, on the whole, than the Jewish *aljamas* that remained under royal or episcopal control (Burgos, Miranda, and Palencia).[139] Smaller *aljamas* were revitalized by an infusion of newcomers, as the Jews who had escaped conversion and death sought to leave major towns.[140] But in one particular sense, the cortes of 1371 proved to be a turning point for the Jewish fortunes in Castile. King Enrique made no effort to defend the Jews against the procurators' vitriol or to remind the assembly that the Jews possessed ancient privileges granted and confirmed by generations of Castilian kings, his predecessors. He merely protected his right to continue employing Jewish fiscal agents in his administration. In other words, Enrique reduced the reasons for tolerating the Jews to their usefulness to the Crown.[141] The strategy adopted by the town procurators was yielding the desired results. Without the royal endorsement of their privileges, the Jews' position in the kingdom was becoming ever more tenuous. By pushing for stripping the Jews of their charters and relegating them to an inferior juridical status, the townsmen created an opening—still small but growing—for a society in which there would be no place for Jews.

139. Cadiñanos Bardeci, "Los judíos de Belorado y sus contornos," 235.
140. Luis Suárez Fernández, *Judíos espanoles en la edad media* (Madrid: Ediciones Rialp, 1980), 217; Angus MacKay, "Popular Movements and Pogroms in Fifteenth-Century Castile," *Past and Present* 50 (1971): 38–39.
141. Suárez Fernández, *Monarquía hispana y revolución Trastámara*, 58.

BIBLIOGRAPHY

Archives

Archivo de la catedral de Burgos
Archivo de la catedral de León
Archivo de la catedral de Palencia
Archivo histórico nacional, sección de clero y sección de códices
Archivo municipal de Burgos
Archivo municipal de León
Archivo municipal de Miranda de Ebro
Archivo municipal de Palencia
Biblioteca nacional
Biblioteca de la real academia de la historia

Published Primary Sources

Abajo Martín, Teresa, ed. *Documentación de la catedral de Palencia (1035–1247)*. Palencia: Ediciones J. M. Garrido Garrido, 1986.
Abner of Burgos (Alfonso of Valladolid). *Mostrador de Justicia*. Edited by Walter Mettmann. Vol. 1. Opladen: Westdeutscher Verlag, 1994.
Abrahams, Israel, ed. *Hebrew Ethical Wills*. Philadelphia: Jewish Publication Society of America, 1954.
Alvarado Planas, Javier, and Gonzalo Oliva Manso, eds. *Los fueros de Castilla*. Madrid: Boletín Oficial del Estado, 2004.
Baer, Fritz (Yitzhak), ed. *Die Juden im Christlichen Spanien. Erster Teil, Urkunden und Regesten*. Vol. 2. Kastilien, Inquisitionsakten. Berlin: Im Schocken Verlag, 1936.
Barrios García, Angel, ed. *Documentación medieval de la catedral de Ávila*. Salamanca: Ediciones Universidad de Salamanca, 1981.
Burns, Robert Ignatius, ed. *Las siete partidas*. Translated by Samuel Parsons Scott. Vols. 1–5. Philadelphia: University of Pennsylvania Press, 2001.
Cantar de mío Cid (The Poem of the Cid). Translated by Rita Hamilton. Manchester: Manchester University Press, 1975.
Cantera Burgos, Francisco, ed. *Fuero de Miranda de Ebro*. Madrid: CSIC, 1945.
Cole, Peter, ed., trans. *The Dream of the Poem: Hebrew Poetry from Muslim and Christian Spain, 950–1492*. Princeton. Princeton University Press, 2007.
de Berceo, Gonzalo. *Miracles of Our Lady*. Translated by Richard Terry Mount and Annette Grant Cash. Lexington: University Press of Kentucky, 1997.

de Ureña y Smenjaud, D. Rafael, ed. *El fuero de Zorita de los Canes*. Madrid: Establecimiento tipografico de Fortanet, 1911.

———, ed. *El fuero de Cuenca: Formas primitiva y sistemática; Texto Latino, texto Castellano y adaptación del fuero de Iznatoraf*. Cuenca: Ediciones de la Universidad de Castilla-La Mancha, 2003. Facsimile reproduction of the first edition [1936].

de Ureña y Smenjaud, Rafael, and Adolfo Bonilla y San Martín, eds. *Fuero de Usagre*. Madrid: Hijos de Reus, 1907.

Domínguez, Gregoria C., César A. Álvarez, and José A. Martín Fuertes, eds. *Colección documental del archivo diocesano de Astorga*. León: Centro de Estudios e investigación "San Isidoro," 2001.

Francisco Pacheco, Joaquín, Fermín de la Puente y Apezechea, Pedro Gómez de la Serna, Francesco de Paula Díaz y Mendoza, Gregorio López, and Gregorio López de Tovar, eds. *Los codigos españoles, concordados y anotados*. Vols. 1–12. Madrid: Imprenta de la publicidad, 1847–51.

Garrido Garrido, José Manuel, and F. Javier Pereda Llarena eds. *Documentación de la catedral de Burgos*.Vols. 1–5, 804–1316. Burgos: Ediciones J. M. Garrido Garrido,1983–84.

González Díez, Emiliano, ed. *Colección diplomatica del concejo de Burgos (884–1369)*. Burgos: Institutos de estudios castellanos, 1984.

Gutiérrez Cuadrado, Juan, ed. *Fuero de Bejár*. Salamanca: Universidad de Salamanca, 1974.

Ibarra y Marín, Joaquín, ed. *Fuero juzgo en Latin y Castellano*. Madrid: La Real Academia Española, 1815.

Ibn Daud, Abraham. *The Book of Tradition (Sefer ha-Qabbalah)*. Edited and translated by Gerson D. Cohen. Philadelphia: Jewish Publication Society of America, 1967.

Lea, Henry Charles, ed. "Acta Capitular del Cabildo de Sevilla." *American Historical Review* 1, no. 2 (1896): 220–25.

Lizoain Garrido, José Manuel, Araceli Castro Garrido, and F. Javier Peña Pérez, eds. *Documentación del monasterio de Las Huelgas de Burgos*. Vols. 1–10, 1116–1400. Burgos: J. M. Garrido Garrido, 1985–91.

López Dapena, Asunción, ed. *Cuentas y Gastos (1292–1294) del rey D. Sancho IV El Bravo (1284–1295)*. Maracena: Publicaciones del Monte de Piedad y Caja de Ahorros de Cordoba, 1984.

López de Ayala, Pero. *Crónicas*. Edited by José Luis Martín. Barcelona: Planeta, 1991.

———. *Rimado de Palacio*. Madrid: Real Academia Española, 2012.

MacDonald, Robert A., ed. *Espéculo: Texto jurídico atribuido al rey de Castilla Don Alfonso X, el Sabio*. Madison, Wisc.: Hispanic Seminary of Medieval Studies, 1990.

———, ed. *Libro de las Tahurerías: A Special Code of Law, Concerning Gambling, Drawn Up by Maestro Roldán at the Command of Alfonso X of Castile*. Madison, Wisc.: Hispanic Seminary of Medieval Studies, 1995.

Martín, José Luis, and Javier Coca, eds. *Fuero de Salamanca*. Salamanca: Ediciones de la Diputación de Salamanca, 1987.

Martín Fuertes, José Antonio, María del Carmen Rodríguez López, and María Jesús Pradal García, eds. *Colección documental del archivo municipal de León (1219–1400)*. León: Centro de Estudios e Investigación "San Isidoro," 1998.

Martínez Díez, Gonzalo, ed. *Leyes de Alfonso X*. Vol. 2, *Fuero real: Edición y analisis critico*. Ávila: Fundación Sánchez Albornoz, 1988.

Millares Carlo, Agustín, ed. *Fuero de Madrid*. Madrid: Publicaciones del Archivo de Villa, 1994.

Mínguez Fernández, José María, Marta Herrero de la Fuente, and José Antonio Fernández Flórez, eds. *Colección diplomática del monasterio de Sahagún*. Vols. 1–7 (857–1500). León: Centro de Estudios e Investigación "San Isidoro," 1976–97.

Muños y Romero, D. Tomás, ed. *Colección de fueros municipales y cartas pueblas*. Vol. 1. Madrid: Imprenta de Don José Maria Alonso, 1847.

Oceja Gonzalo, Isabel, ed. *Documentación del monasterio de San Salvador de Oña*. Vols. 1–4, 1032–1350. Burgos: Ediciones J. M. Garrido Garrido, 1983–86.

Ortiz de Zuñiga, Diego. *Análes eclesiasticos y seculares*. Vol. 2. Madrid: 1795.

Palacín Gálvez, Maria del Carmen, and Luis Martínez García, eds. *Documentación del hospital del rey de Burgos (1136–1277)*. Burgos: Ediciones J. M. Garrido Garrido, 1990.

Peset Reig, Mariano, and Juan Gutiérrez Cuadrado, eds. *Fuero de Úbeda*. Valencia: Universidad de Valencia, 1979.

Pharr, Clyde, ed. *The Theodosian Code and Novels and the Simondian Constitutions*. Princeton: Princeton University Press, 1952.

Powers, James, trans. *The Code of Cuenca: Municipal Law on the Twelfth-Century Castilian Frontier*. Philadelphia: University of Pennsylvania Press, 2000.

Rivera Romero, Victoriano, ed. *La Carta de fuero concedida á la ciudad de Córdoba por el rey D. Fernando III*. Córdoba: Imprenta, librería y litografía del Diario, 1881.

Rodríguez de Lama, Ildefonso, ed. *Colección diplomatica medieval de la Rioja*. Vols. 1–4, 923–siglo XIII. Logroño: Servicio de Cultura de la Excma. Diputación Provincial, 1976–89.

Rosell, Cayetano, ed. *Cronicas de los reyes de Castilla*. Vol. 1. Madrid: Atlas, 1953.

Sáez, Emilio, Carlos Sáez, José Manuel Ruiz Asencio, José María Fernández Catón, Mauricio Herrero Jiménez, José Antonio Martín Fuertes, Vicente García Lobo, and José María Fernández del Pozo, eds. *Colección documental del archivo de la catedral de León*. Vols. 1–17, 775–1685. León: Centro de Estudios e investigación "San Isidoro," 1987–97.

Sánchez, Galo, ed. *Fueros castellanos: De soria y Alcalá de Henares*. Madrid: Centro de Estudios Históricos, 1919.

———, ed. *Libro de los fueros de Castiella*. Barcelona: Ediciones El Albir, 1981.

Scott, Samuel Parsons, ed. *The Visigothic Code (Forum Judicum)*. Translated by Samuel Parsons Scott. Littleton, Colo.: Fred B. Rothman, 1982.

Serrano, D. Luciano, ed. *Colección diplomatica de San Salvador de el Moral*. Valladolid: Cuesta, 1906.

———, ed. *Fuentes para la historia de Castilla*. Vol. 2, *Cartulario del Infantado de Covarrubias*. Madrid: Gregorio del Amo, 1907.

———, ed. *Cartulario de San Millán de la Cogolla*. Madrid: Centro de Estudios Históricos, 1930.

Simonsohn, Shlomo, ed. *The Apostolic See and the Jews: Documents, 492–1404*. Vol. 1. Toronto: Pontifical Institute of Mediaeval Studies, 1988.

Tanner, Norman P., ed. *Decrees of the Ecumenical Councils*. Vol. 1, *Nicaea I to Lateran V*. London: Sheed and Ward; Washington, D.C.: Georgetown University Press, 1990.

Tejada y Ramiro, Juan, ed. *Colección de canones y de todos los concilios de la iglesia de España y de America*. Vol. 3: Madrid, 1861; vol. 5: Madrid, 1863.

Thacker, Shelby, and José Escobar, trans. *Chronicle of Alfonso X*. Lexington: University of Kentucky Press, 2002

Ubierto Arteta, Antonio, ed. *Crónicas anónimas de Sahagún*. Zaragoza: Universidad de Zaragoza, 1987.

Secondary Sources

Abulafia, David. "'Nam iudei servi regis sunt, et semper fisco regio deputati': The Jews in the Municipal Fuero of Teruel (1176–77)." In *Jews, Muslims and Christians in and around the Crown of Aragon: Essays in Honour of Professor Elena Lourie*, edited by Harvey J. Hames, 97–126. Leiden: Brill, 2004.

Abulafia, Anna Sapir. *Christians and Jews in the Twelfth-Century Renaissance*. New York: Routledge, 1995.

———. *Christian-Jewish Relations, 1000–1300: Jews in the Service of Medieval Christendom*. Harlow: Pearson, 2011.

Alvarez Reyero, Antonio D. *Crónicas episcopales Palentinas*. Palencia: 1898.

Amador de los Ríos, José. *Historia social, politica, y religiosa de los judíos de España y Portugal*. Vols. 1–3. Madrid: Ediciones Turner, 1984.

Amran, Rica. "El arzobispo Rodrigo Jiménez de Rada y los judíos de Toledo: La Concordia del 16 junio de 1219." *Cahiers de linguistique et de civilisation hispaniques médiévales* 26 (2003): 73–85.

———. *Judíos y conversos en el reino de Castilla: Propaganda y mensajes políticos, sociales y religiosos (siglos XIV–XVI)*. Valladolid: Junta de Castilla y León, 2009.

Andrés, P. Alfonso. "El Hospital del Emperador en Burgos." *Boletín de la comisión provincial de monumentos históricos y artísticos de Burgos* 23, nos. 88–89 (1944): 382–90.

Assis, Yom Tov. "Jewish Moneylenders in Medieval Santa Coloma de Queralt." In *Jews and Conversos: Studies in Society and the Inquisition*, edited by Yosef Kaplan, 21–38. Jerusalem: Magnes Press, 1985.

———. *The Jews of Santa Coloma de Queralt: An Economic and Demographic Case Study of a Community at the End of the Thirteenth Century*. Jerusalem: Magnes Press, 1988.

———. "Jewish Attitudes to Christian Power in Medieval Spain." *Sefarad* 52 (1992): 291–304.

———. "Welfare and Mutual Aid in the Spanish Jewish Communities." In *Moreshet Sepharad: The Sephardi Legacy*, edited by Haim Beinart, 1:318–45. Jerusalem: Hebrew University Press, 1992.

———. *The Golden Age of Aragonese Jewry: Community and Society in the Crown of Aragon, 1213–1327*. London: Littman Library of Jewish Civilization, 1997.

———. *Jewish Economy in the Medieval Crown of Aragon, 1213–1327: Money and Power*. Leiden: Brill, 1997.

Astren, Fred. *Karaite Judaism and Historical Understanding*. Columbia: University of South Carolina Press, 2004.

de Ayala Martínez, Carlos. *La monarquía y Burgos durante el reinado de Alfonso X*. Madrid: Ediciones de la Universidad Autónoma de Madrid, 1984.

de Ayala Martínez, Carlos, and Francisco Javier, Villalaba Ruiz de Toledo. "Las cortes bajo el reinado de Alfonso X." In *Las cortes de Castilla y León, 1188–1988: Actas de la tercera etapa del congreso científico sobre la historia de las cortes de Castilla y León, 1988*. Valladolid: Cortes de Castilla y León, 1990, 1:239–70.

Baer, Yitzhak. *A History of the Jews in Christian Spain*. Translated by Louis Schoffman. Vols. 1–2. Philadelphia: Jewish Publication Society of America, 1992–93.

———. "The Origins of Jewish Communal Organization in the Middle Ages." In *Binah: Studies in Jewish History, Thought and Culture*, edited by Joseph Dan, 1:59–82. New York: Praeger, 1989.

Bagby, Albert. "The Jew in the Cántigas of Alfonso X, el Sabio." *Speculum* 46, no. 4 (1971): 670–88.

Ballesteros Beretta, Antonio. *Alfonso X el sabio*. Barcelona: Ediciones "El Albir," 1984.

Baron, Salo. *History and Jewish Historians*. Philadelphia: Jewish Publication Society of America, 1964.

Barrero García, Ana-María. "El proceso de formación del derecho local medieval a través de sus textos: Los fueros Castellano-Leoneses." In *I semana de estudios medievales: Nájera, del 6 al 11 de agosto de 1990*. Logroño: Gobierno de la Rioja, 1990, 91–131.

Bartlett, Robert. *The Making of Europe: Conquest, Colonization, and Cultural Change, 950–1350*. Princeton: Princeton University Press, 1993.

Barton, Thomas W. "Constructing a Diocese in a Post-Conquest Landscape: A Comparative Approach to the Lay Possession of Tithes." *Journal of Medieval History* 35, no. 1 (2009): 1–33.

———. "Jurisdictional Conflict, Strategies of Litigation and Mechanisms of Compromise in Thirteenth-Century Tortosa." *Recerca* 14 (2012): 201–48.

———. *Contested Treasure: Jews and Authority in the Crown of Aragon*. University Park: Pennsylvania State University Press, 2015.

Beceiro Pita, Isabel. "La vinculación de los judíos a los poderes señoriales castellanos (siglos XII–XV)." In *Xudeus e Conversos na Historia*, edited by Carlos Barros, 2:95–109. Santiago de Compostela: Editorial de la Historia, 1994.

Beinart, Haim. "The Jews in Castile." In *Moreshet Sepharad: The Sephardi Legacy*, edited by Haim Beinart, 1:11–43. Jerusalem: Hebrew University Press, 1992.

———. *Los judíos en España*. Madrid: Editorial MAPFRE, 1992.

Berend, Nora. *At the Gate of Christendom: Jews, Muslims and "Pagans" in Medieval Hungary, c. 1000–c.1300*. Cambridge: Cambridge University Press, 2001.

Berger, David. "Mission to the Jews and Jewish-Christian Contacts in the Polemical Literature of the High Middle Ages." *American Historical Review* 91, no. 3 (1986): 576–91.

Bianchini, Janna. *The Queen's Hand: Power and Authority in the Reign of Berenguela of Castile*. Philadelphia: University of Pennsylvania Press, 2012.

Bisson, Thomas. *The Crisis of the Twelfth Century: Power, Lordship, and the Origins of European Government*. Princeton: Princeton University Press, 2009.

Blumenkranz, Bernhard. "The Roman Church and the Jews." In *Essential Papers on Judaism and Christianity in Conflict*, edited by Jeremy Cohen, 193–230. New York: New York University Press, 1991.

Bonachía Hernando, Juan Antonio. *El concejo de Burgos en la baja edad media (1345–1426)*. Valladolid: Universidad de Valladolid, 1978.

———. "Algunas cuestiones en torno al estudio de la sociedad bajomedieval Burgalesa." In *La ciudad de Burgos: Actas del congreso de historia de Burgos*. León: Junta de Castilla y León, 1985, 59–82.

———. *El señorio de Burgos durante la baja edad media (1255–1508)*. Valladolid: Universidad de Valladolid, 1988.

Bonachía Hernando, Juan Antonio, and Julio Antonio Pardos Martínez. *Catálogo documental del archivo municipal de Burgos, sección historica*. Vol. 1, 931–1515. Salamanca: Junta de Castilla y León, 1983.

Bonfil, Robert. *Jewish Life in Renaissance Italy*. Translated by Anthony Oldcorn. Berkeley: University of California Press, 1994.

Bonnassie, Pierre. *From Slavery to Feudalism in South-Western Europe*. Translated by Jean Birrell. Cambridge: Cambridge University Press, 1991.

Bönnen, Gerold. "Worms: The Jews between the City, the Bishops, and the Crown." In *The Jews of Europe in the Middle Ages (Tenth to Fifteenth Centuries): Proceedings of the International Symposium Held at Speyer, 20–25 October 2002*, edited by Christoph Cluse, 449–58. Turnhout: Brepols, 2004.

Bonner, Michael. "The Naming of the Frontier: 'Awāsim, Thughūr, and the Arab Geographies." *Bulletin of the School of Oriental and African Studies, University of London* 57, no. 1 (1994): 17–24.

Burns, Robert I. *The Crusader Kingdom of Valencia: Reconstruction on a Thirteenth-Century Frontier*. Cambridge, Mass.: Harvard University Press, 1967.

———. *Medieval Colonialism: Postcrusade Exploitation of Islamic Valencia*. Princeton: Princeton University Press, 1975.

———. *Muslims, Christians, and Jews in the Crusader Kingdom of Valencia: Societies in Symbiosis*. Cambridge: Cambridge University Press, 1984.

———. "The Significance of the Frontier in the Middle Ages." In *Medieval Frontier Societies*, edited by Robert Bartlett and Angus MacKay, 307–30. Oxford: Clarendon Press, 1989.

———. "Introduction to the Seventh Partida." In *Las Siete Partidas*, vol. 5, *Underworlds: The Dead, the Criminal, and the Marginalized*, edited by Robert I. Burns, xix–xlvi. Philadelphia: University of Pennsylvania Press, 2001.

———. "Jews and Moors in the *Siete Partidas* of Alfonso X the Learned: A Background Perspective." In *Medieval Spain: Culture, Conflict, and Coexistence; Studies in Honour of Angus MacKay*, edited by Roger Collins and Anthony Goodman, 46–62. New York: Palgrave Macmillan, 2002.

Cadiñanos Bardeci, Inocencio. "Los judíos de Belorado y sus contornos." *Sefarad* 54 (1994): 227–51.

———. "Precisiones sobre la sinagoga de Miranda de Ebro." *Sefarad* 54 (1994): 41–45.

Cantera Burgos, Francisco. "La judería de Miranda de Ebro (1099–1350)." *Sefarad* 1 (1941): 89–140.

———. "La judería de Miranda de Ebro (1350–1492)." *Sefarad* 2 (1942): 325–75.

———. "Nuevas inscripciones hebraicas leonesas." *Sefarad* 3 (1943): 329–58.

———. "La judería de Burgos." *Sefarad* 12 (1952): 59–104.

———. "Nuevo hallazgo epigráfico en León." *Sefarad* 14 (1954): 119–21.

———. "La judería de Calahorra." *Sefarad* 15 (1955): 353–72; and *Sefarad*, 16 (1956): 73–112.

———. "Las juderías españolas y el camino de Santiago." In *XII semana de estudios medievales*, 1974. Pamplona: Diputación Foral de Navarra, 1976, 75–119.

Cantera Montenegro, Enrique. "Cuadernos de investigación medieval: Guía crítica de temas históricos." In *Los judíos en la edad media hispana*. Madrid: A–Z, 1986.

———. *Las juderías de la diocesis de Calahorra en la baja edad media*. Logroño: Instituto de Estudios Riojanos, 1987.

———. "Cristianos y judíos en la meseta norte castellana: La fractura del siglo XIII." In *Del pasado judío en los reinos medievales hispánicos: Afinidad y distanciamiento*, edited by Yolanda Moreno Koch and Ricardo Izquierdo Benito, 45–88. Cuenca: Ediciones de la Universidad de Castilla-La Mancha, 2005.

Caputo, Nina. *Nahmanides in Medieval Catalonia: History, Community, and Messianism*. Notre Dame: University of Notre Dame Press, 2007.

Carlé, Maria del Carmen. *Del concejo medieval castellano-leones*. Buenos Aires: Instituto de Historia de España, 1968.

Caro Dugo, María Auxiliadora. "Pleitos entre judíos y cristianos en el derecho municipal Castellano-Leonés." In *Proyección histórica de España en sus tres culturas: Castilla y León, América y el Mediterráneo*. Madrid: Junta de Castilla y León, 1993, 37–43.

Carpenter, Dwayne. *Alfonso X and the Jews: An Edition of and Commentary on Siete Partidas 7.24 "De los judíos."* Berkeley: University of California Press, 1986.

———. "Social Perception and Literary Portrayal: Jews and Muslims in Medieval Spanish Literature." In *Convivencia: Jews, Muslims, and Christians in Medieval Spain*, edited by Vivian Mann, Thomas Glick, and Jerrilynn Dodds, 61–81. New York: The Jewish Museum, 1992.

Carrera de la Red, Fatima M. "Huellas de las culturas árabe y hebrea en torno al monasterio de Sahagún." *Archivos Leoneses* 46 (1992): 375–90.

———. "Árabes y judíos en la documentación del monasterio de Sahagún." In *Proyección histórica de España en sus tres culturas: Castilla y León, América y el Mediterráneo.* Madrid: Junta de Castilla y León, 1993, 1:45–51.

Carrete Parrondo, Carlos. "El repartimiento de Huete de 1290." *Sefarad* 36 (1976): 121–40.

Casado Alonso, Hilario. "Las relaciones poder real-ciudades en Castilla en la primera mitad del siglo XIV." In *Genesis medieval del estado moderno: Castilla y Navarra (1250–1370).* Valladolid: AMBITO Ediciones, 1987, 193–215.

Castaño, Javier. "Una fiscalidad sagrada: Los 'treinta dineros' y los judíos de Castilla." *Studi medievali* 42, fasc. 1 (2001): 165–204.

———. "Los documentos hebreos de León en su contexto prenotarial." In *Judaísmo hispano: Estudios en memoria de José Luis Lacave Riaño,* edited by Elena Romero, 2:459–81. Madrid: Junta de Castilla y León, 2002.

Castaño, Javier, and José Luis Avello. "Dos nuevos epitafios hebreos de la necrópolis del Castro de los judíos (Puente del Castro, León)." *Sefarad* 61 (2001): 299–318.

Castro, Américo. *España en su historia: Cristianos, moros y judíos.* Barcelona: Crítica, 2001.

Catlos, Brian. "Contexto y conveniencia en la corona de Aragón: Propuesta de un modelo de interacción entre grupos etno-religiosos minoritarios y mayoritarios." *Rivista d'história medieval* 12 (2001–2): 259–68.

———. *The Victors and the Vanquished: Christians and Muslims of Catalonia and Aragon, 1050–1300.* Cambridge: Cambridge University Press, 2004.

———. *Muslims of Medieval Latin Christendom: c. 1050–1614.* Cambridge: Cambridge University Press, 2014.

Chazan, Robert. "Anti-Usury Efforts in Thirteenth-Century Narbonne and the Jewish Response." *American Academy for Jewish Research* 41–42 (1973–74): 45–67.

———. *Church, State, and Jew in the Middle Ages.* West Orange, N.J.: Behrman House, 1980.

———. *Daggers of Faith: Thirteenth-Century Christian Missionizing and Jewish Response.* Berkeley: University of California Press, 1989.

———. *Barcelona and Beyond: The Disputation of 1263 and Its Aftermath.* Berkeley: University of California Press, 1992.

———. *The Jews of Medieval Western Christendom, 1000–1500.* Cambridge: Cambridge University Press, 2006.

Clemente Ramos, Julián. "Estructuras dominales castellanoleonesas: Palencia en los siglos XII y XIII." *Studia Zamorensia* 7 (1986): 433–45.

Cohen, Jeremy. *The Friars and the Jews.* Ithaca: Cornell University Press, 1982.

———. *Living Letters of the Law: Ideas of the Jew in Medieval Christianity.* Berkeley and Los Angeles: University of California Press, 1999.

———. "Christian Theology and Anti-Jewish Violence in the Middle Ages: Connections and Disjunctions." In *Religious Violence between Christians and Jews: Medieval Roots, Modern Perspectives*, edited by Anna Sapir Abulafia, 44–60. New York: Palgrave, 2002.

———. "*Synagoga conversa*: Honorius Augustodunensis, the Song of Songs, and Christianity's 'Eschatological Jew.'" *Speculum* 79, no. 2 (2004): 309–40.

Cohen, Mark. *Under Crescent and Cross: The Jews in the Middle Ages*. Princeton: Princeton University Press, 1994.

Colmeiro, Manuel. *Introducción a las Cortes de los antiguos reinos de Leon y Castilla*. Vols. 1–2. Madrid: 1883–84.

Constable, Olivia Remie. "Regulating Religious Noise: The Council of Vienne, the Mosque Call and Muslim Pilgrimage in the Late Medieval Mediterranean World." *Medieval Encounters* 16 (2010): 64–95.

———. "Merchants and Cross-Cultural Commerce in the Medieval Mediterranean World." In *History as Prelude: Muslims and Jews in the Medieval Mediterranean*, edited by Joseph V. Montville, 131–54. Lanham, Md.: Lexington, 2011.

———. "Clothing, Iron, and Timber: The Growth of Christian Anxiety about Islam in the Long Twelfth Century." In *European Transformations: The Long Twelfth Century*, edited by Thomas F. X. Noble and John Van Engen, 279–313. Notre Dame: University of Notre Dame Press, 2012.

Craddock, Jerry R. "La cronologia de las obras legislativas de Alfonso X El Sabio." AHDE 51 (1981): 365–418.

———. "The Legislative Works of Alfonso el Sabio." In *Emperor of Culture: Alfonso X the Learned of Castile and His Thirteenth-Century Renaissance*, edited by Robert I. Burns, 183–98. Philadelphia: University of Pennsylvania Press, 1990.

Crespo Álvarez, Macarena. "Judíos, préstamos y usuras en la Castilla medieval: De Alfonso X a Enrique III." *Edad media: Revista de historia* 5 (2002): 179–215.

Crusafont, Miquel, Anna Balaguer, and Philip Grierson, eds. *Medieval European Coinage*. Vol. 6, *The Iberian Peninsula*. Cambridge: Cambridge University Press, 2013.

Dahan, Gilbert. *La polémique chrétienne contre le judaïsme au Moyen Âge*. Paris: Albin Michel, 1991.

Davies, Horton, and Marie-Hélène Davies. *Holy Days and Holidays: The Medieval Pilgrimage to Compostela*. London: Associated University Presses, 1982.

Deimann, Wiebke. *Christen, Juden und Muslime im mittelalterlichen Sevilla*. Münster: Lit, 2012.

Delibes de Castro, Germán, *Historia de Palencia*. Vol. 1, *De la prehistoria a la época medieval*. Palencia: Ediciones Cálamo, 2002.

del Valle Curieses, Rafael. "Archivo municipal de Palencia: Privilegios y cartas reales concedidos a la ciudad en la edad media (regesta y comentarios)." In *Actas del I congreso de historia de Palencia, vol. 2, Fuentes documentales y edad media*. Palencia: Excma. Diputación Provincial de Palencia, 1985, 115–51.

de Mateo Herrerías, Ángeles. "La pluridad cultural del espacio leonés altomedieval (siglos IX–XI). In *Proyección histórica de España en sus tres culturas: Castilla y León, América y el Mediterráneo*. Junta de Castilla y León, 1993, 211–18.

de Moxó, Salvador. "Los judíos castellanos en el reinado de Alfonso XI." *Sefarad* 35 (1975), 131–50; *Sefarad* 36 (1976): 37–120.

———. "Los judíos castellanos en la primera mitad del siglo XIV," in *Simposio "Toledo judaico,"* Toledo 20–22 Abril 1972, 1:79–103. Toledo: Centro Universitario, 1973.

Díaz Esteban, Fernando. "La ampliación de la sinagoga de Carrión y sus inscripciones." In *Judaísmo hispano: Estudios en memoria de José Luis Lacave Riaño*, edited by Elena Romero, 2:519–35. Madrid: Junta de Castilla y León, 2002.

Dillard, Heath. *Daughters of the Reconquest: Women in Castilian Town Society, 1100–1300*. Cambridge: Cambridge University Press, 1984.

Ecker, Heather. "How to Administer a Conquered City in Al-Andalus: Mosques, Parish Churches and Parishes." In *Under the Influence: Questioning the Comparative in Medieval Castile*, edited by Cynthia Robinson and Leyla Rouhi, 45–65. Leiden and Boston: Brill, 2005.

Elukin, Jonathan. *Living Together, Living Apart: Rethinking Jewish-Christian Relations in the Middle Ages*. Princeton: Princeton University Press, 2007.

Escrivá, José María. *La abadesa de Las Huelgas*. Madrid: Editorial Luz, 1944.

Esteban Recio, María Asunción. *Palencia a fines de la edad media: Una ciudad de señorío episcopal*. Valladolid: Universidad de Valladolid, 1989.

Estepa Díez, Carlos, and Julio Valdeón Baruque, eds. *Burgos en la edad media*. Valladolid: Junta de Castilla y León, 1984.

Estow, Clara. *Pedro the Cruel of Castile, 1350–1369*. Leiden: Brill, 1995.

———. "The Economic Development of the Order of Calatrava, 1158–1366." *Speculum*, 57, no. 2 (1982): 267–91.

Fancy, Hussein. "Theologies of Violence: The Recruitment of Muslim Soldiers by the Crown of Aragon." *Past and Present* 221 (November 2013): 39–73.

Fernández, Luis. "La abadia de Sahagún e el obispado de Palencia durante los siglos XIII y XIV." *Archivos Leoneses* 50 (1971): 209–29.

Fernández Espinar, Ramon. *Manual de historia del derecho español*. Vol. 1, *Las Fuentes*. Madrid: Editorial Centro de Estudios, 1990.

Fernández de Madrid, Alonso. *Silva palentina*. Vol. 3. Palencia: "El Diario Palentino," 1942.

Fernández del Pozo, José M. "Razones económicas de un conflicto en el camino de Santiago." In *El camino de Santiago: La hospitalidad monástica y las peregrinaciones*, edited by Horacio Santiago-Otero, 211–16. Valladolid: Junta de Castilla y León, Consejería de Cultura y Turismo, 1992.

Fita, Fidel. "La aljama hebrea de Belorado: Documentos históricos." *BRAH* 29 (1896): 338–45.

Frago Gracia, Juan Antonio. "El fuero de Cuenca: Lengua, cultura y problemas del romanceamiento." *Boletín de la Real Academia Española* 79, no. 278 (1999): 319–54.

Francisco Rivera, Juan. "Notas sobre el episcopologio Palentino en los siglos XIII Y XIV." *Anuario de Estudios Medievales* 9 (1974–79): 407–24.

Freedman, Paul. *The Origins of Peasant Servitude in Medieval Catalonia.* Cambridge: Cambridge University Press, 1991.

Fuencisla G. Casar, María. "El tratamiento de los judíos en los fueros de la familia Cuenca-Teruel." *Revue des etudes juives* 144, nos. 1–3 (January–September 1985): 27–37.

Gaibrois de Ballesteros, Mercedes. *Historia de reinado de Sancho IV de Castilla.* Vols. 1–3. Madrid: Tip. de la Revista de archivos, bibliotecas y museos, 1922–28.

Galinsky, Judah. "Jewish Charitable Bequests and the Hekdesh Trust in Thirteenth-Century Spain." *Journal of Interdisciplinary History* 35, no. 3 (2005): 423–40.

———. "An Ashkenazic Rabbi Encounters Sephardic Culture: R. Asher b. Jehiel's Attitude Towards Philosophy and Science." Edited by Dan Diner. *Jahrbuch des Simon-Dubnow-Instituts/Simon Dubnow Institute Yearbook* 8 (2009): 191–211.

———. "On Popular Halakhic Literature and the Jewish Reading Audience in Fourteenth-Century Spain." *Jewish Quarterly Review* 98, no. 3 (2008): 305–27.

———. "On the Heritage of R. Yehudah ben ha-Rosh, Rabbi of Toledo: A Chapter in an Exploration of the Responsa Literature of Christian Spain." *Pe'amim* 128 (2010–11): 175–210 [Hebrew].

Gampel, Benjamin. *The Last Jews on Iberian Soil: Navarrese Jewry, 1479 to 1498.* Berkeley: University of California Press, 1989.

———. "Does Medieval Navarrese Jewry Salvage Our Notion of *Convivencia*?" In *In Iberia and Beyond: Hispanic Jews between Cultures*, edited by Bernard Dov Cooperman, 97–122. Newark: University of Delaware Press, 1997.

———. "'Unless the Lord Watches Over the City . . .': Joan of Aragon and His Jews, June–October 1391." In *New Perspectives on Jewish-Christian Relations: In Honor of David Berger*, edited by Elisheva Carlebach and Jacob Schacter, 65–89. Leiden: Brill, 2012.

García de Cortázar, José Ángel. "El Camino de Santiago y la articulación del espacio en Castilla." In *XX semana de estudios medievales, 1993.* Pamplona: Gobierno de Navarra, 1994, 157–83.

García de Valdeavellano, Luis. *Curso de historia de las instituciones españolas: De los orígenes al final de la edad media.* Madrid: Ediciones de la Revista de Occidente, 1968.

García Sanz de Baranda, Julian. *La ciudad de Burgos y su concejo en la Edad Media.* Vols. 1–2. Burgos: El Monte Carmelo, 1967.

García Serrano, Francisco. *Preachers of the City: The Expansion of the Dominican Order in Castile (1217–1348).* New Orleans: University Press of the South, 1996.

García-Gallo, Alfonso. *Manual de historia del derecho español.* Vol. 1. 2nd ed. Madrid: Artes Gráficas y Ediciones, 1964.

———. "Los fueros de Toledo." *AHDE* 45 (1975): 341–488.

———. "La obra legislativa de Alfonso X: Hechos e hipotesis." *AHDE* 54 (1984): 97–161.

García y García, Antonio. "En torno al derecho romano en la España medieval." In *Estudios en Homenaje a Don Claudio Sanchez Albornoz en sus 90 Años*. Buenos Aires: Instituto de Historia de España, 1985, 3:59–72.

———. "Judíos y moros en el ordenamiento canonico medieval." In *Actas del II congreso internacional Encuentro de las Tres Culturas*. Toledo: Ayuntamiento de Toledo, 1985, 176–80.

Gautier-Dalché, Jean. *Historia urbana de Leon y Castilla en la edad media (siglos IX–XIII)*. Madrid: Siglo XXI de España, 1979.

———. "L'organisation des cortes de Castille et León." In *Las cortes de Castilla y León en la edad media: Actas de la primera etapa del congreso científico sobre la historia de las cortes de Castilla y Leon, Burgos, 1986*. Valladolid: Cortes de Castilla y León, 1988, 1:269–88.

Gil, José S. *La escuela de traductores de Toledo y los colaboradores judíos*. Toledo: Instituto Provincial de Investigaciones y Estudios Toledanos, 1985.

Glick, Thomas F. *Islamic and Christian Spain in the Early Middle Ages*. Princeton: Princeton University Press, 1979.

———. "*Convivencia*: An Introductory Note." In *Convivencia: Jews, Muslims, and Christians in Medieval Spain*, edited by Vivian Mann, Thomas Glick, and Jerrilynn Dodds, 1–9. New York: George Braziller, 1992.

———. *Islamic and Christian Spain in the Early Middle Ages*. Rev. 2nd ed. Leiden: Brill, 2005.

González, Julio. *El reino de Castilla en la epoca de Alfonso VIII*. Vol. I, *Estudio*. Madrid: Escuela de Estudios Medievales, 1969.

———. *Historia de Palencia*. Vol. 1, *Edades antigua y media*. Palencia: Excma. Diputación Provincial de Palencia, 1984.

González Alonso, Benjamín. "Poder regio, cortes y regimen politico en la Castilla bajomedieval (1252–1474)." In *Las cortes de Castilla y León en la edad media: Actas de la primera etapa del congreso científico sobre la historia de las cortes de Castilla y Leon, Burgos, 1986*. Valladolid: Cortes de Castilla y León, 1988, 2:203–54.

González Díez, Emiliano. "Formación y desarrollo del dominio señorial de la iglesia Palentina (1035–1351)." In *Actas del I congreso de historia de Palencia*. Vol. 2, *Fuentes documentales y edad media*. Palencia: Excma. Diputación Provincial de Palencia, 1985, 275–308.

González Jiménez, Manuel. "Frontier and Settlement in the Kingdom of Castile (1085–1350)." In *Medieval Frontier Societies*, edited by Robert Bartlett and Angus MacKay, 49–74. Oxford: Clarendon Press, 1989.

———. "Las cortes de Castilla y León y la organización municipal." In *Las cortes de Castilla y León en la edad media: Actas de la primera etapa del congreso científico sobre la historia de las cortes de Castilla y Leon, Burgos, 1986*. Valladolid: Cortes de Castilla y León, 1988, 2:351–75.

González Paz, Carlos Andrés. "The Role of Mercenary Troops in Spain in the

Fourteenth Century: The Civil War." In *Mercenaries and Paid Men: The Mercenary Identity in the Middle Ages*, edited by John France, 331–43. Leiden: Brill, 2008.

Graboïs, A. "L'Abbaye de Saint-Denis et les Juifs sous l'abbatiat de Suger." *Annales: Économies, sociétés, civilisations* 24 (1969): 1187–95.

Grayzel, Solomon. *The Church and the Jews in the XIIIth Century*. New York: Hermon Press, 1966.

———. "The Papal Bull Sicut Judeis." In *Essential Papers on Judaism and Christianity in Conflict*, edited by Jeremy Cohen, 231–59. New York: New York University Press, 1991.

Grierson, Philip. *The Coins of Medieval Europe*. London: Seaby, 1991.

Gross, Georg. "Las cortes de 1252: Ordenamiento otorgado al concejo de Burgos en las cortes celebradas en Sevilla el 12 de Octubre de 1252 (según el original)." *Boletín de la Real Academia de la Historia* 182 (1985): 95–114.

Grossman, Abraham. "Relations between Spanish and Ashkenazi Jewry in the Middle Ages." In *Moreshet Sepharad: The Sephardi Legacy*, edited by Haim Beinart, 1:220–39. Jerusalem: Hebrew University Press, 1992.

Gutwirth, Eleazar. "Jewish Moneylending in 14th Century Castile: The Accord of the Puebla de Alcocer." In *Proceedings of the Tenth World Congress of Jewish Studies*. Division B. Vol. 2, *The History of the Jewish People*. Jerusalem: World Union of Jewish Studies, 1990), 151–58.

Hames, Harvey J. *The Art of Conversion: Christianity and Kabbalah in the Thirteenth Century*. Leiden: Brill, 2000.

———. *Like Angels on Jacob's Ladder: Abraham Abulafia, the Franciscans and Joachimism*. Albany: State University of New York Press, 2007.

———. "Truly Seeking Conversion? The Mendicants, Ramon Llull and Alfonso de Valladolid." *Morgen-Glantz* 20 (2010): 41–61.

———. "Through Ramon Llull's Looking Glass: What Was the Thirteenth-Century Dominican Mission Really About?" In *Ramon Llull i el "lul·lisme": Pensament i llenguatge; Actes de les jornades en homenatge a J. N. Hillgarth i A. Bonner*, edited by Maria Isabel Ripoll and Margalida Tortella, 51–74. Palma: Edicions UIB, 2012.

Hernández, Francisco J. *Las rentas del rey: Sociedad y fisco en el reino castellano del siglo XIII*. Vol. 1, *Estudio y documentos*. Madrid: Fundación Ramón Areces, 1993.

Hillgarth, J. N. *The Spanish Kingdoms, 1250–1516*. Vol. 1, *1250–1410: Precarious Balance*. Oxford: Clarendon Press, 1976.

Hinojosa Montalvo, José. "La sociedad y la economía de los judíos en Castilla y la corona de Aragón durante la Baja Edad Media." In *II Semana de estudios medievales: Nájera, 5 al 9 de agosto de 1991*, 79–109. Logroño: Instituto de Estudios Riojanos, 1992.

Howell, Martha C. *Commerce before Capitalism in Europe, 1300–1600*. Cambridge: Cambridge University Press, 2010.

Huidobro y Serna, Luciano. "La judería de Pancorbo (Burgos)." *Sefarad* 3 (1943): 155–66.

Huidobro y Serna, Luciano, and Francisco Cantera Burgos. "Juderias burgalesas (Beleña, Belorado)." *Sefarad* 13 (1953): 35–59.

———. "Los judíos en Aguilar de Campóo." *Sefarad* 14 (1954): 335–52.

Idel, Moshe. "Jewish Thought in Medieval Spain." In *Moreshet Sepharad: The Sephardi Legacy*, edited by Haim Beinart, 1:261–81. Jerusalem: Hebrew University Press, 1992.

Iglesia Ferreirós, Aquilino. "Derecho municipal, derecho señorial, derecho regio." *Historia. Instituciones. Documentos* 4 (1977): 115–97.

———. "Fuero real y Especulo." *AHDE* 52 (1982): 111–91.

Izquierdo Benito, Ricardo. "Los judíos de Toledo en el contexto de la ciudad." *Espacio, Tiempo y Forma* 6, series 3 (1993): 79–102.

Jordan, William Chester. "Jews on Top: Women and the Availability of Consumption Loans in Northern France in the Mid-Thirteenth Century." *Journal of Jewish Studies* 29 (1978): 39–56.

———. "Jewish-Christian Relations in Mid-Thirteenth Century France: An Unpublished Enquête from Picardy." *Revue des études juives* 138 (1979): 47–54.

———. "An Aspect of Credit in Picardy in the 1240s: The Deterioration of Jewish-Christian Financial Relations." *Revue des études juives* 142 (1983): 141–52.

———. "Women and Credit in the Middle Ages: Problems and Directions." *Journal of European Economic History* 17, no. 1 (1988): 33–62.

———. *The French Monarchy and the Jews: From Philip Augustus to the Last Capetians*. Philadelphia: University of Pennsylvania Press, 1989.

———. "Jews, Regalian Rights, and the Constitution in Medieval France." *AJS Review* 23 (1998): 1–16.

———. "Jew and Serf in Medieval France Revisited." In *Jews, Christians and Muslims in Medieval and Early Modern Times: A Festschrift in Honor of Mark R. Cohen*, edited by Arnold E. Franklin, Roxani Eleni Margariti, Marina Rustow, and Uriel Simonsohn, 248–56. Leiden: Brill, 2014.

Kantorowicz, Ernst H. *The King's Two Bodies: A Study in Mediaeval Political Theology*. Princeton: Princeton University Press, 1997.

Katz, Jacob. *Exclusiveness and Tolerance: Studies in Jewish-Gentile Relations in Medieval and Modern Times*. Oxford: Oxford University Press, 1961.

Kelley, Mary Jane. "Ascendant Eloquence: Language and Sanctity in the Works of Gonzalo de Berceo." *Speculum* 79 (2004): 66–87.

Kisch, Guido. *The Jews in Medieval Germany: A Study of Their Legal and Social Status*. Chicago: University of Chicago Press, 1949.

Klein, Elka. *Jews, Christian Society, and Royal Power in Medieval Barcelona*. Ann Arbor: University of Michigan Press, 2006.

Kriegel, Maurice. *Les juifs à la fin du Moyen Âge dans l'Europe méditerranéenne*. Paris: Hachette, 1979.

Lacave, José Luis. "Un testamento hebraico fragmentario de Miranda de Ebro." *Sefarad* 46 (1986): 271–79.

———. *Juderías y sinagogas españolas*. Madrid: Editorial MAPFRE, 1992.
Ladero Quesada, Manuel. *Las ciudades de la corona de Castilla en la baja edad media (siglos XIII al XV)*. Madrid: Arco Libros, 1996.
Ladero Quesada, Miguel Ángel. *Fiscalidad y poder real en Castilla (1252–1369)*. Madrid: Editorial Complutense, 1993.
———. "Castile: An Overview (Thirteenth to Fifteenth Centuries)." In *The Jews of Europe in the Middle Ages (Tenth to Fifteenth Centuries): Proceedings of the International Symposium held at Speyer, 20–25 October 2002*, edited by Christoph Cluse, 151–62. Turnhout: Brepols, 2004.
Langmuir, Gavin. "The Jews and the Archives of Angevin England: Reflections on Medieval Anti-Semitism." *Traditio* 19 (1963): 183–244.
———. "Tanquam Servi": The Change in Jewish Status in French Law about 1200." In *Toward a Definition of Antisemitism*. Berkeley: University of California Press, 1990, 167–94.
———. "Thomas of Monmouth: Detector of Ritual Murder." In *Toward a Definition of Antisemitism*. Berkeley: University of California Press, 1990, 209–36.
La real academia de la historia. *Cortes de los antiguos reinos de León y de Castilla*. Vols. 1 and 2. Madrid: 1861–63.
Lazar, Moshe. "Alfonso de Valladolid's *Mostrador de justicia*: A Polemical Debate between Abner's Old and New Self." In *Judaísmo Hispano: Estudios en memoria de José Luis Lacave Riaño*, edited by Elena Romero, 1:121–34. Madrid: CSIC, 2002.
Lea, Henry Charles. "Ferrand Martinez and the Massacres of 1391." *American Historical Review* 1, no. 2 (1896): 209–19.
León Tello, Pilar. "Nuevos documentos sobre la judería de Haro." *Sefarad* 15 (1955): 157–69.
———. *Judíos de Ávila*. Ávila: Diputación Provincial de Ávila, 1963.
———. "Legislación sobre judíos en las cortes de las antiguos reinos de León y Castilla." In *Papers of the Fourth World Congress of Jewish Studies*. Jerusalem: World Union of Jewish Studies, 1968, 55–63.
———. *Los judíos de Palencia*. Palencia: Publicaciones de la Institución Tello Téllez de Meneses, 1967.
———. *Judíos de Toledo*. Vols.1–2. Madrid: CSIC, 1979.
———. "Disposiciones sobre judíos en los fueros de Castilla y Leon." *Sefarad* 46 (1986): 279–93.
———. "La estancia de judíos en castillos." *Anuario de Estudios Medievales* 19 (1989): 451–67.
Lerner, Robert E. *The Feast of Saint Abraham: Medieval Millenarians and the Jews*. Philadelphia: University of Pennsylvania Press, 2000.
Lewis, Archibald. "The Closing of the Mediaeval Frontier, 1250–1350." *Speculum* 33, no. 4 (1958): 475–83.
Liebes, Yehuda. *Studies in the Zohar*. Translated by Arnold Schwartz, Stephanie Nakache, and Penina Peli. Albany: State University of New York Press, 1993.

Linage Conde, Antonio. "El parallelismo jurídico-político entre las cortes y los fueros: A propósito del de Sepúlveda." In *Las cortes de Castilla y León, 1188–1988: Actas de la tercera etapa del congreso científico sobre la historia de las cortes de Castilla y León, 1988.* Valladolid: Cortes de Castilla y León, 1990, 1:213–21.

Linder, Amnon. "The Legal Status of the Jews in the Roman Empire." In *The Cambridge History of Judaism.* Vol. 4, *The Late Roman-Rabbinic Period,* edited by Steven T. Katz, 128–73. Cambridge: Cambridge University Press, 2008.

Linehan, Peter. *The Spanish Church and the Papacy in the Thirteenth Century.* Cambridge: Cambridge University Press, 1971.

———. "The Spanish Church Revisited: The Episcopal *Gravamina* of 1279." In *Authority and Power: Studies on Medieval Law and Government Presented to Walter Ullmann on His Seventieth Birthday,* edited by Brian Tierney and Peter Linehan, 127–47. Cambridge: Cambridge University Press, 1980.

———. "A Tale of Two Cities: Capitular Burgos and Mendicant Burgos in the Thirteenth Century." In *Church and City: Essays in Honour of Christopher Brooke,* edited by David Abulafia, Michael J. Franklin, and Miri Rubin, 81–110. Cambridge: Cambridge University Press, 1992.

———. *The Ladies of Zamora.* Manchester: Manchester University Press, 1997.

Lizoain, José Manuel, and Juan José García. *El monasterio de Las Huelgas de Burgos: Historia de un señorio cisterciense burgales (siglos XII y XIII).* Burgos: Ediciones J. M. Garrido Garrido, 1988.

Lomax, Derek. *The Reconquest of Spain.* London: Longman, 1978.

López Gallegos, Silvia, and Ana María Martín Montero. "Las características socioculturales de los enclaves judíos en la Castilla pleno medieval." In *Actas del V congreso de arqueología medieval española.* Valladolid: Junta de Castilla y León, 2001, 1:141–52.

López Mata, Teófilo. "Moreria y judería [de Burgos]." *Boletín de la Real Academia de la Historia* 129 (1951): 335–84.

Lourie, Elena. "A Society Organized for War: Medieval Spain." *Past and Present* 35 (1996): 54–76.

Lower, Michael. *The Barons' Crusade: A Call to Arms and Its Consequences.* Philadelphia: University of Pennsylvania Press, 2005.

MacDonald, Robert A. "Problemas politicos y derecho Alfonsino considerados desde tres puntos de vista." *AHDE* 54 (1984): 25–53.

MacKay, Angus. "Popular Movements and Pogroms in Fifteenth-Century Castile." *Past and Present* 50 (1971): 33–67.

MacKay, Angus, and Vikki Hatton. "Anti-Semitism in the *Cantigas de Santa Maria.*" In *Society, Economy and Religion in Late Medieval Castile,* edited by Angus MacKay, ix. London: Variorum Reprints, 1987.

Mandianes Castro, Manuel. "La personalidad del judío en la obra de Martino de León." In *Santo Martino de León: Ponencias del I congreso internacional sobre Santo Martino en el VIII centenario de su obra literaria (1185–1985).* León: Isidoriana Editorial, 1987, 89–95.

Mansilla Reoyo, D., ed. *Catálogo documental del archivo catedral de Burgos (804–1416)*. Madrid and Barcelona: CSIC, 1971.

Marcus, Ivan. *Rituals of Childhood: Jewish Acculturation in Medieval Europe*. New Haven: Yale University Press, 1987.

Mark, Barry R. "Kabbalistic Tocinofobia: Américo Castro, Limpieza de Sangre and the Inner Meaning of Jewish Dietary Laws." In *Fear and Its Representations in the Middle Ages and Renaissance*, edited by Anne Scott and Cynthia Kosso, 152–86. Turnhout: Brepols Publishers, 2002.

Martínez Díez, Gonzalo. "El fuero real y el fuero de Soria." AHDE 39 (1969): 545–62.

———. "Los comienzos de la recepción del derecho romano en España y el fuero real. In *Diritto commune e diritti locali nella storia dell'Europa: Atti del Convegno di Varenna (12–15 giugno 1979)*. Milan: A. Giuffre, 1980, 253–62.

———, ed. *Fueros locales en el territorio de la provincia de Burgos*. Biblioteca universitaria Burgalesa. Burgos: Caja de Ahorros Municipal de Burgos, 1982.

———. *Leyes de Alfonso X*. Vol. 2, *Fuero real: Edición y analisis critico*. Avila: Fundacion Sanchez Albornoz, 1988.

———. *Alfonso VIII, rey de Castilla y Toledo*. Burgos: Editorial La Olmeda, 1995.

Martínez García, Luis. *El hospital del rey de Burgos: El señorío medieval en la expansion y en la crisis (siglos XIII y XIV)*. Burgos: Ediciones J. M. Garrido Garrido, 1986.

Martínez Liébana, Evelio. *El dominio señorial del monasterio de San Benito de Sahagún en la baja edad media (siglos XIII–XV)*. Ph.D. diss., Universidad Complutense de Madrid, 1990.

———. "La aljama de Sahagún en la transición del siglo XIV al XV." Hispania 53, part 2, no. 184 (1993): 397–429.

Martínez Llorente, Félix J. "En torno al procedimiento judicial alto-medieval judeocristiano en el reino de León: La 'Karta inter christianos et iudeos de foros illorum' (1091)." In *Proyección histórica de España en sus tres culturas: Castilla y León, América y el Mediterráneo*. Valladolid: Junta de Castilla y León, 1993, 1:205–10.

Martínez Marina, Francisco. *Teoría de las cortes o grandes juntas nacionales de los reinos de León y Castilla*. Vols. 1–3. Madrid: 1913.

Martínez Sopena, Pascual. "El camino de Santiago y la articulación del espacio en tierra de Campos y León. In *XX semana de estudios medievales 1993*. Pamplona: Gobierno de Navarra, 1994), 185–211.

McCulloh, John M. "Jewish Ritual Murder: William of Norwich, Thomas of Monmouth, and the Early Dissemination of the Myth." Speculum 72 (1997): 698–740.

Melechen, Nina. "Calling Names: The Identification of Jews in Christian Documents from Medieval Toledo." In *On the Social Origins of Medieval Institutions: Essays in Honor of Joseph F. O'Callaghan*, edited by Donald Kagay and Theresa Vann, 21–34. Leiden: Brill, 1998.

———. "Loans, Land, and Jewish-Christian Relations in the Archdiocese of Toledo." In *Iberia and the Mediterranean World of the Middle Ages*, edited by Larry Simon, 1· 185–215. Leiden: Brill, 1995.

———. "The Jews of Medieval Toledo: Their Economic and Social Contact with Christians from 1150–1391." Ph.D. dissertation, Fordham University, 1999.
Menocal, Maria Rosa. *The Ornament of the Word: How Muslims, Jews, and Christians Created a Culture of Tolerance in Medieval Spain.* Boston: Little, Brown, 2002.
Merchán Fernández, Carlos. *Los judíos de Valladolid: Estudio histórico de una minoría influyente.* Valladolid: Diputación Provincial de Valladolid, 1976.
Meyerson, Mark. *The Muslims of Valencia in the Age of Fernando and Isabel: Between Coexistence and Crusade.* Berkeley: University of California Press, 1991.
———. "Bishop Ramon Despont and the Jews of the Kingdom of Valencia." *Anuario de estudios medievales* 29 (1999): 641–53.
———. *A Jewish Renaissance in Fifteenth-Century Spain.* Princeton: Princeton University Press, 2004.
———. *Jews in an Iberian Frontier Kingdom: Society, Economy, and Politics in Morvedre, 1248–1392.* Leiden: Brill, 2004.
Miceli, Paola. "El derecho consuetudinario en Castilla: Una crítica a la matriz romántica de las interpretaciones sobre la costumbre." *Hispania: Revista Española de Historia* 63, part 1, no. 213 (2003): 9–27.
Milton, Gregory B. "Christian and Jewish Lenders: Religious Identity and the Extension of Credit." *Viator* 37 (2006): 301–18.
———. *Market Power: Lordship, Society, and Economy in Medieval Catalonia (1276–1313).* New York: Palgrave Macmillan, 2012.
Mínguez, José María. "La transformación social de las ciudades y las cortes de Castilla y León." In *Las cortes de Castilla y León en la edad media: Actas de la primera etapa del congreso científico sobre la historia de las cortes de Castilla y Leon, Burgos, 1986.* Valladolid: Cortes de Castilla y León, 1988, 2:15–43.
Mitre Fernández, Emilio. *Los judíos de Castilla en tiempo de Enrique III: El pogrom de 1391.* Valladolid: Universidad de Valladolid, 1994.
Monsalvo Antón, José. *Teoría y evolucion de un conflicto social: El antisemitismo en la corona de Castilla en la baja edad media.* Madrid: Siglo XXI de España Editores, 1985.
———. "Cortes de Castilla y León y minorías." In *Las Cortes de Castilla y León en la edad media: Actas de la primera etapa del congreso científico sobre la historia de las cortes de Castilla y Leon, Burgos, 1986.* Valladolid: Cortes de Castilla y León, 1988, 2:145–91.
Montes Romero-Camacho, Isabel. "Antisemitismo sevillano en la baja edad media: El pogrom de 1391 y sus consecuencias." In *Actas del III colloquio de historia medieval andaluza: La sociedad medieval andaluza; Grupos no privilegiados.* Jaén: Duputación Provincial de Jaén, 1984, 57–75.
———. *Los judíos en la edad media española.* Madrid: Arco Libros, 2001.
———. "La aljama judía de Sevilla en la baja edad media." In *El Patrimonio hebreo en la España medieval*, edited by Alberto Villar Movellán and María del Rosario Castro Castillo, 25–52. Cordoba: Universidad de Cordoba, 2004.
———. "Las minorías étnico-religiosas en la Sevilla del siglo XIV: Mudéjares y

judíos. In *Sevilla, siglo XIV*, edited by Rafael Valencia, 135–55. Seville: Fundación José Manuel Lara, 2006.

Mundill, Robin R. *England's Jewish Solution: Experiment and Expulsion, 1262–1290*. Cambridge: Cambridge University Press, 1998.

———. "Medieval Anglo-Jewry: Expulsion and Exodus." In *Judenvertreibungen in Mittelalter und früher Neuzeit*, edited by Friedhelm Burgard, Alfred Haverkamp, and Gerd Mentgen, 75–97. Hannover: Hahn, 1999.

———. *The King's Jews: Money, Massacre and Exodus in Medieval England*. London: Continuum, 2010.

Netanyahu, Benzion. *The Origins of the Inquisition in Fifteenth Century Spain*. New York: Random House, 1995.

Nieto Soria, José Manuel. "Los judíos de Toledo en sus relaciones financieras con la monarquia y la iglesia (1252–1312)." Part 1, *Sefarad* 41 (1981): 301–19; part 2, *Sefarad* 42 (1982): 79–102.

———. "Los judios como conflicto jurisdiccional entre monarquia e iglesia en la Castilla de fines del siglo XIII: Su casuistica." In *Encuentro de las tres culturas: Actas del II congreso internacional, 3–6 Octobre 1983*. Toledo: Ayuntamiento de Toledo, 1985, 243–52.

———. *Fundamentos ideológicos del poder real en Castilla*. Madrid: EUDEMA, 1988.

———. *Iglesia y poder real en Castilla: El Episcopado (1250–1350)*. Madrid: Universidad Complutense, 1988.

———. "Religión y política en la Castilla bajomedieval: Algunas perspectives de análisis en torno al poder real." *Cuadernos de Historia de España* 76 (2000): 99–120.

Nieva Ocampo, Guillermo. "Los dominicos de Castilla: La genesis de una corporación privilegiada en la baja edad media." In *Servir a Dios y servir al rey: El mundo de los privilegiados en el ámbito hispánico, ss. XIII–XVIII*, edited by Guillermo Nieva Ocampo, Silvano G. A. Benito Moya, and Andrea Navarro, 13–47. Salta: Mundo Editorial, 2011.

Nirenberg, David. *Communities of Violence: Persecution of Minorities in the Middle Ages*. Princeton: Princeton University Press, 1996.

———. "Conversion, Sex, and Segregation: Jews and Christians in Medieval Spain." *American Historical Review* 107, no. 4: (2002): 1065–93.

———. "Figures of Thought and Figures of Flesh: 'Jews' and 'Judaism' in Late-Medieval Spanish Poetry and Politics." *Speculum* 81, no. 2 (April 2006): 398–426.

———. "Deviant Politics and Jewish Love: Alfonso VIII and the Jewess of Toledo." *Jewish History* 21 (2007): 15–41.

———. *Anti-Judaism: The Western Tradition*. New York: W. W. Norton, 2013.

Novikoff, Alex. "Between Tolerance and Intolerance in Medieval Spain: An Historiographic Enigma." *Medieval Encounters* 11 (2005): 7–36.

———. *The Medieval Culture of Disputation: Pedagogy, Practice, and Performance*. Pennsylvania: University of Pennsylvania Press, 2013.

O'Brien, Bruce. *God's Peace and King's Peace: The Laws of Edward the Confessor*. Philadelphia: University of Pennsylvania Press, 1999.

O'Callaghan, Joseph. "The Cortes and Royal Taxation during the Reign of Alfonso X of Castile." *Traditio* 27 (1971): 379–98.

———. *A History of Medieval Spain*. Ithaca: Cornell University Press, 1975.

———. "Sobre la promulgación del *Especulo* y del *Fuero real*." In *Estudios en homenaje a Don Claudio Sánchez Albornoz en sus 90 años*. Buenos Aires: Instituto de Historia de España, 1985, 3:167–79.

———. "Las cortes de Castilla y León (1230–1350)." In *Las cortes de Castilla y León en la edad media: Actas de la primera etapa del congreso científico sobre la historia de las cortes de Castilla y Leon, Burgos, 1986*. Valladolid: Cortes de Castilla y León, 1988, 1:155–81.

———. *The Cortes of Castile-León, 1188–1350*. Philadelphia: University of Pennsylvania Press, 1989.

———. *The Learned King: The Reign of Alfonso X of Castile*. Philadelphia: University of Pennsylvania Press, 1993.

———. "Las cortes de Fernando IV: Cuadernos ineditos de Valladolid 1300 y Burgos 1308." In *Alfonso X, the Cortes, and Government in Medieval Spain*. Aldershot: Ashgate, 1998, 13:1–14.

———. "Alfonso X and the Partidas." In *Las siete partidas*. Vol. 1, *The Medieval Church*, edited by Robert I. Burns, xxx–xxxix. Philadelphia: University of Pennsylvania Press, 2001.

———. *Reconquest and Crusade in Medieval Spain*. Philadelphia: University of Pennsylvania Press, 2003.

Oikonomides, Nicolas. "The Jews of Chios (1049): A Group of Excusati." In *Intercultural Contacts in the Medieval Mediterranean*. London and Portland, Ore.: Frank Cass, 1996, 218–25.

Palacio Sanchez-Izquierdo, María Luisa. "El monasterio de San Zoilo de Carrion: Jurisdiccion, franquezas y privilegios." In *Actas del I congreso de historia de Palencia*. Vol. 2, *Fuentes documentales y edad media*. Palencia: Diputación Provincial de Palencia, 1985, 65–73.

Palacios Alcaine, Azucena, ed. *Alfonso X el Sabio: Fuero Real*. Barcelona: PPU, 1991.

Patschovsky, Alexander. "The Relationship between the Jews of Germany and the King (11th–14th Centuries): A European Comparison." In *England and Germany in the Middle Ages*, edited by Alfred Haverkamp and Hanna Vollrath, 193–218. Oxford: Oxford University Press, 1996.

Patton, Pamela. *Art of Estrangement: Redefining Jews in Reconquest Spain*. University Park: Pennsylvania State University Press, 2012.

Pérez, Joseph. *Los judíos en España*. Madrid: Marcial Pons Historia, 2005.

Pérez Martín, Antonio. "El Fuero real y Murcia." *AHDE* 54 (1984): 55–96.

Pick, Lucy K. "Rodrigo Jiménez de Rada and the Jews: Pragmatism and Patronage in Thirteenth-Century Toledo." *Viator* 28 (1997): 203–22.

———. *Conflict and Coexistence: Archbishop Rodrigo and the Muslims and Jews of Medieval Spain*. Ann Arbor: University of Michigan Press, 2004.

Piskorki, Wladimir. *Las Cortes de Castilla en el período de tránsito de la edad media a la moderna*. Translated by Claudio Sánchez Albornoz. Barcelona: Ediciones Albir, 1977.
Post, Gaines. *Studies in Medieval Legal Thought: Public Law and the State, 1100–1322*. Princeton: Princeton University Press, 1964.
Pounds, N. J. G. *An Economic History of Medieval Europe*. London: Longman, 1974.
Powers, James F. "Frontier Municipal Baths and Social Interaction in Thirteenth-Century Spain." *American Historical Review* 84, no. 3 (June 1979): 649–67.
Procter, Evelyn. "The Towns of Leon and Castille as Suitors before the King's Court in the Thirteenth Century. *English Historical Review* 74, no. 290 (January 1959): 1–22.
———. *Curia and Cortes in León and Castile, 1072–1295*. Cambridge: Cambridge University Press, 1980.
Quintana Prieto, Augusto. "Guillermo de Taillante, abad de Sahagún y cardinal de la iglesia romana." *Anthologica annua* 26 (1979): 11–83.
Ray, Jonathan. "Beyond Tolerance and Persecution: Reassessing Our Approach to Medieval Convivencia." *Jewish Social Studies* 11, no. 2 (2005): 1–18.
———. *The Sephardic Frontier: "The Reconquista" and the Jewish Community in Medieval Iberia*. Ithaca: Cornell University Press, 2006.
———. "The Jews between Church and State in Reconquest Iberia: The Evidence of the Ecclesiastical Tithe:" *Viator* 38, no. 1 (2007): 155–65.
———. "The Jew in the Text: What Christian Charters Tell Us about Medieval Jewish Society." *Medieval Encounters* 16 (2010): 243–67.
Reilly, Bernard. *The Kingdom of León-Castilla under Queen Urraca, 1109–1126*. Princeton: Princeton University Press, 1982.
———. *The Kingdom of León-Castilla under King Alfonso VI, 1065–1109*. Princeton: Princeton University Press, 1988.
———. *The Kingdom of León-Castilla under King Alfonso VII, 1126–1157*. Philadelphia: University of Pennsylvania Press, 1998.
Reiner, Avraham (Rami). "From Rabbenu Tam to R. Isaac of Vienna: The Hegemony of the French Talmudic School in the Twelfth Century." In *The Jews of Europe in the Middle Ages (Tenth to Fifteenth Centuries): Proceedings of the International Symposium Held at Speyer, 20–25 October 2002*, edited by Christoph Cluse, 273–82. Turnhout: Brepols, 2004.
Reinhardt, Klaus. "La exegesis escrituristica de Santo Martino." In *Santo Martino de León: Ponencias del I congreso internacional sobre Santo Martino en el VIII centenario de su obra literaria (1185–1985)*. León: Isidoriana Editorial, 1987, 583–94.
Richardson, H. G. *The English Jewry under Angevin Kings*. London: Methuen, 1960.
Rodríguez Díez, Matias. *Historia de la ciudad de Astorga*. Vol. 2. Facsimile edition. León: Editorial Celarayn, 1981.
Rodríguez Fernández, Justiniano. "Judería de Sahagún." *Archivos Leoneses* 7, no. 14 (1953): 5–77.
———. *La judería de la ciudad de León*. León: Centro de Estudios e Investigación "San Isidoro," 1969.

———. *Las juderías de la provincia de León*. León: Centro de Estudios e Investigación "San Isidoro," 1976).

Romano, David. "Alfonso X y los judíos: Problemática y propuestas de trabajo." *Anuario de Estudios Medievales* 15 (1985): 151–77.

———. "Aljama frente a judería, call y sus sinómimos." In *De historia judía hispánica*. Barcelona: Publicaciones Universitat de Barcelona, 1991, 347–54.

———. "Judíos hispánicos y mundo rural." *Sefarad* 51 (1991): 353–67.

———. "Marco juridico de la minoría judía." In *De historia judía hispánica*. Barcelona: Publicaciones de la Universitat de Barcelona, 1991, 261–91.

Roth, Cecil. *The History of the Jews of Italy*. Philadelphia: Jewish Publication Society of America, 1946.

Roth, Norman. "Jewish Collaborators in Alfonso's Scientific Work." In *Emperor of Culture: Alfonso X the Learned of Castile and His Thirteenth-Century Renaissance*, edited by Robert I. Burns, 59–71. Philadelphia: University of Pennsylvania Press, 1990.

———. "The Civic Status of the Jew in Medieval Spain." In *Iberia and the Mediterranean World of the Middle Ages*, edited by P. E. Chevedden, D. J. Kagay, and P. G. Padilla, 139–61. Leiden: Brill, 1996.

———. "Two Jewish Courtiers of Alfonso X Called Zag (Isaac)." *Sefarad* 43 (1983): 75–85.

Rowe, Nina. *The Jew, the Cathedral, and the Medieval City*. Cambridge: Cambridge University Press, 2011.

Rubin, Miri. *Gentile Tales: The Narrative Assault on Late Medieval Jews*. New Haven: Yale University Press, 1999.

Rubio Hernández, Ángel Jesús. "El Libro Rimado de Palacio: Datos sobre la inoperatividad de las cortes de Castilla y León en el siglo XIV." In *Las cortes de Castilla y León, 1188–1988: Actas de la tercera etapa del congreso científico sobre la historia de las cortes de Castilla y León, 1988*. Valladolid: Cortes de Castilla y León, 1990, 1:319–32.

Rucquoi, Adeline. "Pouvoir royal et oligarchies urbaines d'Alfonso X à Fernando IV de Castille." In *Genesis medieval del estado moderno: Castilla y Navarra (1250–1370)*. Valladolid: AMBITO Ediciones, 1987, 173–92.

———. *Valladolid en la edad media*. Vol. 1, *Genesis de un poder*. Valladolid: Junta de Castilla y León, 1987.

Ruiz, Teofilo. "Burgos: Society and Royal Power, 1250–1350." Ph.D. diss., Princeton University, 1973.

———. "The Transformation of the Castilian Municipalities: The Case of Burgos." *Past and Present* 77 (November 1977), 3–32.

———. *Sociedad y poder real en Castilla*. Barcelona: Editorial Ariel, 1981.

———. "Oligarchy and Royal Power: The Castilian Cortes and the Castilian Crisis 1248–1350." *Parliaments, Estates and Representation/Parlements, états et representation* 2, no. 2 (1982): 95–101.

———. "Une royauté sans sacre: La monarchie castillane du Bas Moyen Age." *Annales* (May–June 1984): 429–53.

———. "Burgos y el comercio castellano en la baja edad media: economia y mentalidad." in *La ciudad de Burgos: Actas del congreso de historia de Burgos*. León: Junta de Castilla y León, 1985, 37–55.

———. "Unsacred Monarchy: The Kings of Castile in the Late Middle Ages." In *Rites of Power: Symbolism, Ritual and Politics Since the Middle Ages*, edited by Sean Wilentz, 109–44. Philadelphia: University of Pennsylvania Press, 1985.

———. *Crisis and Continuity: Land and Town in Late Medieval Castile*. Philadelphia: University of Pennsylvania Press, 1994.

———. "Judios y christianos en el ambito urbano bajomedieval: Avila y Burgos, 1200–1350." In *Xudeus e Conversos na Historia*, edited by Carlos Barros, 2:69–93. Santiago de Compostela: Editorial de la Historia, 1994.

———. "Trading with the 'Other': Economic Exchanges between Muslims, Jews, and Christians in Late Medieval Northern Castile. In *Medieval Spain: Culture, Conflict, and Coexistence; Studies in Honour of Angus MacKay*, edited by Roger Collins and Anthony Goodman, 63–78. New York: Palgrave Macmillan, 2002.

———. *From Heaven to Earth: The Reordering of Castilian Society, 1150–1350*. Princeton: Princeton University Press, 2004.

———. *Spain's Centuries of Crisis: 1300–1474*. Malden, Mass.: Wiley-Blackwell, 2011.

Ruiz de la Peña, Juan Ignacio. "La political antijudaica del Obispo don Gutierre de Toledo (1377–1389)." *Archivos Leoneses* (1974): 263–89.

Ruiz Gómez, Francisco. "Aljamas y concejos en el reino de Castilla durante la edad media." *Espacio, Tiempo y Forma*." Series 3, *Historia medieval* 6 (1993): 57–78.

———. "Juderias y aljamas en el mundo rural de la Castilla medieval." In *Xudeus e Conversos na Historia*, edited by Carlos Barros, 2:111–52. Santiago de Compostela, 1994.

Rustow, Marina. *Heresy and the Politics of Community: The Jews of the Fatimid Caliphate*. Ithaca: Cornell University Press, 2008.

Salcedo Izu, Joaquín. "La autonomia municipal según las cortes Castellanas de la Baja Edad Media." *AHDE* 50 (1980): 223–42.

Salvador Martínez, H. *La convivencia en la España del siglo XIII: Perspectivas alfonsíes*. Madrid: Ediciones Polifemo, 2006.

Sánchez, Galo. "Para la historia de la redacción del antiguo derecho territorial castellano." *AHDE* 6 (1929): 260–328.

Sánchez-Albornoz, Claudio. *Una ciudad de la España cristiana hace mil años: Estampas de la vida en León*. 5th ed. Madrid: Ediciones Rialp, 1966.

———. *Spain, a Historical Enigma*. Vol. 2. Translated by Colette Joly Dees and David Sven Reher. Madrid: Fundacion Universitaria Española, 1975.

Sánchez-Lafuente Pérez, Jorge, and José Luis Avello Álvarez. *El mundo judío en la Península Ibérica: Sociedad y economía*. Cuenca: Alderabán Ediciones, 2012.

Saperstein, Marc. "The Preaching of Repentance and the Reforms in Toledo of 1281." In *Models of Holiness in Medieval Sermons*, edited by Beverly Mayne Kienzle, 157–74. Louvain-la-Neuve: Fédération Internationale des Instituts d'Études Médiévales, 1996.

Schmandt, Matthias. "Cologne, Jewish Centre on the Lower Rhine." In *The Jews of Europe in the Middle Ages (Tenth to Fifteenth Centuries): Proceedings of the International Symposium Held at Speyer, 20–25 October 2002*, edited by Christoph Cluse, 367–78. Turnhout: Brepols, 2004.

Scholem, Gershom. *Major Trends in Jewish Mysticism*. 3rd ed. New York: Schocken, 1995.

Schorsch, Ismar. *From Text to Context: The Turn to History in Modern Judaism*. Hanover, N.H.: Brandeis University Press, 1994.

Schreckenberg, Heinz. *Die christlichen Adversus-Judaeos-Texte (11.–13. Jh.), mit einer Ikonographie des Judenthemas bis zum 4. Laterankonzil*. Frankfurt am Main: Peter Lang, 1991.

Skolnik, Fred, and Michael Berenbaum, eds. *Encyclopedia Judaica*. Vol. 1. 2nd ed. Detroit: Keter, 2007.

Septimus, Bernard. "Piety and Power in Thirteenth-Century Catalonia." In *Studies in Medieval Jewish History and Literature*, edited by Isadore Twersky, 1:197–230. Cambridge, Mass.: Harvard University Press, 1979.

———. *Hispano-Jewish Culture in Transition: The Career and Controversies of Ramah*. Cambridge, Mass.: Harvard University Press, 1982.

———. "Hispano-Jewish Views of Christendom and Islam." In *In Iberia and Beyond: Hispanic Jews between Cultures*, edited by Bernard Dov Cooperman, 43–65. Newark: University of Delaware Press, 1998).

Shatzmiller, Joseph. *Shylock Reconsidered: Jews, Moneylending, and Medieval Society*. Berkeley: University of California Press, 1990.

Shoval, Ilan. "'Servi regis' Re-Examined: On the Significance of the Earliest Appearance of the Term in Aragon, 1176." *Hispania Judaica Bulletin* 4 (2004): 22–69.

Silver, Daniel Jeremy. *Maimonidean Criticism and the Maimonidean Controversy, 1180–1240*. Leiden: Brill, 1965.

Simon, Larry. "Jews in the Legal Corpus of Alfonso el Sabio." *Comitatus* 18 (1987): 80–97.

———. "Intimate Enemies: Mendicant-Jewish Interaction in Thirteenth-Century Mediterranean Spain." In *Friars and Jews in the Middle Ages and Renaissance*, edited by Steven McMichael and Susan Myers, 53–80. Leiden and Boston: Brill, 2004.

Simonsohn, Shlomo. *The Apostolic See and the Jews*. Vol. 7, *History*. Toronto: Pontifical Institute of Mediaeval Studies, 1991.

Sivan, Hagith. "The Invisible Jews of Visigothic Spain." *Revue des études juives* 159, nos. 3–4 (2000): 369–85.

Soifer, Maya. *See* Soifer Irish, Maya

Soifer Irish, Maya. "'You Say That the Messiah Has Come . . .': The Ceuta Disputation (1179) and Its Place in Christian Anti-Jewish Polemics of the High Middle Ages." *Journal of Medieval History* 31 (2005): 287–307.

"Beyond *Convivencia*: Critical Reflections on the Historiography of Interfaith Relations in Christian Spain." *Journal of Medieval Iberian Studies* 1, no. 1 (2009): 19–35.

———. "The Castilian Monarchy and the Jews (Eleventh to Thirteenth centuries). In *Center and Periphery: Studies on Power in the Medieval World in Honor of William Chester*

Jordan, edited by Katherine L. Jansen, Guy Geltner, and Anne E. Lester, 39–49. Leiden: Brill, 2013.

———. "Tamquam domino proprio: Contesting Ecclesiastical Lordship over Jews in Thirteenth-Century Castile." *Medieval Encounters* 19 (2013): 536–41.

———. "The Problem of Old Debts: Jewish Moneylenders in Northern Castile (Belorado and Miranda de Ebro, ca. 1300)." *Sefarad* 74, no. 2 (2014): 279–302.

Soloveitchik, Haym. "Pawnbroking: A Study in Ribbit and of the Halakah in Exile." *Proceedings of the American Academy for Jewish Research* 38 and 39 (1970–71): 203–68.

———. "Jewish and Provençal Law: A Study in Interaction." In *Mélanges Roger Aubenas*. Montpellier: Faculté de Droit et des Sciences Économiques de Montpellier, 1974, 711–23.

Szpiech, Ryan. "Polemical Strategy and the Rhetoric of Authority in Abner of Burgos/Alfonso of Valladolid." In *Late Medieval Jewish Identities: Iberia and Beyond*, edited by Carmen Caballero-Navas and Esperanza Alfonso, 55–76. New York: Palgrave Macmillan, 2010.

———. *Conversion and Narrative: Reading and Religious Authority in Medieval Polemic*. Philadelphia: University of Pennsylvania Press, 2013.

Stacey, Robert. "Jewish Lending and the Medieval English Economy." In *A Commercializing Economy: England 1086 to c. 1300*, edited by Richard Britnell and Bruce Campbell, 78–101. Manchester and New York: Manchester University Press, 1995.

———. "Jews and Christians in Twelfth-Century England: Some Dynamics of a Changing Relationship." In *Jews and Christians in Twelfth-Century Europe*, edited by Michael Signer and John Van Engen, 340–54. Notre Dame: University of Notre Dame Press, 2001.

Stow, Kenneth. "Papal and Royal Attitudes toward Jewish Lending in the Thirteenth Century." *AJS Review* 6 (1981): 161–84.

———. *Alienated Minority: The Jews of Medieval Latin Europe*. Cambridge, Mass.: Harvard University Press, 1992.

———. "The Good of the Church, the Good of the State: The Popes and Jewish Money." In *Christianity and Judaism: Papers Read at the 1991 Summer Meeting and the 1992 Winter Meeting of the Ecclesiastical History Society*, edited by Diana Wood, 237–52. Oxford: Blackwell, 1992.

Suárez Bilbao, Fernando. "Algunas noticias sobre Judíos en la provincial de Palencia." In *Actas del II congreso de historia de Palencia*. Vol. 2, *Fuentes documentales y edad media*. Palencia: Excma. Diputación Provincial de Palencia, 1990, 609–25.

———. *El fuero judiego en la España cristiana: Las fuentes jurídicas, siglos V–XV*. Madrid: Dykinson, 2000.

Suárez Fernández, Luis. *Documentos acerca de la expulsión de los judíos*. Valladolid: CSIC, 1964.

———. *Judíos españoles en la edad media*. Madrid: Ediciones Rialp, 1980.

———. *Monarquía hispana y revolución Trastámara*. Madrid: Real Academia de la Historia, 1994.

Tartakoff, Paola. *Between Christian and Jew: Conversion and Inquisition in the Crown of Aragon, 1250–1391*. Philadelphia: University of Pennsylvania Press, 2012.

Ta-Shema, Israel. "Between East and West: Rabbi Asher b Yehiel and His Son Rabbi Ya'aqov." In *Studies in Medieval Jewish History and Literature*, edited by Isadore Twersky and Jay M. Harris, 3:179–96. Cambridge, Mass.: Harvard University Press, 2000.

Toch, Michael. *Peasants and Jews in Medieval Germany: Studies in Cultural, Social, and Economic History*. Aldershot: Ashgate, 2003.

Tolan, John. "Une *convivencia* bien précaire: La place des juifs et des musulmans dans les sociétés chrétiennes ibériques au Moyen Âge." In *La Tolérance: Colloque international de Nantes, mai 1998, Quatrième centenaire de l'édit de Nantes*, edited by Guy Saupin, Rémy Fabre, and Marcel Launay, 386–90. Rennes: Presses Universitaires de Rennes, Centre de Recherche sur l'histoire du Monde Atlantique, 1999.

Transier, Werner. "Speyer: The Jewish Community in the Middle Ages." In *The Jews of Europe in the Middle Ages (Tenth to Fifteenth Centuries): Proceedings of the International Symposium Held at Speyer, 20–25 October 2002*, edited by Christoph Cluse, 435–47. Turnhout: Brepols, 2004.

Twersky, Isadore, ed., *Rabbi Moses Nahmanides (Ramban): Explorations in His Religious and Literary Virtuosity*. Cambridge, Mass.: Harvard University Press, 1983.

Valdeón Baruque, Julio. *Los judíos de Castilla y la revolución Trastámara*. Valladolid: Universidad de Valladolid, 1968.

———. "Las cortes castellanas en el sigle XIV." *Anuario de Estudios Medievales* 7 (1970–71): 633–44.

———. "La judería toledana en la guerra civil de Pedro I y Enrique II." In *Symposio "Toledo judaico," Toledo 20–22, Abril 1972*. Toledo: Publicaciones del Centro, 1973, 107–31.

———. "Las cortes de Castilla y León en tiempos de Pedro I y de los primeros Trastámaras (1350–1406)." In *Las cortes de Castilla y León en la edad media: Actas de la primera etapa del congreso científico sobre la historia de las cortes de Castilla y Leon, Burgos, 1986*. Valladolid: Cortes de Castilla y León, 1988, 1:185–217.

———. "Judios y mudéjares en tierras Palentinas (siglos XIII–XV)." In *Actas del II congreso de historia de Palencia. Vol. 2, Fuentes documentales y edad media*. Palencia: Excma. Diputación Provincial de Palencia, 1990, 359–75.

———. *Judíos y conversos en la Castilla medieval*. Valladolid: Universidad de Valladolid, 2000.

Vallecillo Ávila, Manuel. "Los judíos de Castilla en la alta edad media." In *Cuadernos de historia de España*. Buenos Aires: Instituto de Investigaciones Históricas, 1950, 14:17–110.

Vicente Niclós, José. "San Martin de León y la controversia con los judíos en el siglo XII." In *La controversia judeocristiana en España (desde los orígenes hasta el siglo XIII)*. Madrid: CSIC, 1998, 243–52.

Villalon, Andrew L. J. "'Seeking Castles in Spain': Sir Hugh Calveley and the Free Companies' Intervention in Iberian Warfare (1366–1369)." In *Crusaders, Condottieri, and Cannon: Medieval Warfare in Societies around the Mediterranean*, edited by L. J. Andrew Villalon and Donald J. Kagay, 305–28. Leiden: Brill, 2003.

Viñayo González, Antonio. *San Martín de León y su apologética antijudía*. Madrid and Barcelona, 1948.

Vose, Robin. *Dominicans, Muslims and Jews in the Medieval Crown of Aragon*. Cambridge: Cambridge University Press, 2009.

Watt, J. A. "The Jew, the Law, and the Church: The Concept of Jewish Serfdom in Thirteenth-Century England." In *The Church and Sovereignty c. 590–1918*, edited by Diana Wood, 153–72. Oxford: Basil Blackwell, 1991.

Webster, Jill R. "Conversion and Co-existence: The Franciscan Mission in the Crown of Aragon." In *Iberia and the Mediterranean World of the Middle Ages*, edited by P. E. Chevedden, D. J. Kagay, and P. G. Padilla, 163–77. Leiden: E. J. Brill, 1996.

Wilkins, Constance. *Pero López de Ayala*. Boston: Twayne, 1989.

Wolf, Kenneth Baxter. *Conquerors and Chroniclers of Early Medieval Spain*. 2nd ed. Liverpool: Liverpool University Press, 1999.

Wolff, Philippe. "The 1391 Pogrom in Spain: Social Crisis or Not?" *Past and Present* 50 (1971): 4–18.

Wolfson, Elliot. "Ontology, Alterity, and Ethics in Kabbalistic Anthropology." *Exemplaria: A Journal of Theory in Medieval and Renaissance Studies* 12, no. 1 (2000): 129–55.

Yuval, Israel. *Two Nations in Your Womb: Perceptions of Jews and Christians in Late Antiquity and the Middle Ages*. Translated by Barbara Harshav and Jonathan Chipman. Berkeley and Los Angeles: University of California Press, 2006.

INDEX

Aaron of Lincoln, 35
Abelgas, 198n116
Abner of Burgos (later Alfonso of Valladolid), 80, 158, 159
Abraam of Burgos, 97
Abraam the Fat (of Dueñas), 97
Abrafan Pardal, and wife Ourodueña (of Astorga), 197–98
Abrafan Royuelo (of León), 201
Abraham Cordiella (tax collector), 126
Abraham el Barchilón, 124, 250
Abraham Enpollegar (of Palenzuela), 66, 70
Abraham Ruvielo (of León), 66, 128–29
Abulafia, Abraham (rabbi; kabbalist), 156n20, 157n24, 158–59n28
Abulafia, David, 29nn36–37, 30
Abulafia, Joseph ben Todros (rabbi), 163
Abulafia, Meir ben Todros ha-Levi (rabbi; Ramah), 36, 81,152–54, 155, 156
Abulafia, Todros ben Joseph ha-Levi (rabbi), 155, 157n23, 163–66
Abulafia, Todros ben Judah (poet), 165n53, 194n100
adelantados (elders), in Burgos, 169
agriculture and farming: Alfonso XI's efforts to turn Jews into farmers, 246, 249; diezmos de los ganados, 67; mill rights, 61; viticulture, 61–63
Aguilar de Campóo: Alfonso X, Fuero real legislation of, 7, 39, 181; attacks on Jews in, 228; mill rights owned by Jews, 61; moneylenders in, 70, 133; royal grant of Jewish revenues to church of Santa María in, 28, 102n99; Santa María de Aguilar (monastery), 98, 102n99, 125–26, 130; Santa María la Real (monastery), 61, 120; tax collection in, 125–26, 140

Alarcón, 46n113, 181
Alba de Tormes, 191n95
albedí (Jewish judge), 44, 49, 169
Albelda, 140n33
alcabala (sales tax), 66
Alcalá de Guadaíra, 145
Alcalá de Henares, 184, 191, 233, 245
alcaldes (judges): challenges to Jewish right to separate judges, 172, 202–5, 237, 238, 248; collection of debt and, 197, 202–5, 209, 210, 211–13, 216, 217; fueros on, 41, 42, 43, 47, 49; Palencian bishop's right to appoint, 138, 139; tax collection cases and, 125–26; and tithes, 110
Alcaraz, 46n113
Alfonso, Infante (son of Pedro I), 127
Alfonso I of Aragon, 25, 42, 58, 59
Alfonso V of León, 54
Alfonso VI of Castile-León: death of, 25; Jewish contribution to royal income under, 22–24; Jewish notables at court of, 24, 35, 124; Miranda, fueros and privileges of, 216; royal donations of Jewish taxes to church, 22, 83, 96; Toledo, conquest of, 7–8, 22–23
Alfonso VII of Castile-León: Calatalifa charter (1141), 20; death of, 27; Jewish notables at court of, 35; Karaite Judaism, suppression of, 35–36, 166; pardon of attackers of Jews by, 25, 55, 133; royal authority over Jews, 25–27, 31; royal donations of Jewish taxes to church, 96
Alfonso VIII of Castile: Burgos as capital city, 7; "castles" of Jews and, 27, 55–56; fueros granted by, 43, 47; Jewish notables at court of, 35; Libro de los fueros and, 48; Palencia and, 133, 135–36, 139, 141; papacy

and conciliar legislation on Jews, 104, 106; royal authority over Jews, 27–33; royal donations of Jewish taxes to church, 96, 98; towns, reliance on prosperity of, 32

Alfonso IX of León, 27, 32, 62n48

Alfonso X *el Sabio* ("the Wise") of Castile, 178–89, 259; Algeciras, misappropriation of funds for siege of, 163–64, 166, 193–94, 250; Burgos *aljama* and, 71; Burgos dispute over Jewish *alcaldes*, 203; *caballeros villanos*, emergence of, 173; *Cantigas de Santa María* (attrib.), 225–26; coinage and monetary policies, xi, 172–73; collaboration of Christian and Jewish scholars under, 157–58, 178; cortes legislation and, 234–35, 242, 247–49, 250, 254–55; ecclesiastical complaints to Pope Nicholas III about, 129–30; effects of policies on Jewish-Christian relations, 16; *Espéculo*, 164, 181n43; fiscal pressure on Jews under, 16, 175–76, 189; *Fuero real* legislation of, 7, 39, 85, 164, 175, 180–85, 187–88, 190, 199, 234–35, 254; Holy Roman Emperor, quest to become, 110, 189, 191; impact of legislation, 187–89; Jewish *aljama* reforms and legislative initiatives, 163–66; Jewish notables at court of, 163; legislation compared to *dhimma* system, 5n21; *Libro de las Tahurerías*, 74n98; mendicant friars and, 143; Miranda, *portero* granted to Jews of, 216; moneylending and, 16, 164–65, 175–76, 188, 189, 190–94; papacy and conciliar legislation on Jews, 110–11, 112; royal donations of Jewish taxes to church under, 94, 98–99; Sahagún, dispute between Jews and abbot in, 142, 168–69; *Las siete partidas*, 85, 164, 165, 166, 175, 180, 182n51, 185–87, 191, 208n149; tax hike on *aljamas* under, 16, 175, 193–94, 204–5

Alfonso XI of Castile: *aljama* economy, policies aimed at reviving, 194; *captio* issued by, 214; charter of privilege (1335) to Jews, 170–71, 174, 240; on collection of debts owed to Jews, 122, 194–95, 210, 214, 217–19; cortes legislation and, 234, 236, 238–40, 243–47, 251–52, 255; death, 170; Fernando III's reign compared, 170, 171, 172; Jewish moneylending, ban on, 194, 233, 245–47, 249; Jewish tax collectors under, 126–27; prohibition on Christians as moneylenders, 191; royal donations of Jewish taxes to church, 94, 99n88, 101

Alfonso de Espina, 159n28

Alfonso de la Cerda, Infante, 137

Alfonso Núñez (royal judge), 119

Alfonso of Valladolid (formerly Abner of Burgos), 80, 158, 159

Algeciras: defeat of Muslims at, 170; misappropriation of funds for siege of, 163–64, 166, 193–94, 250

aljamas (self-governing Jewish communities): "battles of privileges" with *concejos*, 237–38, 247–49; Belorado, collection of debt in, 206–10; Camino, network of *aljamas* along, 64–65; categories and sizes, 68–71; Christian sources recognizing existence of, 44; cortes legislation, responses to, 237–40; fortifications of *judería* and, 48–49; *Libro de los fueros* and, 48–49; Miranda de Ebro, collection of debt in, 210–20; royal jurisdiction in, 50–51

almojarifes (treasurers): Jews as, 26, 27, 36, 124, 153, 171, 249–51

Almoravid (bishop of Calahorra), 86

altars: Jewish rents assigned for illumination of, 95

Alvaro Carillo (bishop of Palencia), 137, 138, 139

Alvito (bishop of León), 21, 95

Amador de los Ríos, José, 141n35

Annales Toledanos, 25n21

anti-Jewish discourse: *caballeros villanos* and, 231–33; church in Spain and, 84–89, 130–31, 146–47; collection of debts and, 196, 205; deicide, Jews accused of, 224–25; of Enrique II of Trastámara and Civil War of 1360s, 16, 146, 221–22, 226, 227, 249, 252–53; growing estrangement between Christians and Jews from late thirteenth century, 11–12, 171–74; host desecration,

223, 224n9, 225; "Jew" as insult, 177; Martínez, Ferrán, inflammatory preaching of, 86, 145–47, 260; monarchy, policies of, 11–12, 16, 84, 174–78, 195; moneylending and, 176–77, 224–25; ritual murder, 85–86, 186, 223, 224n9, 225. *See also* cortes legislation

anti-rationalism/rationalism debate, 152–55

Aragon: attacks on Jews in, 9–10, 146, 147, 260n137; church and Jews in, 80, 83n24, 89n45, 111, 116, 128, 131, 143–45; collection of debt in, 208n148; conversion to Christianity in, 159; cortes legislation, Jewish responses to, 239; fiscal pressures on Jews, 176; *fueros*, 29, 42; Kabbalah in, 15, 152; moneylending in, 111, 121, 195; Muslim soldiers recruited by, 38n71; public offices, dismissal of Jews from, 171; royal jurisdiction over Jews in, 30–31n43, 34, 36–37, 38, 100n91, 166–67; social tensions in Jewish *aljamas*, 152, 160, 162n41

Asher ben Yehiel (rabbi; Rosh), 154–55, 161n38, 166

Assis, Yom Tov, 34, 83n24, 161, 176

Astorga: Camino's role in Jewish life and, 68, 70; *Castro de los judíos* in, 56; collection of debts in, 197–98, 201n124; Jewish carpenter in, 70n83; moneylenders in, 70; royal donations of Jewish taxes to ecclesiastical bodies, 101n96

Astudillo, 102

Atienza, 100n94, 181

attacks on/massacres of Jews: Alfonso XI's charter of privileges and, 171; Algeciras, punishments associated with misappropriation of funds for siege of, 163–64, 166, 193–94, 250; cortes legislation and, 227, 260–61; by English mercenaries under Black Prince, 228; under Enrique II of Trastámara and Civil War of 1360s, 227–29, 260; Haro *judería*, sacking of, 187n74, 212n158; Martínez, Ferrán, inflammatory sermons of, 145–47; Miranda de Ebro, attacks on *judería*, 219;

under Queen Urraca, 25–26, 55, 133; reconquest affecting, 55; synagogues destroyed, 27, 95, 131, 145, 228; synagogues turned into churches, 86; in Toledo (1110), 25, 55; in Toledo (1335), 227; violence of 1391, 86, 146, 147, 260–61

Augustine of Hippo and Augustinian doctrine, 77, 85, 124

Ávila, 26, 72, 98, 158–59n28, 228n22

Los Bachilleres de los Ciento, 71–72

badges and signs. *See* dress requirements and distinguishing signs

Baer, Fritz (Yitzhak), 14, 43–44n100, 57, 159, 161, 162, 163, 164, 171, 172, 193n100

Baeza, 46n113

Bano Papieto, 109

Barcelona, 153, 160–61, 163, 167

Barcelona Disputation (1263), 79–80, 144

Baron, Salo, 10

Barton, Thomas, 34

bastonarios (judicial combatants), 22–23

Bejár, 46n113

Belorado: after 1391, 261; Camino's role in Jewish life and, 64, 65, 70, 206; city taxes, Jewish contributions to, 45; collection of debt in, 206–10, 243; *fuero*, 42, 58, 59; *judería* and *aljama* of, 206–7; moneylenders in, 70; royal fortifications, Jewish payments for upkeep, 57; San Miguel de Pedroso monastery, Jews as witnesses for, 60; semi-urban settlements of Jews, 7; urban boom along Camino de Santiago, 4

Bembibre, 68

Benedictines, 82, 101

Berenguela (queen of Castile), 32

Bertrand du Guesclin, 228

Bianchini, Janna, 32

Black Death, 170

"Black Legend," 9

Black Prince (Edward, Prince of Wales), 228

blacksmithing, 61

Blanca of Portugal (abbess of Las Huelgas de Burgos), 117

blasphemy prohibitions and punishments, 183
Bonfil, Robert, 6n23
Boniface VIII (pope), 137
Book of the Bahir, 156
Briviesca: after 1391, 261; attacks on Jews in, 228n22; Camino's role in Jewish life and, 64, 66, 70; city taxes, Jewish contributions to, 45; *fuero*, 41, 58; Jewish physician in, 70n83; moneylenders in, 70; royal donations of Jewish taxes to ecclesiastical bodies, 100–101; royal fortifications, Jewish payments for upkeep, 57; semi-urban settlements of Jews, 7; on subsidiary Camino route, 54
Buitrago, 181
Burgos (city): *adelantados* (elders) in *aljama* of, 169; after 1391, 261; Alfonso X, *Fuero real* legislation of, 181; anti-rationalism in, 153–54; *caballeros villanos*, emergence of, 173–74; Camino's role in Jewish life and, 54, 64, 66–68, 70–71; cathedral and chapter, 1, 101n96, 127, 143; city taxes, Jewish contributions to, 45; collection of debts owed to Jews, 122–23; cortes legislation in, 239; Dominicans, 143; exemption of Jews from city taxes, dispute over, 248–49; *fuero*, 48; Hospital del Emperador, 22, 73, 96, 111; Hospital del Rey, 2, 60, 93, 123, 192; importance to history of Jewish experience in medieval Iberia, 6–7; jurisdiction over Jews by Las Huelgas, 97–98; mixed Jewish-Muslim-Christian community, 1–2, 72–73; population of, 68n77, 69; prohibition of gambling houses in, 56n17; royal fortifications, Jewish payments for upkeep, 57; San Pedro de Cardeña (Cluniac monastery), 1; Santa Clara de Burgos, 229n24; Santa María la Real (Las Huelgas; Cistercian convent), 1, 62, 63, 83, 90, 92, 93, 97–98, 100, 117, 123; separate *alcaldes* for Jews, dispute over, 71, 202–5, 237, 248; size and importance of Jewish community, 64, 67–68, 70–71; St. Clare, order of, 102; tanneries, Hospital del Rey, 2, 93; tax collection by Jews, 127–28; Tenebregosa Street (*judería*), 1; thirty *dineros* tax in, 109; tithes on Jews in, 109–11, 127; urban boom along Camino de Santiago and, 1–2, 4, 19; usury investigation in, 191–92; viticulture in area of, 62–63
Burgos, Francisco Cantera, 53, 210
Burns, Robert L., 5n21

caballeros villanos (urban knights): anti-Jewish sentiments of, 231–33; cortes, townsmen in, 32, 230–31; descendants of foreign merchants, 59; emergence of, 173–74; royal alliance with, 12; as tax collectors, 250; tax exemptions, 45n106
Cáceres, 177n31
Çag de Haro (royal official), 125–26
Çag de la Maleha (Alfonso X's tax collector), 163, 193, 250
Çag el Levi (tax collector of Burgos), 66
Çag Merdohay (tax collector), 68
Çag Nihoray (of Palencia), 140
Çahagui/Çaguy Pardo (Jewish creditor of Miranda), 213, 215
Calahorra, 56, 67, 68, 109–10
Calatalifa charter (1141), 20, 31
Calatrava, 36
Camino de Santiago, 14, 53–74; "castles" and fortified settlements, Jews living in, 27, 48–49, 55–58, 63; economic and urban boom along, 1–2, 4, 19, 42, 54; Jewish population numbers, 58–59, 67–71; mingling of Jews, Christians, and Muslims, 71–74; origins of Jewish settlement in, 53–55; pilgrims on, 1–2, 53–54, 72–73, 96; role of road network in lives of Jews, 64–68; trade and commercial activities, 59–61, 65–66; violence between Jews and Christians, *fuero* provisions for, 58–59; viticulture, 61–63. *See also specific cities and towns*
Cantar de mío Cid, 189–90

INDEX

Cantigas de Santa María (attrib. Alfonso X), 225–26
captiones limiting collection of debts, 214, 244
Caro Dugo, María Auxiliadora, 44n104
Carrión: attacks on Jews in, 25, 55, 133; on Camino route, 54; fuero, 169; Karaite Judaism in, 35–36; San Zoilo de Carrión (monastery), 120; tax payments from, 68n76; urban boom along Camino de Santiago and, 4
cartas de personería, 234n41
Castile and León: Edict of 1492 expelling Jews, 19, 124, 260; ethnic and religious mix in, 1–2, 4, 59. See also Jews and Christians in medieval Northern Castile; monarchy; reconquest; and specific cities and towns
"castles" and fortified settlements, Jews living in, 27, 48–49, 55–58, 73–74
Castriello (Castil de Judíos), 56n17, 68, 73
Castro, Américo, 8
Castrojeriz (Castil de Judíos), 4, 6n24, 54n5, 55
Castro Urdiales, 100, 127
Catlos, Brian, 9n36, 84n25
Cea, 55, 68, 133
Christian names: Jews forbidden to use, 188, 254, 255, 256
Christians and Christianity: Alfonso X, collaboration of Christian and Jewish scholars under, 157–58, 178; debts to moneylenders, disinclination to pay, 189–90, 202; Fuero real, crimes against Christianity in, 183–84; jizya poll tax of Muslim rulers on Christians and Jews, 37; Kabbalah and, 156–60; mingling of Jews, Christians, and Muslims, 71–74; moneylending, Christian views on, 114–15; moneylending, forbidden to Christians, 112, 114, 164–65, 175–76, 190–92, 195; sexual relations, cross-cultural, 160, 165–66, 182, 187; social interactions between Jews and non-Jews, restrictions on, 160, 165–66, 182, 184, 186–87, 188,
254–57; tithes on Jewish properties formerly owned by Christians, 103, 104–8, 109–11, 127. See also church and Jews in Northern Castile; Jews and Christians in medieval Northern Castile
church and Jews in Northern Castile, 14–15, 258; anti-Jewish discourse and, 84–89, 130–31, 146–47; concejos, Jews siding against ecclesiastical bodies with, 140–41; jurisdiction over Jews granted by crown to ecclesiastical bodies, 96–98, 141–42; land acquisitions and economic contacts between clergy and Jews, 89–93; leasing of monastic estates as means of paying debts, 119–20; mendicant orders in Spain, 15, 79, 88, 94, 102, 131, 143–44, 158; missionizing and polemics, 15, 77, 79–81, 131, 134–35, 142–45; reconquest and, 82–83; religious controversy with Jews, reluctance to engage in, 83–84; royal grants of Jewish revenues to ecclesiastical bodies, 5–6, 21–22, 26–28, 82–84, 94–102; royal jurisdiction over Jews and, 89; tax collectors, Jewish, 123–30; theoretical discourse compared to lived experience, 77–82. See also church councils; moneylending; Palencia; papacy and conciliar legislation on Jews
church councils: Lateran III (1179), 184; Lérida (1229), 87; Montpelier (1195), 184; Palencia (1388), 87; Paris (1213), 184; Rouen (1074), 183–84; Salamanca (1335), 87; Tarragona (1239), 87, 184; Valladolid (1228), 87, 107; Valladolid (1322), 87, 130; Vienne (1311–12), 85n30, 87, 114, 121; Zamora (1312–13), 15, 87, 121, 122, 130, 244, 255. See also Fourth Lateran Council
Cidellus (Joseph ha Nasi ben Ferruziel), 24, 35
Cisneros, 25, 55, 68
Cistercians, 82, 101
Civil War of 1360s. See Enrique II of Trastámara and Civil War of 1360s
Clare, St., order of, 102
Clement V (pope), 112

Cluniac order, 95
Cohen, Jeremy, 183n52
Cohen, Mark, 5–6n22
coinage and currency, xi, 11, 173
collection of debts, 196–220; anti-Jewish discourse and, 196, 205; in Belorado, 206–10, 243; *captiones* limiting, 214, 244; communal consent and legislation, 198–200, 206; contract regulating, 65; cortes legislation and, 122, 239, 240, 242–45; disinclination of Christians to pay, 189–90, 202; from ecclesiastical sources, 121–23; fiscal pressure from monarchy and, 16, 169, 192, 194–95, 204–5, 212; intercommunal processes for, 196–98; Jewish *alcaldes*, disputes regarding, 202–5; *merinos*, 193, 198, 200, 208, 211, 215, 216, 218, 219; in Miranda de Ebro, 210–20, 243; old or long-term debts, 202–5, 242–43; property transactions covering, 196–98, 200–202; from single women and widows, 200–201. *See also entregas* and *entregadores*; *porteros*
commercial activities, merchants, and trade, 59–61, 65–66
communal life. *See* cultural, religious, and communal life after 1250
concejos (municipal councils): *aljamas* compared, 44; "battles of privileges" with *aljamas*, 237–38, 247–49; Belorado, collection of debt in, 206–10; Burgos, judges for mixed cases in, 71, 202–5, 237; *caballeros villanos*, 173, 231; *fueros* generally granting right to form, 42; Jews siding against ecclesiastical institutions with, 140–41; Miranda de Ebro, collection of debt in, 210–20; Palencian episcopate, *concejo*'s dispute with, 15, 132, 135–41; royal power versus, 23; *vecinos*, rights and duties of, 44–46. *See also* taxation paid to *concejo*
conciliar legislation. *See* papacy and conciliar legislation on Jews
Constable, Olivia Remie, 121n69, 196n108
conversion: to Christianity, 80, 86, 144, 146, 158, 159, 226, 245; to Islam, 185; to Judaism, 183, 185
convivencia, 2, 8–9, 16, 178–79n34
Córdoba: conquest of, 38, 151, 178; *Fuero juzgo* granted to, 179; *fuero of* Fernando III, 181; tithes on Jews in, 110
Coria, 40n80, 41, 177n31
cortes legislation, 16, 221–57, 258; Alfonso X's legislation affecting, 187–89; analysis of, 240–41; as anti-Jewish discourse, 221–30; attacks on Jews and, 227, 260–61; *caballeros villanos*, 173–74; *cartas de personería*, 234n41; "castles" of Jews and Muslims, proposals to appropriate, 16; Christian names, Jews forbidden to use, 188, 254, 255, 256; church involvement in, 87–88; collection of debts and, 122, 239, 240; customary Castilian privileges and norms, willingness to overthrow, 256–57; dress requirements and distinguishing signs, 188, 236, 254–57; Enrique II of Trastámara and Civil War of 1360s, 221–22, 226, 227, 249, 252–53, 256, 261; inclusion of townsmen in cortes, 32, 230–31; Jewish responses to, 237–40; Martínez, Ferrán, and, 146–47; moneylending and, 112, 177, 188–89, 190, 232–33, 235, 241–49; on public offices, 249–53; representative nature of *procuradores* at, 233–34n41; royal control of, 231, 234–37; social origins of anti-Jewish sentiments of, 230–37; social separation measures, 254–57; tax exemptions for Jews, 45; tax farmers/collectors, Jews as, 129, 232, 249–52; wet-nurse prohibitions, 188, 235, 254, 255, 256. *See also cuadernos*
credit. *See* collection of debts; moneylenders and moneylending
Crónica del rey don Pedro Primero (Pero López de Ayala), 219
cuadernos (cortes legislation booklets), 16, 93, 178, 222–24, 226–27, 230, 234–37, 240–41
Cuenca: adoption of Code by other towns, 46; conquest of, 27; *fuero*, 28–29, 31, 39, 40, 41, 43–46, 48, 51

cultural, religious, and communal life after 1250, 15–16, 151–69; European/Ashkenazi orbit, move into, 152–56; Kabbalah, 15–16, 151, 155–63; messianic movements, 157, 158–59; rationalism/anti-rationalism debate, 152–55; reconquest, migration south after, 151–52, 172; royal control of Jewish communal affairs, 152, 166–69; sexual relations, cross-cultural, 160, 165–66, 182, 187; social interactions between Jews and non-Jews, restrictions on, 160, 165–66, 182, 184, 186–87, 188, 254–57; social tensions and social reform within *aljamas*, 152, 160–66
currency and coinage, xi, 11, 173

David of Haro (witness), 64–65
debt collection. *See* collection of debts
Decretales of Gregory IX, 185n67
deicide, Jews accused of, 224–25
dhimma system, 3n10, 5
Diago Martínez (debtor in Miranda), 213n159, 214
Diago Pérez (public scribe of Haro), 213, 215
Diego (bishop of León), 95
Diego López de Haro, lord of Vizcaya, 212
dietary laws, Jewish, 61, 69, 160
diezmos de los ganados (tithe on livestock), 67
distinguishing signs. *See* dress requirements and distinguishing signs
Domingo Cabrero de Villada, 90
Domingo García de Luna, 198n116
Domingo Laínez, and wife, 58n24, 61
Dominic, St., 132, 134–35
Dominicans: Franciscans, preaching agreement with, 144; missionizing of Jews and, 79, 80, 88, 131, 142–45; in Palencia, 88, 131, 132, 134–35, 142–45; royal donations of Jewish revenues to, 89n45, 102; royal patronage of, 143–44; on usury, 111
dominus villae or *señor*, 47, 49–51
dress requirements and distinguishing signs: Alfonso X, legislation of, 187, 188, 254; cortes legislation on, 188, 236, 254–57; Fourth Lateran Council on, 33, 80–81, 103, 105–6, 172; in France, 236
Dueñas, 68, 92, 97, 100–101

ecclesiastical institutions. *See* church and Jews in Northern Castile
Edict of 1492 expelling Jews, 19, 124
Edward, Prince of Wales (Black Prince), 228
Edward I of England, 29n37, 85
Edward the Confessor, Laws of, 34
Elukin, Jonathan, 10n39
England: fiscal pressures on Jews in, 176; mercenaries under Black Prince, attacks on Jews by, 228; royal jurisdiction over Jews in, 34–35; *servi regis* principle in, 29; urban settlements, Jewish preference for, 6n23, 67n74
Enrique II Trastámara of Castile and Civil War of 1360s: anti-Jewish rhetoric of, 16, 146, 221–22, 226, 227, 249, 252–53, 256; attacks on Jews and, 227–29, 260; on collection of debts by Jews, 220; cortes legislation and, 221–22, 226, 227, 249, 252–53, 256, 261; invasion of Castile by, 16, 101; Jewish military resistance against, 57n20, 74n99; Martínez, Ferrán, inflammatory preaching of, 145; Miranda de Ebro, attacks on *judería*, 219; royal donations of Jewish taxes to church, 33n53, 83, 94, 101, 102
Enrique III of Castile, 145–46
entregas and *entregadores* (professional collection of old debts to Jews): in Belorado and Miranda de Ebro, 208, 210–16, 218–19; cortes legislation and, 236, 240, 242, 244, 246, 249; ecclesiastical use of Jewish credit, 122–23, 130; *porteros* distinguished, 192n97; royal policies and, 175–76, 192–93, 198–200, 202–3, 205
Espéculo (Alfonso X), 164, 181n43
Estow, Clara, 252n118
Etsi iudaeos (papal bull, 1205), 108
expulsions: Edict of 1492, 19, 124, 260; Gonzalo Martínez de Oviedo's proposal for Jews from Castile (1339), 245n88; of Jews from France, 1; Louis IX threatening

expulsions (cont.)
  Jews (1253), 246; of Muslims from Castile, 172, 178

Fancy, Hussein, 38n71
Fernando I of León, 5n20, 21–22, 82, 94–95
Fernando II of Aragon, 171
Fernando II of León, 27, 116
Fernando III of Castile: Alfonso XI's reign compared, 170, 171, 172; Burgos, judges for mixed cases in, 204; Córdoba *fuero*, 181; grants of Jewish jurisdiction to ecclesiastical bodies, 97; *Libro de los fueros* and, 48; papacy and conciliar legislation on Jews, 33, 105, 106, 108–9, 172, 255; reconquest triumphs of, 170, 171, 178; revenue from Jewish taxes, 33; translation of Visigothic code, 179
Fernando IV of Castile: Belorado, collection of debt in, 207, 209–10; cortes legislation and, 239, 248; disputed succession, 119, 137; *fuero* of Haro confirmed by, 187n74; grants of Jewish taxes to ecclesiastical bodies, 94, 98n83, 99n88, 100–102; mendicant orders and, 144; Miranda, collection of debt in, 216, 217, 218; Palencia, dispute between bishop and *concejo* in, 137, 138, 139, 140, 141n36; on royal income from Jews, 194, 209
Fernán González, count of Castile, 6n24, 54
Ferrant Martínez (of Miranda), 213, 215
Ferrant Yuannes (suitor), 60
fonsadera (tax paid in lieu of military obligation), 45, 125–26, 135
foreign settlement in northern Castile, 4, 59
fortified settlements and "castles," Jews living in, 27, 48–49, 55–58, 73–74
Forum iudicum/Liber iudicum (Visigothic Code), 5, 41n86, 179
fossataria (payment in lieu of military service), 22
Fourth Lateran Council (1215), 103–8; on blasphemy, 183; Castilian resistance to edicts of, 15, 104–8; dress requirements for Jews, 33, 80–81, 103, 105–6, 172; *Fuero real* of Alfonso X and, 181; heavy and immoderate usury condemned by, 103, 107, 115, 121; on Jews holding public offices, 124, 128; tithes on Jewish properties formerly owned by Christians, 103, 104–8
Frago Gracia, Juan Antonio, 46n112
France: badge required of Jews, 236, 255; edict of 1253 ordering Jews to live by labor or commerce, 246; expulsion of Jews from, 1; fiscal pressures on Jews in, 176; royal jurisdiction over Jews in, 34, 35; *servi regis* principle in, 29; trade and commercial activities of Jews in, 60; urban settlements, Jewish preference for, 6n23
Franciscans, 80, 102, 111, 144, 157
Frederick I Barbarossa (Holy Roman Emperor), 29n37
Frederick II (Holy Roman Emperor), 29
freedom of worship: Alfonso X's legislation protecting, 182, 186
Frómista, 68n76, 120
frontier, concept of, 2–4
Fuencisla G. Casar, María, 44n104
Fuero juzgo, 179, 181, 183
Fuero real legislation of Alfonso X, 7, 39, 85, 164, 175, 180–85, 187–88, 190, 199, 234–35, 254
fueros, 39–52; Alfonso X, *Fuero real* legislation of, 7, 39, 85; on collection of debt, 199; conquest, expansionism, and colonization shaping terms of, 38; continuing use following *Fuero real* legislation, 187; defined and described, 4; *Libro de los fueros de Castilla*, 14, 31–32, 40–41, 48–52, 56, 57, 60, 168, 169n69, 188, 190, 199; published editions of, 14; relations between Jewish and Christian communities in, 42–46; royal involvement in urban affairs and Jewish civic status, 46–52; royal protection, agreement on Jews living under, 40; sections dedicated to Jews, 5, 7; variability of Jewish

provisions in, 39–42; violence between Jews and Christians, provision for, 58–59. *See also specific towns*

Galinsky, Judah, 154n11, 154n13, 161n38
gambling prohibitions, 56n17, 73
García (bishop of Burgos), 127
Garcia de Valdeavellano, Luis, 21n6
García-Gallo, Alfonso, 181n43
García Martínez (*alcalde* of Miranda de Ebro), 211–13, 215
García Sánchez de Maderuelo and wife, 119–20
García-Serrano, Francisco, 131
García y García, Antonio, 86–87
Garçi Ferrandez de Villamayor (royal governor), 207, 215
Gerardo (bishop of Palencia), 141n36
Germany: jurisdiction over Jews by ecclesiastical bodies in, 97n79; royal jurisdiction over Jews in, 34; *servi regis* principle in, 29–30
Gerona, 155
Gerondi, Jonah (rabbi), 153, 167n63
"golden age" of Jews in Iberia, 11
Gonzalo (bishop of Burgos), 110–11
Gonzalo de Berceo: *Los milagros de nuestra señora*, 85–86
Gonzalo García Gudiel (archbishop of Toledo), 122
Gonzalo Martínez de Oviedo, 245n88
Gregory IX (pope), 107–9, 111–13, 121, 128, 133–34, 185n67
Guillaume de Broue, 84
Guillermo (abbot of San Benito de Sahagún), 90–91
Gutierre (abbot of San Benito de Sahagún), 77–78, 89
Gutierre de Toledo (bishop of Oviedo), 86

Hames, Harvey, 79
Haro: Camino's role in Jewish life and, 66, 70; "castle" given to Jews of, 56, 57; cortes of, 232, 250; *fuero*, 14, 40, 42, 47, 51, 57, 187n74, 188; moneylenders of, 66, 70; 211, 212, 215, 217; sacking of *judería* (1288), 187n74, 212n158
Hasidei Ashkenaz, 156
Hatton, Vicki, 226n13
Haui Moreno (representing Jewish creditors of Miranda), 215–16
hekdesh, 161
Henry II of England, 34–35
Hernández, Francisco, 194
Honorius (Byzantine emperor), 123
Honorius III (pope), 33, 104–6, 172
Horna, 200–201
Hoscrispe, 118
host desecration, accusations of, 223, 224n9, 225
Huete, Partition of (1290), 67–68, 70, 73n96

ibn Daud, Abraham: *Sefer ha-Qabbalah* (1161), 35–36
ibn Ezra, Judah, 26, 36
ibn Ezra, Moses, 26
ibn Salib, Yishaq, 24
ibn Shoshan, Joseph, 27
infurción (tax paid by Jews jointly with *concejo*), 45
inheritance laws, 184–85, 194, 195, 249
Innocent III (pope), 103–4, 106, 108, 186n70
Innocent IV (pope), 109
internal frontier, concept of, 3–4
Iohan Mathe of Burgos, 125
Isaac ben Solomon Ibn Sadoq, 193n100
Isaac ha-Cohen (rabbi), 155, 156
Isaac the Blind (rabbi), 155
Isabel I of Castile, 171
Isidore of Seville, 77, 95
Islam. *See* Muslim kingdoms in Iberia; Muslims in Castile
Israel Israeli of Toledo (rabbi), 154
Italy: Genoa, tribute paid by Jews for St. Lorenzo in, 95n70; Papal States, Jews in, 84; urban settlements, Jewish preference for, 6n23
Iuçe Finistriella (representative of cathedral chapter of Calahorra), 92
iudex (judge), 44, 45, 51n141

Iuseph de Levanza (seller of mill rights), 61
Iznatoraf, 28n35, 46n113

Jacob ha-Cohen (rabbi), 155, 156
Jaén, 98, 228
James I of Aragon, 144, 167, 244n81
Jerez, cortes legislation in, 188, 190, 235, 255
Jewish law, fines for violations of, 50
Jewish responses to powers in Christian society, 258–59; cortes legislation, 237–40; royal jurisdiction, 35–37, 168–69; taxes, imposition of, 36–37, 166
Jews and Christians in medieval Northern Castile, 1–16, 257–61; central role of northern regions, 1–8; conquest, expansionism, and colonization shaping relationship, 38; *convivencia*, 2, 8–9, 16, 178–79n34; diachronic approach to, 9–12; documentation issues and source materials, 8, 12–14; Edict of 1492 expelling Jews, 19, 124, 260; growing estrangement from late thirteenth century, 11–12; mingling of, 71–74; semi-urban settlements, Jews inhabiting, 6–7. *See also* anti-Jewish discourse; Camino de Santiago; Christians and Christianity; church and Jews in Northern Castile; cortes legislation; cultural, religious, and communal life after 1250; monarchy
jizya poll tax of Muslim rulers, 37
Joachim of Fiore, 157
Johan Urtiz (of Miranda), 213
John of Abbeville, 87n39, 106, 107
Jordan, William Chester, 30n40, 208n149
Joseph ha-Nasi ben Ferruziel (Cidellus), 24, 35
Juan (bishop of Burgos), 117
Juan, Infante (son of Alfonso X and regent to Alfonso XI), 101n96, 137, 236, 251
Juan I: anti-Jewish discourse of, 146–47; Martínez, Ferrán, inflammatory preaching of, 145
Juan Alfonso (bishop of Palencia), 136, 139
Juan de Padilla (lessee of monastic land), 120
Juçef Haraçon (of Burgos), 63

Judah ben Asher (rabbi), 155, 161n38
juderías: "castles" and fortified settlements, Jews living in, 27, 48–49, 55–58, 73–74; mingling of Jews, Christians, and Muslims, 71–74; segregation, trend towards, 73, 188, 256
judicial combat, 23–24
Justinian I (Byzantine emperor): *Corpus iuris* of, 180
Juzme of Haro (moneylender), 213n159, 214

Kabbalah, 15–16, 151, 155–63
Karaite Judaism in Castile, 35–36, 166
Kimhi, David, 153–54
Kisch, Guido, 29
Klein, Elka, 153n6, 167
Kriegel, Maurice, 30n40

"lachrymose conception of Jewish history," 10, 171
Ladero Quesada, Miguel Ángel, 4n19
land. *See* real property
Langmuir, Gavin, 30
Laredo, 127
Las Navas de Tolosa, battle of (1212), 27, 32, 38, 151
Lateran III (1179), 184
Lateran IV. *See* Fourth Lateran Council
leasing of monastic estates for paying money debts, 119–20
León (city): *aljama*'s negotiations with *concejo*, 71, 237–38; Camino's role in Jewish life and, 54, 65, 66; *Castro de los judíos* near, destruction of, 27, 55–56, 62n48, 95; cathedral of, 229n24; *fuero*, 54–55; mingling of Jews, Christians, and Muslims, 71–72; royal grant of Jewish revenues to church of Santa María de, 21–22; San Miguel de Escalada, 128–29; Santa María de León, 95, 116; Santa María de Otero (convent), 119; Santa María de Regla, 92; urban boom along Camino de Santiago and, 1–2, 4, 19; viticulture, 62
León Tello, Pilar, 98, 223n7
Lérida, legatine council of (1229), 87

INDEX

Lerma, 42n90, 64, 68
Lewis, Archibald, 3–4n14
Liber iudicum. *See Forum iudicum*
Libro de las Tahurerías (Alfonso X), 74n98
Libro de los fueros de Castilla, 14, 31–32, 40–41, 48–52, 56, 57, 60, 168, 169n69, 188, 190, 199
Libros de Repartimiento (land registers), 151
Liebes, Yehuda, 157n23, 163n45
Linehan, Peter, 138n26, 143
Llerena, 240
Llorente, don (butcher in León), 72
Logroño, 4, 54, 68, 216n166
Lope Días de Haro, 187n74, 206n142, 250
Louis IX of France, 29n37, 84, 85, 246
Lull, Raymond, 79, 80

MacKay, Angus, 226n13
Madrid, 40, 205n140, 245, 247, 251
Mael (or Mair) and Merian (mill owners, in Aguilar de Campóo), 61
Maimonides (Moses ben Maimon) and Maimonidean rationalism, 16, 152, 153; *Mishneh Torah*, 153; *Treatise on Resurrection*, 153
Mansilla de las Mulas, 65, 66, 68, 92
Marcus, Ivan: *Rituals of Childhood*, 9
María de Molina, 137, 244, 251
Marinids, 170, 171
Martín Domínguez (canon at León and Astorga), 116–17
Martín Martínez (of Miranda), 213
Martin of León, St., 77, 78, 89
Martín Pérez (canon at León), 117n51
Martínez, Ferrán (inflammatory anti-Jewish preacher), 86, 145–47, 260
Martínez, H. Salvador, 178–79n34
Martínez Díez, Gonzalo, 42n91, 181n43, 181n45
Martini, Raymond, 79
martiniega (tax paid by Jews jointly with *concejo*), 45
massacres. *See* attacks on/massacres of Jews
Mauricio (bishop of Burgos), 105, 106–8, 111
Mayorga, 68

Medina de Pomar, 7, 59, 64, 68, 70, 118, 200
Meir bar Simon of Narbonne: *Milhemet Mizvah*, 114, 115
Melechen, Nina, 117n52, 119n62
Melun, Ordinance of (1230), 29n37
mendicant orders in Spain, 15, 79, 88, 94, 102, 131, 143–44, 158. *See also specific orders*
merchants. *See* commercial activities
merino major (regional royal representative), 193, 200, 218
merinos (royal officials): collection of debt and, 198, 208, 211, 215, 216, 219; enforcing tithes, 110; *fueros* on, 49, 51; in Palencia, 137; tax collection cases and, 126
messianic movements, 157, 158–59
Meyerson, Mark, 11n40, 30–31n43, 176, 260
Miceli, Paola, 41n86
migration of Jews south after reconquest, 151–52, 172
Miguel (abbot of Santa María la Real, Aguilar de Campóo), 61
Los milagros de nuestra señora (Gonzalo de Berceo), 85–86
Milhemet Mizvah (Meir bar Simon of Narbonne), 114, 115
mill rights, 61
Milton, Gregory B., 191n93
minyan, 69
Miranda de Ebro: after 1391, 261; attacks on *judería* (1360), 219, 228; Camino's role in Jewish life and, 55, 64–65, 68–71; collection of debt in, 210–20, 243; foreigners settling in, 59; *fuero*, 216n166; Jewish tailor in, 70n83; *judería* and *aljama* of, 206; semi-urban settlements, Jews inhabiting, 7
missionizing and polemics, 15, 77, 79–81, 131, 134–35, 142–45. *See also* conversion
mixed Christian-Jewish cases: separate *alcaldes*, 202–5; witness testimony in, 43, 47, 107, 169, 172, 197
monarchy, ca. 1050–ca. 1250, 14, 19–52, 257–58; compared to others in Europe, 33–35, 37–38; conquest, expansionism, and colonization shaping, 38; ecclesiastical

301

monarchy (cont.)
  bodies, royal grants of Jewish revenues to, 5–6, 21–22, 26–28, 82–84, 94–102; ecclesiastical jurisdiction over Jews granted by, 96–98, 141–42; evolution of royal jurisdiction over Jews, 5, 20–33; Jewish notables employed by, 24, 26, 27, 35, 124; Jewish responses to royal jurisdiction, 35–37; Jews as *servi regis*, 5, 28–32, 37–38, 45, 51; Jews employed as tax collectors/tax farmers, 66–67, 70, 123–30; moneylending, 84, 85; reconquest and, 5, 8, 12, 14, 24, 35; religious controversy with Jews, reluctance to engage in, 83–84; royal jurisdiction over Jews accepted by church, 89; settlement of Jews in municipalities on royal lands, 19–20. *See also fueros; and specific rulers*
  monarchy, ca. 1250–ca. 1370, 16, 170–220; anti-Jewish discourse and policies, 11–12, 16, 84, 174–78, 195; changing relationship with Jewish community, 170–78; collection of Jewish debts and, 196–220; cortes legislation and, 231, 234–37; fiscal pressures on Jews, 16, 169, 175–77, 189–95, 204–5, 212; Jewish communal affairs, tighter control of, 152, 166–69; Jewish notables employed by, 157–58, 163, 167; Jewish responses to royal jurisdiction, 168–69; Jews as *servi regis*, 174; legislative program of Alfonso X, 178–89; moneylending and fiscal pressure on Jews, 189–95. *See also* Alfonso X; collection of debt; *and specific rulers*
moneylenders and moneylending: Alfonso X and, 16, 164–65, 175–76, 188, 189, 190–94; anti-Jewish discourse and, 176–77, 224–25; biblical passages on, 113, 224–25; Camino's role in Jewish life and, 66, 70; Christians forbidden to lend at interest, 112, 114, 164–65, 175–76, 190–92, 195; Christian views on, 114–15; church and monarchy profiting from and restricting, 84, 85; cortes legislation and, 112, 177, 188–89, 190, 232–33, 235, 241–49;

Council of Vienne on, 114, 121; Council of Zamora on, 121, 122; ecclesiastical use of Jewish credit, 113–23; as economic necessity, 113, 115, 117, 121; fiscal pressure from monarchy and, 189–95; Fourth Lateran Council on, 103, 107, 115, 121; *Fuero real* on, 190; gentile intermediaries in intra-Jewish loans, 164; Gregory IX condemning, 111–13, 133–34; Jewish usury banned by Alfonso XI, 194, 233, 245–47, 249; Jewish views on, 113–14; leasing of monastic estates and, 119–20; origins of Jewish involvement, 60; rates, 111, 112, 121, 188–89, 190, 235, 242; social reforms of R. Abulafia concerning, 164–65; tax burdens affecting, 12, 193–94, 195. *See also* collection of debts
Monsalvo Antón, José, 223n7, 226n15, 233
Montpelier, Council of (1195), 184
Mose Abaltax (of Saldaña), 67, 70
Mose Amordosiel (of Burgos), 60
Mose of Pancorbo (witness), 64–65
Moses ben Maimon. *See* Maimonides
Moses ben Nahman (Nahmanides), 36, 153, 163n45
Moses ben Simeon of Burgos (rabbi), 155
Moses de León (rabbi), 157n23, 162–63
Mosse Aramas and wife Cinfa (creditors), 201–2
Moxó, Salvador de, 246
mudéjars. *See* Muslims in Castile
mules: petition to prevent Jews from riding, 65
Muneo, 118
Munio of Zamora (Dominican bishop of Palencia), 137, 138n26, 144
Muslim kingdoms in Iberia: Almoravid intolerance of Jews, 36, 54, 105; anti-Jewish measures and fears of Jews fleeing to, 105; Calatrava as Jewish refuge city, 36; concept of frontier, 3n11; dhimma system, 3n10, 5; Granada, 151, 171; jizya poll tax, 37; Marinids, 170, 171. *See also* reconquest
Muslims in Castile (*mudéjars*): in Burgos,

2; contracts with Christians, 9n36; expulsions of, 172, 178; *Fuero real* on, 182, 183, 184–85; mingling of Jews, Christians, and Muslims, 71–74; moneylending and, 191n93, 192, 245; Palencian community, 97, 136, 138; rebellion of mid-1260s, 172, 179; royal jurisdiction over, evolution of, 20; sexual relations, cross-cultural, 160, 165–66, 182, 187; as slaves, merchants, and refugees, 3; social interactions between Jews and non-Jews, 160, 165–66, 182, 184, 186–87, 188, 254–57; tithes on properties formerly owned by Christians, 104, 110

Nahmanides. *See* Moses ben Nahman
Nájera, 4, 54, 58, 68, 227
names, restrictions on, 188, 254, 255, 256
Netanyahu, Benzion, 226n15, 241n71, 260n137
Nicholas III (pope), 129–30
Nieto Soria, José Manuel, 99n88, 101n96
Nirenberg, David, 5n21, 9–10, 177
Novikoff, Alex, 80

O'Callaghan, Joseph, 38, 180n40
Oña, 7, 66, 68, 70, 125
Oro Sol and son, 61
Oviedo, 68, 86

Pablo Christiani (convert), 144
Pablo de Santa María, 159n28
Palencia (episcopal city), 15, 132–47; after 1391, 261; Alfonso X, *Fuero real* legislation of, 7, 181; assaults on Jews in, 25, 26; Camino's role in Jewish life and, 54, 66, 67, 68, 69; city taxes, Jewish contributions to, 45; *concejo*, episcopal dispute with, 15, 132, 135–41, 258; cortes of, 244, 248, 251; Dominicans in, 88, 131, 132, 134–35, 142–45; importance to history of Jewish experience in medieval Iberia, 6; missionizing of Jews in, 131, 134–35, 142–45; moneylending in, 133–34; origins and population of Jewish community, 8n31, 132–34; royal grant of jurisdiction over Jews to bishop of, 96–97, 101, 132, 136, 137, 139, 140–42; royal grants of Jewish revenues to, 33; San Pablo (Dominican monastery), 102, 135, 229n24; strong ecclesiastical presence, 134–35; taxation of Jews, 135–36; tax collection from Jews and Muslims, 135–36, 138; tax collectors, Jews as, 129; tower of bishop, burning of, 137, 138, 141n35

Palencia, legatine council of (1388), 87
Palenzuela, 66, 67, 68, 70
Pancorbo: Camino's role in Jewish life and, 66, 70; moneylenders of, 66, 70, 211, 212, 215, 217; semi-urban settlements, Jews inhabiting, 7; on subsidiary Camino route, 54; Villanueva de los Judíos/Villanueva de Pancorbo near, 57–58, 61
papacy and conciliar legislation on Jews, 15, 103–31; dress requirements, 33, 80–81, 103, 105–6, 172; Jewish credit, ecclesiastical use of, 113–23; Jewish tax collectors and, 123–30; proper place of Jews within Christian community, 103–4; public offices, exclusion of Jews from, 123–24, 128; royal assistance in enforcing, 104–6; royal income from Jews and resistance to, 33, 105, 106–8; thirty *dineros* tax, 108–9; tithes on Jewish properties formerly owned by Christians, 103, 104–8, 109–11, 127. *See also* moneylending; *and specific councils and popes*
papal bulls: *Etsi iudaeos* (1205), 108; *Sicut judeis* (1199), 186n70
Papal States, Jews in, 84
Paredes de Nava, 68, 228
parias (tributes paid by *taifa* kingdoms), 22
Paris, Council of (1213), 184
particiones, 67–68
Partition of Burgos (1286, 1287), 68, 194
Partition of Huete (1290), 67, 70, 73n96, 169n70, 187n74, 206, 213nn157–58
Patschovsky, Alexander, 29n39
Patton, Pamela, 226n13
Pedro (bishop of León), 95n70

Pedro, Infante (brother of Fernando IV), 28n33, 98n83, 244, 251
Pedro I of Castile: on collection of debt, 204–5n135, 219, 220n177; cortes legislation and, 225n12, 233n37, 245, 252–53, 255–56; ecclesiastical bodies, grants of Jewish revenues to, 94; English mercenaries, assaults on Jews by, 228; Enrique II, rebellion of, 221, 226, 227, 249, 252–53; Miranda de Ebro, attacks on *judería*, 219, 228; pro-Jewish reputation of, 252; on segregation of Jews, 73
Pedro II of Aragon, 27, 56
Pedro de San Esteban (priest), 118
Pedro Gomez Barroso (archbishop of Seville), 147
Pedro Lobónez of Valdelafuente, 202
Pedro of Briviesca, 98
Pedro Sarracín (dean of cathedral chapter of Burgos), 63, 91
Pedro Tenorio (archbishop of Toledo), 145n51
Pelagius (bishop of León), 95n70
Pelayo (bishop of Astorga), 90
Pelayo (bishop of León), 21
Peñafiel, 68, 181
Pero Ferrandez of Oña, 125
Pero López de Ayala, 219, 225, 227
"perpetual servitude," doctrine of, 108, 113, 124
Peter the Venerable of Cluny, 85
Philip II Augustus of France, 35
Philip IV the Fair of France, 1
Pick, Lucy, 89, 105
pogroms. *See* attacks on/massacres of Jews
polemics and missionizing. *See* missionizing
Polo Pérez (tax collector), 212, 214
population and community sizes, Jewish, 58–59, 67–71
portazgo (toll), 22, 65, 93, 96, 133
porteros (debt collectors): cortes legislation and, 242; *entregadores* distinguished, 192n97; fiscal pressure from monarchy and, 175, 181, 192, 200, 201n121, 211, 215, 216, 217; origins of, 60, 192

Post, Gaines, 231n29
Powers, James, 29n36
procuradores. *See* cortes legislation
property. *See* real property
Provence, Jews of, 1, 153–54
public offices: *albedí*, 44, 49, 169; *almojarifes*, Jews as, 26, 27, 36, 124, 153, 171, 249–51; cortes legislation on, 249–53; *dominus villae* or *señor*, 47, 49–51; *iudex*, 44, 45, 51n141; monarchy, Jewish notables employed by, 24, 26, 27, 35, 124, 157–58, 163, 167; papal/conciliar exclusions of Jews from, 123–24, 128; tax farmers/collectors, Jews as, 66–67, 70, 123–30, 232, 249–52; *vedín*, 49–51; *venditores*, 43. *See also alcaldes*; *entregas* and *entregadores*; *merinos*; *porteros*
Puente del Castro, 95

Quintana de la Cuesta, 118
Quintana Palaçio, 202
Quintanilla, 202

Ra'aya Mehemna, 161–62
Rabi and brother Cemal (rural property owner, Vegamediana), 62, 90
Rabi Çahagui/Çaguy (Jewish creditor of Miranda), 213, 215
Raimundo (bishop of Palencia), 28, 96–97, 133
Ramah. *See* Abulafia, Meir ha-Levi
Ramon Berenguer IV (count of Barcelona), 34
Ramon de Penyafort, 79, 144, 185n67
Ramon Despont (bishop of Valencia), 131
Rashi, 153n7
rationalism/anti-rationalism debate, 152–55
Ray, Jonathan, 10, 167, 174n18
real property: agriculturalists, efforts to turn Jews into, 246, 249; clergy and Jews, economic contacts between, 89–93; collection of debt and, 196–98, 200–202; inheritance laws, 184–85, 194, 195, 249; interfaith transactions, 60–62, 92, 126, 196–98; leasing of monastic estates as

means of paying debts, 119–20; *Libros de Repartimiento*, 151; prohibition on Jews buying land from Christian taxpayers, 172, 174; tithes on Jewish properties formerly owned by Christians, 103, 104–8, 109–11, 127

reconquest: attacks on Jews and, 55; changing status of Jews in Spain and, 172–73; church and, 82–83; Córdoba, conquest of, 38, 151, 178; Cuenca, conquest of, 27; historiographical interest in frontier and, 2–3; Las Navas de Tolosa, battle of, 27, 32, 38, 151; Marinids, 170, 171; migration of Jews south after, 151–52, 172; monarchy and, 5, 8, 12, 14, 24, 35; Nasrid kingdom of Granada, 171; relationship between Jews and Christians shaped by, 38; Seville, conquest of, 38, 48, 151, 178; taxation of Jews and, 5, 14, 35; Toledo, conquest of, 7–8, 22–23. *See also* cultural, religious, and communal life after 1250

rediezmo (extra tithe for church of Burgos), 127

Reilly, Bernard, 8n31, 25n21

religious life. *See* cultural, religious, and communal life after 1250

Rimado de palacio, Pero López de Ayala, 225

Rioturbio, 127

ritual murder, accusations of, 85–86, 186, 223, 224n9, 225

Rodrigo (bishop of Palencia), 118

Rodrigo Jiménez de Rada (archbishop of Toledo), 80–82, 89, 105–6

Rodrigo de Padrón (archbishop of Santiago de Compostela), 88n43

Rodríguez Fernández, Justiniano, 117n51

Roman law, 16, 41n86, 175, 179, 180, 208n149, 231n29, 234n41

Rosell, Cayetano, 14

Rosh. *See* Asher ben Yehiel

Roth, Norman, 31n44, 44n104, 171n5, 193n100

Rouen, Council of (1074), 183–84

Ruiz, Teofilo, 2n6, 69n79, 101n96, 109n20, 118n58, 179, 181n44, 185, 232

Sabbath observance, 164

Sahagún: Alfonso X, *Fuero real* legislation of, 7, 181; assaults on Jews in, 25, 26; Camino's role in Jewish life and, 54, 64, 65–66, 67, 68; dispute between *concejo* and abbot, 135, 140–41, 168–69, 258; *fuero*, 45n106, 169; importance to history of Jewish experience in medieval Iberia, 6; Jewish cemetery in, 78, 91; jurisdiction over Jews given to abbot of, 26–27, 96, 97, 140–41, 142; royal interference in Jewish affairs in, 168–69; San Benito de Sahagún (monastery), 26–27, 77–78, 89, 90–91, 93, 96, 135, 140–41, 168–69; urban boom along Camino de Santiago and, 4

Salado, 170

Salamanca, 41, 44–45n106, 110

Salamanca, Council of (1335), 87

Salamon del Portiello (monastic lessee), 92

Saldaña, 25, 55, 67, 70, 133

Salomón Atrugel (vineyard seller), 62, 90

Salomon Bien Veniste (tax collector of Burgos), 66

Samuel of Belorado (royal tax collector), 70, 125, 207, 212n157

Samuel the carpenter (of Astorga), 70n83, 194

Sánchez, Gálo, 48, 181n45

Sánchez-Albornoz, Claudio, 224

Sancho, don (brother of Enrique II), 206n142

Sancho III Garcés (el mayor) of Navarre, 54, 55, 82

Sancho IV of Castile: Burgos, judges for debt collection cases in, 71, 203–4; on collection of debt, 199–200, 205; cortes legislation and, 235, 242, 250; on *entregadores* in Toledo, 122; Haro *judería*, sacking of, 187n74, 212n158; Jewish tax collectors employed by, 124, 125–26; León *aljama*'s negotiations with *concejo*, 237–38; mendicant friars and, 144; Miranda, collection of debt in, 216, 217; Palencia, dispute between bishop and *concejo* in, 136, 138n26, 139; prohibition of gambling houses and *Castil de judíos*, 56n17; royal

Sancho IV of Castile (cont.)
  donations of Jewish taxes to church under, 94, 99–100; royal income from Jews under, 194, 195; as Infante Sancho, 110, 136, 163, 192, 193
San Esteban, 118
San Isidoro (monastery), 77
San Martín de Albelda, 100
San Miguel de Escalada (monastery), 201
San Millán de la Cogolla (monastery): land donated to, 58n24, 61
San Pedro de Arlanza (monastery), 119–20
San Salvador de Oña (monastery), 58n24, 125, 202
Santa Coloma de Queralt, 191n93
Santa María de Carracedo (monastery), 127
Santa María de Otero de las Dueñas (convent), 92
Santa María de Rioseco (Cistercian monastery), 118, 200
Santa María de Zamora (convent), 138n26
Santander, 127
Santo Domingo de la Calzada, 4
San Vicente de la Barquera, 127
Saperstein, Marc, 163
Saul of Mansilla (creditor), 201
Scholem, Gershom, 156n20, 157n23
Sefer ha-Qabbalah (ibn Daud), 35–36
sefirot, 156, 157
Segovia, 65, 110, 228
semi-rural settlements, Jews inhabiting, 6–7, 69–70
Semuel Franco (monastic lessee), 92
señales (earnest money), 208
señor or *dominus villae*, 47, 49–51
Sento Cidicaro (of Villadiego), 66, 67, 70
Septimus, Bernard, 152, 162, 163n45
servi regis: Jews as, 5, 28–32, 37–38, 45, 51, 112, 140, 174
Seville: Camino's role in Jewish life and, 66; conquest of, 38, 48, 151, 178; cortes of, 234; *Fuero juzgo* granted to, 179; Jewish settlement after reconquest, 151; Martínez, Ferrán, inflammatory preaching of, 145–47; tithes on Jews in, 110
sexual relations, cross-cultural, 160, 165–66, 182, 187
shochet, 69
shoe making regulations in León, 238
Sicut judeis (papal bull; 1199), 186n70
Las siete partidas (Alfonso X), 85, 164, 165, 166, 175, 180, 182n51, 185–87, 191, 208n149
signs and badges. *See* dress requirements and distinguishing signs
Simeon ben Yohai (rabbi), 157, 163n45
Simon, Larry, 5n21, 183n52
Simonsohn, Shlomo, 85n30
Sivan, Hagith, 4n18
social interactions between Jews and non-Jews: restrictions on, 160, 165–66, 182, 184, 186–87, 188, 254–57
social life. *See* cultural, religious, and communal life after 1250
Solomon ben Abraham of Montpelier, 153
Solomon ben Adret of Barcelona (rabbi), 36, 158n28, 167
Solomon ben Ferruziel, 24
Soria, 40n80, 155, 156, 181
Spiritual Franciscans, 157
Stacey, Robert, 67n74
Stow, Kenneth, 3n10, 225
Suárez Bilbao, Fernando, 5n20
Suárez Fernández, Luis, 260
Summa de Poenitentia (Ramon de Penyafort), 185n67
sumptuary legislation. *See* dress requirements and distinguishing signs
synagogues: community ability to support, 69; construction, enlargement, maintenance, and decoration, 86, 87, 107, 134, 145, 147; destruction of, 27, 95, 131, 145, 228; freedom to worship in, 186; locations, 72, 73; messianists assembling in, 158; turned into churches, 86

tanneries: Hospital del Rey, Burgos, 2, 93
Tariego, 68, 137
Tarragona, Council of (1239), 87, 184

Tartakoff, Paola, 159
taxation of Jews: debt collection and, 204–5, 212; ecclesiastical bodies, royal grants of Jewish revenues to, 5–6, 21–22, 26–28, 82–84, 94–102; estimating Jewish population from tax records, 67–68; evolution into royal prerogative, 5, 20–33; growing estrangement from Christian community and, 11–12; increasing rates of, 16, 175, 193–94, 195, 204–5; individual exemptions of wealthy Jews, 162; Jewish response to imposition of, 36–37, 166; Palencia, dispute between bishop and *concejo* in, 135–36, 138, 139, 140; papacy and conciliar legislation against Jews, royal resistance to, 33, 105, 106–8; significance of royal income from, 22–24, 32–33, 38, 170, 194; thirty *dineros* tax, 108–9; threats by Enrique II regarding, 229; tithes on Jewish properties formerly owned by Christians, 103, 104–8, 109–11, 127; Toledo, head tax on Jews in, 105–6, 108
taxation paid to *concejo*: *caballeros villanos* exempted, 45n106; Jewish duties and exemptions, 45, 248–49
taxes: *alcabala*, 66; *fonsadera*, 45, 125–26, 135; *fossataria*, 22; *infurción*, 45; *jizya* poll tax of Muslim rulers, 37; *martiniega*, 45; *parias*, 22; *portazgo*, 22, 65, 93, 96, 133; thirty *dineros* tax, 108–9. *See also* tithes
tax farmers/collectors, Jews as, 66–67, 70, 123–30, 232, 249–52
Tello (bishop of Palencia), 105, 106
tercias (third of tithe), 66, 99n89, 118, 203n130
Tertullian, 77
Teruel (Aragon), 29
testimony of witnesses in Christian-Jewish cases, 43, 47, 107, 169, 172, 197
Theodosian Code, 184n59
Third Lateran Council (1179), 184
thirty *dineros* tax, 108–9
Tierra de Campos, 133
Tikkunim, 161
tithes: *diezmos de los ganados*, 67; on Jewish properties formerly owned by Christians, 103, 104–8, 109–11, 127; *rediezmo*, 127; *tercias*, 66, 99n89, 118, 203n130
Toch, Michael, 60
Toledo: anti-rationalism/rationalism debate in, 153–55; collection of debts owed to Jews in, 122; conquest of, 7–8, 22–23; *fuero*, 23, 41; *Fuero juzgo* granted to, 179; head tax on Jews in, 105–6, 108; *hekdesh* in, 161n38; massacre of Jews (1110), 25, 55; massacre of Jews (1355), 227; papacy and conciliar legislation on Jews, 105–6; Santa Justa, 117n52; social reforms of *aljama* in, 162–66; tithes on Jews in, 109; Trastámara revolution, Jewish defense of Toledo against, 57n20
Toledot Yeshu, 183
Tomás de León (archdeacon), 116
Toro, 102, 144, 177, 229, 253, 260
Tortosa, 140n33
trade. *See* commercial activities
Trastámara rebellion. *See* Enrique II Trastámara of Castile and Civil War of 1360s

Urban IV (pope), 109–10
urban knights. *See caballeros villanos*
Urraca (queen of Castile-León), 25, 133
Usagre, 40n80, 177n31
usury. *See* collection of debts; moneylending

Valderas, 70
Valladolid: attacks on Jews in, 228; Camino route, location away from, 54; Camino's role in Jewish life and, 66–67; cortes of, 73, 162, 174, 189, 190, 191, 204, 205, 234, 235, 242, 244, 247, 252, 255n128; debt collection in, 204, 205
Valladolid, Council of (1228), 87, 107
Valladolid, Council of (1322), 87, 130
Varon (moneylenders' agent in Miranda), 66, 213
vecinos (citizens), Jews as, 43, 44–47
vedin (Jewish judge), 49–51
Vegamediana, 62, 90
venditores (public sellers of commodities), 43

Vienne, ecumenical Council of (1311–12), 85n30, 87, 114, 121
Villadiego, 7, 60, 67, 68, 70, 120, 192, 228
Villanueva de los Judios/Villanueva de Pancorbo, 57–58, 61
Violante (mother of Sancho IV), 193
violence between Jews and Christians: *fuero* provisions for, 58–59
Visigothic Spain: Jews in, 4n18, 5, 41n86, 175, 179, 181
viticulture: Jewish involvement in, 61–63
Vose, Robin, 79, 80, 143, 144

Watt, J. A., 30n41
wet-nursing, interfaith, 166, 183–84, 188, 235, 254, 255, 256
witness testimony in Christian-Jewish cases, 43, 47, 107, 169, 172, 197

Yago of Aranda (creditor), 119–20
Yuanez de Vitoria of Miranda, 213

Yuçaf Abenguinano (rabbi) and son Yafiel, 127
Yuçaf de Écija (*almojarife mayor* of Alfonso XI), 251n116
Yuçaf, son of Todros El Leui (of Burgos), 127
Yusuf Cordiella (of Palenzuela), 66, 70
Yuval, Israel: *Two Nations in Your Womb*, 9

Zag ben Mair Ibn Susan (Shushan), 193n100
Zag Garzon, 127
Zamora, 138n26, 205, 209
Zamora, Council of (1312–13), 15, 87, 121, 122, 130, 244, 255
Zaragoza, 161
Zarza, Samuel, 228n22
Zohar (*The Book of Splendor*), 152, 156–57, 159–60, 161, 162–63
Zorita, 27, 46n113

Jews and Christians in Medieval Castile: Tradition, Coexistence, and Change was designed and typeset in Quadraat with Optima display type by Kachergis Book Design of Pittsboro, North Carolina. It was printed on 60-pound House Natural Smooth, and bound by Sheridan Books of Chelsea, Michigan.

www.ingramcontent.com/pod-product-compliance
Lightning Source LLC
Chambersburg PA
CBHW020315010526
44107CB00054B/1848